MIRACLES

The miracle stories of the founders and saints of the major world religions have much in common. Written by international experts, this *Companion* provides an authoritative and comparative study of miracles in not only Hinduism, Islam, Buddhism, Christianity and Judaism, but also indigenous or traditional religions. The authors promote a discussion of the problems of miracles in our largely secular culture, and of the value of miracles in religious belief. The miracles of Jesus are also contextualized through chapters on the Hebrew Bible, Classical culture to the Romans, Second Temple and early rabbinic Judaism, and early Christianity. This book provides students with a scholarly introduction to miracle, which also covers philosophical, medical and historical issues.

Graham H. Twelftree is Distinguished Professor of New Testament, Regent University, Virginia Beach. His previous publications include *Jesus the Exorcist: A Contribution to the Study of the Historical Jesus* (1993), *Jesus the Miracle Worker: A Historical and Theological Study* (1999), *In the Name of Jesus: Exorcism Among Early Christians* (2007) and *People of the Spirit: Exploring Luke's View of the Church* (2009). He is also on the editorial board of the *Journal for the Study of the Historical Jesus*.

D0145576

CAMBRIDGE COMPANIONS TO RELIGION
A series of companions to major topics and key figures in theology and religious studies. Each volume contains specially commissioned chapters by international scholars which provide an accessible and stimulating introduction to the subject for new readers and non-specialists.

Other titles in the series

Continued at the back of the book

THE CAMBRIDGE COMPANION TO

MIRACLES

Edited by Graham H. Twelftree

CAMBRIDGE
UNIVERSITY PRESS

CAMBRIDGE UNIVERSITY PRESS
Cambridge, New York, Melbourne, Madrid, Cape Town, Singapore,
São Paulo, Delhi, Dubai, Tokyo, Mexico City

Cambridge University Press
The Edinburgh Building, Cambridge CB2 8RU, UK

Published in the United States of America by Cambridge University Press, New York

www.cambridge.org
Information on this title: www.cambridge.org/9780521899864

© Cambridge University Press 2011

First published 2011

Printed in the United Kingdom at the University Press, Cambridge

A catalogue record for this publication is available from the British Library

Library of Congress Cataloging-in-Publication Data

The Cambridge companion to miracles / edited by Graham H. Twelftree.
    p. cm. – (Cambridge companions to religion)
  ISBN 978-0-521-89986-4 (Hardback) – ISBN 978-0-521-72851-5 (Paperback)
1. Miracles. I. Twelftree, Graham H.
BL487.C36 2011
202'.117–dc22

                     2010045138

ISBN 978-0-521-89986-4 Hardback
ISBN 978-0-521-72851-5 Paperback

To Bob Sivigny
and all the other librarians who support our work

Contents

Notes on contributors

David Basinger is Professor of Philosophy and Ethics and Chair of the Division of Teacher Education at Roberts Wesleyan College. He has edited *Religious Tolerance through Humility* (with James Kraft, 2008) and has written *Religious Diversity: A Philosophical Assessment* (2002), *The Case For Freewill Theism* (1996) and *The Openness of God* (with Richard Rice, William Hasker, John Sanders and Clark Pinnock, 1994).

Barry L. Blackburn is Professor of New Testament, Atlanta Christian College. He has written *Theios Anēr and the Markan Miracle Traditions: A Critique of the Theios Anēr Concept as an Interpretative Background of the Miracle Traditions Used by Mark* (1991).

Fiona Bowie is Senior Lecturer in Social Anthropology at the University of Bristol. Her initial fieldwork looked at the relationship between the Bangwa of Cameroon, West Africa, and the Focolare Movement. Current research interests include the Bangwa diaspora, adoptive parenting and child circulation, and comparative notions of the afterlife. She has edited *Cross-Cultural Approaches to Adoption* (2004) and written *The Anthropology of Religion* (2nd edn 2006).

Colin Brown is Professor of Systematic Theology, Fuller Theological Seminary. His books include *Miracles and the Critical Mind* (1984), *Jesus in European Protestant Thought* (1985), *Christianity and Western Thought* (1990), *Karl Barth and the Christian Message* (1999) and he edited *The New International Dictionary of New Testament Theology* (1986).

Ralph Del Colle is Associate Professor of Theology, Marquette University. His publications include *Christ and the Spirit: Spirit-Christology in Trinitarian Perspective* (1994) and he is a co-editor of the *International Journal of Systematic Theology*.

Gavin Flood is Professor of Hindu Studies and Comparative Religion at the University of Oxford where he is also the academic director for the Oxford Centre for Hindu Studies. His publications include *An Introduction to Hinduism* (1996), *The Ascetic Self: Subjectivity, Memory and Tradition* (2004) and *The Tantric Body: The Secret Tradition of Hindu Religion* (2006).

Robert Garland is Roy D. and Margaret B. Wooster Professor of the Classics at Colgate University and was Director, Division of the Humanities. His books include *Daily Life of the Ancient Greeks* (1998; 2nd edn 2009), *The Eye of the Beholder* (1995), *Religion and the Greeks* (1994) and *Introducing New Gods* (1992).

Rupert Gethin is Professor of Buddhist Studies and Co-Director of the Centre for Buddhist Studies in the Department of Theology and Religious Studies at the University of Bristol and, since 2003, President of the Pali Text Society. He has published *Sayings of the Buddha: New Translations from the Pali Nikāyas* (2008), *The Foundations of Buddhism* (1998) and *The Buddhist Path to Awakening: A Study of the Bodhi-Pakkhiya Dhamma* (1992, 2nd edn 2001).

Niels Christian Hvidt is Associate Professor at the Institute of Public Health at the University of Southern Denmark and his publications include *Miracles – Encounters of Heaven and Earth* (2002), *Does Faith Move Mountains* (with Christoffer Johansen, 2004), *Christian Prophecy – the Post-Biblical Tradition* (2007), *Do Mountains Move Faith?* (with Christoffer Johansen, 2008) and *The Art of Miracles* (with Elisabeth Assing Hvidt, 2008).

Robert A. Larmer is Professor of Philosophy at the University of New Brunswick and author of *Water into Wine? An Investigation of the Concept of Miracle* (1988) and *Questions of Miracle* (1996). He is a past president of the Canadian Society of Christian Philosophers and has served on the executive boards of the Canadian Philosophical Association and the Evangelical Philosophical Society.

Michael P. Levine is Winthrop Professor of Philosophy in the School of Humanities, University of Western Australia. His publications include *Politics Most Unusual: Violence, Sovereignty and Democracy in the 'War on Terror'* (with Damian Cox and Saul Newman, 2009), *Integrity and the Fragile Self* (with Damian Cox and Marguerite LaCaze, 2003), *Pantheism: A Non-Theistic Concept of Deity* (1994) and *Hume and the Problem of Miracles: A Solution* (1988).

R. Walter L. Moberly is Professor of Theology and Biblical Interpretation in the Department of Theology and Religion, Durham University. He has written most recently, *The Bible, Theology, and Faith* (2000), *Prophecy and Discernment* (2006) and *The Theology of the Book of Genesis* (2009).

Lidija Novakovic is Associate Professor of Religion (Biblical Studies/New Testament) in the Department of Religion at Baylor University. Her publications include *Messiah, the Healer of the Sick: A Study of Jesus as the Son of David in the Gospel of Matthew* (2003) and she is a co-editor of *The Dead Sea Scrolls: Hebrew, Aramaic, and Greek Texts with English Translations*, vols. 3 and 6B.

James Carleton Paget is Senior Lecturer in New Testament Studies at Cambridge University and Fellow and Tutor of Peterhouse. His publications include

The Epistle of Barnabas: Outlook and Background (1994) and he is the co-editor of *The New Cambridge History of the Bible*, vol. i.

Kenneth Seeskin is Philip M. and Ethel Klutznick Professor of Jewish Civilization at Northwestern University. His books include *Jewish Philosophy in a Secular Age* (1990), *Searching for a Distant God: The Legacy of Maimonides* (2000), *Autonomy in Jewish Philosophy* (2001), *The Cambridge Companion to Maimonides* (2005) and *Maimonides on the Origin of the World* (2005).

David Thomas is Professor of Christianity and Islam at the University of Birmingham. Among his recent publications are *Early Muslim Anti-Christian Polemic: Abu 'Isa al-Warraq's 'Against the Incarnation'* (2002), *Christian Doctrines in Islamic Theology* (2008) and he is the lead editor for *Christian–Muslim Relations, A Bibliographical History*, vol. 1 *(600–900)* (2009).

Graham H. Twelftree is Distinguished Professor of New Testament, School of Divinity, Regent University, Virginia Beach. His previous publications include *Jesus the Exorcist: A Contribution to the Study of the Historical Jesus* (1993), *Jesus the Miracle Worker: A Historical and Theological Study* (1999), *In the Name of Jesus: Exorcism Among Early Christians* (2007) and *People of the Spirit: Exploring Luke's View of the Church* (2009). He is also a member of the editorial board of the *Journal for the Study of the Historical Jesus* (Brill).

Benedicta Ward is a sister of the Anglican Community of Sisters of the Love of God, the Reader in the History of Christian Spirituality at the University of Oxford and a supernumerary fellow at Harris Manchester College. Among her publications are *Miracles and the Medieval Mind* (1982), *The Venerable Bede* (2002), *Christ Within Me: Prayers and Meditations from the Anglo-Saxon Tradition* (2008), *A True Easter: The Synod of Whitby 664 AD (2007)* and *Anselm of Canterbury* (2009).

Acknowledgements

Special thanks is offered to Jacqueline Duckett and Alicia Eichmann, my research assistants, and to the large cadre of anonymous readers who helped in the development of the following chapters. The editors, Kate Brett and Laura Morris at Cambridge University Press, along with their teams, are also to be thanked for their detailed and long-suffering support of this project. I would also like to thank Ann Lewis, the volume's copy-editor.

Graham H. Twelftree

Introduction: Miracle in an age of diversity

GRAHAM H. TWELFTREE

In their various ways, atheist, agnostic and believer alike negotiate the problem of miracle: their possibility, their apprehension and, if any, their meaning. But for the first time in recent history it is increasingly obvious that we do not travel alone. Not only is this the experience of those living in the West, those cultures extending from the rim of the north Atlantic. With greater communication, travel, immigration and trade, it is apparent that miracle is also a problem in the East for the Hindu, Muslim and Buddhist, as well as for the Christian and Jew in the global south.

Not since the religions of Egypt, Syria, Persia and Asia Minor found their way into the Graeco-Roman world have the boundaries between so many cultures been so porous[1] and the problem of miracle so interesting. In the Graeco-Roman world, late in the second century CE, the philosopher Celsus (probably in Alexandria) was pouring scorn on Christians who, 'for a few obols make known their sacred lore in the middle of the market-place and drive demons out of people and blow away disease' (Origen, *Against Celsus* 1.69). In the same period, the philosopher-satirist Lucian of Samosata (modern Samsat in southeast Turkey) says in relation to the followers of Peregrinus: 'By Zeus, it would be nothing unnatural if, among all those dolts [who witnessed his death] that there are, some should be found to assert that they were relieved of quartan fevers by him' (*The Passing of Peregrinus* 28). In poking fun at such views he said, 'we have a powerful antidote to such poisons [the stories] in the truth and in sound reason brought to bear everywhere. As long as we make use of this, none of these empty foolish lies will disturb our peace' (*The Lover of Lies* 40).

But the temper of our time is different. It is not simply that we live in a postmodern world in which some members of the intelligentsia have exchanged their dogmas and absolutes for a plurality of possibilities and narratives. Nor is it that Charles Taylor can

pronounce our Western world 'disenchanted'.[2] That is, it is not that
the enchanted world of our predecessors with its spirits, demons,
moral forces, and a cosmos testifying to divine activity and purposes,
is lost to us.[3] Rather, as Taylor goes on to discuss, our age is also
characterized by a religious diversity that is experienced not only by
social elites, but by everyone in society. There is, especially in the
West, no longer a cultural obligation to believe in God to the point
that many feel it easier not to believe. Moreover, it is not simply that
there is a decline in Jewish and Christian believers, nor is it that it is
now possible to be a Hindu or a Muslim or a Buddhist. It is, in short,
that there is a variety of ways of being a materialist or spiritual or
religious, and relating to a god.[4]

Not surprisingly, one expression of the variety of possible ways of
existing in relation to a god and the world is seen in the responses to the
idea of miracle. We will see in the chapters below that the category of
miracle has been abandoned by many. Also, some religious traditions
have distanced themselves from miracle at various times in their histories, and more so in recent times. As well, there are ongoing deep
philosophical objections to miracle from some quarters, even among
thinkers who claim affiliation to major religious traditions. Yet, perhaps surprisingly, what follows will also show that a significant pro-
portion of the population of the Western world – for example around
three-quarters of those in the United States[5] and 38 per cent in Britain[6] –
continue to believe in miracles. At least in part, these figures give voice
to R. G. Collingwood's view that 'if the rationalist had any intelligence
he would see that his attacks on religion are too easy to be sound, and
that there must be a catch somewhere'.[7] Or, perhaps, this persistent
belief in miracle can be claimed as evidence that we are religious
animals.[8]

In the light of our experience of this increasing diversity and,
therefore, potential misunderstanding of each other, part of the
purpose in writing these essays, and bringing them together, is to aid
dialogue among readers to help mutual understanding of how a
particular faith (or lack of it) relates to the issue of miracle. Some of
the chapters, such as those related to Christianity, bring order and
clarity to, and guide the reader through, the growing mountain of
literature in that particular field. Chapters on other areas, such as
the Hebrew Bible and traditional religions, are either charting new
ground or bringing to our attention material that may be little known
and understood; this is especially the case with respect to the chapters
on the major religions that arose in the East.

The various chapters on miracle in antiquity and the Middle Ages in Part II of this volume are of intrinsic value in contributing to our knowledge. They also provide depth and historical perspective for discussing miracle in Islam, Christianity, Judaism and in contemporary secular society. Moreover, a number of these chapters help understand and interpret the gospel traditions about Jesus, who has dominated and continues to be important in Western debates about miracle. Hence, the miracles of Jesus will come into view again, for example, in the chapter on the history of the debates about miracle.

However, the following pieces, written independently by diverse specialists, are not intended to be an exhaustive treatment of the subject. Instead, these chapters are best read as a number of core samples recovered by those who have drilled down at strategic points in the past and in the cultures we now share, at least to some extent, exposing not only the surface expression evident in the various claims to miracle, but also the deep-seated structures that have given rise to the views on miracle in these times and traditions.

FUNDAMENTAL ISSUES

In the opening chapter of Part I, David Basinger shows there is no standard way of defining a miracle. While most theists assume a miracle to be due in part to intentional divine activity, there is debate over the type of divine activity. Some assume that God directly manipulates the natural order while others assume that God predetermines that nature will bring about miraculous events. Theists also differ on the natural explicability of the event. Some limit miracles to events that could never have a natural explanation while others claim that an event can be a miracle even if a natural explanation is available.

Robert Larmer (Chapter 2) defines a miracle as a dramatic supernatural intervention in nature that furthers God's purposes. He explores the meaning of a miracle, so defined, for science, philosophy and theology. With regard to science, he argues that miracles do not violate the laws of nature and thus there is no necessary conflict between the evidence for miracles and the evidence which supports belief in the laws of nature. At the philosophical level, he argues that methodological naturalism is not metaphysically neutral and it questionably restricts what form explanations may take and whether God can be conceived as acting directly in the world. Theologically, he argues that miracles can serve both for believer and non-believer alike as evidence for God and his ongoing activity in creation.

MIRACLES IN ANTIQUITY AND THE MIDDLE AGES

In the first of the historical chapters of Part II, Walter Moberly (Chapter 3) notes that as divine activity in the Hebrew Bible can vary from the ordinary to the extraordinary it is understandable that there is, arguably, no Hebrew word for miracle. Instead, characteristic terminology such as 'signs and wonders' depicts existentially engaging moments which are meant to engender Israel's praise of God. Moberly also notes that 'miracles' in the Hebrew Bible are associated primarily with Moses, Elijah and Elisha, and not more widely. Although the stories about these figures can give the impression that they are wielding magical power under their control, hints in the text direct the reader towards understanding the power as deriving from YHWH. It is tempting for both sceptic and believer to offer rationalized explanations for 'miracle' stories, yet such an approach tends to produce an alternative account rather than explaining the existing narrative. The great distance in time between us and the accounts, and the difficulty in determining their literary genre, as well as other traditions having similar stories, make it probably impossible to determine what actually happened. So a more fruitful approach, Moberly suggests, is not to isolate the 'miraculous' from its narrative context but to seek the possible original and enduring significance of the material as a whole.

According to Robert Garland (Chapter 4), terminological difficulties also abound in the study of 'miracle' in the Greek and Roman world. This is due largely to the fact that there was no clear division between religion and magic. In contrast to the Christians, for whom miracles were the signifiers *par excellence* of God's power over the phenomenal world, the Graeco-Romans regarded such events primarily as a cause of wonder. A particularly rich source of evidence for miraculous occurrences is the battlefield, where such occurrences commonly took the form of the fulfilment of a contractual agreement between a human and a deity in which the deity, perhaps operating within the parameters of cause and effect, paid humans either retrospectively or prospectively for cultic activity. Another important function of miracles was to advance the cause of a new god who was seeking incorporation within the community. This aspect of the miraculous finds important expression in the collections of healing accounts associated first with Isis and then, more prolifically, with Asclepius. Miracle workers, evidence for whom is largely confined to the Archaic period, seem to have operated for the most part at the edge of the Greek-speaking world. Such figures are frequently regarded with scorn in our sources. Though Tacitus tells the story of the Emperor Vespasian curing two invalids, the second-century CE satirist Lucian continues the tradition of mocking those with pretensions to working miracles. Reports of miracles featured prominently in the battle between Christianity and polytheism, being cited as evidence on both sides of the superior power of each other's God or god.

Recognizing the difficulty of finding a uniform understanding of miracle across the various expressions of Judaism in the Second Temple and early rabbinic period, in Chapter 5 Lidija Novakovic identifies three groups of miracle workers that were active in this period: exorcists, sign prophets, and charismatic miracle workers. An increased interest in exorcism is documented in a number of writings, but there are only two full accounts about a contemporary figure engaging in such practice. The so-called sign prophets include various individuals in pre-70 Palestine who promised, though failed, to perform miraculous signs similar to those in the biblical traditions about the exodus and conquest. The two most prominent charismatic miracle workers were Ḥoni and Ḥanina ben Dosa, who were known not only for their miraculous abilities but also for their piety and kindness. Yet, early rabbinic literature does not show much interest in miracles until the transition to the Talmudic era because of their contested use in halakhic arguments.

Generally speaking, Jewish authors from this period take pains to distinguish extraordinary events taking place in their midst from magical practices, especially in cases that require the employment of certain objects and rituals. The most common strategy was to ascribe miracles to God's power and magic to human agency. The last section of this chapter offers a short discussion of the expected eschatological wonders. Even though no Jewish text unambiguously ascribes the execution of such miracles to a human figure, this is done in the accounts of Jesus' miracles in early Christian literature.

No figure in antiquity has more miracle stories associated with him than Jesus. Barry Blackburn (Chapter 6) notes that the importance of miracle stories in the portrait of Jesus in the gospels, including how they were used to convey his self-understanding, his relationship to God, his ministry, along with the later significance Jesus was given by Christians, has led to the development of sophisticated critical tools for evaluating the historicity of the stories. Blackburn concludes that central to his ministry, Jesus probably performed many miracles, exorcizing demons, healing the sick and raising the dead. In turn, Jesus believed himself to be God's agent or royal Messiah, overthrowing the evil one, inaugurating the kingdom of God and heralding its consummation. Further, for those with the eyes of faith, the miracles, taken in the light of the Resurrection, became revelations of the cosmic identity of Jesus.

In Chapter 7, James Carleton Paget then examines the miraculous in Christianity until the middle of the third century CE, noting that, from the perspective of twenty-first-century scepticism, it is difficult to evaluate this aspect of Christianity which was taken for granted. Nevertheless, significant questions remain. Is there a clear development in miracle from the sober Paul to the extravagance of the apocryphal literature? Why are miracles so little mentioned in some of the important early Christian writers such as Justin, Irenaeus and Tertullian? How important was miracle as the trump card in the expansion of Christianity? How important was the charge of magic against Christians in their attitude to and use of miracles?

In the Middle Ages, Benedicta Ward (Chapter 8) tells us, miracle stories proliferate in relation to saints, shrines, holy places, relics, pilgrimages, liturgy and daily life. They were taken to attest to the reality of God's presence on earth, and in this the stories were consistent with those in the gospel. A change, however, took place in the eleventh and twelfth centuries; the outward mechanics of miracle mattered less than the interior miracle of salvation and goodness of life. For example, with no historical warrant, miracle stories accrued to the figure of the Virgin Mary who, in turn, was credited with miracles connected with her relics. Although the question of 'how' rather than 'why' returned to centre stage, stories (disengaged from any actual events) could be changed and elaborated at will. In any case, though St Bernard said that love was the greatest miracle, the sick and needy remained keenly interested in him and other such figures as practical miracle workers. The very vagueness of some of the records of the cures, Ward suggests, may point to their authenticity. However, in seeking details and in the concern for character (in the face of heretics and bad people being able to perform a miracle), the evolving canonization process set aside these stories, favouring signs (signa) of redemption linked to virtue. Nevertheless, that miracle remains of interest in the major religions of the contemporary world is obvious from the second part of this book.

MIRACLES IN THE MAJOR RELIGIONS

Recognizing and defining a 'traditional' people and 'traditional' religion can be problematic. In Chapter 9, Fiona Bowie notes that the term 'traditional' is often used as a residual category for all those who do not fit into a named world religion. It also carries connotations of primitivism on the one hand and authenticity or purity on the other. Those who practise so-called traditional religions in many parts of the world are also followers of or are influenced by world religions, and are part of wider global economic systems. Accepting a category of 'traditional religion' we do, however, recognize that for many people so defined the Western positivist distinctions between natural and supernatural, or science and religion, do not hold. For these people there is an expansion of the category of nature to include unseen forces, discarnate entities and an active force that links animate and inanimate people and objects within a single moral system. What might appear as miraculous to a Western observer may to traditional religionists appear to be a normal, if unusual, occurrence. The acceptance of unseen forces and their operation in the world is not confined to traditional religions, but their place within the scheme of things is more normative and easily accepted in 'traditional' societies that do not operate with a predominantly materialist paradigm. The paradox Bowie alludes to is that if we define something as miraculous, it is almost by definition not part of the cosmology of a 'traditional religion'. The ways in which spirits, deities and psychic powers operate will vary from one society to another, but their veracity and ubiquity are taken for granted.

Gavin Flood (Chapter 10) shows that Hinduism links cosmology and a psychology of meditation, seeing state of mind and the world of experience as coterminous. What appear to be miracles or disruptions of natural law, therefore, are not seen to go against natural law, but are the result of a yogin's mastery of the higher levels of the universe using natural law to change causation in the natural world. These feats include leprosy being cured, a girl being transformed into a plant, levitation, bilocation, and ash or fruit or red powder for tilak marks being manifest on finger tips. However, as detachment from the world of sense and desire is the goal of liberation, these miraculous powers are discouraged as distractions and dangerous in creating desires in the yogin. In more recent times, Western understandings of miracles have been fused with traditional Hindu accomplishments so that while the wonder of an event is maintained, rationalists offer their explanations.

For Muslims not only did Muḥammad perform miracles (for example, miraculous feedings, healings, an army drinking from water emerging from his fingers, and his foretelling the future), but everything associated with him, such as his clothing, was thought to have miraculous powers. Further, the Qur'ān is also considered miraculous in its beauty and in being the presence of the eternal among people.

The development of Islamic religious thought took place in the context of engagement with other faiths, including Christianity. This gave rise to literature that includes miracles associated with the Prophet. In Chapter 11 on miracle in Islam, David Thomas shows that miracles were part of the disagreements between Muslims and Christians in particular. Muslims argued that Jesus' divine status is not guaranteed by miracles, for miracle working is also associated with figures such as Moses, Elijah, Elisha and Ezekiel. And Muḥammad is also credited with providing food for his followers, just as Jesus provided wine for his. As the debate matured, Muslim interest turned from comparing miracles to arguing that God alone is to be credited with miracles, removing human agency so reducing Jesus to no more than a channel of God's power. These debates, and even Muslim theologians who took a rationalist approach, had little impact on the followers of saintly individuals. These Ṣūfīs were seen as so close to God that he became visible through them and their marvellous activities.

In Chapter 12 on miracle in early Indian Buddhism, Rupert Gethin points out that, in common with other religions of that sub-continent, Buddhist texts consider an individual's ability to carry out extraordinary feats – flying through the air, passing through solid objects and making things appear or disappear, for example – as not due to direct divine circumvention or modification of the natural order. Rather, the wondrous feats of the Buddha and his followers are taken to be the direct and natural consequence of the extraordinary power of the mind, that is accomplished through the mastery of deep concentration by the individual. Yet, the Buddha is said to be alerted by the excitement caused by miracles and to pronounce the monastic rule that such powers should not be displayed before the laity as they neither aroused nor strengthened faith. However, the wish to marginalize the miraculous is a more recent feature to be credited to the rationalist and ethical sensitivities of some Buddhist apologists. Notwithstanding the monastic rule, there is no question of the value of the Buddha's and monks' practice of miraculous powers, which in manifesting reality can also attract followers and encourage the faithful. In any case, individuals besides those who have attained full mastery of the mind can be protected and healed by the power of truth, while the miracles associated with various points in the career of the Buddha are accessible to all in the literature and the representations at sacred sites.

Although sometimes marginal to Christianity, as for some of the sixteenth-century Reformers, and sometimes its focus of attention, as among contemporary Pentecostals, Ralph Del Colle says in Chapter 13 that the testimony of miracles has never been absent from Christianity. In turn, Del Colle argues that Christians understand miracles in terms of two foci. St Thomas Aquinas expressed one, the ontological aspect. Presupposing the relations between God and creation in terms of causality, Thomas defined a miracle as the work of God against the order of nature. Yet, God does not violate the created order, but acts in miracle to perfect it. With the Enlightenment considering the laws of nature no longer reflecting divine participation, miracle came to be understood as either a violation of what God or nature had constituted, or miracles were thought irrelevant to reason which grasped truth. However, some continued to defend the authenticity of at least the biblical miracles so that the other focal point for Christians' understanding of miracle, its intentional aspect, is that it becomes the basis for witness or Christian apologetics. Miracles are signs, perhaps received in ecstatic experience, that point to the mystery of God.

According to Kenneth Seeskin, in Jewish philosophy miracles have been regarded with ambivalence (Chapter 14). Denying them would be to set aside the story of God's saving power, but their acceptance may court chaos. Some early rabbis concluded, therefore, that they could have no significance in a legal dispute. Medieval thinkers attempted to reconcile divine freedom (implying the possibility of extraordinary action) and metaphysical perfection (implying immutability). Maimonides, for example, sought a middle ground between arguing not that miracles occurred, but that they could, and are to be explained rationally. However, if, according to the common view, God is revealed only in the extraordinary there must be a power at work other than God. Spinoza would not have this and famously proposed an identification of God with nature. In more recent times some Jewish thinkers have distrusted the numinous aspect of religion, of which miracle is a part, as a distraction from the clear commands of God. For, as Seeskin concludes, no matter how extraordinary, miracles raise as many questions as they answer so that they can only be effective in the light of prior convictions.

MIRACLE TODAY

The twenty-first-century reader of this book is likely to have been at least significantly shaped by Western thought and to be an heir to the history of debates about miracle that is outlined in Chapter 15. Colin Brown shows not only that miracle was a potent factor in the early growth of Christianity, but also that, early in Western tradition, individuals such as Eusebius of Caesarea and St Augustine were caught up in the need to defend miracle both in the Christian canon as well as among their contemporaries. Brown draws attention to critical periods and figures – the fourth and fifth centuries, St Thomas Aquinas, the Reformation and Counter-Reformation, the Age of Enlightenment and the flowering of scepticism, the nineteenth-century struggle with rationalism and supernaturalism – ending with the twentieth century. He concludes that there was a tendency for philosopher and apologist to interact with each other, while ignoring biblical scholars, historians and sociologists.

This conclusion sets the scene for Chapter 16, Michael Levine's discussion of philosophers on miracle. In his view, of all the questions raised in relation to miracle, the only philosophically significant one is whether anyone is or has ever been justified epistemologically in believing not that a miracle *could* but *has* occurred. In his discussion, Levine engages with, for example, Francis Beckwith, John Haldane, Richard Swinburne and Nicholas Wolterstorff. He shows that no advance has been made on David Hume's argument that even if miracles have occurred, no one has ever been justified (on epistemological and sound evidential grounds) in believing that a miracle has taken place. It has been the fashion to use Bayes' theorem to calculate the probability of a miracle occurring. However, Levine asserts that this approach is otiose until the prior question of evidence is resolved, at which point the theorem adds only complexity rather than clarity to Hume's argument. Above all this, Levine suggests that it is the signifi-cance of miracle for religious belief and life that is both important and ignored, philosophers preferring to give attention to the problem of whether miracles are consistent with science.

This question of the significance of miracle can be taken as the point of departure for Niels Christian Hvidt and his exploration of the impact on patients of faith in healing miracles in Chapter 17. Relying on a number of contemporary studies he is able to show that faith in an active and interactive God is an important factor in a patient's handling of a health crisis. However, although nothing indicates that belief in miracles itself is a sign of any religious pathology, particular concep-tions of God, perhaps as using sickness as punishment, can lead to coping negatively. Believing in miracles can in some instances also cause patients to refuse treatment or in other cases demand unwar-ranted extension of treatment. Yet, belief in a living and active God has been shown to sustain believers by strengthening their relationship of trust with God as they pray, even when no miracle occurs. Although, traditionally, the faith of a patient has been seen as a private matter, this chapter raises the question of the important distinction between religious neurosis and healthy faith and takes up the case that, where patients show signs of using belief in the miraculous to escape reality, qualified psychologists and religious professionals can be called on to help the patients so that the best health and spiritual care can be made available to them.

THEMES AND QUESTIONS

Placing these chapters next to each other means that readers will be able to see the patterns in and parallels between periods and traditions. It will also become obvious that, across the various cultures and religions, the nature and understanding of miracle has varied considerably and continues to do so. This opens up the discussion of the place, if any, and then importance of miracles in an expression of faith and its practice. To explore this point further, miracle is important for all the major religious traditions, not least in relation to their founders, and sometimes later key figures. However, the question arises: what is to be concluded in the light of similar miracles being found in different religions? Just as Jesus fed a crowd with a small amount of food, so did Mahākassapa, a chief disciple of the Buddha. Not only is Jesus said to walk on water, give sight to the blind and miraculously feed multitudes, there are also stories of Ṣūfī saints accomplishing the same feats. Both Jesus and Buddha are said to have had miraculous births. Also, there are stories of Jews, Ṣūfīs and Christians acting as exorcists.[9] Further, for example, as Christians have claimed that 'truth' would set people free, so a Buddhist is able to heal a sick boy through a statement of truth. Are we to conclude, echoing David Hume, that these claims from conflicting religions, particularly as they relate to establishing the origin of the religions, cancel out each other and discredit the testimony of the witnesses?[10]

In any case, on the one hand, these chapters should prompt considerable sobriety and engender careful reflection in religious readers who will not be able to escape questioning the value and propriety of exclusive claims regarding their belief in miracles. For in these pages we are being invited into worlds and world views that, though different from each other, are equally sophisticated and highly valued by their inhabitants. It may now be difficult to repeat St Augustine's statement: '[T]he miracles allegedly performed in the pagan temples are not worthy of comparison with those performed at the shrines of our martyrs' (*City of God* 22.10).

On the other hand, readers who are not religious or do not consider it possible to establish that miracles have taken place, will be caused to consider how the religious claims, and those who make them, are to be interpreted. Put another way, reading these chapters together should help readers who either have a Western mind-set, or are heavily indebted to and influenced by it, to see that they may have become blind to the relativity inherent in their explanations of their world. An unwillingness to acknowledge the reality of the enchanted world of others might, therefore, be justly perceived as another expression of cultural or intellectual colonialism.[11]

Apart from this most obvious point of the varied yet important place of miracle in all cultures and religions, there are a number of other pedal notes – recurring themes – heard through the text that also merit careful attention and raise their own questions. First, as already suggested, a prominent repeated theme extending beyond the first chapter is the problem of defining a miracle. Some traditions and people did not and do not have a word for miracle, others may have the word, but define it radically differently from others. For a Christian a miracle might be an unusual event resulting from divine intervention, but for a Buddhist it would be the natural expression of the power of the mind of a holy man. Philosophers also, as will become clear, variously define miracles.

Second, another topic that will surface from time to time and in various ways is the ambiguity of miracle. An event seen and understood by some, but missed or at least supposedly misunderstood by others, has led more than one tradition to hold that miracles could neither create faith in the unbeliever nor strengthen the belief of the already faithful. Perhaps, then, a miracle can only be perceived (or not) and interpreted against an existing world view – faith, religion or community – and its set of perceptions. In other words, perhaps, a miracle is no more than my way of seeing as extraordinary what another sees as ordinary.

Similarly, as in the Hebrew Bible and also for Baruch Spinoza, for example, since false prophets could perform miracles, other ways of knowing God and his representatives were thought needed to prevent the faithful from being led astray. Concomitantly, in the tapestry of what follows in this book, the relationship between miracle and magic and the problem of the detection of the latter is a thread that is brought to the surface from time to time.

The ambiguity of miracle will, therefore, often be seen to be expressed in a third theme: the problem of the meaning of miracle. They might equally be claimed as evidence for the goodness of the deity or as for his tragic neglect of those who do not experience the mercy or marvel. Or, miracles could be taken as evidence of an incompetent creator meddling in an unfinished or imperfect work. Alternatively, according to some, if miracles occur in a world overseen by a perfect, all-powerful creator, they must have been planned from the beginning. Yet, how do the Jews interpret a God who saves them from Pharaoh, but not from Hitler? Perhaps, as Kenneth Seeskin says in Chapter 14, 'true faith has nothing to do with fortune'. Or, perhaps miracles do not mean anything independent of an existing religious conviction: no more than an eclipse of the sun can be evidence of a god's quotidian intervention can a healing be credited to his or her beneficence.

Or, perhaps, for those in Western civilizations who are detached from an interpretative community and from spiritual attainment, and for whom the windows to transcendence have been closed, the perception of a miracle, as Kenneth Woodward has suggested, is relocated in the theatre of the questing self. The miracle becomes a sign of the God within us all. 'Where classical miracle stories inspired fear and awe, inducing worship of God and admiration of the saint, modern miracles tend to inspire admiration of the divinity that is the self.'[12] This perspective, Woodward supposes, explains why so many, against the current of contemporary culture, have come to believe in God and miracles. 'It is a way of saying that in the privacy of individual experience, where all meaning resides, I have come to believe in myself.'[13]

Fourth, another recurring theme, that is also an expression of the ambiguity of miracles, is that there is a problem of miracle, and it may be considerably exacerbated, in the border disputes along the uncertain boundaries between cultures. For, to varying degrees, miracles have been involved in the clash and competition between religions. This gives rise to hints in the pages below of the view that miracles are of doubtful value in proselytizing.

In line with this, there is the problem of using miracle to establish the divine or special status of the miracle worker. For example, as we have noted, in the tenth-century battles with the Christians, Muslims pointed out that if the miracles of Jesus are also seen in the life of Moses there can be no difference between them as prophets.

Fifth, a theme that may not be immediately obvious through what follows is that there is scattered evidence of the fluctuating fortunes of miracles. This can be seen, for example, in both Buddhism and, surprisingly, in the early years of the Christian tradition. Also, both of these traditions responded to rationalism in the late nineteenth and early twentieth centuries by distancing themselves from the miraculous.

In Judaism as well there are those who see no need for miracles, associating them with the mythology of earlier times.[14]

Finally, from time to time, key individuals will come to the fore in what follows. Not only founding figures of the various religions – Moses, Buddha, Jesus, Muḥammad – but there will also be evidence of other individuals of brilliance who have given attention to the problem of miracle, and whose views still merit our consideration, such as St Augustine, Abū Bakr al-Bāqillānī, St Thomas Aquinas, Baruch Spinoza and David Hume.

This book does not claim to cover all the territory, and may not answer all the questions raised by a thoughtful person. Nevertheless, in this collection of essays an attempt has been made to provide more than enough raw material for fruitful discussion, questioning and reflection on the perennial set of problems associated with the idea of miracle.[15]

Notes

1   Cf. Franz Cumont, *The Oriental Religions in Roman Paganism* (New York: Dover, 1956), 196–7, and the discussion by Hans-Josef Klauck, *Magic and Paganism in Early Christianity: The World of the Acts of the Apostles* (Edinburgh: T&T Clark, 2000), 1.

2   Charles Taylor, *A Secular Age* (Cambridge, MA: Belknap, 2008), 29–30; cf. the review of Taylor by Martin Jay, 'Faith-Based History', *History and Theory* 48 (2009), 76–84.

3   See the brief discussion of the 're-enchantment' of the present by Robert J. Wallis and Megan Aldrich, 'Introduction: Enchantment, Disenchantment, Re-enchantment', in *Antiquaries and Archaists: The Past in the Past, the Past in the Present*, ed. Megan Aldrich and Robert J. Wallis (Reading: Spire, 2009), 9–13.

4   Cf. Taylor, *A Secular Age*, 437. In what Quentin Smith, 'The Metaphilosophy of Naturalism', *Philo* 4 (2001), 195–215, calls the 'Desecularization of academia that evolved in Philosophy Departments since the late 1960s' (196–200), a similar diversity is reflected in the guild of philosophers.

5   George D. Gallup, *The Gallup Poll: Public Opinion, 1995* (Wilmington: Scholarly Resources, 1996), and the discussion by Niels Hvidt in Chapter 17.

6   International Social Survey Program (ISSP), *International Social Survey Program: Religion II, 1998 (ICPSR 3065)* (Ann Arbor: Inter-university Consortium for Political and Social Research, 2001), 61.

7   R. G. Collingwood, *Speculum Mentis or the Map of Knowledge* (Oxford: Oxford University Press, 1924), 148; cf. 146–53.

8   Cf. Jonathan Benthall, *Returning to Religion: Why a Secular Age is Haunted by Faith* (London and New York: Tauris, 2008), for example, 191.

9 Andrew Rippen and Jan Knappert, ed. and trans., *Textual Sources for the Study of Islam* (Chicago: University of Chicago Press, 1986), 161 ('Legends of 'Abd al-Qadir al-Jilani'); Graham H. Twelftree, *In the Name of Jesus: Exorcism Among Early Christians* (Grand Rapids: Baker Academic, 2007), 35–54.

10 David Hume, 'Of Miracles', in *Enquiries Concerning Human Understanding*, 3rd edn, ed. L. A. Selby-Bigge, rev. and notes P. H. Nidditch (Oxford: Oxford University Press, 1975), 109–31 (121–2). See the discussion in Bruce Langtry, 'Miracles and Rival Systems of Religion', *Sophia* 24 (1985), 21–31; cf. Richard G. Swinburne, 'Miracles', *Philosophical Quarterly* 18 (1968), 320–8 (325); Robert Larmer, *Water Into Wine? An Investigation of the Concept of Miracle* (Montreal: McGill-Queen's University Press, 1986), 108.

11 Cf. Ronald Hutton, *Shamans: Siberian Spirituality and the Western Imagination* (London: Hambledon, and New York: Continuum, 2001), 67, and Fiona Bowie's discussion below in Chapter 9.

12 Kenneth L. Woodward, *The Book of Miracles: The Meaning of the Miracle Stories in Christianity, Judaism, Buddhism, Hinduism and Islam* (New York: Simon & Schuster, 2000), 384.

13 *Ibid.*, 385. In this connection Andrew M. Greeley, *Religion as Poetry* (New Brunswick and London: Transaction, 1996), 91, can be noted as reporting that, for example, 14 per cent of atheists in Britain and 30 per cent in Germany believe in miracles.

14 See Hermann Cohen, *Religion of Reason out of the Sources of Judaism*, trans. Simon Kaplan (Atlanta: Scholars Press, 1995) and the discussion by Kenneth Seeskin in Chapter 14.

15 To aid this discussion, each chapter is followed by a 'further reading' list, and the single most important item identified by each of the contributors is starred (*).

Further reading

Woodward, Kenneth L., *The Book of Miracles: The Meaning of the Miracle Stories in Christianity, Judaism, Buddhism, Hinduism and Islam* (New York: Simon & Schuster, 2000)

Part I

Fundamental issues

1 What is a miracle?

DAVID BASINGER

The concept of miracle is very important in many religions, as evidence of both God's existence and God's benevolent presence in our world.[1] However, the meaning of 'miracle' often differs significantly, even within a given religion. Moreover, a number of these meanings have generated important critical discussion. The main purpose of this chapter is not to discuss whether miracles do occur (ontological or metaphysical questions) or can be known to occur (epistemological questions). The main purpose is to outline the various meanings or definitions of miracle, note some of the conceptual difficulties, and when relevant share my own perspective.

In its most general sense, a miracle is something quite unusual or unexpected. Some use the term to describe any unexpected event – from an unanticipated job offer, to the rediscovery of a hopelessly lost heirloom, to the rapid, welcomed change in a person's behaviour. More commonly, the term is used in a more restricted manner, being applied only to those very unusual events that we would not have expected to occur, given the relevant natural laws – events such as the survival of a fall from the top of a tall building or the immediate total recovery of a person dying of cancer.

When used in either of these general senses, the events labelled miracles are often assumed to be solely the result of non-purposeful natural activity – that is, are understood to be events we would not have expected, given the natural order, but that are in principle fully explainable naturally. In religious contexts, however, the term 'miracle' has a narrower focus. It is normally applied to unusual, remarkable events that it is assumed would not have occurred in the context in question if not for the *intentional activity of a supernatural being*.

It is here that we encounter our first, and most basic, challenge to the concept of a religious miracle: the contention that belief in the existence of supernatural beings who involve themselves in earthly affairs is not rational. For example, in his very popular and influential book, *The God Delusion*, Richard Dawkins maintains not only that a supernatural creator almost certainly does not exist but that religious faith qualifies as a delusional false belief.[2] Others, both past and present, agree.[3] However, while it is granted by many that these non-theistic critics are justified in believing personally that supernatural interventive agents do not exist, such critics have not, in the estimation of most philosophers of religion, established in an objective, non-question-begging manner that theists cannot justifiably believe both that supernatural beings exist and that such beings intentionally act in our world.[4] And this will be sufficient for our purposes.

INITIAL CLARIFICATIONS

While it is true that religious miracles are usually understood to be events resulting from intentional supernatural activity, more specificity is needed since not all acknowledged supernatural activity is normally considered miraculous. It should first be noted that many religions posit the existence of a number of supernatural beings, some benevolent and others malevolent. For example, many variants of Christianity posit not only the existence of God and other benevolent supernatural beings such as angels but also the existence of Satan and other malevolent supernatural beings such as demons. And it is often acknowledged that unusual, even awe-producing, events are the result of the intentional activity of malevolent supernatural beings. For example, the wonders performed by Pharaoh's sorcerers in the biblical story of the exodus of God's people from Egypt are sometimes considered the activity of a malevolent supernatural agent (Satan), as are some of the unusual events related to the occult or witchcraft.

In most religions, however, 'miracle' is reserved for an event that would not have occurred when and how it did without the intentional activity of a *benevolent* supernatural agent: a being who stands as the main recipient of worship or adoration and is normally referred to as God. In other words, most theists today still hold that 'if we have no reason to think that an event is something done by God, we have no reason to call it a miracle'.[5]

This does not mean for most theists that miracles never involve the intentional activity of beings other than God – for example faith healers or angels. However, it is usually assumed that even in such cases, the ultimate source of the miracle is the power and intentionality of God, who is either working through human or subservient supernatural agents or has bestowed on these agents certain powers.[6]

It is also important to specify further the type of the divine activity most theists have in mind when conceiving of the miraculous. Theists normally hold that many, if not most, events are acts of God (are the result of divine causal activity) in the broad, fundamental sense that God has created the universe, established the laws that govern the natural order, and continues to sustain these natural laws by divine power. In this sense, the birth of a baby or the intricacies of other bodily systems can be said to be acts of God. And some, such as Augustine, have at times referred to divine activity of this sort as miraculous. Most theists, however, also maintain that there are some events – for example, healings – that would not have occurred in the exact manner in which they did if God had not intentionally brought it about that this would be so – that is, if God had not at some point and in some manner directly imposed the divine will on the natural order. Miraculous occurrences, not surprisingly, are normally considered to fall within (be a subset of) this 'direct act of God' category.

Furthermore, while many theists believe that some of their personal, internal religious experiences – for example, an unexpected sense of freedom from long-standing guilt or some form of debilitating obsessive thought – have been divinely induced, it has not been my professional or personal experience that most consider such experiences miraculous. Usually, 'miracle' is reserved for those unusual or unexpected events that are 'public' in the sense that they are, in principle, observable to all as occurrences that would not have been expected to happen, given our understanding of the natural order.

Another, more significant clarification relates to the manner in which events normally considered miracles are experienced by those observing or experiencing them. Many theists believe that God has at times intervened in earthly affairs to punish humanity or encourage obedience. Many Christians believe, for instance, that God sent a plague that killed 70,000 individuals as punishment for one of King David's indiscretions and took the lives of Ananias and Saphira to demonstrate to the early Christian church (and us today) the severe consequences of lying in God's presence. However, while it is normally accepted that such activity was brought about by a benevolent God – a being who is perfectly good and cares for us – such divine activity has seldom, in my experience or reading, been labelled miraculous. 'Miracle' is normally reserved for those observable outworkings of divine activity that we experience as desirable – that we are very pleased have occurred – and for which we are, therefore, grateful. For instance, while many Christians will acknowledge both that a benevolent God can, and sometimes does, intervene directly to 'take believers home' and that God can, and does, sometimes directly heal individuals, only the latter form of intentional divine activity is normally considered miraculous.

Or, to state this important point somewhat differently, while most theists believe that a benevolent God can and does for good reasons bring about events that are experienced at least initially as unpleasant and undesired – for instance, the unexpected and grieved loss of a desired object that has become an 'idol' or a desired relationship that is at its core unhealthy – what qualifies an event as a miracle for most is that its unexpected occurrence evokes at the time it occurs a very *positive* response.[7]

However, what may be viewed as desirable or in a positive manner by one person may not be viewed as such by another. And this exemplifies a very important general epistemological point: that what is considered miraculous is always to some extent contextual – is always relative in part to how the event is perceived by a given person.

As I see it, though, the most significant way in which this subjectivity plays out is not in relation to the personal impact the event in question has on those observing it. Rather, the most significant manifestation of this subjectivity is found in the varying extent to which theists encountering the same unusual, unexpected events will consider them the result of direct divine activity. By definition, whether a given theist will consider an unusual, even awe-producing, event a miracle is always dependent on whether this theist believes the event to be an 'act of God'. However, it is very important to recognize that this determination is almost always a function, in part, of this theist's *prior* understanding of how God works in our world. A good example of the significance of such background beliefs can be found in the differing theistic responses to the activity of faith healers. For those theists who believe that God currently works through men and women of faith to bring about healing that would not have occurred without intentional divine manipulation of the natural order, reported healings can, in principle, still be considered miracles.

However, some Christians question whether many of the 'gifts of the spirit', including the miraculous gift of healing, are still operative today. These individuals do not deny that God has in the past healed through individuals. Nor do they deny that God can and does today miraculously heal individuals directly. But these Christians believe that, while the gift of healing, along with the other gifts, was at one time a necessary way of validating the religious teachings of certain individuals – a way of demonstrating that such individuals were divinely anointed transmitters of religious truth – such validation became unnecessary once God's primary means of doctrinal revelation, the Bible, was completed and available. Or, as stated clearly by one proponent of this position, 'The spiritual gifts were used of the Lord to bring the revelation of His will to [humans]. But when this revelation was committed to writing as it was in the first century, there remained no further purpose to be fulfilled by these gifts.'[8] Thus, for these Christians, the alleged healings performed by individuals today are not considered miraculous, even if the occurrence of the events is granted, as these theists do not currently acknowledge a valid pattern of benevolent divine intervention of this sort in our world.

This is not to say that observing or experiencing a given occurrence – for example, the immediate disappearance of a parent's cancerous growth at a healing service – might not for a given theist lead her or him to affirm a divine action pattern not previously acknowledged. But I see this as the rare exception to the rule. So, I remain convinced that for most theists a necessary condition for labelling an event a miracle is that it be an instantiation of a recognized divine action pattern. And if this is so, then since these patterns differ from theist to theist, it is not surprising that the types of events that will, in principle, be considered miraculous also differ from theist to theist.

CONTINUING CONTROVERSIES

Significant and diverse debates surrounding the definition of 'miracle' abound. However, what probably still generates the greatest amount and intensity of debate is the question of how we are to understand or conceive of the relationship between miraculous events and the laws of nature.

At least since the time of Hume, miracles have often been defined by proponents and critics alike as *violations of natural laws*. While there is no non-controversial understanding of what would constitute a violation of such laws, something like the following seems frequently to be intended by most. Natural laws, it is held, describe actual uniformities that occur in our world. More specifically, they are universal generalizations describing what will happen (or not) under specifiable conditions. Moreover, some of our best-established natural laws confirm for us, for instance, that water does not turn instantly into wine and that a floating body always displaces an amount of fluid the weight of which is equal to its own weight.

But let us assume that water actually did turn instantly into wine or that someone were to walk on water. We would then, it is argued, be required to acknowledge not only the occurrence of an event that our knowledge of natural laws gives us good reason to believe will not occur; more importantly, we would then be required to acknowledge the occurrence of an event for which we could justifiably conclude no natural explanation could ever be forthcoming. And, thus, proponents of this line of reasoning conclude, we would be justified in assuming that the relevant natural laws had been violated.[9]

One oft-repeated critical response is that to conceive of a violation of natural laws in this manner is incoherent. Natural laws, it is argued, are simply statements that describe 'the actual course of events'. Thus, we could never find ourselves justifiably claiming both that our current set of natural laws is adequate and that some acknowledged occurrence is a violation of these laws in the sense that it is a true counter-instance to these laws – is an event for which no natural explanation could ever be forthcoming. Events that are true counter-instances to current laws might well occur. But to acknowledge that an event is a true counter-instance to established laws only demonstrates the law(s) in question to be inadequate since we must always be willing, in principle, to expand our natural laws to accommodate any occurrence, no matter how unusual. So a violation of our natural laws – if viewed as a true counter-instance to true (adequate) laws – is conceptually impossible.[10]

Many, though, view this criticism as question-begging. To maintain that natural laws accurately describe the natural order, it is noted, is to say only that they correctly predict what will occur under a specified set of *natural conditions*. But to maintain that an event is a miraculous counter-instance to a set of natural laws – for instance, that water has turned into wine – is not to maintain that some event has occurred under the exact set of natural conditions covered by these laws. It is to maintain, rather, that an additional non-natural causal force, namely direct divine activity, was also present in this case. Thus, even if we grant that a fully natural counter-instance to a set of natural laws would require an expansion of our natural laws to accommodate this occurrence, such expansion would not be required for a counter-instance that was the result in part of non-natural causal forces. So since it cannot be demonstrated in an objective, non-question-begging manner that supernatural activity is impossible – since it cannot be demonstrated that forces from outside the natural system cannot influence observed activity in our world – the concept of a divinely induced true counter-instance to natural laws remains coherent.[11] And if this is so, then *for those who grant that a true counter-instance to a natural law can rightly be labelled a violation regardless of the type of causal factors involved,*[12] a violation of natural laws can be considered a coherent concept.

Since I agree with most philosophers of religion that supernatural causal activity in our world can justifiably be assumed to occur, I not surprisingly agree that to define a miracle as a true counter-instance to natural laws (and thus as a 'violation' in this sense) is not conceptually incoherent.[13] However, is it wise for a theist to define a miracle as a true counter-instance to natural laws? That is, should a theist embrace a conceptual understanding of the miraculous as an observable event that could never be fully explained by any set of natural laws, even those established in the future?

It is *very important* at this point to distinguish between the claim that a given occurrence was in fact the result of solely natural causal factors and the claim that this occurrence could have been the result of natural causal factors alone. If we assume, as we are, that miracles are by definition in part the result of intentional supernatural activity – are not, in fact, the result of natural factors alone – then a miraculous occurrence must itself, as an event token, always be considered permanently inexplicable naturally. But this leaves open the question of whether the label of 'miracle' should be reserved for only those occurrences that are permanently inexplicable in the sense that no event of this type could ever be given a fully natural explanation – is an event type that nature could never produce on its own. And this continues to be the subject of considerable debate.

Those theists and non-theists who believe it unwise to conceive of a miracle as a permanently inexplicable event type offer a straightforward, seemingly compelling argument. To define a miracle as permanently inexplicable in this sense allows a person to claim that any given event is actually a miracle only if we are, or could be, in a position to state with certainty or high probability that a given type of event could never be given a fully natural explanation. However, the scientific enterprise is continually discovering new, often startling and unexpected, information about the causal relationships which operate in our universe. And the annals of science record numerous instances in which counter-instances to supposedly well-established natural laws were later demonstrated – sometimes only after significant conceptual shifts – in fact to be consistent with such laws or revisions thereof. Accordingly, would it not be the height of scientific provincialism for a theist (or anyone else) ever to decide, solely on the basis of the data presently available, that it was now justifiable to label a given occurrence permanently inexplicable naturally? Given our necessarily limited understanding of the true nature of reality, would not the more reasonable response to even the most unusual of anomalies be for theists to assume that the scientist should continue to run tests indefinitely or simply label the occurrence a 'freak event' and await the occurrence of similar phenomena before seriously investigating further?[14]

A number of philosophers are not convinced. Richard Swinburne, for instance, makes a distinction between repeatable and non-repeatable anomalies and then states the following:

> We have to some extent good evidence about what are the laws of nature, and some of them are so well established and account for so many data that any modification of them which we could suggest to account for the odd counter-instance would be so clumsy and *ad hoc* as to upset the whole structure of science. In such cases the evidence is strong that if the purported counter-instance occurred it was a violation of the law of nature. There is good reason to believe that the following events, if they occurred, would be violation of the laws of nature: levitation; resurrection from the dead in full health of a man whose heart has not been beating for twenty-four hours and who was dead also by other currently used criteria; water turning into wine without the assistance of chemical apparatus or catalysts; a man getting better from polio in a minute. We know quite enough about how things behave to be reasonably certain that ... these events are physically impossible.[15]

Robert Larmer also believes there are events imaginable that could clearly be identified as permanently beyond the pale of natural explanation. Let us assume, for instance, he asks, that there is a man who claims to have healing powers from God and we are 'able to capture on film occasions when, immediately following the prayers of this man, fingers lost to leprosy were regrown to their original form and length in a matter of seconds, and occasions when eyes severely burned by acid were immediately restored to sight'. And let us further assume that this man can heal any kind of disease and can heal those who are separated from him by various barriers – for example, lead screens or strong electromagnetic fields or great distance.[16] In cases such as this, argues Larmer, it would, in fact, 'require a greater act of faith to interpret such events naturalistically' than to assume that natural explanations could never be forthcoming.[17]

It seems to me, however, that Swinburne and Larmer present us with a false dilemma. They would have us believe that given certain real or imaginable occurrences that are seeming counter-instances to well-established laws, our choice is solely between declaring the type of event in question permanently inexplicable naturally or declaring that there is a fully natural explanation (even if it is yet to be found). But, as I see it, the more reasonable alternative is still the option noted earlier: to acknowledge that the *event type* in question *might* be inexplicable naturally but to continue to search for a natural explanation. To do so would not functionally damage the natural laws in question since, as Swinburne acknowledges, it is only repeatable or frequent counter-instances which falsify natural laws. That is, unless the type of event in question were repeatable naturally or occurred over and over, the practical value of the relevant laws for predicting the behaviour of the natural order would remain.

This is not to say, of course, that the anomalies of the sort envisioned by Swinburne and Larmer would ever as event types in fact be subsumable under natural laws. It is only to say that there is no theoretical or practical need to state with certainty that events of this type could or could not at some point be given a fully natural explanation. It alleviates, for instance, the awkward, undesirable necessity for scientists (or any of us) to make predictions concerning the future limits of scientific explanation.

Furthermore, it is important to remember, to leave open the question of whether any given *type of event* is permanently inexplicable naturally does not require us to deny that any given event itself, *as an event token*, is not in fact the result in part of supernatural design and thus could never be given a fully natural explanation. So to leave open the question of whether a given event type could ever be given a fully natural explanation does not make it less likely that miracles occur.

However, it does have a significant epistemological implication. If we ought always to leave open the question of event type natural explicability, then we will never be in a position to maintain justifiably that a miracle, defined as the type of event for which a natural explanation could never be given, has actually occurred. And this may be one of the reasons why some have chosen not to limit the definition of miracle solely to those types of events that could never be given a natural explanation, accepting as miracles also (or instead) those awe-producing, divinely induced events that have at *present* as event types no fully natural explanation. In the *Catholic Encyclopedia*, for instance, we read that 'a miracle is said to be above nature when the effect produced is above the native powers and forces in creatures of which the *known* laws of nature are the expression'.[18] And in the *American Heritage Dictionary* we read that a miracle is 'an event that *appears inexplicable* by the laws of nature and so is held to be supernatural in origin or an act of God'.[19]

No one denies that this is a coherent conceptualization of the miraculous. However, we have already seen the price to pay for this definition: that an event currently labelled a miracle can lose this distinction, and thus whatever apologetic force it had as an unexplained anomaly, if science does indeed identify a natural cause for the type of event in question. Or, as Theodore Drange rightly states this point, 'If events which cannot at present be explained ... were to come to be explained naturalistically in the future, then, in retrospect, it would need to be said of them that they were never miracles, although they may at one time have (erroneously) been thought to be that'.[20]

There have always been, though, a significant number of theists who do not believe an observable event need be of a type that cannot be explained naturally to be considered miraculous. Take, for instance, the classic story by R. F. Holland. A child riding his toy motorcar strays onto an unguarded railway crossing near his house whereupon a wheel of his car gets stuck down the side of one of the rails. At that exact moment, an express train is approaching with the signals in its favour. Also a curve in the track will make it impossible for the driver to stop his train in time to avoid any obstruction he might encounter on the crossing. Moreover, the child is so engrossed in freeing his wheel that he hears neither the train whistle nor his mother, who has just come out of the house and is trying to get his attention. The child appears to be doomed. But just before the train rounds the curve, the brakes are applied and it comes to rest a few feet from the child. The mother thanks God for the miracle although she learns in due course that there was not necessarily anything supernatural about the manner in which the brakes came to be applied. The driver had fainted, for a reason that had nothing to do with the presence of the child on the line, and the brakes were applied automatically as his hand ceased to exert pressure on the control lever.[21]

The event sequence described in this situation includes no component for which a natural explanation is not available. Boys sometimes play on train tracks, drivers sometimes faint, and the brakes of trains have been constructed to become operative when a driver's hand releases the control lever. But another explanation presents itself in this case: that God directly intervened to cause the driver to faint at the precise moment. And as the theists in question see it, if God did directly intervene in this instance, the event can be considered a miracle, even though a totally natural explanation would also be available.

In short, to generalize, there are a number of theists who do not want to limit the range of the term 'miracle' to only those direct acts of God for which no natural explanation can presently be offered. They want to expand the definition to cover events in relation to which God can be viewed as having directly manipulated the natural order, regardless of anyone's ability to construct plausible alternate natural causal scenarios. To do so, as David Corner points out, allows us to continue to conceive of the miraculous as something 'contrary to our expectations ... an event that elicits wonder, though the object of our wonder seems not so much to be *how* [an event comes to be] as the simple fact *that* [it occurs] when it did'.[22]

It is important to emphasize here that those who allow for, or favour, this 'coincidence' definition of miracle are not thereby saying that any miraculous event can, itself, be considered fully explainable naturally and thus a mere coincidence. That is, while these theists are granting that nature itself could have brought about an event of this type, they are not thereby saying that nature itself did in fact produce fully the event in question. They agree with Corner that a miracle can never be 'a mere coincidence no matter how extraordinary or significant. (If you miss a plane and the plane crashes, that is not a miracle unless God intervened in the natural course of events causing you to miss the flight.)' As an event token, 'an observed occurrence cannot be considered a miracle, no matter how remarkable, unless the "coincidence" itself is caused by divine intervention (i.e. [is] not really a coincidence at all)'.[23]

However, it is in relation to this conception of the miraculous that some have wanted to introduce a different understanding of the nature of the intentional divine activity involved. As just noted, all who affirm the concept of a 'coincidence' miracle agree that while nature left to itself can produce events of the type in question, the specific miraculous event in question would not, itself, have occurred if God had not interrupted the way things would have happened naturally by purposely manipulating the natural order. Furthermore, most in this camp assume God's interventive activity occurs *at the time* of the miraculous occurrence. For instance, most who considered the preservation of the boy's life in Holland's train scenario the result of intentional divine intervention would be assuming that God brought it about that the driver fainted *at the time* the train rounds the bend. And most who believed God brought it about that someone misses a fatal flight would be assuming that God did so *at the time* the person was attempting to reach the airport or board the plane.

However, as philosophers such as Robert Adams have pointed out, there is another way to think of God's activity in this context. We can, Adams tells us, conceive of God creating 'the world in such a way that it was physically predetermined from the beginning' that nature would act in the appropriate way 'at precisely the time at which God foresaw' it would be needed.[24] For example, we can conceive of God creating the world in such a way that a specific individual driving a train would faint at a specific time in order to save the life of a young boy. And we can conceive of God creating the world in such a way that a specific tyre on a specific car would go flat at the exact time required to ensure that the person driving the car would miss a fatal flight.

This perspective is also evident in the thinking of those rabbis mentioned in the Talmud who argued that to maintain that the walls of Jericho came down at the precise time needed to ensure an Israelite victory was the result of divine intervention does not necessitate believing that God intervened in the natural order at the time this event occurred. It can be assumed instead that God determined when setting up the natural order that an earthquake would bring down the walls 'naturally' at the exact time this needed to occur.[25]

In all these cases, to restate the general point, God is still viewed as directly intervening in the sense that God purposely manipulates the natural order to bring about some event that would not have occurred without this intentional divine activity. However, God is not viewed as directly intervening in the sense that God directly manipulates a natural order already in place. It is held, rather, that the intentional divine activity takes place when God was planning how the natural order would operate and not at the time this predetermined natural activity occurred.[26]

As Corner sees it, however, any conception of the miraculous that is built upon supernatural *causation* – that assumes that God is the main *causal force* in the occurrence of the event in question, and thus that the event itself could not have been produced by nature alone – is problematic.[27] First, he points out, the concept of a supernatural causal force overriding or modifying the relevant natural causes is very difficult to explicate coherently.[28] Moreover, he adds, we can meaningfully speak of an agent performing a *basic action* – for example, a person lifting her arm – 'without being committed to a *causal* analysis of what she has done'.[29] Accordingly, he concludes, the best understanding of miracle is not one in which a miraculous occurrence is held to be an instance of supernatural causality superseding or modifying these laws.[30] The best understanding of miracle, rather, is one that views the miraculous as a basic divine action that 'contradicts any reasonable expectations about what is going to happen' but is in need of no causal explanation *vis-à-vis* the natural order.[31]

I agree with Corner that any attempt to explain fully how (or even to conceive of how) some supernatural force can override, suspend or modify the natural order is difficult at best. And I am willing to grant that we can claim coherently and justifiably that an event is the result of intentional divine agency without being in a position to give a complete or even partial causal explanation (although many will wonder whether acknowledging that an event is the result of intentional divine activity does not count as giving a partial causal explanation). However, I do not see this as a meaningful critique of a causal account of the miraculous – of an account of the miraculous that holds the events in question to be the result of supernatural causal forces outside of nature – since to view miracle in this way is not to say one can explain such causation or even understand exactly how such causation is possible. It is simply to make what I see as the coherent and justifiable claim that the event in question would not have come about when and how it did if God had not intentionally decided that this should be so and done what is necessary (whatever that might be) to ensure its occurrence.

Might it not be argued, though, that even this sort of non-causal conceptualization of the miraculous is too narrow? While this conceptualization challenges the standard claim that a miraculous event itself, as an event token, is the result of supernatural causal forces, it can still be assumed that a miracle must be understood to be the result of intentional divine agency – that is, it is still being assumed that a miracle is an event that would not have occurred as it did if God had not intended it to occur in this manner.

But is it necessary to conceive of a miracle as directly involving the intentional activity of God in any way? Most theists, as we have seen, agree with John Hick that whatever else it may be, a miracle 'is an event through which we become vividly and immediately ... aware of God's presence'.[32] That is, most theists believe that a necessary condition for the miraculous is that it be an awe-producing event that *points to* the divine. However, could defining a miracle solely in terms of this effect on individuals be sufficient?

This type of 'affective miracle' is obviously coherent and possible. And it may well be that for some theists, especially those 'liberal' or 'neo-orthodox' theists who believe that the essence of religion lies not in what has actually occurred but rather in the spiritual effect that what occurs has on us, this is the most attractive and useful way of conceiving of the miraculous. However, as noted earlier, for most theists, a necessary condition for the miraculous is that God be directly involved. And even if it is granted that intentional divine activity is not a necessary condition, those theists who believe God can manipulate the natural order will understandably be reticent to believe that God does not at times do so and will thus be very reticent to maintain that only 'affective miracles' occur or that this type of miracle should be given greater emphasis.

CONCLUSION

What then is a miracle? The preceding discussion has hopefully shown that simply to assume there is a standard definition of miracle to which these questions are applied is misguided. There is no one standard religious way of understanding the concept of miracle. Most theists, as we have seen, do conceive of the miraculous as an unusual, unexpected, awe-producing observable event due in part to the intentional activity of a benevolent God. We have also seen, though, that theists differ significantly on the nature of the divine activity in question. Some assume that God directly manipulates the natural order at the time the event occurs. Others assume that God predetermines that nature will bring about the event. Still others assume that God makes us aware of fully natural events as signs of the divine presence and care for us.

And we have seen that theists differ even more significantly on the natural explicability of the event itself. Some assume that the type of event in question is permanently inexplicable naturally. Others assume that while the event itself is permanently inexplicable, the type of event in question is explicable naturally. Still others assume that even the event itself might have a fully natural explanation.

Moreover, each of these definitional understandings of 'miracle' can trigger quite different conceptual, ontological and epistemological questions. Thus, to avoid reductionistic, question-begging treatments of the miraculous, it is important that those discussing any given conception of 'miracle' acknowledge explicitly both that the concept of miracle with which they are working is but one of many and that their analysis is, accordingly, not necessarily relevant to 'miracle' *simpliciter* but rather primarily to the given conception they have chosen to address.

Notes

1 See, for example, Kenneth L. Woodward, *The Book of Miracles: The Meaning of the Miracle Stories in Christianity, Judaism, Buddhism, Hinduism, Islam* (New York: Simon & Schuster, 2000).

2 Richard Dawkins, *The God Delusion* (Boston: Houghton Mifflin, 2006).

3 See, for instance, Christopher Hitchens, *God Is Not Great: How Religion Poisons Everything* (New York: Twelve/Hachette Book Group USA/Warner Books, 2007). Some influential past atheists include John Stuart Mill, Frederick Nietzsche, Bertrand Russell and A. J. Ayer.

4 See, for instance, Alvin Plantinga, *Warranted Christian Belief* (New York: Oxford University Press, 2000) and David Basinger, *Religious Diversity: A Philosophical Assessment* (Burlington: Ashgate, 2002), 31–53. It should also be noted that even some theists – for example, process theists – do not in fact believe that God can unilaterally intervene in earthly affairs. See John Cobb and David Griffin, *Process Theology: An Introductory Exposition* (Philadelphia: Westminster Press, 1976).

5 David Corner, 'The Definition of "Miracle"' in 'Miracles', *Internet Encyclopedia of Philosophy*, n.p. [cited 10 June 2008]. Online: www.iep.utm.edu/mmiracles/.htm

6 J. Randi, *The Faith Healers* (Amherst: Prometheus, 1987); Stanley M. Burgess, Gary B. McGee and Patrick H. Alexander, eds., *Dictionary of Pentecostal and Charismatic Movements* (Grand Rapids: Zondervan, 1988).

7 See, for example, John Hick, *God and the Universe of Faith* (Oxford: Oneworld, 1973).

8 Roy Dunavin, 'The Holy Spirit and Miraculous Spiritual Gifts' (1996), n.p. [cited 15 June 2008]. Online: www.westarkchurchofchrist.org/library/holyspirit.htm. Theists who hold this perspective are normally labelled dispensationalists.

9 I first offered this explication of the concept of a violation of natural laws in Michael Peterson *et al.*, eds., *Reason and Religious Belief* (New York: Oxford University Press, 1991), 157. See also Theodore Drange, 'Science and Miracle' (1998) in *The Secular Web Library: Modern Library*, n.p. [cited 10 June 2008]. Online: www.infidels.org/library/modern/theodore_drange/miracles.html.

10 See, for instance, Alistair McKinnon, '"Miracle" and "Paradox"', *American Philosophical Quarterly* 4 (1967), 308–14 (309–12).

11 See, for instance, Robert Larmer, 'Miracles and the Laws of Nature', in *Questions of Miracle*, ed. Robert Larmer (Montreal: McGill-Queen's University Press, 1996), 40–9; Michael Levine, *Hume and the Problem of Miracles: A Solution*, Philosophical Studies Series 41 (Dordrecht: Kluwer, 1989), 67; and Peter Byrne, 'Miracles and the Philosophy of Science', *Heythrop Journal* 19 (1978), 162–70 (166–9).

12 It must be noted that not all theists who believe that miracles are true counter-instances to natural laws believe that miracles should be considered violations of these laws. Such theists maintain that only

if a true counter-instance to natural laws had solely natural causes could it be considered a true violation of these laws. Hence, since miracles by definition are necessarily the result in part of non-natural causal forces, they maintain that miracles ought not to be conceived of as violations of these laws. This is the view, for instance, of Robert Lamar, who argues that once we understand that the basic laws of nature describe the normal, predictable behaviour of the 'stuff' (mass/ energy) of which the natural order is composed, 'it can be seen that, although a miracle is an event which would never have occurred without the overriding of nature, this in no way entails that a miracle involves a violation of the laws of nature'. Larmer, 'Miracles and the Laws of Nature', 48.

13   Basinger, *Religious Diversity*, 31–53.
14   I first made this point in David Basinger, 'Christian Theism and the Concept of Miracle: Some Epistemological Complexities', *The Southern Journal of Philosophy* 2 (1980), 137–50 (139–40).
15   Richard Swinburne, *The Concept of Miracle* (London: Macmillan, 1970), 31–2.
16   Robert Larmer, 'Miracles and Criteria', in *Questions of Miracle*, ed. Robert Larmer (Montreal: McGill-Queen's University Press, 1996), 76–82 (79).
17   *Ibid.*, 80.
18   Kevin Knight, 'Miracle', in *The Catholic Encyclopedia*, n.p. [cited 12 June 2008]. Online: www.newadvent.org/cathen/10338a.htm.
19   *American Heritage Dictionary* (Boston: Houghton Mifflin, 2000), my emphasis.
20   Drange, 'Science and Miracle'.
21   R. F. Holland, 'The Miraculous', *American Philosophical Quarterly* 2 (1965), 43–51 (43).
22   David Corner, 'Coincidence Miracles' in 'Miracles', *Internet Encyclopedia of Philosophy*, his emphasis.
23   Michael Levine, 'Introduction', in 'Miracles', *Stanford Encyclopedia of Philosophy*, n.p. [cited 10 June 2008]. Online: http://plato.stanford.edu/ entries/miracles/.
24   Robert Merrihew Adams, 'Miracles, Laws and Natural Causation (II)', *Proceedings of the Aristotelian Society* Supplementary volume (1992), 207–24 (209).
25   Midrash *Genesis Rabbah* 5.45; Midrash *Exodus Rabbah* 21.6; and *Pirqê Avôth* (Sayings of the Fathers) 5.6. See also Stephen Howard, 'Miracles', in *Liberal Judaism*, n.p. [cited 15 June 2008]. Online: www.liberaljudaism.org/lj_wherewestand_miracles.htm. This type of divine 'preplanning' will, of course, be acceptable only to those who believe that God decreed all before creation or that God possesses middle knowledge (knows beforehand what will actually happen in each conceivable situation).
26   For theological determinists such as Calvin and Luther, this distinction in a very real sense collapses since, given this model of divine sovereignty, God has in every case decreed both the event and the means

necessary to ensure that it comes about. Thus, Thomas Aquinas can say, for instance, that 'we pray not in order to change the divine disposition but for the sake of acquiring by petitionary prayer what God has disposed to be achieved by prayer'. See *Summa Contra Gentiles* 2a–2ae, q. 83, a.2.4.

27 David Corner, *The Philosophy of Miracle* (New York: Continuum, 2007).
28 *Ibid.*, Chapter 2.
29 *Ibid.*, 3.
30 *Ibid.*, 1–6.
31 *Ibid.*, 14, 15–16.
32 Hick, *God and the Universe of Faith*, 51.

Further reading

Basinger, David, 'Christian Theism and the Concept of Miracle: Some Epistemological Complexities', *The Southern Journal of Philosophy* 2 (1980), 137–50

*Burns, Robert M., *The Great Debate on Miracles* (Lewisburg: Bucknell University Press, 1981)

Corner, David, *The Philosophy of Miracles* (New York: Continuum, 2007)

Earman, John, *Hume's Abject Failure: The Argument Against Miracles* (New York: Oxford University Press, 2000)

Fogelin, Robert, *Defense of Hume on Miracles* (Princeton: Princeton University Press, 2003)

Hambourger, Robert, 'Need Miracles Be Extraordinary?', *Philosophy and Phenomenological Research* 3 (1987), 435–49

Houston, Joseph, *Reported Miracles: A Critique of Hume* (Cambridge: Cambridge University Press, 1994)

Hume, David, 'Of Miracles', in *Enquiries Concerning Human Understanding*, 3rd edn, ed. L. A. Selby-Bigge, rev. and notes P. H. Nidditch (Oxford: Oxford University Press, 1975), 109–31

Larmer, Robert, *Water Into Wine? An Investigation of the Concept of Miracle* (Montreal: McGill-Queen's University Press, 1988)

Larmer, Robert, ed., *Questions of Miracle* (Montreal: McGill-Queen's University Press, 1996)

Levine, Michael P., *Hume and the Problem of Miracles: A Solution*, Philosophical Studies Series 41 (Dordrecht: Kluwer, 1989)

Lewis, C. S., *Miracles* (New York: Macmillan, 1947)

Mackie, J. L., *The Miracle of Theism: Arguments For and Against the Existence of God* (New York: Oxford University Press, 1982)

Swinburne, Richard, *The Concept of Miracle* (London: Macmillan, 1970)

Swinburne, Richard, ed., *Miracles* (New York: Macmillan, 1989)

Williams, T. C., *The Idea of the Miraculous: The Challenge of Science and Religion* (New York: St Martin's, 1991)

Woodward, Kenneth, *The Book of Miracles: The Meaning of the Miracle Stories in Christianity, Judaism, Buddhism, Hinduism and Islam* (New York: Simon & Schuster, 2000)

2 The meanings of miracle

ROBERT A. LARMER

I take a miracle to be: (1) an event which would never have occurred
except through the action of a transcendent rational agent, (2) an event
that has religious significance in the sense that it can reasonably be
viewed as furthering God's purposes and (3) an event of such an extraordinary nature that it is either directly perceived as a supernatural
intervention in the normal order of nature or immediately inferred as
such. If such events occur what do they mean for science, philosophy
and theology?

MIRACLES AND SCIENCE

A common view is that miracles, so defined, necessarily involve
violation of the laws of nature. The assumption seems to be that the
only way a supernatural overriding of the normal course of nature can
take place is by violating some law of nature. If this assumption is
correct two problems arise.

First, it is not clear that the concept of a law of nature being
violated is logically coherent. Three major types of theories are proposed as accounts of the laws of nature: (1) regularity theories, (2) nomic
necessity theories and (3) causal dispositions theories.[1] On all these
theories the concept of a violation of a law of nature is problematic.[2]

On regularity theories, laws of nature are universal generalizations
made on the basis of, and summarily descriptive of, what actually
happens in nature. Such theories imply that no event could violate a
law of nature, since laws of nature are understood simply to describe
what actually happens.[3]

On nomic necessity theories, laws of nature are taken to describe
necessary connections between events. Such theories regard laws of
nature not simply as statements of the actual course of events but as
universal generalizations that support counterfactual conditionals,
namely what must take place *if* such and such occurs. Again, the

implication is that no event could violate a law of nature, since, as William Craig notes, 'so long as natural laws are *universal* generalizations based on experience, they must take account of anything that happens and so would be revised should an event occur which the law does not encompass'.[4]

On causal disposition theories, laws of nature express metaphysically necessary truths regarding causal dispositions possessed by physical things. Such theories hold that physical things have natural tendencies or powers that are a result of their nature and that the laws of nature describe these tendencies or powers. For example, sodium chloride has an atomic structure that disposes it to dissolve in water, all other things being equal and no other causal forces intervening. If something does not dissolve in water under such conditions then it is not salt but something other than salt.[5] As in the case of regularity theories and nomic necessity theories, causal disposition theories imply that no event could violate a law of nature, since laws of nature are taken to express metaphysically necessary truths. It thus becomes clear that defining miracles as involving violation of the laws of nature commits one to the claim that miracles are impossible.

Second, even if sense could be made of the idea of violation of the laws of nature, the claim that a miracle implies such violation opens the door to Humean 'balance of probabilities' type arguments which pit the evidence supporting belief in the laws of nature against the evidence supporting belief in miracles. We thus get arguments along the following lines:

1. A miracle must be defined as violating the laws of nature.
2. The evidence in favour of a miracle inevitably conflicts with the evidence in favour of the laws of nature.
3. The evidence in favour of a miracle cannot exceed, even in principle, the evidence in favour of the laws of nature.
4. Therefore belief in the occurrence of a miracle can never be justified.

Those who accept that a miracle implies violation of the laws of nature, yet who wish to defend the rationality of belief in miracles, are forced to attack the third premise of this argument. This is not an easy task. Even if they are successful in demonstrating there could be circumstances in which there is sufficient evidence to justify belief in the occurrence of a miracle, they are forced to view this evidence as conflicting with another body of evidence we are strongly inclined to accept, namely the evidence which justifies belief in the laws of nature.

The assumption that divine intervention in the natural order necessarily involves violating a law of nature is incorrect.[6] That this assumption is mistaken can be seen by reflecting on the fact that the laws of nature do not by themselves allow the prediction or explanation of any event.[7] Scientific explanations must make reference not only to laws of nature but also to material conditions to which the laws apply.[8] For example, it is impossible to predict what will happen on a billiard table by making reference solely to Newton's laws of motion. One must also make reference to the number of balls on the table and their initial position. Thus, although we often speak as though the laws of nature are in themselves sufficient to explain the occurrence of an event this is not the case. C. S. Lewis notes:

> We are in the habit of talking as if they [the laws of Nature] caused events to happen; but they have never caused any event at all. The laws of motion do not set billiard balls moving: they analyse the motion after something else (say, a man with a cue, or a lurch of the liner, or, perhaps, supernatural power) has provided it. They produce no events: they state the pattern to which every event – if only it can be induced to happen – must conform, just as the rules of arithmetic state the pattern to which all transactions with money must conform – if only you can get hold of any money. Thus, in one sense the laws of Nature cover the whole field of space and time; in another, what they leave out is precisely the whole real universe – the incessant torrent of actual events which makes up true history. That must come from somewhere else. To think the laws can produce it is like thinking that you can create real money by simply doing sums.[9]

This basic distinction between the laws of nature and the 'stuff' of nature, the behaviour of which they describe, implies that miracles can occur without violating any laws of nature. If God creates or annihilates units of mass/energy, or simply causes some of these units to occupy a different position, then he changes the material conditions to which the laws of nature apply. He thereby produces an event that nature would not have produced on its own but breaks no laws of nature. One would not violate or suspend the laws of motion if one were to introduce an extra ball into a group of billiard balls on a billiard table or alter the position of one of the balls already on the table, yet that action would alter the outcome of what would otherwise be expected to happen. Similarly, if God were to create *ex nihilo* a fertilized egg in the body of a virgin no laws of nature would be broken, yet the usual course of nature would have been overridden in such a way as to bring about an event nature would not otherwise have produced.[10]

Two objections are liable to be raised against this line of argument. First, it might be objected that the term 'law of nature' should not be understood in a technical sense but rather more colloquially as meaning simply a well-established regularity of nature. On this understanding a violation of a law of nature would be an event that is a dramatic exception to such a regularity.

Unfortunately for the critic, this suggestion does not reflect even in a non-technical sense, how the term 'law of nature' is actually used. It is possible to think of exceptions to established regularities of nature that would nevertheless not be regarded as violations of the laws of nature. Consider the possible case of a woman who is a virgin and has a fertilized egg implanted in her uterus through a medical procedure. She remains a virgin and nine months later gives birth. We would hardly regard the event of her baby's birth as involving a violation of some law of nature.

The critic might protest that justice has not been done to his suggestion. Granted that we must distinguish between laws of nature and regularities of nature, it is nevertheless true that we are convinced there are established regularities of nature that in the absence of extraordinary circumstances admit of no exceptions. Could not such exceptions be plausibly viewed as violations of the laws of nature?

One can accept that, all other things being equal, there is good evidence that some regularities of nature suffer no exceptions and that virgins not giving birth falls into this category. The believer in a miracle, however, contends that all other things were not equal; in the instance of a miracle God intervenes into nature to produce an event that would not otherwise occur. Those who believe in the Virgin Birth hold that it is analogous to our hypothetical case of a virgin who through medical procedures had a fertilized egg implanted in her uterus. It is analogous not in the means by which the result of a virgin birth is achieved but rather by virtue of the fact that in neither case are 'all other things equal'. In our hypothetical case, a human agent, the doctor, intervenes to change a material situation to which the laws of nature apply, thus producing an event that would not otherwise occur. In the case of the Virgin Birth, a divine agent, God, intervenes to change a material situation to which the laws of nature apply, thus producing an event that would not otherwise occur. Both cases are exceptions to a well-established regularity of nature but in neither case are 'all other things equal', and in neither case is there any reason to suppose that the laws of nature were violated.

Second, it might be objected that on the account of miracle that has been given at least one law of nature must be broken since the creation, annihilation or moving of material entities by a non-physical agent involves the creation or destruction of energy and thus violates the Principle of the Conservation of Energy. William Stoeger, for example, claims that 'direct divine intervention ... would involve an immaterial agent acting on or within a material context as a cause ... This is not possible ... if it were ... energy ... would be added to a system spontaneously and mysteriously, contravening the conservation of energy.'[11]

This objection fails to take into consideration an important distinction between two forms of the Principle. The Principle is commonly stated either as 'Energy can neither be created nor destroyed', or 'In an isolated system the total amount of energy remains constant'. It is routinely assumed that these two statements are logically equivalent. This assumption is mistaken. From the proposition 'Energy can neither be created nor destroyed' the proposition 'In an isolated system the total amount of energy remains constant' can be deduced. But from the proposition 'In an isolated system the total amount of energy remains constant' the proposition 'Energy can neither be created nor destroyed' cannot be deduced. The latter claim involves a greater ontological commitment than the former.

The significance of this distinction is considerable. Theists cannot accept the claim that energy can neither be created nor destroyed, since it not only rules out miracles but creation *ex nihilo*.[12] Theists can, however, accept the claim that energy is conserved in an isolated system. They reject not the well-evidenced scientific claim that energy is conserved in an isolated system but the speculative metaphysical claim that nature is an isolated system not open to the causal influence of God. In short, they are in a position to affirm the Principle when it is formulated as a scientific law and not as a metaphysical commitment which excludes the possibility of theism.

Conceiving of a miracle as involving the creation or annihilation of energy does not imply violation of the Principle of the Conservation of Energy, so long as there is good reason to adopt the scientific rather than the metaphysical form of the Principle. Accepting the occurrence of a miracle does not commit one to denying the vast body of experimental evidence supporting the conservation of energy in an isolated system. Rather, it commits one to arguing that any attempt to move from the scientific formulation of the Principle to its metaphysical formulation is ill-founded.

That such attempts are questionable seems evident. All that any experiment can show is that energy was conserved in an isolated system on a particular occasion or series of occasions. This evidence is neutral regarding the further question of whether there exists something capable of creating or destroying energy. If the move from the scientific to the metaphysical form of the Principle is to be justified it must be on the grounds that there exists no evidence that energy is ever created or destroyed and that the metaphysical form provides an explanation of *why* the weak form holds true. This move is problematic on several counts.

First, the theist is able to provide an alternative explanation of the scientific form's truth. The theistic conception of the universe as a contingent reality in which secondary physical causes operate equally explains why the scientific form holds true. Appealing to the metaphysical form and insisting that energy can neither be created nor destroyed attributes necessary existence to energy rather than to God, making it clear that the metaphysical form of the Principle functions not simply as a statement of observed regularity in nature but as a defining postulate of physicalism.

Second, the metaphysical form is at odds with the Big Bang theory of the origin of the universe. This theory is interpreted as implying an absolute beginning to the mass/energy that composes the universe. It is possible to accept both the scientific form of the Principle and the Big Bang theory but it is hard to see how acceptance of the metaphysical form of the Principle is consistent with Big Bang cosmology, since it would imply that the mass/energy making up the universe had no beginning.

Third, the metaphysical form of the Principle cannot be used to reject accounts of miracles. Given a positive body of evidence for miracles, it will not do to attempt to frame a balance-of-probabilities argument designed to show conflict between the experimental evidence taken to support belief in the Principle of the Conservation of Energy and the evidence in favour of miracles. The occurrence of miracles conceived as instances of creation or annihilation of energy conflicts not with any positive scientific evidence supporting belief in the Principle but rather with the negative claim that no events occur which involve the creation or annihilation of energy. Faced with reports of events whose occurrence constitutes positive evidence that energy *can* be created or destroyed, it begs the question to dismiss such events or to argue that they are antecedently improbable on the ground that they imply the falsity of the metaphysical form of the Principle.[13]

I conclude that it is incorrect to define a miracle as a violation of the laws of nature. This implies that Humean balance-of-probabilities arguments, depending as they do upon an assumed conflict between evidence that supports belief in the laws of nature and evidence in favour of miracles, are fundamentally misguided inasmuch as there exists no necessary conflict between the two bodies of evidence and thus no need to pit them against each another. There is, therefore, no reason to hold that belief in miracles is unscientific.

MIRACLES AND PHILOSOPHY

At a philosophical level, many theists and non-theists insist that methodological naturalism is a prerequisite of investigating the world. A core claim of methodological naturalism is that no event should be explained as directly caused by a non-natural agent.

Adherents of methodological naturalism typically assert that it is metaphysically neutral. They assume that the methodology one employs can be neatly separated from one's beliefs about the nature or possible nature of reality. Not only is this assumption far from self-evidently true; it seems false. If, for example, I believe that there exist, or may possibly exist, mental states which play a causal role in determining bodily behaviour it makes no sense to adopt methodological behaviourism, since its adoption guarantees the development of psychological theories in which mental states either do not exist or play no causal role in bodily behaviour. Only if I am already convinced that mental states do not exist or play no causal role does it make sense to insist on methodological behaviourism as a prerequisite of developing psychological theories.

Similarly, methodological naturalism seems a sensible approach to scientific theorizing if one believes that non-natural agents do not exist or that if they do exist they never intervene in the operation of the physical universe. If, however, one believes that non-natural agents may exist and might possibly intervene in the operation of the universe it will seem wrong to adopt a methodology which forbids positing such intervention. Insisting that methodological naturalism be adopted implicitly commits one either to the claim that non-natural agents do not exist or to the claim that if they do exist they never intervene on the natural order. This begs the important question of whether such claims can be justified.

A possible objection is that it would be wrong to operate on the assumption that non-natural agents interfere with the natural order and thus it is permissible to take as a working assumption that if such agents exist they do not intervene on the natural order. This objection misses the mark. Advocates of methodological naturalism do not typically propose it as an assumption which allows that in certain instances the evidence could be such as to justify belief in the intervention of a non-natural agent. Rather, they insist that it is never in principle legitimate to posit such intervention. Methodological naturalism functions, therefore, not as a tentative working assumption but as an explanatory straitjacket. It guarantees that if miracles occur they can never be recognized as such but must be forever regarded as events with some unknown physical cause or else summarily dismissed as not actually occurring.

Another attempt to justify methodological naturalism is to claim that it is an inductive generalization based on the results of science. Given the success that science has achieved in explaining the events and structures of the world in terms of natural causes, it is claimed that the adoption of methodological naturalism is justified.

Such an attempt is inadequate on several grounds. First, it fails to take into consideration methodological naturalism's commitment to a natural explanation of all physical events regardless of the event's nature or the context in which it occurs. Far from being an inductive generalization open to disproof, methodological naturalism appears an a priori rejection of the possibility of there ever existing sufficient evidence to postulate a non-natural cause for a physical event. The willingness of those espousing methodological naturalism to reject the possibility of explaining a physical event by anything other than a natural cause and their insistence that 'in dealing with questions about the natural world, scientists *must* act as if they can be answered without recourse to supernatural powers'[14] suggests that methodological naturalism is typically espoused as something other than an inductive generalization subject to falsification.

Second, the suggestion that methodological naturalism can be justified on inductive grounds assumes without argument that prior to the rise of modern science theologians and philosophers typically inferred that God was the immediate cause of any physical event they did not understand and that this was the basis upon which miracle claims were made. Richard Bube, for example, claims without any supporting argument that 'in earlier days it was both possible and common to sustain a religious interpretation of the world by looking directly to God as the immediate Cause of those physical and biological events that human beings were then unable to describe or understand'.[15]

This claim is false. It is historically and philosophically naive to suggest that thinkers such as Augustine and Aquinas were willing to make miracle claims simply on the basis of ignorance. Both distinguished between direct (primary) and indirect (secondary) divine action. Both held that miraculous interventions in nature take place but neither argued for such interventions on the basis of ignorance of how secondary causes operate. Nor are Augustine and Aquinas unique in this respect. The philosophy and theology of the Middle Ages was too sophisticated to allow the positing of direct divine action solely on the basis of ignorance of natural causes.[16]

Third, the suggestion that methodological naturalism can be justified on inductive grounds assumes that the progress of science has provided natural explanations of events traditionally thought to be the result of supernatural intervention. The widespread acceptance of this claim obscures the fact that it is typically asserted rather than argued for. This is unfortunate. It is far from evident that the progress of science has made it easier to provide a natural explanation of events traditionally viewed as miracles.

With regard to the events that are understood as central miracles of the Christian faith, the advance of science has diminished rather than enhanced the prospect of explaining them naturalistically. For example, advances in our knowledge of physiology have made it more, not less, difficult to provide natural explanations of events such as the Virgin Birth or the Resurrection. It is precisely the difficulty of providing a natural explanation of these events that leads many critics to deny that they occurred; though this is to beg the question of whether it should be assumed that all events can be explained naturalistically.

Two further points should be made as regards the issue of miracles and methodological naturalism. First, the methodological naturalist does not provide an alternative naturalistic explanation of events such as the Virgin Birth or the Resurrection but rather the hope that some day such an explanation will be forthcoming. This insistence that the issuing of promissory notes concerning the future availability of naturalistic explanations is always to be preferred over the possibility of explaining an event in terms of non-natural causes invites the question of what grounds can be given for thinking that no matter what the event or the context in which it occurs an explanation in terms of non-natural agency is not to be countenanced.

Assuming there are good grounds for thinking that events traditionally regarded as miracles have occurred, those who posit nonnatural intervention are in a position to be more respectful of the scientific enterprise than is the methodological naturalist. Faced with examples such as the Virgin Birth or the Resurrection, the methodological naturalist must be prepared to reject or revise the presumed laws of nature which led him to expect different results. This places him in the position of questioning what on other grounds appear to be accurate statements of the laws of nature. In short, he is forced to adopt a position of radical scepticism concerning the claims of science as it presently stands, all the while issuing promissory notes of questionable value concerning what science will in the future be able to explain in terms of natural causes. The methodological naturalist provides not an alternative naturalistic explanation but rather the hope that some day such an explanation will be forthcoming, despite the fact that the advance of science makes it increasingly unlikely that an explanation in terms of natural causes will emerge. This is in contrast to those who are open to the possibility of non-natural intervention in nature. Positing non-natural explanations of events traditionally viewed as miracles enables one to offer an account of how it is possible to accept the occurrence of such extraordinary events without abandoning the basic trustworthiness of our scientific knowledge of how nature works. For those who are open to the possibility of non-natural intervention, the issue is not whether we are entitled to trust our knowledge of how nature behaves in the absence of nonnatural intervention but whether there occur events which indicate intervention into the usual order of nature.

Second, the events traditionally viewed as miracles do not occur as simple anomalies but as parts of a larger pattern that itself needs explanation. For example, in the case of the Virgin Birth, Mary does not inexplicably find herself pregnant while still a virgin but has a vision in which she is told she will become pregnant through the power of God. Joseph, understandably concerned about Mary's pregnancy, is reassured in a dream of Mary's fidelity, and Elizabeth, Mary's cousin and herself unexpectedly pregnant, prophetically recognizes the importance of the child Mary carries.[17] Any naturalistic account of the Virgin Birth requires not only an explanation of how a virgin could be pregnant with a male child but also an explanation of the larger teleological pattern in which the event is embedded.

I conclude that methodological naturalism is far from metaphysically neutral. As typically employed, it constitutes a questionable philosophical restriction on what form explanations may take and whether God may be conceived as directly acting in the world.

WHAT MIRACLES MEAN FOR THEOLOGY

Traditionally, the events regarded by believers as miracles were thought to have apologetic value as regards convincing non-believers of the existence, nature and purposes of God. The claim that Jesus fulfilled the Old Testament prophecies of a coming Messiah and that his miracles are confirmation that in him the Messiah has arrived was regarded by first- and second-century Christian apologists as the strongest argument for Christianity. F. F. Bruce comments that,

> in the proclamation of the apostles the argument from prophecy
> and the argument from miracle coincided and culminated in the
> resurrection of Jesus. This was the supreme messianic sign, the
> greatest demonstration of the power of God ... the conclusive
> fulfilment of those prophecies which pointed to the Messiah.[18]

Early apologists were aware that the evidential value of miracles did not reside simply in the fact that they are unusual events. Origen (c. 185–c. 254), who was prepared to say that without miracles the early Church could not have been established, did not define an event as a miracle solely on the basis that it was unusual. The mighty works of Jesus were to be judged miracles not merely because they constitute dramatic exceptions to the usual course of nature but also by virtue of the fact that they fulfilled Old Testament prophecies concerning the Messiah.[19] Similarly, he held that the miracles of the apostles and later Christians must be understood not just as exceptions to the usual course of nature but as furthering the transforming and healing work of the Church (Against Celsus 1.46).

This apologetic has fallen on hard times. Several lines of argument are typically employed against it. One of the best known is David Hume's fourth a posteriori argument in 'Of Miracles'. He claims that since miracles are reported in rival religions these various reports must be regarded as cancelling one another out.[20]

This is not a strong objection. It seems reasonable that a merciful God might perform miracles of healing in different religions, even though those religions may not be completely accurate in their various doctrines.[21] Further, the question of whether miracle claims are taken equally seriously in all religions is a factual one, as is the question of whether miracle claims in various religions are equally well-evidenced, as is the question of whether certain religions can accommodate the concept of miracle.[22] Hume cannot from his armchair decree that all miracle reports are on an equal footing or that they must be taken as contrary facts.

A second objection commonly asserted is that miracles can only be believed in if one is already a theist, since to call an event a miracle is to presuppose the existence of God. On this view, it is one's belief in theism that enables one to call an unusual event a miracle.[23] Events traditionally described by believers as miracles cannot, therefore, have apologetic value.

This view is mistaken. It confuses two distinct questions: the first being 'Is one committed to the truth of theism once one calls an event a miracle?', the second being 'Must one already be committed to the truth of theism in deciding whether an event is best explained as being a miracle?' Although it is true that to call an event a miracle is to commit oneself to the truth of theism, this scarcely implies that one must already be a theist before one can consider whether a particular event is best described as a miracle. To insist otherwise is analogous to insisting that a corpse could never be considered evidence for the existence of a murderer. Granted that once one calls a corpse a homicide victim one commits oneself to the existence of a murderer, if the best explanation of the corpse is the existence of a murderer then the corpse constitutes good evidence for the existence of a murderer. Similarly, although it is true that once one calls an event a miracle one commits oneself to the existence of God, if the best explanation of the event is the existence of God then the event constitutes evidence for God.

Assuming there is good evidence that an unusual event occurred, it is legitimate to draw upon the concepts of theism in attempting to explain it, even if one does not as yet accept the truth of theism. The links between theory and evidence can be supplied by the theory to be tested, so long as these links are not used in such a way as to guarantee that the theory is positively instantiated whatever the evidence. What is required in deciding whether an event should be termed a miracle is that one be able to entertain theism as a hypothesis and consider whether the event is best explained by the theistic hypothesis or a naturalistic hypothesis. If affirming the existence of God would render the event more comprehensible than otherwise then the event is independent evidence that God exists.

A third objection that is frequently raised against the apologetic significance of miracles is that if they occur they imply that God is a bumbler who, not getting things right initially, finds it necessary to intervene in nature to correct his mistakes. Underlying this objection is the presumption that an all powerful, all knowing, all good God would create the universe in such a way as to make miracles unnecessary. Thus David Jenkins insists that, 'a God ... [who inserts] additional causal events from time to time into ... [the] universe to produce particular events or trends ... would be a meddling demigod, a moral monster and a contradiction of himself ... God is not an arbitrary meddler nor an occasional fixer'.[24]

This line of argument has a decidedly deistic flavour. The implicit claim seems to be that the perfection of God implies that his creation of the universe be along the lines of a maintenance-free machine. On this view, the relation of God to creation appears to be that, apart from originating and upholding the existence of the physical universe, God must leave the natural order absolutely alone. Creation may be designed in the sense that its initial boundary conditions lead to certain felicitous results but any subsequent direct intervention is out of the question.

The assumption that God's perfection implies that he never intervene in the natural order is dubious. The analogy of a maintenance-free machine is scarcely the only analogy available for modelling the relation between God and nature. A musical instrument is as much a product of design as a maintenance-free machine but it is designed precisely to be intervened upon. More fundamentally, if creation includes free rational agents there appears no a priori reason to think that in interacting with such agents God must operate solely through secondary causes or that he might not intervene in the natural order in response to their choices. Indeed such a creation seems to require that God intervene. F. R. Tennant notes that,

> if ... the world ... [has] a derived or devolved activity permitted to it, as relatively independent of its self-limited Creator; and if any of God's creatures are in their lesser way also creators: then ... why should not God encounter obstacles within His own created world? ... The deists were so shocked at the attribution of anything like arbitrariness to the Deity that, in their zeal to rule it out, they ... removed all possibility of God's directivity, of adaptation of immutable purpose to emergent needs. In their haste to eliminate from the idea of God the very anthropic quality of caprice and changefulness, they ascribed to Him the equally anthropic qualities of indifference and impassive obstinacy.[25]

A fourth objection to the apologetic worth of miracles is that if they occur they reveal an arbitrary and unfair God. Jordan Sobel writes that, 'a fair God would presumably want miracles not to be "sporadic" and distributed arbitrarily to only some of otherwise similar potential beneficiaries. In this somewhat attenuated way, evidence for miracles ... can be evidence ... that God does not exist.'[26]

Why a miracle is granted in one instance but not in another is no easy question. This should come as no surprise, since it is essentially an aspect of the problem of evil. It could as easily be asked why certain other goods such as intelligence or beauty are not more evenly distributed throughout creation. A number of points, however, undermine the prima facie force of the objection that in performing miracles for some but not others God would be revealed as unjust.

First, although apparently similar cases have different outcomes, the difficulty of judging whether such cases are similar in all relevant details should not be underestimated. Further, God may have a number of equally effective means of accomplishing his purposes in individuals' lives other than performing a miracle. It also deserves emphasis that those experiencing miracles do not have noticeably less suffering in their lives than those who do not. Indeed, they frequently experience more suffering. Paul, who experienced many miracles, reports that, in addition to routinely experiencing hunger, thirst and sleeplessness, he was scourged five times with thirty-nine lashes, beaten with rods three times, shipwrecked three times, and was once stoned and left for dead (2 Cor. 11.23–7). Jesus frequently reminded his listeners that those to whom much is given much is required and this seems true in the case of those who receive miracles.

Second, it seems that God often performs a miracle through the instrumentality of a human agent. God does not directly heal Paul of his blindness, but rather instructs Ananias to go to Paul as the instrument through whom God will heal Paul. This requires a considerable step of faith on Ananias' part, since Paul was known as someone who 'breathed threats and murder against the disciples of the Lord' (Acts 9.1–2). This raises the possibility that there are occasions when God wishes to perform a miracle but is frustrated by the fact that the person through whom he wishes to work does not cooperate.

Third, in certain instances, it seems that miracles may not occur because of a settled climate of disbelief. Mark notes that in the location where Jesus grew up many people refused to take him seriously. He goes on to record that Jesus 'could do no mighty work there, except that He laid His hands on a few sick people and healed them' (Mark 6.5).

Other considerations of why miracles occur in one instance but not in another could be mentioned but enough has been said to make questionable the claim that because we cannot always say why a miracle occurs for one person but not another this requires the conclusion that God is unjust.

SUMMING UP

In discussing the meanings of miracle in relation to science, philosophy and theology, I have argued for a number of key claims, which, by way of a brief summary, I now list. First, it is a mistake to argue that miracles imply violation of the laws of nature and thus that belief in miracles is inherently unscientific. Second, to attempt on the basis of methodological naturalism to rule out ever describing an event as a miracle is to beg important questions regarding both the nature of God and what can count as a legitimate explanation. Third, events plausibly viewed as miracles can constitute evidence for the existence of a theistic God. Fourth, although it may be difficult to discern why a miracle occurs in one instance but not in another, the occurrence of miracles does not imply that God is unjust.

The conclusion to be drawn is that on scientific, philosophical and theological grounds belief in miracles is entirely rational. Far from being an embarrassment to religious faith, they are signs of God's love for, and continuing involvement in, creation.

Notes

1 Stephen S. Bilynskyj, 'God, Nature and the Concept of Miracle', Ph.D. diss., University of Notre Dame (1982). William Lane Craig, *Reasonable Faith: Christian Truth and Apologetics* (Wheaton: Crossway, 1994), 143–4.

2 For a fuller discussion, see Hendrik van der Breggen, 'Miracle Reports, Moral Philosophy and Contemporary Science', Ph.D. diss., University of Waterloo (2004).

3 Alistair McKinnon, '"Miracle" and "Paradox"', *American Philosophical Quarterly* 4 (1967), 308–14 (309). A fatal flaw for such theories is that the laws of nature do not by themselves allow prediction of what will take place, but rather in conjunction with a set of initial conditions not specified by the laws. This point also applies to nomic necessity theories.

4 William Lane Craig, 'Creation, Providence and Miracles', in *Philosophy of Religion: A Guide to the Subject*, ed. Brian Davies (Washington: Georgetown University Press, 1998), 136–62 (153). Richard Swinburne,

The Concept of Miracle (London and Basingstoke: Macmillan, 1970), 26–8, attempts to make sense of the notion of a violation of a law of nature, by defining violations as non-repeatable counter-instances to laws of nature. His attempt seems unsuccessful. As Martin Curd, 'Miracles as Violations of Laws of Nature', in *Faith, Freedom, and Rationality: Philosophy of Religion Today*, ed. Jeff Jordan (Lanham: Rowman & Littlefield, 1996), 171–84 (182), notes, the proposal 'that "All A's are B" is a genuine law even though there is a nonrepeatable instance of an A that is not B . . . is logically impossible: if "All A's are B" is a genuine law then *all* A's are B without exception'.

5 van der Breggen, 'Miracle Reports', 91. Also Rom Harré, 'Laws of Nature', in *A Companion to the Philosophy of Science*, ed. William Newton-Smith, Blackwell Companions to Philosophy (Malden: Blackwell, 2000), 213–23 (220).

6 Hume's use of the term 'violation' seems to have been influential in the adoption of this view. See Robert M. Burns, *The Great Debate on Miracles: From Joseph Glanvill to David Hume* (London: Associated University Presses, 1981), 234–6.

7 William Alston, 'The Place of the Explanation of Particular Facts in Science', *Philosophy of Science* 38 (1971), 17–20.

8 I am taking the term 'law of nature' to refer to a scientific law which is in fact true. By 'scientific law' I do not mean simply a general regularity in the observable world. Rather, I mean the theoretical laws which serve to explain the general regularities discovered by scientists. Thus, although the term 'law of nature' refers to a universal conditional that may in principle be confirmed or disconfirmed on the basis of empirical evidence this conditional will contain terms which refer not directly to observed regularities, but to unobservable entities which serve to explain observed regularities of nature. In defence of this usage of the term, it seems clear that regularities in nature, such as the fact that virgins do not usually give birth, may be explicable by reference to the laws of nature, but it does not seem plausible to view them as being themselves laws of nature.

9 C. S. Lewis, *Miracles: A Preliminary Study* (New York: Macmillan, 1947), 71.

10 *Ibid.*, 72.

11 William Stoeger, 'Describing God's Action in the World in Light of Scientific Knowledge of Reality', in *Chaos and Complexity: Scientific Perspectives on Divine Action*, ed. Robert John Russell, Nancey Murphy and Arthur Peacocke (Vatican City: Vatican Observatory Foundation and The Center for Theology and the Natural Sciences, 1995), 239–61 (244).

12 An essential claim of theism is that God causes the universe to exist. If the universe is conceived to be composed of forms of mass/energy and energy that can neither be created nor destroyed, then this claim is false.

13 Robert Larmer, *Water Into Wine? An Investigation of the Concept of Miracle* (Montreal: McGill-Queen's University Press, 1988), 71–3.

14 Douglas Futuyma, *Science on Trial* (New York: Pantheon, 1983), 170, emphasis added.

15 Richard Bube, *Putting It All Together* (New York: University Press of America, 1995), 57.

16 John M. Reynolds, 'God of the Gaps', in *Mere Creation*, ed. William Dembski (Downers Grove: InterVarsity, 1998), 327.

17 Matt. 1.18–25; Luke 1.5–2.52.

18 F. F. Bruce, *The Apostolic Defence of the Gospel*, 2nd edn 1967 (London: InterVarsity, 1979), 12.

19 The combined evidential strength of dramatic miracles plus Old Testament prophecies displays the epistemic virtue of unification. Unification gives a theory strength that is greater than the total of adding up the strengths of the component parts of that theory. See W. C. Myrvold, 'A Bayesian Account of the Virtue of Unification', *Philosophy of Science* 70 (2003), 399–423.

20 David Hume, 'Of Miracles', in *Enquiries Concerning Human Understanding*, 3rd edn, ed. L. A. Selby-Bigge, rev. and notes P. H. Nidditch (Oxford: Oxford University Press, 1975), 109–31 (121–2).

21 Joseph Houston, *Reported Miracles: A Critique of Hume* (Cambridge: Cambridge University Press, 1994), 204.

22 Houston, *Reported Miracles*, 204–5. Also David K. Clark, 'Miracles in the World Religions', in *In Defense of Miracles*, ed. R. Douglas Geivett and Gary R. Habermas (Downers Grove: InterVarsity, 1997), 202–5.

23 See, for example, J. L. Mackie, *The Miracle of Theism* (Oxford: Oxford University Press, 1982), 27.

24 David Jenkins, *God, Miracle, and the Church of England* (London: SCM, 1987), 63–4.

25 F. R. Tennant, *Miracle and its Philosophical Presuppositions* (Cambridge: Cambridge University Press, 1925), 91.

26 Jordan Howard Sobel, *Logic and Theism: Arguments For and Against Beliefs in God* (Cambridge: Cambridge University Press, 2004), 309. Also James Keller, 'A Moral Argument Against Miracles', *Faith and Philosophy* 12 (1995), 54–78.

Further reading

Brown, Colin, *Miracles and the Critical Mind* (Grand Rapids: Eerdmans, 1984)

*Burns, Robert M., *The Great Debate on Miracles* (East Brunswick: Associated University Presses, 1981)

Campbell, George, *Dissertation on Miracles*, 2 vols. (1762) 3rd enlarged and corrected edn (Edinburgh: Bell & Bradfute, 1797)

Corner, Mark, *Signs of God* (Burlington, VT: Ashgate, 2005)

Earman, John, *Hume's Abject Failure* (Oxford: Oxford University Press, 2000)

Fogelin, Robert J., *A Defense of Hume on Miracles* (Princeton: Princeton University Press, 2003)

Geivett, R. Douglas and Gary R. Habermas, eds., *In Defence of Miracles* (Downers Grove: InterVarsity, 1997)

Grant, Robert M., *Miracle and Natural Law in Graeco-Roman and Early Christian Thought* (Amsterdam: North Holland, 1952)

Houston, Joseph, *Reported Miracles: A Critique of Hume* (Cambridge: Cambridge University Press, 1994)

Hume, David, 'Of Miracles', in *Enquiries Concerning Human Understanding*, 3rd edn, ed. L. A. Selby-Bigge, rev. and notes P. H. Nidditch (Oxford: Oxford University Press, 1975), 109–31

Jaki, Stanley L., *Miracles and Physics* (Front Royal: Christendom, 2004)

Larmer, Robert, *Water Into Wine? An Investigation of the Concept of Miracle* (Montreal: McGill-Queen's University Press, 1988)

Lewis, C. S., *Miracles: A Preliminary Study* (New York: Macmillan, 1947)

Moule, C. F. D., ed., *Miracles: Cambridge Studies in their Philosophy and History* (London: A. R. Mowbray, 1965)

Mozley, J. B., *Eight Lectures on Miracles*, 3rd edn (London: Longmans, Green, 1890)

Mullin, Robert Bruce, *Miracles and the Modern Religious Imagination* (London: Yale University Press, 1996)

Newman, John Henry, *Two Essays on Biblical and on Ecclesiastical Miracles* (London: Longmans, Green, 1890)

Sherlock, Thomas, *The Trial of the Witnesses of the Resurrection of Jesus* (1729) (Edinburgh: J. Robertson for W. Gray, 1769)

Swinburne, Richard, *The Concept of Miracle* (New York: Macmillan, 1970)

Whately, Richard, *Historic Doubts Concerning the Existence of Napoleon Bonaparte*, 2nd edn (London: George Routledge & Sons, 1890)

Part II
Miracles in antiquity and the Middle Ages

3 Miracles in the Hebrew Bible

R. WALTER L. MOBERLY

If one is to make some progress towards understanding 'miracle' in the Hebrew Bible (HB), then certain initial cautionary notes need to be sounded. First, there is arguably no Hebrew word for 'miracle'; which is arguable because sometimes HB translations do render particular Hebrew words as 'miracle'. The issue here is a recurrent problem in biblical interpretation, for many of the common terms that interpreters use – 'conversion' or 'history' or 'theology' – cannot be straightforwardly translated into biblical Hebrew (or septuagintal Greek). This does not make such terms unusable, but it does necessitate that they be used with care. For although there may be continuity between what we mean by these terms and what is going on in the biblical text, there may also be difference; and that difference may be partly or wholly obscured if we are insufficiently self-critical in use of a familiar and apparently convenient interpretative category. So, for example, there is a danger that in using the familiar English word 'miracle' with reference to the HB one may import familiar implications and overtones from historic debates – such as Hume's famous definition of a miracle as 'a violation of the laws of nature',[1] although the notion of an autonomous natural world was unknown to the writers of the HB.[2]

Second, and related, an interest in 'miracle' may well introduce distinctions in relation to divine action within the HB which are absent within the biblical text. For within the HB there is a wide spectrum and continuum of divine actions, which happen in both ordinary and extraordinary ways, sometimes with human or other agency and sometimes without. The fact that God does something may indeed make that action or event extraordinary; but the extraordinary as such is not seen as the particular locus of divine action. The interest that many contemporary believers or sceptics may have in, say, finding, or disproving, evidence for the reality of God in the realm of the extraordinary owes far more to the conceptual legacy of the debates of the eighteenth century than it does to the content of the HB. 'Proceed with caution' must therefore be the principle underlying our discussion of 'miracle' in this chapter.

TERMINOLOGY AND USAGE

If care with terminology is crucial for accurate understanding, then terminology may be a useful place to begin this study.[3] Among the various words used in relation to our concern, the most frequently used are ʾoth ('sign') and mopheth ('wonder'). A recurrent idiom, especially in Deuteronomy and texts influenced by Deuteronomy, is that ʾoth and mopheth are conjoined in the plural (often with other terms also) as a formulaic depiction of YHWH's acts of delivering Israel from Egypt (Deut. 4.34; 6.22; 7.19; 26.8; 29.2; 34.11; Ps. 135.9) – though these acts of deliverance can also be characterized as niphlaʾoth, 'wonders' (Exod. 3.20; Judg. 6.13; Mic. 7.15; see below).

Yet ʾoth and mopheth can each be used in its own right (the former more often than the latter). Commonly in HB narratives both ʾoth and mopheth depict extraordinary acts or events which accompany a verbal message and are meant to have some existential probative significance, to engender not just intellectual assent to the message but also appropriate attitude and action. Thus, the astonishing actions that Moses is enabled to perform for a possibly incredulous Israel are designated each as a 'sign' (ʾoth) to engender responsiveness (Exod. 4.1–9, esp. 8); when Samuel anoints a bemused Saul as ruler he also reassures him by telling him of events that will soon happen to him, events which are 'signs' (ʾoth) that this is all from YHWH (1 Sam. 10.7, 9); comparably, a man of God's pronouncement of coming destruction of the altar in Jeroboam's Bethel is accompanied by an indicative 'sign' (mopheth, 1 Kgs. 13.3, 5).

The existentially persuasive nature that YHWH's 'signs' should have for Israel is spelled out in several key texts. When Israel fails on the borders of the promised land, YHWH says to Moses, 'How long will they refuse to believe in me, in spite of all the signs [ʾoth] that I have done among them?' (Num. 14.11).[4] The point is expressed positively in Deuteronomy 4.34–5, that the 'signs and wonders' and other things that YHWH did in Egypt are 'so that you would acknowledge that the LORD is God; there is no other besides him'. This is most memorably displayed in the story of Elijah's contest with the prophets of Baal on Mount Carmel (1 Kgs. 18), where, despite the lack of explicit use of ʾoth or mopheth, the deuteronomic conceptuality is present when the people respond to YHWH's fire from heaven with the confession that 'The LORD indeed is God' (18.39); this is not something that the people did not, in principle, already know, but it is an understanding that is now 'brought to life'. Thus existential responsiveness is clearly a goal of 'signs and wonders', though Numbers 14.11 (whose sentiments are expressed at length in Ps. 106) fully recognizes that this desired responsiveness may not be forthcoming, as it was not in the paradigmatic generation in the wilderness.

The other prime Hebrew root for our concerns is pl', 'wonder'/'be wonderful', whose basic sense appears to be 'concerned above all with the insurmountable contrast between what is possible for human beings and what is possible for God'.[5] The notion that God can realize that for which humans deeply long but which appears utterly beyond their reach, at least at the time, is expressed axiomatically in certain famous texts. When an elderly and post-menopausal Sarah can only respond to the promise of a son with laughter (ironic and mocking in tone, one imagines), YHWH says to Abraham, 'Is anything too wonderful [pl'] for the LORD?' (Gen. 18.14). This wording is picked up both in Jeremiah's prayer of amazement at YHWH's promise to restore the land of Judah as symbolized by Jeremiah's purchase of a field, and in YHWH's response to Jeremiah: 'See, I am the LORD, the God of all flesh; is anything too hard [pl'] for me?' (Jer. 32.17, 27).

In another prophetic text, when YHWH depicts to a diminished and demoralized community a restored and flourishing Jerusalem in which life is as it should be, an anticipated response of incredulity is instantly met:

> Thus says the LORD of hosts: Old men and women shall again sit in the streets of Jerusalem, each with staff in hand because of their great age. And the streets of the city shall be full of boys and girls playing in its streets. Thus says the LORD of hosts: Even though it seems impossible [pl'] to the remnant of this people in these days, should it also seem impossible [pl'] to me, says the LORD of hosts?
> (Zech. 8.4–6)

The psalmist also looks back on a divine reversal of human actions and expectations (Ps. 118.22–3).

In each of these passages we have a comparable axiomatic formulation that what is impossible for humans is possible for God. Since only Sarah's conception of Isaac looks at all eligible for Hume's categorization as 'a violation of the laws of nature'[6] it is indicative of the fact that within the HB the 'impossible' thing that YHWH does is 'impossible' less in theoretical than in existential terms. It is also in line with the common observation of theologians that, generally speaking, 'miracles' are better thought of not as 'violation of the laws of nature' but rather as 'enhancement', 'a temporary elevation of powers beyond the natural'.[7]

The most common form of *pl'* is the Niphal participle in the plural used as a noun, *niphla'oth*, 'wonders', whose own most common occurrence is in the psalms. It can be instructive to focus on the use of this word in the psalter, not least because the primary narrative accounts of acts of God generally use no particular term to depict what is happening. The poetic parallelisms are illuminating for grasping the resonances and associations of 'wonders'; while the psalms also reveal how God's 'wonders' are to be thought about and responded to. In the following examples I italicize both the English word that represents *niphla'oth*, and its parallel term. Consider, for example:

> Let them thank the LORD for *his steadfast love* [*hesed*],
> for *his wonderful works* to humankind. (Ps. 107.8, 15, 21, 31)
> They forgot God, their Saviour,
> who had done *great things* in Egypt,
> *wondrous works* in the land of Ham,
> and *awesome deeds* by the Red Sea. (106.21–2)
> Remember *the wonderful works* he has done,
> his *miracles* [*mophetim*],[8] and the *judgements he has uttered* ...
> (105.5)
> We will tell to the coming generation
> the *glorious deeds* of the LORD, and his *might*,
> and *the wonders* that he has done. (78.4)
> Declare his *glory* among the nations,
> his *marvellous works* among all the peoples.   (96.3)

Here *niphla'oth* are associated with *hesed*, the prime term within the HB for YHWH's covenant commitment to Israel, with YHWH's deliverance of Israel from the power of Egypt, with the giving of *torah* at Sinai, and with the display of divine power that redounds to the praise and glory of God. Generally speaking, it is everything that God does in Israel's foundation story in Exodus to Deuteronomy that is depicted as 'wonders' (it is the HB equivalent of the Christian celebration of the death and resurrection of Jesus as God's decisive action *pro nobis*).

Also of note are the verbs within the psalter that govern *niphla'oth* and which indicate the stance that Israel should adopt. These wonderful acts are to be the focus of mind and heart and speech for Israel in various ways: those who use the psalms are to *remember/not forget*

(Pss. 78.11; 105.5), *declare/proclaim/tell of* (9.2 [ET 1], 26.7; 96.3), *tell of/teach children* (78.4), *meditate on* (119.27; 145.5), *consider* (106.7), *believe in* (78.32), *give thanks for* (107.8, 15, 21, 31) God's wonderful acts. Grateful celebration, confident proclamation, trusting reflection, and an identity to be passed on are the notes that are sounded.

To be sure, the psalms are well aware that not everything in life goes as one might like or hope for – indeed, the lament is the single most common type of psalm. Within the psalter as a whole, however, this is not seen as incompatible with the celebration of God's wonderful acts. Even if, of course, there may be moments when any celebration becomes existentially beyond a person's or community's reach, this does not deny that Israel's identity is still fundamentally constituted by God's wonderful acts and Israel's grateful response to them.

One final aspect of the usage of 'wonders' in the psalter is the emphasis that YHWH alone does them (Pss. 72.18; 86.10; 136.4). Although this language could be taken to be a theoretical or in-principle denial of the power of any other deity, its contextual significance is to direct Israel's praise to YHWH, and YHWH alone. In other words, the psalms' emphasis here is probably to be understood in the same way as the affirmation in the Shema that YHWH is 'one', that is the 'one and only', the sole focus and recipient for Israel's allegiance and devotion (Deut. 6.4–9). Whatever other deities might do, the characteristic HB emphasis is that YHWH is *incomparable* (no other deity is the match of YHWH), and that *only he, and no other, has done wonders for Israel* (so to transfer allegiance elsewhere would be foolish ingratitude). Thus the plagues narrative depicts the initial wondrous acts worked by Moses and Aaron being matched by the Egyptian magicians, though this is ascribed not to other deities but rather to 'secret arts' (Exod. 7.11, 22; 8.3 [ET, 8.7]). But not only do the Egyptian magicians run out of ability to keep up (8.14 [ET, 8.18]), but even at the outset their staffs-turned-snakes are swallowed up by Aaron's (7.12). There may in some sense be 'wondrous acts' beyond Israel, but they do not compare with what YHWH does for Israel.

Beyond the psalter, one other instance of *niphla'oth* especially merits attention, Exodus 34.10, where YHWH says to Moses:

> I hereby make a covenant. Before all your people I will perform marvels [*niphla'oth*], such as have not been performed in all the earth or in any nation; and all the people among whom you live shall see the work of the LORD; for it is an awesome thing that I will do with you.

Interpreters generally assume that *niphla'oth* here should have the same sense that it generally has (as in the psalms), and that therefore it depicts what YHWH does in addition, and subsequently, to making the covenant, such as the divine actions in the narratives of Numbers.[9]

Contextually, however, the mention of *niphla'oth* surely makes better sense not as something other than the covenant making (the text continues with covenantal stipulations, and does not shift focus away from Sinai) but rather as a redescription of it, an interpretation of its significance. Israel's sin with the golden calf in Exodus 32.1–6, while still at Sinai where the covenant has just been made, is presented as a breaking of the covenant that is paradigmatic apostasy – a kind of equivalent to committing adultery on one's wedding night. The subsequent narrative in Exodus 32.7–34.9 explores the issue of whether there can be any future for Israel as YHWH's covenant people, and the initial account looks doubtful. Ultimately, however, the issue is resolved through Moses' intercession eliciting the self-revelation of YHWH as merciful and gracious, a God of steadfast love (Exod. 33.19; 34.6–7), and this is the basis on which the covenant is renewed. In context, the covenant making/renewal with a faithless 'stiff-necked' people (32.9; 33.3, 5), who remain stiff-necked even after Moses' intercession and YHWH's self-revelation (34.9), is astonishing. Thus the text applies *niphla'oth*, the regular word for YHWH's acts on behalf of Israel, to the divine mercy which enables their continuance as the people of YHWH through a renewed covenant; Israel's very existence will thereby be a testimony to others of the amazing grace of God. In essence, the greatest 'miracle' is love.

THE DISTRIBUTION OF 'MIRACLES'

Contrary to a common assumption that 'miracles' occur throughout the HB, they occur primarily in clusters in two locations: the Moses narratives in Exodus and Numbers, and the Elijah and Elisha narratives in 1 Kings 17–2 Kings 13. It is not, of course, that there are no 'miracles' elsewhere, but that these are the predominant locations.[10] Moses, Elijah and Elisha are paradigmatic prophetic figures, each of whom matches the designation applied to Jesus by the disciples on the Emmaus Road: 'a prophet mighty in deed and word before God and all the people' (Luke 24.19). In general terms there is clearly a sense that some people are so responsive towards God that they become channels for God's power to be displayed.

However, it does not follow that God's power always takes the 'wonderful' form it takes with these three figures. The figure in the HB history books who receives more space than any other is David, the man 'after God's own heart' (1 Sam. 13.14). Yet no 'miracles' are ascribed to him. To be sure, his youthful conquest of Goliath could readily be construed as 'wondrous' (*pl'*), though the biblical text itself nowhere does so. The consistent form of God's presence and working with David is 'providential', from his initial anointing by Samuel (16.1–13) through his being preserved from shedding Israelite blood while on the run from Saul,[11] or in YHWH's causing the counsel of Ahithophel to be disregarded (2 Sam. 17.14) so that David would regain his throne from Absalom.

Similarly, within the prophetic books, the figure about whom we have the fullest narrative account is Jeremiah, and no 'miracle' is ascribed to him. To be sure, Jeremiah remains alive, despite his powerful enemies, and in that (providential) sense God's initial promise to 'deliver' him (Jer. 1.8) is fulfilled (so that he does not suffer the fate of Uriah ben Shemaiah, 26.20–4; cf. 36.26). Yet Jeremiah's message provokes strong opposition from people in powerful places and is only heeded by few; he is maltreated (38.1–13), and the last we hear of him is that he is taken to Egypt against his will by people actively resisting his message (42–3). Jeremiah is not a lesser prophet because he suffers and is not an agent of any deeds of power; the searching character of his message and his integrity in adversity have long been recognized as lying at the heart of faithful response to vocation.

Why 'miracles' should cluster in some contexts and be absent in others is unclear, and is open to many different kinds of explanation – for example, differing kinds of opposition to the prophetic upholders of Israel's faith, differing developments within the history of the tradition, differing assumptions on the part of the writers. Whatever the explanation, however, one clear implication of the overall canonical portrayal is that God's call and God's action are worked out in many and varied ways.

'MIRACLES' AND 'MAGIC'

Problems that affect understanding and use of the term 'miracle' apply no less to the term 'magic'. 'Magic' tends to be a loaded term, and is often used to depict that which is done by others of whom one in some way disapproves (for example, 'we practise religion, which is personal and relational, while you/they practise magic, which is impersonal and manipulative'). Nonetheless, at least some distinctions can serve useful heuristic purposes, not least when contrasts are made with the normative Jewish and Christian mode of seeking divine action, which is through prayer whose realization depends on God.

In this context, interpreters have often noted how some HB narratives, perhaps especially those that portray Elijah and Elisha, seem to envisage the unusual power that these figures display as, in some way, 'in their possession', 'under their control', often in association with their wielding a staff or cloak, rather than as a divine bestowal in answer to prayer.[12] Even if the power belongs to God, the human appears to decide how it is to be wielded. Whether or not one wants to call this 'magical', such displays of power look prima facie similar to the kind of thing that often is called 'magic'.

The point here is not the reputation that an Elisha might acquire, as when an officer tells the king of Aram that Elisha 'tells the king of Israel the words that you speak in your bedchamber' (2 Kgs. 6.12), for this may be read as popular awe of Elisha. It is rather the narrator's authoritative telling:

> Elijah answered the captain of fifty, 'If I am a man of God, let fire come down from heaven and consume you and your fifty'. Then fire came down from heaven, and consumed him and his fifty.
>
> (2 Kgs. 1.10, 12)

> Elisha said to him, 'Where have you been, Gehazi?' He answered, 'Your servant has not gone anywhere at all'. But he said to him, 'Did I not go with you in spirit when someone left his chariot to meet you? ... Therefore the leprosy of Naaman shall cling to you, and to your descendants forever.' So he left his presence leprous, as white as snow.
>
> (5.25–7)

Although the issues are complex, I offer one general observation. Although often the narrator tells the story starkly, at least sometimes there is the narrative equivalent of a zoom lens which allows the reader to see and hear something (words on a prophet's lips, often in private conversation) that makes sense of what is happening in categories familiar elsewhere in the HB. In the famous contest on Mount Carmel, Elijah prepares confidently, yet the fire of YHWH falls only in response to his prayer (1 Kgs. 18.36–8). When the Shunammite woman comes to Elisha, Elisha says to an over-protective Gehazi, 'Let her alone, for she is in bitter distress; the LORD has hidden it from me and has not told me' (2 Kgs. 4.27). When Elisha's servant is fearful of a surrounding Aramean army, Elisha prays that

YHWH would open his eyes, which happens and enables him to see 'horses and chariots of fire all around Elisha' (6.17; fire is a prime symbol of YHWH's presence, Exod. 3.2; 19.18).

In other words, the interpretations that have been given to these stories are such as to conform them somewhat, in varying degrees, to the 'normal' understanding of life with YHWH as attested elsewhere in the HB; that is, the interpretative move is away from what looks like 'magic' towards personal interaction with God. To be sure, the stories for the most part have been allowed to stand in their strangeness. But one may suggest that we can already see at work, in the way at least some of the stories have been shaped and preserved, an instinctive tendency which developed much more fully in classic biblical commentary: to conform the unfamiliar to the familiar. Thus in the Targum, for example, Elisha's words when Elijah is taken up to heaven become, 'My master, my master, who did more good for Israel by his prayer than chariots and horsemen'.[13]

WHAT ACTUALLY HAPPENED?

This question is, of course, easier to ask than to answer – at least, if one is to do more than just appeal to theological and philosophical axioms as to the possibility, or impossibility, of 'miracles'. Although interpreters' first principles undoubtedly make a difference to how they read, such principles need to be complemented by attention to specific particularities. For it is perfectly feasible to believe in the possibility of 'miracles' generally, and yet still be uncertain what to make of particular instances.[14] Moreover, since the kind of 'miraculous' actions ascribed to Moses, Elijah and Elisha are also well attested in the literature of other religious traditions,[15] Jews and Christians, whose instincts are likely to be positive towards what is attested in the Bible, need to have criteria of judgment that are sufficiently nuanced to do justice to non-biblical material also.

One obvious temptation, which comes into and goes out of fashion but which probably never entirely goes away, is to rationalize accounts of 'miracle'. In its own way, of course, this is to do what we have just noted in the previous section – to conform the unfamiliar to the familiar, only in terms of 'common sense' or apologetic persuasiveness rather than the normative principles of religious life. The appeal of such an approach is likely to vary from case to case and from interpreter to interpreter.

For example, with a simple repointing of the Hebrew text, from
ʿorᵉbim to ʿarabim, the ravens who fed Elijah become Arabs (1 Kgs.
17.2–7), if one is so inclined[16] – though one thereby loses the resonances with numerous comparable motifs in other ancient texts.[17]
Alternatively, with regard to the puzzling story of the axe-head, which
is lost in water but which Elisha makes to float by throwing a stick into
the water (2 Kgs. 6.1–7), G. H. Jones confidently asserts:

> It seems that he had adopted a simple and practical method of
> fishing out the axe-head with a pole or stick. The water was
> probably deep, but he managed either to raise the axe-head by
> inserting the tip of his stick into it, or else by moving it along the river
> bed into a shallower part from which it could be lifted out by hand.[18]

The main problem, however, is that this rationalizing move does not
really account for the narrative in the text so much as replace it by an
alternative, apparently more comprehensible, narrative. In this particular case, there appears to be an implicit evaluation of the biblical story,
that it is a testimony to the hagiographic and exaggerating imagination
of popular piety. So greatly is Elisha revered that even an ordinary
action becomes transformed into an extraordinary – a wonderful person
does wonderful things. The scenario is feasible. However, as is characteristic of such an approach, the possible symbolic dimensions of the
biblical portrayal are simply passed over in silence.

The rationalizing instinct not infrequently appears in the service of
faith with an apologetic function. Such treatment is perhaps especially
applied to the Exodus account of the plagues and Israel's crossing of the
Red Sea, where there is a long history of rationalizing accounts so that
people can see that the foundational biblical narrative is indeed cred-
ible/true.[19] A noteworthy recent example is Colin Humphreys' *The
Miracles of Exodus: A Scientist's Discovery of the Extraordinary
Natural Causes of the Biblical Stories*, a tour de force where the
subtitle well sums up the book. Humphreys says:

> A natural explanation of the events of the Exodus doesn't to my
> mind make them any less miraculous. As we will see, the ancient
> Israelites believed that their God worked in, with, and through
> natural events. What made certain natural events miraculous was
> their timing: for example, the River Jordan stopped flowing precisely
> when the Israelites were assembled on its banks and desperate to
> cross ... I believe this natural explanation [an earthquake] makes
> this miracle more, not less, believable.[20]

Humphreys is undoubtedly correct in his general point about Israelite belief in divine action; and undoubtedly the timing of an event can have the kind of existential impact we noted as characteristic of 'signs' and 'wonders'. However, he does not ask the question whether Israel also believed in divine actions that were not 'in, with, and through natural events', and, if so, how one understands the difference. The difficult issue of evaluation becomes whether Humphreys may not, in trying to make the biblical narrative 'more, not less, believable', in fact replace it with an alternative narrative whose rationalized/naturalistic account of divine action ('more dramatic than the traditional interpretation ... truly astonishing, amazing, and inspirational')[21] is more acceptable to a contemporary believer with a scientific outlook who is puzzled by, but sympathetic towards, the Bible.

Two brief examples must suffice. For the first plague in Egypt (Exod. 7.14–24) Humphreys suggests that:

> toxic red algae were caused to bloom by this combination of very hot weather [the Egyptian summer] and the nutrient rich water [in the Nile Delta]. The resulting toxins killed the fish ... and the dead fish caused the river to stink, just as described in the book of Exodus.[22]

This looks fine on its own terms. But what recedes from sight (Humphreys does not discuss it) is that in the biblical account the river is changed because of the action of Moses – 'he lifted up the staff and struck the water in the river, and all the water in the river was turned to blood, and the fish in the river died' – and indeed because of the comparable action of the Egyptians as well – 'but the magicians of Egypt did the same by their secret arts; so Pharaoh's heart remained hardened' (Exod. 7.20–2). In other words, the timing of the event (which Humphreys recognizes in the initial quotation above to be important, maybe all-important), which in the biblical narrative is linked to specific human actions at a particular moment, disappears in favour of an account of processes over a period of time. But if it is suggested that the point is that Pharaoh and Moses came down to the river just on the day on which the toxic red algae were beginning to have visible effect – that is, wonderful timing – then the narrative's linkage of the turning to blood with the action of Moses and the Egyptian magicians would be mistaken and misleading.

Second, the story of the manna in the desert (Exod. 16) has a long history of rationalizing interpretations, going back at least to the time of Josephus.[23] Humphreys (whose interest in the story relates to identifying the geographical location of the Desert of Sin) appeals to the known fact that the stem of the tamarisk tree, when bitten by a particular insect, 'exude[s] a sweet, sticky substance that falls to the ground and solidifies' and argues that 'the biblical description of manna fits so well the present-day manna that I believe we can say, beyond reasonable doubt, that the manna the Israelites ate in the desert was a natural substance produced by suitable trees'. According to Humphreys, the manna disappears when the sun grows hot, because insects eat it; a specimen of manna could be kept in a jar because its high sugar content preserved it; and tamarisk trees are plentiful (thus producing the necessary large quantity of manna) in the Hisma Desert, which is where the biblical Desert of Sin is now to be located.[24]

One should note, however, that when Humphreys cites 'the key points as recorded in the book of Exodus' he cites only parts of 16.14-16, 21, 31-5.[25] Not only does the biblical text's framing concern with the manna as a divine test disappear from view ('I will test them, whether they will follow my instruction or not', 16.4) but, more importantly, so does the fact that the manna behaves differently at the end of each week: Israel is to collect double on the sixth day, this manna will not go off when kept overnight (as it does every other day), and no manna appears on the seventh day, the Sabbath (16.22-30). One suspects that it is precisely because this resists the rationalizing account of manna as the natural product of the tamarisk tree that Humphreys lets it drop out of sight. So the question remains: Is one left with the biblical account better understood, or an alternative account?

WHAT KIND OF TEXT?

Literature, like film, relates to life in a huge variety of ways. One of the key insights of biblical scholarship is that biblical literature is not different from literature generally in this regard. Therefore the fact that one should take any biblical text, and not just those portraying 'miracle', seriously as a literary work in its own right, does not enable one to know precisely how the text relates to 'life'. That requires further judgment as to the genre of the text, judgment which needs to be informed by a wide range of factors, a few of which will briefly be noted here.

First, there is the way in which a 'miracle' narrative is told. The storyline of Jonah, for example, is consistently 'larger-than-life' – an unusually reluctant prophet, the hardest possible assignment, an unparalleled success, and yet a resultant sulk on Jonah's part; the most common adjective in the story is 'big' (*gadol*) – there is a big city, big wind, big storm, big fish, etc. (Jonah 1.2, 4, 17 [Heb. 2.1]); and the story ends with a punchline question. Thus there are plenty of clues as to the genre of the text, clues towards which historic debates about the logistics of a whale swallowing Jonah have been distinctly tone-deaf.

More generally, those HB narratives which portray 'miracle' do not differ from HB narratives elsewhere, in that they offer a dramatized narrative in which, among other things, the reader is enabled to know what the characters say, analogous to the conventions of fiction and film (as in my reference above to 'the narrative equivalent of a zoom lens'). Such speech belongs to the conventions of an enacted presentation that seeks to engage its audience, rather than to modern historiographical conventions.[26]

Sensitivity to narrative convention also entails a heuristic willingness to bracket questions that the narrator (like any good storyteller) wants to be bracketed. For example, there are two HB narratives in which there is the 'miracle' of an animal speaking: the snake in Genesis 3, and the she-ass in Numbers 22. Each time, however, the narrator presents this as part of the fabric of the story (as in, say, Aesop's Fables), rather than as an issue in its own right. Particularly interesting is the donkey's speech in Numbers 22.28–30. This is indeed momentous within the story: 'Then the LORD opened the mouth of the donkey...'. But the point of what the donkey says is to highlight for Balaam his inability to see the significance of her unprecedented behaviour (in going off the road, and then in not going at all), for which he has hit her three times, despite long familiarity with her ways: 'Am I not your donkey, which you have ridden all your life to this day? Have I been in the habit of treating you in this way?' Balaam's inability to see the obvious, that something must be wrong, exemplifies the blindness (induced by greed) that has come upon him.[27] But Balaam within the story, and the story's implied reader, will only attend to what the donkey says if they, as it were, allow her to say it. That is, the donkey's point about her unprecedented behaviour cannot be heard if one trumps it by asking a prior question about her speaking at all. It is not difficult to imagine possible lines along which a conversation might run: Balaam: 'But how can you speak to me?'; Donkey: 'I can do so because YHWH has opened my mouth'; Balaam: 'But since your speaking is no less unprecedented and even more remarkable than your previous erratic behaviour, you must first tell me what this means'. If a question leads one away from the point of the story, one is most likely stepping outside the conventions with which the narrator is working; which ought to be suggestive for the genre of the material one is reading.[28]

Finally, there are factors which play around persons or events that appear 'larger than life'. Certain people who make a memorable impact tend quickly to become the focus of stories that exemplify that impact. We sometimes speak of a person becoming 'a legend in his/her lifetime'. Within Britain, Winston Churchill was such a figure, and stories about him, and sayings ascribed to him, still circulate nearly half a century after his death. One of the things one quickly realizes is that it is extremely difficult to distinguish between sayings and stories whose origin with Churchill is accurately attested, and those which are *ben trovato*, that is 'well-invented' in the sense that they convey something that is genuinely characteristic of Churchill. Further back in history, one finds the same thing with a figure like St Francis of Assisi. When one reads of St Francis preaching to attentive birds, or healing the wolf of Gubbio who leads a reformed wolfish life thereafter, one can be in little doubt that these stories convey something that was characteristic of Francis, as someone who made an impact on animals as well as people. But precisely what 'really happened' it is impossible to say, because one cannot at this distance make precise discriminations as to what is, and is not, *ben trovato*.

It is likely that the HB presents us with a similar phenomenon. Its notable figures have become inseparable from the responses they generated, and the contemporary reader is hardly in a position to distinguish which is which. Although this can often trigger either a rationalizing reading in an attempt to make the distinction anyway, or else a dismissive or credulous reading stance, other reading strategies are more likely to be fruitful. On the one hand, evaluation should be directed to the material as a whole, without separating out the 'miracle' within it, as it is judgments about the plausibility and significance of the whole (judgments which may of course be differentiated) which tend to be decisive for most readers, whether religiously believing or not. On the other hand, the obstacles that impede the quest for what 'really happened' do not similarly impede enquiry into the possible significance, both original and enduring, of the HB 'miracles' in terms of their symbolic and existential implications for understanding God and life in the world.

Notes

1 David Hume, 'Of Miracles', in *Enquiries Concerning Human Understanding*, 3rd edn, ed. L. A. Selby-Bigge, rev. and notes P. H. Nidditch (Oxford: Oxford University Press, 1975), 109–31 (114).

2 On continuity and discontinuity between ancient and modern experiences and accounts of 'nature', see John Rogerson, 'The Old Testament View of Nature: Some Preliminary Questions', in *Instruction and Interpretation*, ed. A. S. van der Woude, Oudtestamentische Studien 20 (Leiden: Brill, 1977), 67–84.

3 For more comprehensive surveys, see Yair Zakovich, 'Miracle (OT)', in *The Anchor Bible Dictionary*, vol. IV: *K–N*, ed. David Noel Freedman *et al.* (New York: Doubleday, 1992), 845–56; Franz-Elmar Wilms, *Wunder im Alten Testament*, Schlüssel zur Bibel (Regensburg: Pustet, 1979); and Paul A. Kruger, *'oth'*, *'mopheth'*, *'pl'*, in *New International Dictionary of Old Testament Theology & Exegesis*, ed. Willem A. VanGemeren (Carlisle: Paternoster, 1997), vol. I, 331–3, vol. II, 879–81, vol. III, 615–17; also see R. Albertz, *'pl'* ni. to be wondrous', in Ernst Jenni and Claus Westermann, *Theological Lexicon of the Old Testament*, vol. II (Peabody: Hendrickson, 1997; ET by Mark Biddle from German of 1971, 1976), 981–6, and J. Conrad, *'pele'*, in *Theological Dictionary of the Old Testament*, vol. XI, ed. G. J. Botterweck, H. Ringgren and H.-J. Fabry (Grand Rapids and Cambridge: Eerdmans, 2001; ET by David Green from German of 1987–8), 533–46.

4 Although the NRSV of Num. 14.11 represents the most common construal of the Hebrew, where the second occurrence of the preposition *'b^e'* that follows the verb for 'believe' is taken to mean 'in spite of', as in Isa. 5.25b (cf. F. Brown, S. R. Driver and C. A. Briggs, *A Hebrew and English Lexicon of the Old Testament* (Oxford: Oxford University Press, 1907), *'b'* III.7), it may be noted that it would be possible to construe the Hebrew as having two objects to the verb juxtaposed in apposition to each other (i.e. 'believe in me, in all the signs'), such that the signs would be an object of belief alongside YHWH himself.

5 J. Conrad, *'pele'* in *Theological Dictionary of the Old Testament*, ed. G. J. Botterweck and H. Ringgren, trans. J. T. Willis, G. W. Bromiley and D. E. Green, 8 vols. (Grand Rapids: Eerdmans, 1974), II, 535.

6 What is envisaged is not a virginal conception, as with Mary's conception of Jesus, but rather that, as a result of YHWH's action, the elderly Sarah will conceive after intercourse with Abraham (Gen. 21.1–2).

7 Keith Ward, *Divine Action* (London: Collins, 1990), 172. Ward is unimpressed by Hume's definition, which he considers 'misleading in almost every respect' (179).

8 Presumably NRSV here renders *mophetim* as 'miracles' so as to avoid repetition with the antecedent 'wonderful works'; but 'signs' would be a preferable rendering.

9 S. R. Driver, *Exodus*, Cambridge Bible for Schools and Colleges (Cambridge: Cambridge University Press, 1911), 368.

10 There is also a high level of 'miracle' in Dan. 1–6. However, these narratives are different from those featuring Moses or Elijah and Elisha in at least two ways: the figure of Daniel is not integral to the 'miraculous', and the 'miracles' happen at the divine behest without human mediation. In both these ways the portrayal of 'miracle' is consistent with the role of the book of Daniel as 'resistance literature' which gives hope to the powerless.

11 This motif works out in striking ways. Abigail is a willing agent (1 Sam. 25.30–1), as is David himself when he deceives Achish about the targets of his raids and makes sure that no one is left alive who might tell the Philistine king what was really going on (27.8–12). But when it seems that David has no choice but to fight with the Philistines against Saul and the Israelite army, then the suspicions of the Philistine commanders other than Achish ensure David's non-participation in shedding Israelite blood (1 Sam. 29).

12 Although Moses' actions are often comparable to those of Elijah and Elisha, the narrator tends to specify that Moses acts at YHWH's behest in a way that is not so with these other prophets.

13 Daniel Harrington and Anthony Saldarini, *Targum Jonathan of the Former Prophets*, Aramaic Bible 10 (Edinburgh: T&T Clark, 1987), 267.

14 See the statement of position, characteristic of many Christian Old Testament scholars, by H. H. Rowley, *The Faith of Israel* (London: SCM, 1956), 57–9.

15 There is a useful collection of material in Theodor H. Gaster, *Myth, Legend and Custom in the Old Testament* (London: Duckworth, 1969).

16 A rationalizing tendency here is ancient (though is not evidenced in the ancient versions), and includes the suggestion that ʿorᵉbim means 'the inhabitants of the city of Oreb'. See Louis Ginzberg, *The Legends of the Jews*, vol. vi (Philadelphia: JPS, 5729/1968), 317.

17 See Gaster, *Myth*, 498–503.

18 G. H. Jones, *1 and 2 Kings*, 2 vols., New Century Bible (London: Marshall, Morgan & Scott, 1984), vol. ii, 422.

19 The most influential modern treatment is Greta Hort, 'The Plagues of Egypt', *Zeitschrift für die alttestamentliche Wissenschaft* 69 (1957), 84–103, and *Zeitschrift für die alttestamentliche Wissenschaft* 70 (1958), 48–59. Humphreys acknowledges her work as 'classic'. A naturalistic construal of the plagues based on Hort can also be found in James Hoffmeier, *Israel in Egypt* (New York and Oxford: Oxford University Press, 1996), 144–9; K. A. Kitchen, *On the Reliability of the Old Testament* (Grand Rapids: Eerdmans, 2003), 249–54; and, with greater nuance, Nahum Sarna, *Exploring Exodus: The Heritage of Biblical Israel* (New York: Schocken, 1987), 68–78.

20 Colin Humphreys, *The Miracles of Exodus: A Scientist's Discovery of the Extraordinary Natural Causes of the Biblical Stories* (London and New York: Continuum, 2003), 5. For the importance of timing in Humphreys' account, cf. 256, 271, 337.

21 *Ibid.*, 339.

22 *Ibid.*, 118.

23 Josephus, *Jewish Antiquities* 3.31: 'to this day all that region is watered by a rain like that which, as a favour to Moses, the Deity then sent down for men's sustenance'. There is a useful account of the nature of the manna that occurs naturally in the Sinai peninsula, and of the similarities and differences between it and the biblical manna, in Driver, *Exodus*, 153–4.

24 Humphreys, *Miracles*, 290, 291, 292.

25 *Ibid.*, 288–9.

26 One of the major differences between a modern 'History of Israel' and the biblical histories is that the modern genre is presented in an analytical, non-dramatized form; which is one reason why, whatever its merits, it is less engaging to the general reader than the biblical original.

27 For a reading of the whole narrative, see R. W. L. Moberly, *Prophecy and Discernment*, Cambridge Studies in Christian Doctrine (Cambridge: Cambridge University Press, 2006), 138–47.

28 Rabbinic tradition made an interestingly different move. Balaam's ass was included among 'ten things which God created on the eve of the [first] Sabbath', other items in the list including the manna, the rainbow, the tables of stone, and the opening up of the earth to swallow the wicked (*b. Pesahim* 54a). The logic of the list appears to be that its items are all non-human, with a possible corollary that an understanding of God's 'miraculous' action as enhancing human capability cannot here apply and so must be otherwise explained.

I am grateful to friends in the Durham Old Testament Research Seminar, and also to Brent Strawn, for their suggestions which have considerably improved this chapter.

Further reading

Albertz, R., '*plʾ* ni. to be wondrous', in Ernst Jenni and Claus Westermann, *Theological Lexicon of the Old Testament*, vol. ii (Peabody: Hendrickson, 1997; ET by Mark Biddle from German of 1971, 1976), 981–6

Conrad, J., '*peleʾ*', in *Theological Dictionary of the Old Testament*, vol. xi, ed. G. J. Botterweck, H. Ringgren and H.-J. Fabry (Grand Rapids and Cambridge: Eerdmans, 2001; ET by David Green from German of 1987–8), 533–46

Gaster, Theodor H., *Myth, Legend and Custom in the Old Testament* (London: Duckworth, 1969)

Ginzberg, Louis, *The Legends of the Jews*, vol. vi (Philadelphia: JPS, 5729/1968)

Hort, Greta, 'The Plagues of Egypt', *Zeitschrift für die alttestamentliche Wissenschaft* 69 (1957), 84–103, and *Zeitschrift für die alttestamentliche Wissenschaft* 70 (1958), 48–59

Hume, David, 'Of Miracles', in *Enquiries Concerning Human Understanding*, 3rd edn, ed. L. A. Selby-Bigge, rev. and notes P. H. Nidditch (Oxford: Oxford University Press, 1975), 109–31

Humphreys, Colin J., *The Miracles of Exodus: A Scientist's Discovery of the Extraordinary Natural Causes of the Biblical Stories* (London and New York: Continuum, 2003)

Kruger, Paul A., *ʾoth'*, *'mopheth'*, *'pl'*, in *New International Dictionary of Old Testament Theology & Exegesis*, ed. Willem A. VanGemeren (Carlisle: Paternoster, 1997), vol. I, 331–3, vol. II, 879–81, vol. III, 615–17

Moberly, R. W. L., *Prophecy and Discernment*, Cambridge Studies in Christian Doctrine (Cambridge: Cambridge University Press, 2006)

Rogerson, John, *The Supernatural in the Old Testament* (Guildford and London: Lutterworth, 1976)

'The Old Testament View of Nature: Some Preliminary Questions', in *Instruction and Interpretation*, ed. A. S. van der Woude, Oudtestamentische Studiën 20 (Leiden: Brill, 1977), 67–84

Ross, J. P., 'Some Notes on Miracle in the Old Testament', in *Miracles: Cambridge Studies in the Philosophy and History*, ed. C. F. D. Moule (London: Mowbray, 1965), 43–60

Ward, Keith, *Divine Action* (London: Collins, 1990), 170–89

Wilms, Franz-Elmar, *Wunder im Alten Testament*, Schlüssel zur Bibel (Regensburg: Pustet, 1979)

Zakovich, Yair, *The Concept of Miracle in the Bible* (Tel Aviv: MOD, 1990)

*Zakovich, Yair, 'Miracle (OT)', in *The Anchor Bible Dictionary*, vol. IV: *K–N*, ed. David Noel Freedman *et al.* (New York: Doubleday, 1992), 845–56

4 Miracles in the Greek and Roman world

ROBERT GARLAND

In Christological terms a miracle is a *sēmeion* ('sign') or, more prosaic-ally, an *ergon* ('deed'), these being the words most commonly used by Jesus to describe the miracles he performs. Other words found in the gospels include *teras* ('wonder') and *dunamis* ('power'). Collectively they imply that miracles were primarily perceived as signifiers that had far greater value and meaning than simply their impact upon the phenomenal world; or as St Augustine (*City of God* 22.10) put it, their purpose was that 'faith may prosper'.

In Graeco-Roman terms, by contrast, a miracle was regarded more as a sociological event, one that generated a sense of astonishment and wonder in those who witnessed it. This can be deduced from the fact that the nearest Greek and Latin equivalents for 'miracle' in the pre-Christian era are *thauma* from *thaumazō* and *miraculum* from *miror*. Both verbs (*thaumazō* and *miror*) mean literally 'to wonder at, be amazed at'. In other words, both languages highlight the reaction of spectators to 'that which is amazing'. Since what is amazing is not invariably or necessarily the same as what is miraculous, it follows that neither *thauma* nor *miraculum* carries the same force as the Christian concept of 'miracle'. Faithful to the Greek, the Latin Vulgate renders 'miracle' by *signum*, *prodigium* and *virtus; miraculum* is only used in patristic and later theology. In sum, there is no Greek or Latin word that differentiates an act, sight or occurrence that is 'truly' miraculous from one that is, quite simply, worthy of wonder. In the plainest terms, a goal scored from behind the halfway line could, without hyperbole, have been appropriately deemed 'miraculous'.[1]

It is important to note, however, that *thauma*, meaning 'wonder', may also denote 'trickery', both in the literal and metaphorical sense of the word (as, for instance, in the case of the kind of verbal trickery that is employed by a sophist). Similarly, *thaumatourgos* denotes not only a 'miracle worker' but also a 'juggler or acrobat', while *teratourgos*, 'one who deals in or produces monstrosities or prodigies', is used almost exclusively in a pejorative sense. A more generic term is *goēs*, which denotes 'one who is skilled in the art of deception'. As Georg Luck has aptly observed: 'This is more than a semantic difficulty: it is ultimately a matter of faith',[2] and one that has important cultural implications. The period covered by this chapter extends from the late eighth century BCE to the early centuries of the Christian era, when both paganism and Christianity utilized miracles as propagandist weapons to demonstrate the superiority of their respective belief systems.

THE DIFFICULTY OF DEFINITION

The study of miracles in the Graeco-Roman world is bedevilled by terminological and conceptual difficulties. An extreme position would be to reject the validity of 'miracle' altogether, on the grounds that it had a specific importance and value for Christianity, which was not shared by polytheism. This, however, would be to deny the similarities and continuities between the two religious systems, as well as Christianity's many borrowings from pre-Christian practices, both Jewish and pagan. It is true that 'miracle' comes with Christian baggage and as such is liable to engender what Jaś Elsner and Ian Rutherford call 'wrong expectations in certain aspects of our assumptions about antique religion ... [which] may map only clumsily onto the range of evidence from antiquity'. The fact remains, however, that the pagans believed that something akin to our understanding of the word 'miracle' did indeed occur in the phenomenal world, and this is important for our understanding of the origins of the early Christian mindset.[3]

A second terminological problem has to do with the overlap between magic and religion. H. S. Versnel defines magic as 'a manipulative strategy to influence the course of nature by supernatural ("occult") means'.[4] If we exclude the words 'manipulative' and 'occult', this might equally describe the craft of the miracle worker. The difficulty in establishing clear boundaries between the two enterprises originates in antiquity. Lucian of Samosata, who is a major source for the religious attitudes of the cultural elite in the second century CE, treated magicians and miracle workers with equal scorn. As Anderson puts it, 'Miracle is a term of approval applicable to the work of one's friends, while magic in many but by no means all cases turns out to be the work of one's enemies'.[5] We even encounter the term 'pagan religious magic'. A similar overlap, both essential and linguistic, exists between miracles on the one hand, and omens and prodigies on the other. Both Greek *teras* and Latin *monstrum* can be variously translated as either 'sign, wonder, marvel', or 'monstrosity'. Which translation, we might ask, should we use either for spontaneous combustion or for a cloudburst in a desert region that had never previously experienced rain (Herodotus, *Histories* 1.59.1; 3.10.3)?

In light of these difficulties it is hardly surprising that scholars of Graeco-Roman religion rarely regard miracles as deserving of separate investigation, preferring to subsume them under a broader discussion of the workings of the supernatural.[6] And yet the relative paucity of unambiguous examples has in itself much to tell us about the distinctive way in which the belief system functioned. First, it reminds us that polytheism was not *au fond* a proselytizing religion. Since belief in a multiplicity of deities was, with the exception of the Jews and the Christians, universally accepted throughout the Mediterranean, polytheism per se had little to prove. It follows from this that miracles were chiefly associated either with moments of crisis or with periods when a local pantheon was undergoing expansion, and further that charismatic religious leaders claiming to have the power to work miracles would have been somewhat marginal figures, who posed little threat to polis-centred religion until the advent of the Jesus movement.

RECIPROCITY AND OVER-DETERMINATION

Not every supernatural occurrence can be blithely assimilated to the miraculous. This is true of the majority of instances of divine intervention, in that they represented one side of a semi-contractual agreement between the deity on the one hand and the human recipient of her or his goodwill on the other. An early instance is an inscription that is scratched on the legs of a bronze statuette of a naked youth dated 700–650 BCE in the Boston Museum of Fine Arts (no. 03.997): 'Mantiklos offers me as a tithe to silver-bowed Apollo. Give me something nice in return, Phoebus [Apollo].' When in due course the god responded, as he presumably did, given the petitioner's obliging lack of specificity, we are hardly entitled to conclude that Mantiklos interpreted his windfall as a miracle; more likely he saw it as just deserts, perhaps muttering under his breath, 'And about time too'. Roman religion was founded on the same principle of reciprocity, pithily expressed in the formula, '*Do ut des*', 'I give so that you [the deity] may give'.

We should also note the tendency in polytheistic thinking towards over-determination, which further undermines the attempt to identify the miraculous. Take the pestilence that afflicts the Achaean army at the beginning of Book I of Homer's *Iliad*. Though brought about by Apollo as a way of punishing Agamemnon for rejecting the appeal of his priest Chryses to accept a ransom for the return of his daughter, it has a logical explanation in the weakened condition of the Achaean army, now into the tenth year of conducting a siege in circumstances that made it highly vulnerable to disease. All that is noteworthy is the timing: the exact coincidence between Agamemnon's obstinacy and the plague's outbreak. Similarly when a god breathes *menos* or strength into a hero, thereby empowering him with an extra burst of energy, it is not that a miracle has occurred but that the hero in question, at a timely moment, has experienced an adrenalin rush. Divine intervention therefore operates within the parameters of natural cause and effect, though this in no way diminishes its religious value or significance. Homer also alerts us to the fact that the gods voluntarily limit their power to work miracles. When, for instance, Zeus is tempted to save his son Sarpedon from slaughter by snatching him from the battlefield before he encounters Patroclus, he wisely desists when Hera warns him that should he do so other gods will follow suit (*Iliad* 16.433–47).

A contractual agreement also governed divine intervention in battle. When the runner Philippides encounters Pan on Mount Parthenion on his way back to Marathon with the dispiriting news that the Spartans have declined to render immediate assistance against the vastly superior Persian forces, the goat god, as reported by Herodotus, tells him to relay the following message to his compatriots: 'Why don't you pay me cult [*epimeleia*] since I am well-disposed towards you and have on many occasions already been useful and will be so in the future?' (Herodotus, *Histories* 6.105.2). After their victory, the Athenians repaid Pan by establishing his cult on the slopes of the Acropolis.[7] Constantine, eight centuries later, seems to have been equally averse to interpreting his victory over his rival Maxentius at Saxa Rubra in 312 BCE as miraculous in the Christian sense of the term: his claim to have seen a cross above the sun inscribed with the words *in hoc signo vinces* ('You will conquer in this sign') before the battle suggests that belief in Christ simply enhanced military performance. Both of these examples contrast sharply with the plagues of Egypt, which function as 'signs and wonders' illustrative of the power of the Lord (Exod. 7.3), even though the importance of both Pan and the Christian God increased in consequence of the victories to which they had contributed. Not all instances of supernatural intervention were either contractual or over-determined, of course. It is, however, against this complicated background that we now turn to the two most prominent types of miracles attested in the Graeco-Roman world.

MIRACLES IN THE SERVICE OF A NATIONALIST AGENDA

Referring to Greek religion, A. D. Nock stated axiomatically: 'Miracle proved deity'.[8] Yet only at specific moments in Greek history does this formula hold true. One such moment is the state's foundation. The dispute between Athena and Poseidon for the possession of Athens was, for instance, decided by a contest in which both deities showed off their miraculous powers – the ability to generate an olive tree on the Acropolis in Athena's case, and a jet of salt water in Poseidon's case. There are few reports of miracles in the fifth century BCE except in the period of the Persian Wars, when the Greeks came within a hair's breadth of defeat. Not surprisingly they ascribed their success partly to their gods, principally to Apollo, the primary champion of their cause. His most spectacular miracle was the defence of Delphi, which he achieved by breaking off two peaks from Mount Parnassus and using them to crush the invaders (Herodotus, *Histories* 8.37.2).[9]

In the national consciousness, Roman Republican history was viewed as a series of political and military crises that imperilled the very existence of the state and that had been surmounted in part by miraculous occurrences (for example, the expulsion of Tarquin the Proud in 509 BCE, the defeat of the Etruscans at the battle of Lake Regillus in 499 or 496 BCE, the abating of the devastating plague that afflicted Rome in 293 BCE). Valerius Maximus provides an instructive compilation of these miracles in his book of memorable deeds and sayings, in which he interprets *miraculum* loosely to mean any event that defies human explanation (*Memorable Deeds and Sayings* 1.8). They include sightings of the twins Castor and Pollux, and of the god Mars, in battle, Rome's rescue from plague as a result of the providential arrival of Asclepius' snake, the appearance of Caesar's ghost to C. Cassius before Philippi, a timely Delphic prophecy, and so on. Valerius does not state that he incontrovertibly believes in these miracles; merely that he is reluctant to treat as fiction 'events that have been hallowed by famous literary monuments' (1.8.7). Less literary-minded Romans are likely to have interpreted the stories as proof of the exceptional regard in which their city was held by its gods.

MIRACLES IN THE SERVICE OF RELIGIOUS PROPAGANDA

Another prominent application of miracles was to legitimate the entry of a new deity or the establishment of a sanctuary. The Homeric hymns to Apollo, Demeter and Dionysus all contain accounts of both epiphanies and miracles, which function as foundation charters for the cults in question. As we see from Euripides' *Bacchae*, Dionysus was fully prepared to perform punitive miracles (as well as those of a beneficent kind) when he met with resistance, a fact which suggests that his priests were especially aggressive in the furthering of his (and their) interests.[10] Miracles remained central to his cult in Roman times, albeit ridiculed by non-believers. Livy, writing of the year 186 BCE when the Senate passed a decree outlawing his worship in Italy, scoffed at stories of maenads dipping flaming torches in water and bringing them out alight, alleging that they had previously been coated in a mixture of sulphur and calcium. He was equally dismissive of the report that people were abducted by gods, alleging that they had been attached to machines and hidden in caves (*History* 29.13). Though it is unclear whether Dionysus' cult served a nationalist agenda for Greek-speakers and others in Italy, reports of miracles would certainly have strengthened the cult's appeal among the downtrodden.

The claim to work miracles was regularly deployed in the Hellenistic era to advance the interests of foreign gods, particularly Egyptian. Isidorus (first century BCE), author of the three earliest-surviving Greek hymns to Isis, whose cult eventually spread throughout the Graeco-Roman world, credits the goddess with the power to rescue men, women and children from war, release them from prison, save them from the grip of death, cure them from pain, and protect them when abroad or at sea.[11] Diodorus Siculus (c. 80–29 BCE) provides further testimony to Isis' powers, claiming that 'many who have been given up as lost by their doctors ... are saved by her, while numbers of those who have lost their eyesight or the use of some other part of the body are restored to their previous condition whenever they solicit the goddess' (*Library of History* 1.25.4–5). Another significant Egyptian import was Serapis (the Hellenized form of Osiris-Apis), though his cult never achieved the prominence of Isis. The early Ptolemies founded a Serapeum at Canopus where according to Strabo 'even the most reputable men' had faith in the cures that were performed therein (*Geography* 17.1.17). A well-known inscription from Delos dated to the third century BCE reports that Sarapis caused the authorities to be struck dumb when they sought to oppose the establishment of his cult on their island.[12]

ASCLEPIUS THE HEALER

Miracle stories feature in the *aretalogiai* or aretalogies, quasi-liturgical accounts of the beneficial powers (*aretai*) of gods such as Isis, the earliest examples of which date to the fourth century BCE. It is, however, the *iamata* or cures ascribed to the healing god Asclepius that provide what Versnel has aptly described as the 'first traces of a *structural* advertising function of miracles'.[13] The largest surviving collection derives from Epidaurus in the Argolid. They are preserved on two tablets or *stēlai* of late fourth-century BCE date, which record forty-four cures. In the late second century CE, however, Pausanias (*Description of Greece* 2.27.3) saw six *stēlai*, adding 'in earlier times there were more', so the total number of recorded cures must have eventually been in the hundreds. The fact that the Greeks used the word *iama* from *iaomai*, meaning 'to heal', rather than *thauma*, suggests, however, the cures are to be regarded as routine rather than miraculous, even though they came about in surprising ways.[14] Indeed reports of healing miracles ascribed to a variety of deities abound in the Roman period. Other Asclepiea are known to have preserved *iamata*, including Tricca in mainland Greece, the island of Cos, and Pergamum in Asia Minor, though only one other *stēlē* survives, from Lebena in Crete.[15] We should not, however, assume that all Asclepiea preserved such records, since, as Kee has suggested, there is evidence of a basic split in the Asclepius tradition between miraculous healing and medical intervention.[16]

The *stēlai* were presumably set up by the priesthood, partly to inspire faith among suppliants, and partly to publicize the god's miraculous healing powers to the Greek world at large. Their basic format is as follows: after providing the name and place of origin of the invalid, they identify the nature of his or her ailment before recounting how the god effected the miraculous cure. Often the narrative teaches a simple moral lesson, such as respect for the god's powers and gratitude for his intervention.[17] Asclepius accuses one suppliant of *hubris* and taxes another with failing to bring him a thank-offering. He cures blindness, dumbness, paralysis, lameness, extended pregnancies, infertility, headaches and even baldness. Not surprisingly we rarely hear of him casting out devils, since for the most part these did not trouble the classical imagination. Eventually he was slain by Zeus because of presumptuously raising the dead to life. This detail speaks to a characteristically Greek caveat that may have militated in general against miracle workers – the need to respect human limitations. In the fifth century BCE the priesthood of Apollo fostered Asclepius' elevation to godhead and his cult eventually spread throughout the eastern Mediterranean.[18]

Asclepius was unique among major Greek deities in exhibiting compassion for the human race. He was not only 'the god to whom every law of necessity yields' (Aristides 23.16), but also 'the god most loving to humankind' (Aelian, *On the Nature of Animals* 8.12). This presented a severe challenge to the early Christians, because they cast their god in identical terms, and so they sought to extirpate his cult.[19] There was, however, no expectation that suppliants, once cured, would experience a spiritual transformation and demonstrate exclusive allegiance to Asclepius. It was deemed sufficient that they expressed their gratitude to the god – or rather to his attendant priests – by means of a gift, though this does not exclude the likelihood that they were also placed under a moral obligation to 'spread the word'.

This said, the most eloquent witness to Asclepius' powers is the hypochondriac sophist Aelius Aristides who, after experiencing an epiphany of the god at Smyrna, journeyed to the Asclepieum at Pergamum in 145 CE, where he resided for two years in the (no doubt enervating) company of other highly educated hypochondriacs. Aristides narrates his battle with sickness and recovery in his diaries known as the *Hieroi logoi* or *Sacred Discourses*. He claims that his sufferings were more intense, his fortitude greater and his numerous cures more miraculous than those of any other suppliant. His is the only first-hand literary account from the beneficiary of a miraculous cure that has come down to us from Graeco-Roman antiquity. Aristides epitomizes a new type of pagan that emerged in the second century CE – one that placed his entire well-being in the care of a single deity and made it his goal to be 'at one with the god' (2.23).[20]

MIRACLE WORKERS

Human miracle workers or *thaumatourgoi* constitute a sub-species under the general classification of religious virtuosi, *viz.* holy men, gurus, shamans, exorcists and *magoi* (from which our word 'magician' derives), who filled the void left by a priesthood whose primary function was liturgical and administrative.[21] The commonest types of miracles attributed to them include healing, bilocation (the ability to be in two places at the same time), control over natural forces, walking on water, flying through the air and apotheosis.

They seem to have been prevalent in the Archaic period, as Herodotus indicates, particularly in association with Apollo. Reports of their deeds are largely confined to the fringes of the Greek-speaking world. One such was Aristeas of Procconesus who, 'inspired by Phoebus [Apollo]', visited the land of the one-eyed Arimaspians and Hyperboreans. After Aristeas had been pronounced dead in a fuller's shop, a man from Artaca, recently arrived in town, declared he had seen him on his way to Cyzicus. Returning to the shop to remove the deceased, his relatives discovered the room to be empty. Seven years later Aristeas turned up again in Procconesus, before disappearing again, only to appear for the last time, 240 years later, in Metapontum (*Histories* 4.14–16). Another was Abaris, a native of the land of the Hyperboreans (Apollo's haunt in the winter months), who is said to have 'carried the arrow around the whole world while fasting' – seemingly a reference to Apollo's arrow, which was credited with healing powers (4.36). Herodotus offers no judgment on the claims associated with either Aristeas or Abaris. The Thracian Salmoxis does not get off so lightly. Worshipped by the Thracians as a god, Salmoxis was denounced as a charlatan by Herodotus' Greek informants (4.94–6). They claimed that he faked his resurrection by building a hall with an underground chamber and then went into hiding for three years, after which he popped up again – literally so, perhaps – to the amazement of all.

Even more ridicule attached to the philosopher Empedocles of Acragas (*c.* 492–32 BCE), who is said to have stayed the winds, cured the sick, resuscitated the dead and become a god. His chief claim to fame, however, was the bathetic manner of his death. The most colourful account has him leaping into the volcanic crater of Mount Etna with the intention of faking his apotheosis, only to be revealed as a fraud when the volcano belched up one of his bronze sandals (Diogenes Laertius, *Lives* 8.69). It may be that the reports of his miraculous powers, largely extrapolated from his poetry, aroused such derision that posterity exacted its revenge by assigning him a particularly ignominious death.

One pagan whose reputation as a miracle worker remained largely unsullied into the Christian era was Pythagoras. His biographers Porphyry and Iamblichus claim that rivers spoke to him, that on one occasion he talked to his disciples at Metapontum and Tauromenium on the same day, and that he could predict earthquakes, avert epidemics, lull storms, and calm both rivers and seas.[22] In the absence of any contemporary account of Pythagoras' life, there is no knowing when reports of his wondrous deeds first began to circulate.

Religious personnel are rarely credited with the ability to perform miracles, which is hardly surprising in view of the fact that eligibility to office was based wholly on external qualifications, rather than on intellectual, moral or spiritual attributes. An exception is the priestess of Athena at Pedasa, a city in south-west Turkey, who, whenever any crisis occurred, grew a long beard, an occurrence that allegedly happened three times (Herodotus, *Histories* 1.175).[23] A Hellenistic dynast credited with the power to work healing miracles, however, was Pyrrhus king of Epirus, whose big toe, according to his biographer Plutarch (*Pyrrhus* 3.4), was capable of curing diseases of the spleen when rubbed on the infected area. Like Shelley's heart, it failed to ignite when his corpse was cremated – a minor miracle of sorts.

We hear of no Roman miracle workers, and it may be that here, as in so many other areas of professional expertise, the Greeks claimed a monopoly, particularly in light of the fact that miracle workers were, as we have seen, to some degree perceived as entertainers. An exception involves the introduction of the cult of the Magna Mater into Rome in 204 BCE in the form of a black stone, when a certain Claudia Quinta is said to have miraculously rescued the goddess at the moment when the ship in which she was being conveyed grounded on a sandbank (Ovid, *Fasti* 4.247–8; Herodian, *History* 1.11). This act of devotion has no exact parallel in classical literature and looks forward to the miracles that were performed in the Middle Ages, notably those connected with the construction of Chartres Cathedral. Though other Roman women of exceptional piety were credited with miraculous powers, the miracles they performed were self-vindicating, so to speak, rather than intended for the good of others, as in the case of a Vestal Virgin named Tuccia, accused of breaking her vow of chastity, who proved her innocence by carrying water in a sieve (Valerius Maximus, *Memorable Deeds and Sayings* 8.1. abs. 5).

VESPASIAN'S MIRACULOUS HEALING POWERS

It was not part of the job description of a Roman emperor to be able to perform miracles on behalf of his subjects. True, the Jewish philosopher Philo (*Embassy* 144–5) credited the deified Augustus with the ability not only to 'calm the torrential storm on every side' but also to 'heal plagues that afflicted both the Greeks and the barbarians'. However, extravagant flattery of this sort was routinely offered by those seeking favours or rewards and is part of the language of soteriology. An exception is Vespasian, who according to Tacitus (*Histories* 4.81), while residing in Alexandria before being appointed emperor, was accosted first by a blind man seeking a miraculous cure, who implored him to moisten his cheeks and eyes with spittle, and then by a man with a withered hand, who asked him to stamp on it with his foot. At first Vespasian treated their requests with scorn, but on the advice of some physicians he was eventually persuaded to accept the challenge. Both invalids were instantly cured, Tacitus relates, 'as eye-witnesses continue to report, even at a time when nothing is gained by lying' – in other words, long after Vespasian's death.

Tacitus' account is nicely nuanced. Though he does not dismiss the story outright as fabrication, he falls short of endorsing the claim that Vespasian had miraculous powers. The fact that this event took place in Egypt is, moreover, highly significant, as the first Roman official to proclaim Vespasian emperor was the prefect of Egypt. Since this highly charged political act occurred in Alexandria on 1 July – shortly after the alleged miracles took place[24] – it is therefore likely that the miraculous cures laid the groundwork for the proclamation, and further that Vespasian accepted the challenge with precisely this purpose in mind.

There are no reports of Vespasian performing miracles after his accession. Quite possibly claims to this effect would have been greeted with incredulity in the capital itself. Some at least of the Roman elite were sceptical of miracles, even when there were pressing patriotic motives to encourage belief. Livy, for instance, at the very beginning of his history, indicates that he is dubious of the tradition, datable to the third century BCE, that Rome's first king Romulus underwent apotheosis. Instead he advances a variant claim to the effect that the king was torn to pieces by an angry mob (*History* 1.16.4–8). His scepticism is all the more striking in light of the fact that he risked arousing the displeasure of Augustus, since the 'official' tradition would surely have served to justify the deification of his adoptive father Julius Caesar in 42 BCE.[25]

ALEXANDER OF ABONOTEICHUS

Polytheism's late flowering in the second century CE found expression in a handful of exotic new cults. One of the most successful was an oracular shrine set up by Alexander of Abonoteichus on the southern coast of the Black Sea. The shrine, which offered miraculous healings, took its cue from an alleged epiphany of the healing god Asclepius in the form of a human-headed snake called Glycon. Unfortunately we see Alexander exclusively through the eyes of his hostile biographer Lucian, who visited his shrine in c. 160 CE. Lucian made it his task to expose Alexander's venality and concupiscence – charges that were regularly laid against religious charismatics. He reports that Alexander claimed to work miracles and exercise control over malignant spirits, while advocating an ethical system that cloaked his debauchery. Despite his vitriolic hatred of the seer, however, Lucian does not underestimate his enormous popularity. On the contrary, he uses it to mock the pitiful depths of human ignorance. Alexander, he claims, particularly won the devotion of Paphlagonians who were 'fatheads and simpletons' (*Alexander* 9). As the description exists *in vacuo*, however, there is no reason why Lucian should be given more credibility than the seer he denounces as an impostor. A narrative of Jesus' mission seen through the eyes of a Pharisee would not be substantially different in tone from Lucian's hatchet job on Alexander.

Lucian also despised 'the poor wretches [meaning the followers of Christ] who have convinced themselves that they will become immortal and live for ever'. He added: 'If any charlatan or trickster moves among them with a knack for making money he immediately becomes wealthy by imposing on the simple-witted' (*The Passing of Peregrinus* 13). Not only the dim-witted came in for ridicule. In *Philopseudēs*, or 'Lover of Lies', it is the self-professed seekers after truth, namely the philosophers, who are the butt of his humour. Of all classical authors, Lucian foremost provides evidence of sustained hostility both to miracles and to those who claimed miraculous powers.

APOLLONIUS OF TYANA

Further evidence of the rival claims of Christianity and polytheism to perform miracles is provided by Lucius Flavius Philostratus' unreliable biography of Apollonius of Tyana, written in *c.* 220 CE. Apollonius, whose life spanned the greater part of the first century CE, was a wandering ascetic Neopythagorean philosopher, who travelled extensively in the Roman East accompanied by his disciples. While en route from Persia to India, Apollonius rebuked an apparition [*phasma*], which departed 'gibbering like a ghost' (*Life of Apollonius* 2.4). Back in the Greek-speaking world he saved the Ephesians from the plague (4.10). Moving on to Pergamum, he cured many who were diseased (4.11.1). In Athens he cast a demon from a youth who was addicted to licentiousness (4.20). In Rome he seemingly brought back to life a recently deceased bride, though Philostratus observes that the sage may have observed a spark of life in the girl, which the physicians had overlooked (4.45). Arrived at the Hellespont he put a stop to earthquakes (6.41). In Tarsus he cured a man of rabies, not neglecting to restore the rabid dog to health as well (6.43). Various stories were reported of his death – 'if indeed he died', as Philostratus observes. The most elaborate is that he was placed in chains under suspicion of being a sorcerer and robber. After he had broken them, the doors of the prison opened and he ascended to heaven to the accompaniment of a female choir (8.29–31).

In the late second century CE the cult of Apollonius attracted the patronage of the Severan emperors. Indeed Philostratus notes that he undertook to write his biography at the request of Julia Domna, the wife of Septimius Severus. Seventy years later, around the time of the persecution of the Christians by Diocletian in CE 303, an official in his administration called Hierocles published an anti-Christian polemic entitled *Philalēthēs*, or 'Lover of Truth', in which he compared Jesus unfavourably to Apollonius, partly on the grounds that he performed superior miracles. Whereas Jesus' miracles were limited in scope, Apollonius – so Hierocles alleges – had the power to harness the forces of nature. About a decade later Eusebius, Bishop of Caesarea, published a rebuttal entitled *Against Hierocles*, in which he dismissed Apollonius' feats as 'mere wizardry'.

CHRISTIAN VERSUS PAGAN MIRACLES

As Christianity and polytheism entered into mortal combat, miracles became a major weapon in the arsenal of Christianity. We already encounter a contest in Acts 13.4–12, where Paul demonstrates his superior ability to work miracles over a *magos* named Bar-Jesus (or Elymas). Later when Paul and Barnabas are visiting Lystra in southwest Turkey and heal a cripple, the townsfolk mistake them for Hermes and Zeus respectively. The author of Acts is indicating to his pagan readers that their belief in the supernatural powers of anthropomorphic deities should now be attributed to the apostles.

The Christian response to pagan miracles was politically shrewd. Christians did not deny their validity, but denounced them as the work of demons or spirits.[26] Early evidence of this is in Mark's Gospel, where Jesus charges the twelve disciples with authority over 'unclean spirits' (Mark 6.7; cf. Matt.10.1). Even when demons appear to perform miracles for the good of mankind, they are in reality using them for their own nefarious purposes. Nearly two centuries later, Tertullian, in a discussion of their apparent ability to perform healing miracles, claims that demons 'first cause sickness and then teach remedies that are either novel or paradoxical to the point of seeming miraculous' (Tertullian, *Apology* 22.11).

One of the most illuminating testimonies to the importance of miracles for both religions in this period is in *Contra Celsum* (*Against Celsus*), a tract written in c. 249 CE by the biblical scholar and theologian Origen, who saw himself in debate with learned polytheists. *Against Celsus* offers a vigorous and detailed response to a lost work entitled *Alēthēs logos* (the *True Doctrine*), perhaps the first sustained philosophical polemic against Christianity, which had been written by the Middle Platonic philosopher Celsus some seventy years before. In it Celsus had argued that the miracles performed by polytheists were on a par with those performed by Jesus Christ. Origen, who quotes extensively from Celsus, pays particularly close attention to his description of the wonders performed by Aristeas of Procconesus, alleging that they served no useful function, whereas those ascribed to Jesus 'helped to establish the doctrine spread by him which brought salvation to mankind' (*Against Celsus* 3.28).

Miraculous occurrences were a central feature of a quasi-philosophical movement known as theurgy (from *theourgia*, meaning 'actuating or accessing the divine'). Theurgy drew its inspiration from a collection of hexameter verses called the Chaldean Oracles, which the gods purportedly dictated to Julian the Chaldean and/or his son Julian in the late second century CE. Julian the Theurge is said to have caused a miraculous downpour in 172 CE, when the Roman army was dying from thirst during Marcus Aurelius' campaign in Germany. Other polytheists claimed credit for the miracle, while Christians for their part attributed it to Christ.[27] The fact that polytheists saw themselves in competition with one another for the title of miracle worker tells us much about the disadvantages that they faced in their battle with Christianity.[28]

Theurgy flourished in the late third century CE in line with the rise of Neoplatonism, some of whose proponents, such as Porphyry, valued it as a means to purify the soul. A notable practitioner of the fourth century was Sosipatra, who had a fertilizing effect on crops, consorted with divine beings, and was credited with the ability to be omnipresent.[29] Secret rites that instilled the divine presence in statues of the gods, which thus became capable of performing miracles, were also performed in the name of theurgy. An inscription dated to the late second or third century CE from Stratonikeia in Caria claims that the statues of Zeus and Hecate perform 'good deeds of divine power for the safety of the eternal empire of our lords the Romans', as celebrated daily by hymns sung in honour of the gods.[30] In his discussion of 'the miracles of the gods of the gentiles [*miracula deorum gentilium*]', St Augustine, likening theurgy to magic, claimed that 'most practices of this sort take over people's sensory perceptions by playing with their imagination' (*City of God* 10.16). Like Tertullian two centuries earlier, St Augustine did not deny the efficacy of pagan miracles. After listing many of the examples that we find in Valerius Flaccus, which he culled from a lost work by Varro entitled *On the Roman Race*,[31] he declared that pagan miracles were inferior both in power and scale (*virtute ac magnitudine*) to Christian miracles, which proved that 'our miracles are incomparably superior' (10.16).

CONCLUSION

Though the Greeks and the Romans acknowledged events that were marvellous, they did not invariably apprehend the divine through interference in the laws of nature. Since polytheists by and large have little need to proselytize, there was far less need to publicize the gods' miraculous powers. As a result, a somewhat legalistically framed relationship existed between gods and humans, which was based on an acknowledgement of the gods' superior powers. This meant that their belief system was not reliant on *sēmeia*, unlike Christianity, whose success came to depend largely on widely disseminated reports of miracles that were performed either by Jesus himself or in Jesus' name. The Christian belief in miracles operated more on the level of agitation propaganda, its intent being to bring about a revolutionary change in the collective mindset, whereas its Graeco-Roman equivalent sought primarily to bring about a minor realignment in line with the fluidity of the pantheon, as the fortunes of individual cults waxed and waned. Throughout antiquity, however, it was the case that the most aggressive cults, those, in other words, seeking pan-hellenic and later Roman acceptance, including Dionysus, Asclepius and Isis, relied heavily on reports of miracles.

It is highly unfortunate that Lucian, arguably our most eloquent witness, denounced all miracle workers as charlatans. We should not, however, assume that they were all fraudulent, even though our only counterweight, Philostratus' *Life of Apollonius of Tyana*, is hardly more reliable. Very possibly the audiences that were attracted to magicians and tricksters were not much different from those that were attracted to miracle workers. Hellenistic kings and Roman emperors, though often regarded as divine, were credited with the power to effect the good of their subjects only in general, unspecific terms.

Until Latin took its place alongside Greek and Aramaic as one of the languages in which Christian faith and liturgy found expression, the pagan discourse on miracles was conducted primarily in Greek. The periods of Greek history that were most favourable to reports of miracles were the Archaic and Hellenistic, when Greece was fighting for its freedom in the Persian Wars and when new gods were competing with established gods for entry into the pantheon. In Roman history by contrast, miracles punctuated crisis moments throughout the Republican era. Then in the second century of the Christian era pagan apologists fought an uneven campaign against the claims which their Christian counterparts made on behalf of the miraculous powers of *their* God. In late antiquity the pagan holy man (*theios anēr*) became a significant figure, particularly in urban centres such as Alexandria, Aphrodisias and Athens. However, his spirituality was primarily denoted by his personal conduct and adherence to a philosophical tradition, rather than by his power to work miracles. Such miracles as he did perform, moreover, were largely performed in private.[32] In conclusion, just as Poseidon had lost out to Athena, so paganism eventually lost out to Christianity, not least because its miracles were deemed inferior in value and usefulness.[33]

Notes

1   Greek adjectives such as *paradoxos* ('unexpected') and *deinos* ('terrible'), which are the nearest approximations to 'miraculous', equally lack the intensity of the English.
2   Georg Luck, *Arcana Mundi: Magic and the Occult in the Greek and Roman Worlds: A Collection of Ancient Texts* (Baltimore: Johns Hopkins University Press, 1985), 135.
3   Jaś Elsner and Ian Rutherford, eds., *Pilgrimage in Graeco-Roman and Early Christian Antiquity: Seeing the Gods* (Oxford: Oxford University Press, 2005), 9.
4   H. S. Versnel, 'Magic', *Oxford Classical Dictionary*, 3rd edn, 908–10 (909).
5   Graham Anderson, *Sage, Saint and Sophist: Holy Men and their Associates in the Early Roman Empire* (London and New York: Routledge, 1994), 28. For further discussion of the difference between magic and religion, see J. N. Bremmer, 'The Birth of the Term "Magic"', *Zeitschrift für Papyrologie und Epigraphik* 126 (1999), 1–12.
6   The fullest discussions are Richard Reitzenstein, *Hellenistische Wunderzählungen* (Leipzig: B. G. Teubner, 1906) and Otto Weinreich, *Antike Heilungswunder: Untersuchungen zum Wunderglauben der Griechen und Römer*, Religionsgeschichtliche Versuche und Vorarbeiten 8.1 (Giessen: Töpelmann, 1909), both still useful. H. S. Versnel, *Ter Unus: Isis, Dionysos, Hermes: Three Studies in Henotheism*, Studies in Greek and Roman Religion 6 (Leiden and New York: Brill, 1990) is important for both Isis and Dionysus. Wendy Cotter, *Miracles in Greco-Roman Antiquity* (London and New York: Routledge, 1999) is overwhelmingly Christian in emphasis.
7   For the cult of Pan in Athens, see Robert S. J. Garland, *Introducing New Gods: The Politics of Athenian Religion* (Ithaca: Cornell University

Press, 1992), 58–62. For other marvellous occurrences associated with the battle of Marathon, see Herodotus, *Histories* 6.117.2–3, Plutarch, *Theseus* 35.5 and Pausanias, *Description of Greece* 1.32.5.

8 A. D. Nock, *Conversion: The Old and the New in Religion from Alexander the Great to Augustine of Hippo* (London and New York: Oxford University Press, 1933), 91.

9 Miraculous occurrences reported by Herodotus at the time of the Persian Wars include the sprouting of the sacred olive tree on the Acropolis that had been cut down by the Persians (*Histories* 8.55), and the dust cloud that moved across the Thriasian Plain before the Battle of Salamis (8.65).

10 See Versnel, *Ter Unus*, 165–6, for all the miracles in Euripides, *Bacchae*. Other miracles associated with Dionysus include the transformation of water into wine at a festival of Dionysus at Elis (Paus. 6.26.1–2) and the miraculous appearance of a statue of Dionysus at Magnesia (*Die Inschriften von Magnesia am Maeander*, ed. Otto Kern (Berlin: Spemann, 1900), no. 215).

11 *Supplementum Epigraphicum Graecum* III, nos. 548–51. Apuleius' description in *Metamorphoses* 11.13–14 of the transformation of Lucius from an ass back into human shape, thanks to the good offices (*beneficium*) of Isis is, despite its preposterousness, one of the most moving first-hand accounts of a pagan miracle in classical literature. For miracles associated with Isis, see Versnel, *Ter Unus*, 41, 66, etc.

12 Helmut Engelmann, *The Delian Aretalogy of Sarapis* (Leiden: Brill, 1975).

13 Versnel, *Ter Unus*, 191, emphasis original.

14 I owe this insight to Jon Mikalson. *Inscriptiones graecae*, Editio minor, 4th edn (Berlin, 1924), 121–2. Emma Jeannette Edelstein and Ludwig Edelstein, *Asclepius: A Collection and Interpretation of the Testimonies*, 2 vols. (Baltimore: Johns Hopkins University Press, 1945), vol. I, no. 423; H. Müller, 'Ein Heilungsbericht aus dem Asklepieion von Pergamon', *Chiron* 17 (1987), 193–233.

15 Tricca and Cos: Strabo 8.6.15 (cures recorded on wooden tablets). Pergamum: Christian Habicht, *Die Inschriften des Asclepieions* (= Altertümer von Pergamom 8.3) (Berlin: De Gruyter, 1969), p. 117 no. 86; p. 141, no. 139. Lebena: M. Guarducci, ed., *Inscriptiones Creticae*, 4 vols. (1935–50), vol. I, 17, nos. 17 and 18. In addition, *Oxyrhynchus papyrus* 11.1382, a papyrus of the second century CE, alludes to water that was distributed to the people of Pharos in Alexandria, evidently because it possessed healing qualities.

16 Howard C. Kee, *Miracle in the Early Christian World: A Study in Socio-historical Method* (London and New Haven: Yale University Press, 1983), 86.

17 For the requirements to which those supplicating Asclepius were subject before undergoing the cure, see Elsner and Rutherford, eds., *Pilgrimage in Graeco-Roman and Early Christian Antiquity*, 79–80. They include sexual abstinence and refraining from eating goat's cheese or drinking goat's milk.

18 Edelstein and Edelstein, *Asclepius*, vol. I, nos. 1–336, provides a comprehensive list of all the testimonia relating to the legend of Asclepius.

19 For literary comparisons between Asclepius and Christ, see Edelstein and Edelstein, *Asclepius*, vol. I, nos. 332–6.

20 Regarding the 'truth' of the claims, Charles A. Behr, *Aelius Aristides and the Sacred Tales* (Amsterdam: Hakkert, 1968), 39, writes: 'Many of Aristides' cures seem transient … But he felt that the force of his disease had been blunted by the regimen which the God had set up for him … His attitude became that of a man who did not expect miraculous liberation once and for all. Rather he sought the prolongation of his life and immediate relief from whatever symptom troubled him.' Alex Petsalis-Diomidis, *Truth Beyond Wonders: Aelius Aristides and the Cult of Asklepios* (Oxford: Oxford University Press, 2010) appeared too late for incorporation into this chapter.

21 The pioneering work on religious virtuosi is by Ludwig Bieler, *Theios Anēr: Das Bild des 'Göttlichen Menschen' in Spätantike und Fruhchristentum*, 2 vols. in 1 (Darmstadt: Wissenschaftliche Buchgesellschaft, 1967). See also James P. D. Bolton, *Aristeas of Procconesus* (Oxford: Clarendon Press, 1962); and Graham Anderson, *Sage, Saint and Sophist: Holy Men and their Associates in the Early Roman Empire* (London and New York: Routledge, 1994).

22 Porphyry, *Life of Pythagoras* 27–9; Iamblichus, *Life of Pythagoras* 134–6.

23 Herodotus does not tell us whether hirsutism, a condition due to an abnormality of the endocrine glands, occurred in the same priestess at different times or in different incumbents, but since it is often hereditary and resultant upon acute anxiety, the anecdote is plausible in either case.

24 Interestingly the physicians told Vespasian that he would win *gloria* if he was successful – a term that is most commonly applied to a military victory but obviously highly appropriate in the political context. Vespasian also claimed to have had a supernatural vision in the Serapeum, which foretold his elevation to the imperial purple (Tacitus, *Histories* 4.82).

25 For Livy's treatment of the supernatural, see D. S. Levene, *Religion in Livy*, Mnemosyne, bibliotheca classica Batava 127 (Leiden: Brill, 1993), with pp. 132–3 for Romulus' apotheosis. As T. P. Wiseman, 'History, Poetry, and *Annales*', in *Clio and the Poets: Augustan Poetry and the Traditions of Ancient Historiography*, ed. D. S. Levene and D. P. Nelis, Mnemosyne, bibliotheca classica Batava, Supplementum 224 (Leiden: Brill, 2002), 331–62 (353), notes, Livy's attitude to miracle stories and epiphanies is 'a partisan statement of philosophical scepticism', which was not shared by historians such as Dionysius of Halicarnassus and Plutarch.

26 For demons in general, see the useful collection of sources in Georg Luck, *Arcana Mundi: Magic and the Occult in the Greek and Roman Worlds: A Collection of Ancient Texts* (Baltimore: Johns Hopkins University Press, 1985), 163–225. In pagan usage Greek *daimōn* (Latin

daemon) means simply 'a god, god, or a divine force', though in Platonic thinking it also comes to mean 'a supernatural being or spirit, halfway between the human world and the divine'. The negative connotation in English is predominantly the consequence of Christian propaganda.

27 The earliest surviving reference to the rain miracle is in Tertullian, *Apology* 5.6 (*c.* 197–8). As G. Fowden, 'Pagan Versions of the Rain Miracle of AD 172', *Historia* 36 (1987), 83–95, points out, Tertullian's account 'draws attention ... to the uncertainty that will naturally have assailed an army made up of men of many faiths' (86), and as such it intimates that the prayers of the pagan soldiers were mediated, and thereby appropriated, by the prayers of their Christian counterparts.

28 Fowden, 'Pagan Versions of the Rain Miracle of AD 172', 94.

29 See Silvia Lanzi, 'Sosipatra, la teurga: Una "holy woman" iniziata ai misteri caldaici', *Studi e Materiali di Storia delle Religioni* 70 (2004), 275–94.

30 Mehmet Çetin Sahin and Arminda Lozano, eds., *Die Inschriften von Stratonikeia*, 2 vols. (Bonn: Habelt, 1981–90), vol. I, no. 1101. The translation is that of A. D. Lee, *Pagans and Christians in Late Antiquity* (London and New York: Routledge, 2000), 23–5.

31 For Varro, see H. W. G. Peter, *Historicorum Romanorum reliquiae*, 2 vols. (Stuttgart: B. G. Teubner, 1906), vol. II, 9–25, xxxi–xl. St Augustine's discussion of the Varran miracles is found in *City of God* 18.9–10, 17.

32 For examples of miracles performed by late antique holy men, see Fowden, 'The Pagan Holy Man in Late Antique Society', 50.

33 Jesus' tally according to David E. Aune, 'Magic in Early Christianity', *Aufstieg und Niedergang der römischen Welt* II.23.2 (1980), 1507–57 (1523–4), includes six exorcisms, seventeen cures and eight so-called nature miracles.

In the writing of this chapter, I am most grateful to Georgia Frank, Jon Mikalson, Naomi Rood and an anonymous reader for their invaluable comments and insights.

Further reading

Anderson, Graham, *Sage, Saint and Sophist: Holy Men and their Associates in the Early Roman Empire* (London and New York: Routledge, 1994)

Behr, Charles A., *Aelius Aristides and the Sacred Tales* (Amsterdam: Hakkert, 1968)

Bieler, Ludwig, *Theios Anēr: Das Bild des 'Göttlichen Menschen' in Spätantike und Fruhchristentum*, 2 vols. in 1 (Darmstadt: Wissenschaftliche Buchgesellschaft, 1967)

Blackburn, Barry L., *The Theios Anēr and the Markan Miracle Traditions*, Wissenschaftliche Untersuchungen zum Neuen Testament 2.40 (Tübingen: Mohr, 1991)

Bolton, James P. D., *Aristeas of Procconesus* (Oxford: Clarendon Press, 1962)

Bremmer, J. N., 'The Birth of the Term "Magic"', *Zeitschrift für Papyrologie und Epigraphik* 126 (1999), 1–12

Edelstein, Emma Jeannette and Ludwig Edelstein, *Asclepius: A Collection and Interpretation of the Testimonies*, 2 vols. (Baltimore: Johns Hopkins University Press, 1945)

Elsner, Jaś and Ian Rutherford, eds., *Pilgrimage in Graeco-Roman and Early Christian Antiquity: Seeing the Gods* (Oxford: Oxford University Press, 2005)

Engelmann, Helmut, *The Delian Aretalogy of Sarapis* (Leiden: Brill, 1975)

Fowden, G., 'The Pagan Holy Man in Late Antique Society', *Journal of Hellenic Studies* 102 (1982), 33–59

'Pagan Versions of the Rain Miracle of AD 172', *Historia* 36 (1987), 83–95

Garland, Robert S. J., *Introducing New Gods: The Politics of Athenian Religion* (Ithaca: Cornell University Press, 1992)

Kee, Howard C., *Miracle in the Early Christian World: A Study in Socio-historical Method* (London and New Haven: Yale University Press, 1983)

Lanzi, Silvia, 'Sosipatra, la teurga: Una "holy woman" iniziata ai misteri caldaici', *Studi e materiali di storia delle religioni* 70 (2004), 275–94

Luck, Georg, *Arcana Mundi: Magic and the Occult in the Greek and Roman Worlds: A Collection of Ancient Texts* (Baltimore: Johns Hopkins University Press, 1985)

Nock, A. D., *Conversion: The Old and the New in Religion from Alexander the Great to Augustine of Hippo* (London and New York: Oxford University Press, 1933)

Reitzenstein, Richard, *Hellenistische Wunderzählungen* (Leipzig: B. G. Teubner, 1906)

Versnel, H. S., *Ter Unus: Isis, Dionysos, Hermes: Three Studies in Henotheism*, Studies in Greek and Roman Religion 6 (Leiden and New York: Brill, 1990)

*Weinreich, Otto, *Antike Heilungswunder: Untersuchungen zum Wunderglauben der Griechen und Römer*, Religionsgeschichtliche Versuche und Vorarbeiten 8.1 (Giessen: Töpelmann, 1909)

Wiseman, T. P., 'History, Poetry, and Annales', in *Clio and the Poets: Augustan Poetry and the Traditions of Ancient Historiography*, ed. D. S. Levene and D. P. Nelis, Mnemosyne, bibliotheca classica Batava. Supplementum 224 (Leiden: Brill, 2002), 331–62, reprinted in T. P. Wiseman, *Unwritten Rome* (Exeter: University of Exeter Press, 2008), 243–70

5 Miracles in Second Temple and early rabbinic Judaism

LIDIJA NOVAKOVIC

The time period covered in this chapter encompasses two distinct epochs in Jewish history: the time before the destruction of the temple in 70 CE characterized by diversity, instability and sectarianism, and the time after the destruction of the temple characterized by the rise of rabbinic Judaism, the eventual disappearance of rival sectarian groups, the cessation of sacrificial worship, and the shift of emphasis towards the synagogue and the Torah. In addition, 'from about the middle of the third century BCE *all Judaism* must really be designated "Hellenistic Judaism" in the strict sense', as Martin Hengel repeatedly emphasized.[1] At the same time, however, the differences between Jewish and Hellenistic worldviews and the various degrees of Hellenization of Palestinian and diaspora Judaism should not be overlooked. In some cases, Graeco-Roman concepts provide primary categories for presenting Jewish beliefs and practices. In other instances, the Hellenistic world view is deliberately rejected. This encounter between different cultures has also had an impact on the understanding of miracles in Jewish literature. In some cases, miracles are perceived through the lenses of the Hellenistic surroundings, while in other cases they serve as the means of legitimization of a specifically Jewish perception of reality.

Jewish authors typically present miracles and miracle workers in dialogue with their sacred texts. They all believed that Scripture embodied the will of God and that interpretation of the sacred writings provided for its application to contemporary circumstances. In this process, they engaged in two related types of activities: they reinterpreted traditional biblical accounts about the miracles from Israel's history and used the scriptural framework to interpret the miraculous events from their own time.

THE DIFFICULTY OF DEFINITION

Broadly speaking, miracles are extraordinary events that produce amazement or provoke disbelief because they cannot be explained by natural agencies. Joseph Blenkinsopp defines a miracle as 'an act by which power or energy is transmitted from the supramundane to the mundane level'.[2] Every disruption of the ordinary is potentially a miracle. Whether it will be perceived as a miracle, however, depends on a number of circumstances. Some disruptions of the ordinary can be the result of God's direct intervention into the created world while others can involve human agency. If the latter, extraordinary events can be the result of certain innate abilities of a person or a special technique being applied. To complicate the matter, some disruptions of the ordinary can resemble the extraordinary events that the biblical tradition approves, some can resemble the practices that the biblical tradition repudiates, while some can be the result of new developments without real precedents in the sacred texts.

One way of dealing with these ambiguities is to try to provide an 'emic' definition of miracles, that is, an understanding of miracles based on the terms and adjectives employed by Jewish authors themselves, in contrast to an 'etic' definition of miracles that we impose upon the texts from the outside. Unfortunately, Jewish authors employ a number of terms without ever providing their precise definitions. What is more, they sometimes apply the same terms to both the foreign magical practices which they repudiate and the Jewish rituals which they approve. The diversity of the material from this period only adds to the complexity of an 'emic' definition which, we must conclude, is not readily available.

Another way of dealing with these ambiguities is to draw a distinction between miracles and magic. According to Gerd Theissen, the main difference between the two lies in their social acceptability. 'It is precisely this link with the community and its rules which is missing from ancient magic, and especially that of late antiquity.'[3] Magic is characterized by religious syncretism and the belief in the power of objects and rituals. It can be used for both positive and negative purposes – to heal and harm, protect and attack.[4] Although this definition sometimes corresponds to the perception of magic by Jewish authors themselves, it could prevent us from noticing some important features that characterize supernatural phenomena described in ancient Jewish texts. If, for example, we recognize that 'what Israel and its divine messengers accomplished was a "miracle" or a "sign"', and 'the very same deeds, when performed by non-Israelites, were considered magic or manifestations of idolatry', as Michael Singer notes in his assessment of rabbinic literature,[5] we could be tempted to declare all extraordinary events described in Jewish literature as miracles and none of them as magic.[6] And yet, Jewish authors from this period were quite aware of the resemblance between certain practices conducted in their own midst and similar feats performed by their non-Jewish neighbours and took pains to distinguish them from magic. A common strategy was to ascribe the knowledge of the extraordinary qualities of certain objects and rituals to God's favour and magic to human agency.

In light of the above discussion and the diversity of the material from Second Temple and early rabbinic times we should not expect a consistent understanding of miracles and miracle workers. At the same time, however, it is possible to identify several trajectories with common themes and motives. The following presentation is based on the identification of three major types of miracle workers who were active in this period and shared certain common characteristics: Jewish exorcists, sign prophets, and charismatic miracle workers.

JEWISH EXORCISTS

Exorcistic practices, which were steadily accepted in the Second Temple period, grew out of a changed understanding of God's relationship to the world. References to demonic possession and exorcism are quite rare in the biblical tradition. The reason for this is, as Eric Sorensen explains, 'that demons rarely appear as viable entities that either act beyond divine supervision or are subject to conjuration'.[7] Demonology, which rose in prominence during the Second Temple period, presumes that one segment of spiritual entities became alienated from God and began acting independently.[8] Possession is typically understood as the demonic control of a human body, thoughts and actions, achieved either by demonic embodiment or external influence upon a person. In this world view, bodily afflictions and illnesses are caused by demons. To restore the health and well-being of a person, the demon(s) must be driven out or away with the help of exorcistic techniques.

An increased interest in exorcistic practices is documented in a number of Second Temple writings. One of the earliest accounts of an exorcistic procedure is found in the book of *Tobit*, a fourth- or third-century BCE document which narrates how Tobias, the son of a righteous Jew named Tobit, freed the Jewish maiden Sarah from the wicked demon Asmodeus who killed each of her seven husbands on their wedding nights. Tobias drives Asmodeus away with the help of the fragrant smoke of the heart and liver of a certain fish from the Tigris river, which the angel Raphael, disguised as Tobias' travelling companion, directed him to catch and keep. The legitimacy of this exorcistic technique is provided through the account of its angelic origin.[9]

Another way of justifying exorcistic practices is to ascribe them to prominent biblical figures such as Abraham, David and Solomon. This tendency is well attested in the Qumran writings. The *Genesis Apocryphon*, which combines the traditions of Genesis, *Jubilees* and *1 Enoch*, portrays Abram (Abraham) as an exorcist who expelled a chastising spirit that afflicted the Pharaoh and the members of his household on account of Abram's wife. After Egyptian wizards and healers unsuccessfully tried to heal the Pharaoh, Abram performed an exorcism by laying hands on the Pharaoh's head (*1QapGen* 20.16–29).[10] A passage in *11QPsalms^a* (*11Q5*) ascribes to David the composition of 3,600 psalms, 446 cultic songs, and 4 songs to be performed over the possessed (*11Q5* 27.4–10). *11QApocryphal Psalms^a* (*11Q11*) contain the remains of four psalms, including an unusual recension of Psalm 91 known in rabbinic literature as 'the song of the afflicted'. These four psalms, which were designated to be used in a liturgy for healing the stricken, might have been, according to J. P. M. van der Ploeg, the four compositions attributed to David mentioned in *11Q5*.[11] An association between David and exorcism is also found in *Liber Antiquitatum Biblicarum*, a first-century CE document pseudonymously attributed to Philo. Chapter 60 of this writing contains a song which David played for Saul in order to exorcise the evil spirit from him. It ends with a cryptic prediction that David's descendants will subdue the evil spirit (*LAB* 60.3).

The notion of Solomon's exorcistic skills represents a special trajectory that developed out of a growing tradition about his extraordinary wisdom.[12] One of the fullest expressions of the blossoming legends of Solomon's wisdom is preserved in the *Wisdom of Solomon*, a late first-century BCE or early first-century CE document that defends Jewish faith in a Hellenistic setting and portrays wisdom as a saving force for righteous Israelites. The elaborate praise of Solomon's wisdom in *Wisdom of Solomon* 7.7–22 includes not only his extraordinary discernment and piety but also his encyclopaedic knowledge of the universe, such as the knowledge of the structure of the world, the activity of elements, the powers of spirits, the varieties of plants and the virtues of roots. Solomon's knowledge of the violent force of spirits probably provides the background of the tradition about his power over evil spirits, while his knowledge of plants and roots refers to the botanical knowledge which can be used for healing.

The *locus classicus* of this tradition is found in Josephus'
Antiquities 8.42–9. This is also the only complete account of a Jewish
healer from the Second Temple period who performed an exorcism with
the help of the exorcistic technique traceable to Solomon. The technique consisted of two principal elements: a special root prescribed by
Solomon placed under the seal of a ring and special incantations composed by Solomon. The task of the first element was to drive a demon
out of a possessed person and of the second to prevent the demon from
returning to the victim. Before reporting the actual exorcism, Josephus
describes at some length Solomon's surpassing wisdom and knowledge
granted to him by God. He then explains how a certain Eleazar, his
Jewish countryman, applied Solomon's technique of exorcism in front
of a Roman audience, which included Vespasian, his sons, tribunes and
soldiers. Eleazar used a ring which had under its seal one of the roots
prescribed by Solomon, put it under the possessed man's nose, and drew
the demon out who could not resist the smell of the root under the
ring's seal. After that, Eleazar invoked Solomon's name and recited the
incantations composed by him in order to prevent the demon's return.
Josephus adds that Eleazar verified the occurrence of the miracle by
commanding the demon to overturn a foot-basin which had been filled
with water and placed nearby.

Josephus' account about Eleazar should be examined in conjunction with Josephus' overall view of miracles and magic.[13] Josephus'
attitude towards miracles is somewhat ambiguous. On the one hand,
his writings include a number of traditional miracles. He also appeals
to the witness of Scripture as a text of great antiquity in order to
strengthen its trustworthiness in the eyes of his Hellenistic audience
(*Against Apion* 1.42–3). On the other hand, he has a tendency towards
rationalization that leads him frequently to conclude his reports with
rhetorical disclaimers such as, 'However on these matters everyone is
welcome to his own opinion'.[14] George MacRae's remarks about this
ambivalence in Josephus' writings are still worth repeating: 'The divine
origin of Scripture forbids tampering with it. But the apologist must be
conscious of his doubting readers as well as of his fellow believers, and
Josephus will not refrain from adding, deleting, even offering rational
explanations of some things.'[15] Even if Josephus might not be entirely
free from the rationalistic tendencies typical for the Hellenistic world,
his narration of Israel's past is informed by his belief in divine providence and the conviction that God intervenes in human affairs as
revealed in sacred texts, whose sanctity and inspiration Josephus vigor-
ously defends (*Against Apion* 1.42–3; 2.218–19). This includes not only

normal processes by which God governs the world but also God's miraculous interventions that interrupt the ordinary and produce amazement. Josephus is careful to distinguish genuine miracles that come from God from magic that comes from human trickery. One of the most telling examples is his account of Moses' speech to Pharaoh (*Jewish Antiquities* 2.286). Pharaoh dismisses Moses' miraculous signs with the pretext that the Egyptian priests can also perform such spectacles. In his reply, Moses emphasizes that his own miraculous deeds 'so far surpass their magic [*mageia*] and their art [*technē*] as things divine [*ta theia*] are remote from what is human [*ta anthrōpina*]'. Moses also adds that his miracles do not stem from witchcraft and deception but proceed from God's providence (*pronoia*) and power (*dynamis*). The ensuing miracle that Moses performs is evidently meant to demonstrate the fundamental difference between miracles as divine deeds and miracles as magic and art, although the only difference seems to be the degree and not the quality of the miraculous (*Jewish Antiquities* 2.287). It is certainly true that 'what the Egyptians can do, Moses can do better!'[16]

Josephus' predisposition to approve certain practices when they are performed by Jews is clearly visible in his discussion of the exorcism carried out by his countryman Eleazar. He describes Eleazar's technique of exorcism as an 'art' (*technē*) for the benefit of human beings, even though this term was associated with magic and deception in Moses' speech to Pharaoh. Furthermore, the emphasis falls not on a specific individual who possesses extraordinary abilities but on a specific method of cure that, if performed correctly, guarantees a desired result. Josephus explains that Solomon's wisdom enabled him to leave behind certain 'forms of exorcisms' that were handed down through the transmission of a particular type of cure, which included the use of a special fragrant substance (the root prescribed by Solomon placed in a special ring) and the recitation of exorcistic hymns (incantations composed by Solomon).

The only evidence about magical properties of the seal-ring itself that is mentioned in Josephus' account comes from later documents and artefacts, such as the *Testament of Solomon*, Aramaic magical bowls, the Babylonian Talmud and the *Sepher Ha-Razim*. It would certainly be inappropriate to read the motifs from the legends about Solomon from late antiquity back into Josephus' report. Yet, whatever his sources, Josephus' knowledge of the exorcistic practices associated with Solomon's control over demons and the use of a special ring is undeniable. For all practical purposes, this type of cure is indistinguishable from magic. There is no doubt that Eleazar's successful execution of exorcism in front of a distinguished Roman audience was a source of great pride for Josephus. At the same time, however, his eagerness to include this account in his presentation of his Jewish heritage to the Hellenistic readers could have easily left the impression of a Jewish hero practising magic, which verged on the popular and irrational. Dennis Duling suggests that Josephus might have been motivated by the growing appeal of white magic among the more educated classes.[17] Even so, Josephus is quite unwilling to relegate these practices to the realm of magic. He concludes his report by pointing out that 'when this was done, the understanding and wisdom of Solomon were clearly revealed, on account of which we have been induced to speak of these things, in order that all men may know the greatness of his nature and how God favoured him' (*Jewish Antiquities* 8.49). Josephus thus ultimately ascribes the successful accomplishment of the miracle to God who granted Solomon such unsurpassed prudence and wisdom. He dissociates Eleazar's exorcism from magic by relocating it from the human to the divine domain.

SIGN PROPHETS

Josephus' writings contain several accounts about various individuals who promised to perform certain miraculous signs similar to those associated with the exodus from Egypt and the conquest of Canaan.[18] Since, however, Josephus never reports that they actually performed the promised miracles, some scholars question whether they should even be called miracle workers.[19] Even so, this phenomenon is worth exploring because it points to the role of miracles and miracle workers in the uprisings and resistance movements in Palestine in the first century CE.

The section in Josephus' *Jewish Antiquities* 18.85–7 contains a report about a Samaritan who led an armed band to Mount Gerizim during Pilate's procuratorship. He promised his followers that he would show them the sacred vessels buried there. Josephus explains that the hearers of the Samaritan, 'viewing this tale as plausible, appeared in arms' and 'welcomed to their ranks the new arrivals who kept coming'. The promised revelation of the sacred vessels had revolutionary undertones because it produced not an enthralled but an armed crowd. The whole undertaking was, however, interrupted by Pilate's cavalry and heavy-armed infantry. Josephus concludes this sad report with a note that numerous participants were imprisoned while the principal leaders were executed.

Josephus' account about Theudas in *Jewish Antiquities* 20.97–9 is similar. During the procuratorship of Cuspius Fadus, Theudas claimed to be a prophet and that at his command the Jordan River would divide and provide an easy passage for his followers. Josephus notes that he deceived many with these promises, who took up their possessions and followed him to the Jordan. The endeavour, however, was brought to an end by Fadus who sent a squadron of cavalry to crush it. His soldiers surprised Theudas and his followers, killed many and took others as prisoners. Theudas was beheaded and his head was brought to Jerusalem as a warning against similar undertakings.

In *Jewish Antiquities* 20.169–72, Josephus narrates how during the procuratorship of Felix a certain Egyptian convinced the people to follow him to the Mount of Olives by promising them that the walls of Jerusalem would fall at his command and provide an entrance into the city. When Felix heard this, he sent his armed forces to end the undertaking. Josephus introduces this incident with a summary statement about various 'impostors and deceivers' who persuaded the crowd to follow them into the desert because 'they said that they would show them unmistakable marvels and signs that would be wrought in harmony with God's design' (*Jewish Antiquities* 20.168). Josephus' summary of these incidents in *Jewish War* 2.258–60 includes the qualification that these 'deceivers and impostors' led large crowds into the desert because they promised them the 'signs of freedom' (*sēmeia eleutherias*). Felix understood this endeavour as an incipient insurrection and crushed it violently. A similar incident is reported in *Jewish War* 7.437–41, where Josephus illustrates the madness of the Sicarii with a story about a certain Jonathan who 'won the ear of not a few of the indigent class, and led them forth into the desert, promising them a display of signs and apparitions' (*Jewish War* 7.438). Catullus interpreted the movement as a political uprising and sent his military to crush it even though the crowd was unarmed.

The reliability of these reports has often been questioned. These endeavours clearly do not get Josephus' approval, who calls their leaders not only false prophets (*pseudoprophētai*) but also charlatans (*goētes*), like the magicians at Pharaoh's court (*Jewish Antiquities* 2.286). Josephus' contemptuous comments indicate that he evaluates these incidents in light of Deuteronomy 18.21–2, a text which points to the fulfilment of a prophetic prediction as the confirmation of true prophecy.[20] Josephus regards the first-century Jewish prophets as impostors because the events they announced failed to materialize. His perspective, however, should be differentiated from the perspective of the participants in these episodes, who regularly understand the announced miracles as the 'signs of freedom'. Almost all miraculous events promised by the sign prophets approximate the miraculous events from Israel's salvation history: the parting of the Jordan by Theudas resembles the parting of the Red Sea by Moses during the exodus and the parting of the Jordan by Joshua during the conquest; the fall of the walls of Jerusalem by the Egyptian resembles the fall of the walls of Jericho; the promised signs and apparitions by Jonathan and other desert prophets resemble the wonders in the wilderness associated with the exodus. Likewise, the announced recovery of the sacred vessels on Mount Gerizim by the Samaritan displays the hope based on Deuteronomy 18.15–18 that the messianic prophet, called Taheb in later Samaritan literature, will repossess Mount Gerizim and restore the pure cult there. Time after time, the people seem to expect the occurrence of similar or even greater miracles in anticipation of the inauguration of a new era of salvation. Violent responses of the Roman governors, however, indicate that they understood these endeavours as freedom movements that threatened the stability of the Roman government. Given Josephus' disapproval of all such anti-Roman uprisings, his negative assessment of the sign prophets is hardly surprising.

CHARISMATIC MIRACLE WORKERS

Palestinian miracle workers from the Tannaitic period, Honi the circle-drawer and Hanina ben Dosa, belong to a distinct group of charismatic individuals, who were known not only for their miraculous abilities but also for their piety and kindness.[21] The earliest traditions about Honi and Hanina relate them to ancient hasidic piety.[22] The main characteristics of the hasidic movement include the Galilean location, poverty, good deeds and miraculous power. The miracles ascribed to Honi and Hanina reflect their low socio-economic circumstances. They typically relate to mundane events in which a distressing situation is removed in an inexplicable manner. Most of them take place through prayer, which demonstrates Honis and Hanina's piety and dependence on God. Their special charisma and marginal social location put them in conflict with religious authorities, both the priestly establishment in Jerusalem and the Pharisaic teachers of the Law, who were, like early rabbis in the Tannaitic period, opposed to individual claims of supernatural powers. Yet, the miracles of Honi and Hanina were eventually incorporated into and transmitted through the rabbinic literature. This 'rabbinization' of the miracle traditions, which initially developed outside rabbinic circles, is an interesting social and religious phenomenon. The transmission of Ḥoni's and Ḥanina's miracles through a particular literary context demonstrates, as Joseph Blenkinsopp observes, that 'a miracle is always a social event, indeed a social transaction, never private. That is to say, it does not count as a miracle until it becomes socially visible and is registered as miraculous with a given public and in a specific social situation.'[23]

Very little is known about Ḥoni. The tradition situates him to the first century BCE. His connection to Galilee is not mentioned in the early material. The earliest reference is found in Josephus' *Jewish Antiquities*. In the section that describes the conflict between Hyrcanus II and Aristobulus II, Josephus mentions in passing a certain Onias who was 'a righteous man and dear to God [who] once in a rainless period prayed to God to end the drought, and God had heard his prayer and sent rain' (*Jewish Antiquities* 14.22). Hyrcanus II, hearing about the efficacy of Onias' prayer for rain, tried to convince him to curse his opponent, Aristobulus II. When Onias refused, he was stoned to death (*Jewish Antiquities* 14.23–4). An embellished version of the story of Ḥoni's miraculous generation of rain, which explains his nickname 'the circle-drawer', is found in the Mishnah (*m. Ta'anit* 3.8). Ḥoni's initial prayer for rain was not answered. Ḥoni then drew a circle, stepped into it and prayed for rain again, this time swearing that he would not step outside the circle until God had fulfilled his wish. After a few drops started to fall, Ḥoni objected that it was not enough, causing God to send a heavy rainstorm. Ḥoni objected again, and a moderate rain followed. After more than enough rain has fallen, people asked Ḥoni to pray for the rain to stop, and indeed it did so. A prominent Pharisee Simeon ben Shetah, Ḥoni's contemporary, objected to such an imprudent attitude towards God and threatened him with excommunication, but to no avail because, according to the appended commentary, God granted Ḥoni whatever he asked in prayer, like an indulgent father to a spoiled son. The rabbinic framework of this narrative, the only miracle story about a Tannaitic figure in the Mishnah, accomplishes two different goals: it allows for an inherent critique of Ḥoni's activity and it embraces it under the rabbinic wing. This 'rabbinization' of Ḥoni is further continued in the Babylonian Talmud.[24] The story of Ḥoni's miraculous generation of rain in *b. Ta'anit* 23a downplays the miraculous, possibly even magical elements, provides a scriptural basis for Ḥoni's drawing of a circle, gives him the title 'rabbi', emphasizes the divine origin of the miracle, reduces Ḥoni's activity to prayer, and mentions the Sanhedrin's confirmation of Ḥoni's actions.

The tradition about Ḥanina ben Dosa presents him as a Galilean miracle worker living in the first century CE before the fall of Jerusalem. Ḥanina is occasionally mentioned in the Mishnah (*m. 'Abot* 3.10–11; *m. Soṭah* 9.15; *m. Berakhot.* 5.5), but most references are found in the Talmuds. The mishnaic references are sparse. The tractate *'Abot* does not even mention Ḥanina's miraculous activity but presents him as a teacher of piety and ethics (*m. 'Abot* 3.10–11). Although he is called a 'man of deed' in *m. Soṭah* 9.15, this designation does not necessarily imply his miracle-working capacity but could also refer to his acts of kindness. The only clear reference to Ḥanina's extraordinary ability is found in *m. Berakhot* 5.5. This passage explains that Ḥanina used to pray for the sick and say, 'This one will live', or 'This one will die'. When he was asked about the origin of this remarkable knowledge, he replied, 'If my prayer is fluent in my mouth I know that he is accepted; and if it is not I know that he is rejected'. Similar to Ḥoni, Ḥanina's prayer was exceptionally efficacious. The text, however, does not ascribe to him any miraculous power but only miraculous knowledge. In the Talmuds, Ḥanina's miracles are frequently mentioned, but they are not cited for their own sake – to demonstrate his miraculous power and charisma – but typically serve as illustrations of various halakhic concerns, such as the efficacy of prayer or the proper Sabbath observance.

The literary and theological framework given to the stories about Ḥoni and Ḥanina in early rabbinic literature[25] reveals the key elements that characterize the understanding of miracles in the Tannaitic period and the changes that accompanied its transition to the Talmudic era. The sages in the early period generally showed little interest in miracles, and when they did, they had a tendency to reduce their interference with the created order. One way of accomplishing this goal was to expand God's creative activity to include the creation of certain provisions, such as the manna and the tablets of the Decalogue (*m. 'Abot* 5.6), which allowed the placement of biblical miracles within the created order. Another tendency was to diminish the magical implications of traditional miracles by downplaying human involvement and ascribing the miracles solely to God.[26] The main interests in the early rabbinic literature, especially in the Mishnah, are halakhic topics and related exegetical issues.

Only the Tosefta displays greater interest in the miraculous, but at the same time takes a very critical stance regarding the use of this material in halakhic discussions. Michael Becker argues that this shift in interest was caused by new problems that emerged by the end of the early rabbinic period, which were related to the authority of various 'charismatic' proofs in halakhic discussions. Unlike the earlier phase when miracles were practically a non-issue, they started to play an increasingly significant role in the halakhic debates.[27] The magnitude of this problem is clearly visible in a delightful anecdote about the so-called oven of 'Akhnai, preserved in both Talmuds (*y. Mo'ed Qatan* 3.1; *b. Baba Metzi'a* 59b). After Rabbi Eliezer unsuccessfully tried to persuade other rabbis with the help of arguments, he invoked three miracles. One of the rabbis, however, produced a counter-miracle to show that anybody could cause a miracle to prove a point. Eleazar then appealed to heaven, 'If the Halakha agrees with me, let it be proven from heaven'. God responded by sending a *Bat qol* to reprimand the rabbis, 'Why do you rebuke Rabbi Eliezer, whereas the Halakha agrees with him in every instance'. Rabbi Joshua replied with the citation of Deuteronomy 30.12, 'It is not in heaven', which the other rabbis interpreted to mean that the Torah had already been given at Mount Sinai and no other witnesses, including miracles, were needed. Divine laughter acknowledged rabbinic ingenuity, 'My sons have defeated me, my sons have defeated me'. As indicated by the ending of this tale, the Talmudic era was characterized by the relocation of charismatic authority from the personal charisma of a rabbi to the charisma of the Torah.[28]

ESCHATOLOGICAL WONDERS

In addition to the miracles from Israel's past and the miracles performed in their own time, Jewish authors occasionally wrote about the miracles which they anticipated in the future. These passages describe the end time as the time of wonders that have never happened before. The eschatological marvels are regularly presented as the results of divine intervention into the created world, even though human agency could be implied. In each case, however, the emphasis falls on the perception and the experience of the miraculous rather than on the agent through whom these wonders take place.[29] Within the discussion of actual miracle workers in Second Temple and early rabbinic Judaism this group of miracles represents an anomaly. Yet, these miracles provide the most important conceptual framework for understanding Jesus' miraculous activity. In contrast to the Jewish writings, which are reluctant to ascribe the execution of eschatological miracles to a particular human figure, such as the messiah, Jesus' miracles carried eschatological significance and contributed, albeit indirectly, to the perception of his messianic identity.[30]

One of the earliest descriptions of eschatological miracles is found in *Jubilees*, a Jewish writing from the second century BCE, which retells the narrative of Genesis 1 until Exodus 14 in order to validate some polemical issues, such as the solar calendar, the antiquity of the Jewish law, and eschatology. In *Jubilees* 23.26–30, the author envisions the future age in terms of peace, spiritual renewal, gradual prolongation of the human life span, the slowing down and eventual disappearance of aging, and the restoration of health. The text presumes a gradual change of all life conditions and ascribes all improvements in the quality of human life to God.

The earliest text that associates eschatological miracles with the appearance of the messiah is *4QMessianic Apocalypse* (*4Q521*), a Qumran document from the first century BCE. The second column of fragment 2 contains two lists of eschatological blessings that will take place at God's initiative. Lines 5–8 include a number of divine actions, such as renewing the faithful ones by God's might, glorifying the devout on the throne of an eternal kingdom, releasing captives, giving sight to the blind and raising up those who are bowed down. Lines 12–13 further declare that the Lord will heal the wounded, give life to the dead, preach good news to the poor, satisfy the weak, lead those who have been cast out and enrich the hungry. Although the execution of some or even all of the end-time wonders might imply the agency of the messiah who is mentioned in line 1 of this fragment, the text is strangely silent regarding the implications of human involvement in the divine design. The emphasis falls on the uniqueness of these extraordinary events: 'And the Lord will perform glorious things that have not taken place' (*4Q521* frg. 2 2.11).[31]

4 Ezra, a Jewish apocalyptic writing from the first century CE, also describes the messianic kingdom as the time of wonders: 'And everyone who has been delivered from the evils that I have foretold shall see my wonders' (*4 Ezra* 7.27). The text does not specify what kind of wonders are in view but points out that this will be a time of joy. *2 Baruch* 73.1–7, written around the same time, describes the messianic reign as a paradise *redivivus*, characterized by peace, joy, rest, and the absence of illness, fear, tribulation, premature death and childbirth pains. Expected changes in the behaviour of wild animals resemble similar motifs from the description of the messianic era in Isaiah 11.6–9 and elsewhere. *2 Baruch* 29.3–30.1 describes the messianic time before the resurrection of the dead. The days of the messiah are characterized by constant marvels, such as abundance of food, disappearance of hunger, and the dew of health. Some of these wonders resemble the exodus miracles, such as 'the treasury of manna' which 'will come down again from on high' and serve as food for those living at that time (29.8).

CONCLUSION

Second Temple and early rabbinic authors frequently mention biblical miracles and present them as God's wonderful deeds in Israel's history. At the same time, they offer various reports about miracle workers in their own time. This chapter has identified three major types of these exceptional individuals: exorcists, sign prophets and charismatic miracle workers. An interest in exorcistic techniques is documented in a number of writings from this period, which frequently justify this practice by mentioning its angelic origin or tracing it back to prominent biblical figures. Yet there are only two full reports about contemporary figures performing actual exorcisms: one by Tobias in the book of *Tobit* and another by Eleazar in Josephus' *Antiquities*. Given the proximity of exorcistic and magical practices, Josephus' account about the Jewish exorcist Eleazar takes pains to dissociate him from magic by ascribing his success not to a particular technique but to God. Sign prophets include various individuals in pre-70 Palestine who promised to perform certain miraculous signs. Although no actual miracle is ever reported, the anticipated signs, which typically resemble the miracles associated with the exodus and the conquest, carried recognizable political undertones and played a significant role in various anti-Roman uprisings. Charismatic miracle workers from the Tannaitic period, who were known for their miraculous abilities and piety, are only occasionally mentioned in early rabbinic literature. A greater interest in their miracles in the transition to the Talmudic era mirrors an increased rabbinic interest in miracles in general because of their contested use in halakhic arguments. Eschatological miracles, mentioned in the last section of this chapter, are frequently associated with the anticipated messianic time discussed in apocalyptic literature.

Notes

1   Martin Hengel, *Judaism and Hellenism: Studies in their Encounter in Palestine during the Early Hellenistic Period* (London: SCM, 1974), 104. See also Martin Hengel, *Jews, Greeks and Barbarians: Aspects of the Hellenization of Judaism in the pre-Christian Period* (Philadelphia: Fortress, 1980).

2 Joseph Blenkinsopp, 'Miracles: Elisha and Hanina ben Dosa', in *Miracles in Jewish and Christian Antiquity: Imagining Truth*, ed. John C. Cavadini (Notre Dame: University of Notre Dame Press, 1999), 79.

3 Gerd Theissen, *The Miracle Stories of the Early Christian Tradition* (Philadelphia: Fortress, 1983), 238.

4 *Ibid.*, 239–42.

5 Michael A. Singer, 'Restoring the Balance: Musings on Miracles in Rabbinic Judaism', in *Miracles in Jewish and Christian Antiquity: Imagining Truth*, ed. John C. Cavadini (Notre Dame: University of Notre Dame Press, 1999), 112–13.

6 This concept of magic has been especially criticized by Gideon Bohak, *Ancient Jewish Magic: A History* (Cambridge: Cambridge University Press, 2008), 10, who argues that the understanding of magic as 'a derogatory label one affixes to other people's religion' leads to the erroneous conclusion 'that in Jewish culture too there is no such thing as magic'. In his view, the term 'magic' should be used 'as a heuristic device – a means to gather together a group of related cultural phenomena, texts, and artifacts – and not as an explanatory category' (62).

7 Eric Sorensen, *Possession and Exorcism in the New Testament and Early Christianity*, Wissenschaftliche Untersuchungen zum Neuen Testament 2.157 (Tübingen: Mohr Siebeck, 2002), 49.

8 For the notions of demons and the origin of demonology in Israelite-Jewish religion, see the contributions to the Tübingen Symposium on Demonology published in *Die Dämonen/Demons: Die Dämonologie der israelitisch-jüdischen und frühchristlichen Literatur im Kontext ihrer Umwelt/The Demonology of Israelite-Jewish and Early Christian Literature in Context of their Environment*, ed. Armin Lange, Hermann Lichtenberger and K. F. Diethard Römheld (Tübingen: Mohr Siebeck, 2003).

9 Similarly, in the second section of *1 Enoch* called 'Similitudes' (*1 En.* 37–71), exorcistic practice is endorsed because Enoch hears the angel Phanuel 'expelling the demons' (*1 En.* 40.7). In *1 En.* 69.15 it is the angel Michael who reveals to humans the names of demons that cause illnesses.

10 Cf. Joseph A. Fitzmyer, *The Genesis Apocryphon of Qumran Cave 1 (1Q20): A Commentary*, 3rd edn, Biblica et orientalia 18B (Rome: Pontifical Biblical Institute, 2004); Sidnie White Crawford, *Rewriting Scripture in Second Temple Times* (Grand Rapids: Eerdmans, 2008), 105–29. The *Prayer of Nabonidus* (4Q242) is sometimes regarded as another Qumran report of a successful exorcism, but this document neither mentions an evil spirit nor reports an actual exorcism.

11 J. P. M. van der Ploeg, 'Le Psaume XCI dans une recension de Qumran', *Revue biblique* 72 (1965), 210–17; J. P. M. van der Ploeg, 'Un petit rouleau de psaumes apocryphes (11QPsAp^a)', in *Tradition und Glaube: Das frühe Christentum in seiner Umwelt. Festgabe für Karl Georg Kuhn zum 65. Geburtstag*, ed. Gert Jeremias, Heinz-Wolfgang Kuhn and Hartmut Stegemann (Göttingen: Vandenhoeck & Ruprecht, 1971), 128–39. Besides 11Q11, *4QSongs of the Sage^{a-b}* (4Q510–511) and

4QExorcism ar (4Q560) might have also been used for exorcistic purposes, but they are not ascribed to David or another biblical figure.

12 Dennis C. Duling, 'Solomon, Exorcism, and the Son of David', *Harvard Theological Review* 68 (1975), 237–8.

13 Cf. Gerhard Delling, 'Josephus und das Wunderbare', *Novum Testamentum* 2 (1958), 291–309; George MacRae, 'Miracle in the *Antiquities* of Josephus', in *Miracles: Cambridge Studies in their Philosophy and History*, ed. C. F. D. Moule (London: Mowbray, 1965), 129–47; Otto Betz, 'Miracles in the Writings of Flavius Josephus', in *Josephus, Judaism, and Christianity*, ed. Louis H. Feldman and Gohei Hata (Detroit: Wayne State University Press, 1987), 212–35.

14 Josephus, *Jewish Antiquities* 1.108; 2.348; 3.268; 3.322; 4.158; 8.262; 10.281; 17.354.

15 MacRae, 'Miracle in the *Antiquities* of Josephus', 131–2.

16 Dennis C. Duling, 'The Eleazar Miracle and Solomon's Magical Wisdom in Flavius Josephus' *Antiquitates Judaicae* 8.42–29', *Harvard Theological Review* 78 (1985), 12.

17 *Ibid.*, 23–5.

18 Paul W. Barnett, 'The Jewish Sign Prophets – A.D. 40–70: Their Intentions and Origin', *New Testament Studies* 27 (1981), 679–97.

19 John P. Meier, *A Marginal Jew: Rethinking the Historical Jesus*, vol. II, Anchor Bible Reference Library (New York: Doubleday, 1994), 592.

20 For an analysis of the epistemological structure of the prophetic sign, see Wolfgang J. Bittner, *Jesu Zeichen in Johannesevangelium: Die Messias-Erkenntnis im Johannesevangelium vor ihrem jüdischen Hintergrund*, Wissenschaftliche Untersuchungen zum Neuen Testament 2.26 (Tübingen: J. C. B. Mohr [Paul Siebeck], 1987), 17–87.

21 This type of miracle worker has received significant scholarly attention, especially after Geza Vermes suggested that Jesus of Nazareth also belongs to this category. See Geza Vermes, 'Hanina ben Dosa: A Controversial Galilean Saint from the First Century of the Christian Era', *Journal for the Study of Judaism* 23 (1972), 28–50, and *Journal of Jewish Studies* 24 (1973), 51–64; William Scott Green, 'Palestinian Holy Men: Charismatic Leadership and Rabbinic Tradition', in *Aufstieg und Niedergang der römischen Welt* II.19.2 (1979), 619–47; Dennis Berman, 'Hasidim in Rabbinic Traditions', in *Society of Biblical Literature 1979 Seminar Papers*, vol. II, ed. Paul J. Achtemeier (Missoula: Society of Biblical Literature, 1979), 15–33; Sean Freyne, 'The Charismatic', in *Ideal Figures in Ancient Judaism: Profiles and Paradigms*, Society of Biblical Literature Septuagint and Cognate Studies 12, ed. John J. Collins and George W. E. Nickelsburg (Chico: Scholars Press, 1980), 223–58; Baruch M. Bokser, 'Wonder-Working and the Rabbinic Tradition: The Case of Hanina ben Dosa', *Journal for the Study of Judaism* 16 (1985), 42–92; Michael Becker, *Wunder und Wundertäter im frührabbinischen Judentum: Studien zum Phänomen und seiner Überlieferung im Horizont von Magie und Dämonismus*, Wissenschaftliche Untersuchungen zum Neuen Testament 2.144 (Tübingen: Mohr Siebeck, 2002), 290–378.

22 For the reconstruction of the hasidic movement, see Shmuel Safrai, 'The Teaching of Pietists in Mishnaic Literature', *Journal of Jewish Studies* 16 (1965), 27–31; Shmuel Safrai, 'The Pious (Hasidim) and the Man of Deeds (Hebrew)', *Zion* 50 (1985), 133–54.

23 Blenkinsopp, 'Miracles: Elisha and Hanina ben Dosa', 79.

24 Green, 'Palestinian Holy Men', 628–39.

25 This literature typically comprises the writings that were completed by the third and early fourth century, such as the Mishnah, Tosefta, Mekhilta de Rabbi Yishma'el, Sifra, Sifre Bamidbar and Sifre Devarim.

26 Cf. Becker, *Wunder und Wundertäter im frührabbinischen Judentum*, 271–9.

27 *Ibid.*, 245–9, 388–403; see also Becker's article, 'Miracle Traditions in Early Rabbinic Literature: Some Questions on their Pragmatics', in *Wonders Never Cease: The Purpose of Narrating Miracle Stories in the New Testament and its Religious Environment*, Library of New Testament Studies 288, ed. Michael Labahn and Bert Jan Lietaert Peerbolte (London: T&T Clark, 2006), 51–2.

28 Becker, 'Miracle Traditions in Early Rabbinic Literature', 51.

29 Hans Kvalbein, 'The Wonders of the End-Time: Metaphoric Language in *4Q521* and the Interpretation of Matt 11.5 par.', *Journal for the Study of the Pseudepigrapha* 18 (1998), 87–110.

30 Lidija Novakovic, '*4Q521*: The Works of the Messiah or the Signs of the Messianic Time?', in *Qumran Studies: New Voices, New Questions*, ed. Brent A. Strawn and Michael T. Davis (Grand Rapids: Eerdmans, 2007), 208–31.

31 The Q passage preserved in Matt. 11.2–6 and Luke 7.18–23 contains the closest known parallel to *4Q521*, because both texts go beyond their common scriptural basis in Isa. 61.1 by adding the reference to the resurrection of the dead prior to the reference to preaching good news to the poor.

Further reading

Barnett, Paul W., 'The Jewish Sign Prophets – A.D. 40–70: Their Intentions and Origin', *New Testament Studies* 27 (1981), 679–97

Becker, Michael, *Wunder und Wundertäter im frührabbinischen Judentum: Studien zum Phänomen und seiner Überlieferung im Horizont von Magie und Dämonismus*, Wissenschaftliche Untersuchungen zum Neuen Testament 2.144 (Tübingen: Mohr Siebeck, 2002)

*'Miracle Traditions in Early Rabbinic Literature: Some Questions on their Pragmatics', in *Wonders Never Cease: The Purpose of Narrating Miracle Stories in the New Testament and its Religious Environment*, Library of New Testament Studies 288, ed. Michael Labahn and Bert Jan Lietaert Peerbolte (London and New York: T&T Clark, 2006), 48–69

Betz, Otto, 'Miracles in the Writings of Flavius Josephus', in *Josephus, Judaism, and Christianity*, ed. Louis H. Feldman and Gohei Hata (Detroit: Wayne State University Press, 1987), 212–35

Blenkinsopp, Joseph, 'Miracles: Elisha and Hanina ben Dosa', in *Miracles in Jewish and Christian Antiquity: Imagining Truth*, ed. John C. Cavadini (Notre Dame: University of Notre Dame Press, 1999), 57–81

Bohak, Gideon, *Ancient Jewish Magic: A History* (Cambridge: Cambridge University Press, 2008)

Bokser, Baruch M., 'Wonder-Working and the Rabbinic Tradition: The Case of Hanina ben Dosa', *Journal for the Study of Judaism* 16 (1985), 42–92

Duling, Dennis C., 'The Eleazar Miracle and Solomon's Magical Wisdom in Flavius Josephus' *Antiquitates Judaicae 8.42–29'*, *Harvard Theological Review* 78 (1985), 1–25

Freyne, Sean, 'The Charismatic', in *Ideal Figures in Ancient Judaism: Profiles and Paradigms*, Society of Biblical Literature Septuagint and Cognate Studies 12, ed. John J. Collins and George W. E. Nickelsburg (Chico: Scholars Press, 1980), 223–58

Green, William Scott, 'Palestinian Holy Men: Charismatic Leadership and Rabbinic Tradition', in *Aufstieg und Niedergang der römischen Welt* II.19.2 (1979), 619–47

Hogan, Larry P., *Healing in the Second Temple Period*, Novum Testamentum et Orbis Antiquus 21 (Göttingen: Vandenhoeck & Ruprecht, 1992)

Lange, Armin, Hermann Lichtenberger and K. F. Diethard Römheld, eds., *Die Dämonen/Demons: Die Dämonologie der israelitisch-jüdischen und frühchristlichen Literatur im Kontext ihrer Umwelt/The Demonology of Israelite-Jewish and Early Christian Literature in Context of their Environment* (Tübingen: Mohr Siebeck, 2003)

MacRae, George, 'Miracle in the *Antiquities* of Josephus', in *Miracles: Cambridge Studies in their Philosophy and History*, ed. C. F. D. Moule (London: Mowbray, 1965), 129–47

Singer, Michael A., 'Restoring the Balance: Musings on Miracles in Rabbinic Judaism', in *Miracles in Jewish and Christian Antiquity: Imagining Truth*, ed. John C. Cavadini (Notre Dame: University of Notre Dame Press, 1999), 111–26

Sorensen, Eric, *Possession and Exorcism in the New Testament and Early Christianity*, Wissenschaftliche Untersuchungen zum Neuen Testament 2.157 (Tübingen: Mohr Siebeck, 2002)

Woodward, Kenneth L., *The Book of Miracles: The Meaning of the Miracle Stories in Christianity, Judaism, Buddhism, Hinduism, Islam* (New York: Simon & Schuster, 2000)

6 The miracles of Jesus

BARRY L. BLACKBURN

To peruse Thomas Jefferson's famous redaction of the New Testament, which excises the supernatural, is to be reminded of the prominence of the miraculous in the canonical gospels.[1] There are stories in which Jesus is the object of a miracle.[2] Also, Jesus is said to have uttered prophecies that are taken to be correct[3] and to display knowledge that is portrayed as having a supernatural origin.[4] Moreover, there are nine epiphanies of the risen Christ.[5] Then, in the synoptic gospels Jesus' disciples are credited with the power to exorcise, heal, and raise the dead.[6] However, the number of traditions in any one of these categories is eclipsed by the miracles reportedly performed by Jesus. If parallel accounts are excluded, the gospels narrate, or refer to, at least thirty-five miracles performed by him. It is with these 'miracles of Jesus' that we will concern ourselves in this chapter.

Contemporary readers of the gospels reasonably ask if Jesus performed acts that he and others regarded as miracles. Further, if Jesus acted as a miracle worker, how did he understand the significance of this activity, and what relationship did he see between his miracle working and other aspects of his mission, including his proclamation of the kingdom of God?

The answers to these questions will be prefaced by a description of how Jesus' miracle working is presented in the gospels. Since the portrayals of Jesus' miracle working in the synoptic gospels are strikingly similar, we will first treat the synoptic tradition collectively before casting our gaze towards the Fourth Gospel.

THE MIRACLES OF JESUS IN THE GOSPELS

All three synoptics contain parallel accounts of eleven miracles of Jesus.[7] Four additional stories are common to Matthew and Mark alone.[8] Another story is common to Mark and Luke alone,[9] while Matthew and Luke alone possess two in common.[10] Matthew alone reports three miracles,[11] Mark alone two[12] and Luke alone seven.[13] Obviously, these evangelists regarded Jesus' miracle working as a major aspect of his work.

The miracles of Jesus in the synoptics can be classed into several types. Prominent are healings and exorcisms. Collectively, the synoptics narrate or refer to seven exorcisms and thirteen healings. These healings vary greatly; there are three accounts of the healing of blindness, two of leprosy, and one each of persons who suffered from fever, paralysis, a shrivelled hand, a haemorrhage, deafness, a crippled body, dropsy and a severed ear. Moreover, exorcisms and healings are the only two types appearing in the summaries of Jesus' miracles with only one exception (Matt. 11.4–5/Luke 7.22). In addition to this summary, which involves the raising of the dead, the synoptics mention two instances of such a feat.[14] Other categories of miracles are rarer; there are four gift miracles, one rescue miracle, one epiphany and one punishment miracle.[15] All seven, of course, qualify as so-called 'nature miracles' (see n. 39 below).

In the synoptics, Jesus' miracles are tied to his proclamation of the coming kingdom, a connection that is rare in miracle stories, but more common in summaries of Jesus' ministry and in accounts of the disciples' activities (for example, Mark 1.39/Matt. 4.23/Luke 4.44; Mark. 3.14–15/Matt 10.1; Mark 6.12–13/Luke 9.6). In addition, in Matthew 12.28/Luke 11.20, Jesus deduces that the kingdom has come upon his hearers if he is exorcizing demons by God's power. Finally, the evangelists summarize Jesus' message with 'kingdom of God' (or 'Heaven' in Matt.) and, simultaneously, prominently feature his miracles.

The miracles of Jesus in the synoptics are sometimes motivated by Jesus' compassion or mercy. This is stated in eight stories and in one Matthean summary.[16]

The question of Jesus' identity is found throughout the synoptic miracle traditions. To be sure, his miracles are expressions of his prophetic status,[17] but they also are connected with his messiahship and divine sonship. The demons declare his identity as 'the Son of God' long before any human recognizes it.[18] In three stories human suppliants appeal to Jesus as 'the Son of David'.[19] Once Jesus heals as evidence that he is the 'Son of man' with authority to forgive sins.[20] Finally, in Matthew 14.33, the disciples worship Jesus as the Son of God after he walked on the sea.

'Faith' is a regular motif in the synoptic miracle stories.[21] Repeatedly Jesus provides miracles for those who are confident of his help; he ignores the sceptical.[22] When in Nazareth, due to unbelief Jesus could 'do no deed of power there, except that he laid his hands on a few sick people and cured them' (Mark 6.5). Only once is Jesus said to provide a miracle to those who have lost their faith, namely, for the disciples during a storm on the Sea of Galilee (Mark 4.35–42/Matt. 8.23–7/ Luke 8.22–5).

In the synoptics, Jesus' miracles rarely lead the recipient or others to faith.[23] They do, however, exert an impact on those who witness or hear about them. For example, the crowds respond positively to his reputation as an exorcist and healer.[24]

As in the synoptics, so in the Fourth Gospel, Jesus is a powerful miracle worker. The Johannine presentation, however, is distinctive. First, John narrates only seven miracles – far fewer than any synoptic – and five are without parallel.[25] Within the seven there are two gift miracles (wine, bread), three healings (a son with an unspecified illness, a lame man and a blind man), an epiphany (walking on the sea) and a resurrection (Lazarus). It is curious that the Fourth Gospel intimates nothing concerning Jesus' reputation as an exorcist, whereas in the synoptics exorcisms appear alongside healings as the two staples of Jesus' thaumaturgy.[26]

Like the synoptic authors, the Johannine evangelist knows Jesus as the Messiah (for example, John 1.17), the means of entry into the kingdom (for example, 3.3–7; 7.37–9; 14.6), but for this author Jesus' miracles are not *dunameis* ('mighty deeds'), but rather *sēmeia* ('signs') revealing him as the giver of '[eternal] life' (for example, 20.30–1). The evangelist sometimes coordinates a sign with an 'I am' saying that interprets the miracle.[27] As the source of eternal life, Jesus is the Messiah, the Son of God. Thus the Johannine signs are functions of that identity.[28]

Although, as we have seen, the synoptics portray Jesus' miracles as acts of compassion, the Fourth Gospel never does. Conversely, in the latter, Jesus twice (John 9.3; 11.4, 40; cf. 5.17) performs a miracle in order that the works and glory of the Father might be revealed through the Son – a motive absent from the synoptics.

As in the synoptics, but to a lesser extent, the Gospel of John depicts Jesus' miracle working as a magnet for crowds.[29] The Johannine diminution of this motif is possibly motivated by the evangelist's portrayal of Jesus as one who 'came to what was his own, and his own people did not accept him' (John 1.11; cf. 12.37–41).

As we have noted, in the synoptics faith in Jesus is normally not the result of witnessing a miracle, but is a prerequisite for receiving one. The fourth evangelist, however, intended that the signs would lead his audience to faith (John 20.30–1), and often he notes that the signs engendered such faith.[30] Even when Jesus performs a sign at another's behest (2.3–5; 4.47–50; 11.22–7), the evangelist refrains from using language denoting faith.

Despite these differences, the synoptics and John paint similar portraits of Jesus the miracle worker. He is said to have worked many wonders – healings, gift miracles, epiphanies and resuscitations, which were functions of his identity as the messianic Son of God and were manifestations of the kingdom. These miracles were not always given in response to faith, but they were never granted to the sceptical or hostile. Nevertheless, these deeds are said to have had a powerful impact on the populace, and were largely responsible for the following that Jesus mustered, at the head of which he represented a political threat to Jerusalem and Rome.

THE MIRACLES OF JESUS IN HISTORY

Since Jesus' career occurred during the final years of the 20s (CE), and since the gospels were composed during the last thirty-five years of the first century, there is a considerable interval from the death of Jesus (c. 30 CE) to the composition of Mark, the earliest gospel, usually dated in the latter half of the 60s. This hiatus, combined with the possibility that the gospels may have been written outside of Palestine and were written in Greek rather than the Aramaic mother tongue of Jesus, permits the possibility that Jesus' mission differed, perhaps substantially, from the gospels' portrait.

According to the gospels, healing and exorcism constitute the types of miracle most commonly performed by Jesus. In the synoptics there are seven exorcisms, of which five are attested by at least two gospels. The number of synoptic healings totals thirteen, with seven attested by two or more gospels. The Gospel of John adds three healing stories and one mention of Jesus' healings in general. It is therefore reasonable to conclude that of the types of miracles attributed to Jesus, healings and exorcisms have the most cogent claim to historicity.

By 'historicity' I mean that Jesus performed what he and his disciples believed were exorcisms and miraculous healings. Whether these deeds were actually miraculous, that is, cannot be accounted for by natural causes, transcends the boundaries of this chapter. Such a decision would depend on whether or not one's world view and historical method would permit a positive verdict with regard to a putative miracle.

Nevertheless, among Jesus scholars, irrespective of their faith commitments or ideology, there is general consensus that healings and exorcisms were integral to Jesus' career.[31] First, there are the sheer number of healings and exorcisms. It is improbable that all of these accounts were borrowed from pre-existing stories or were created out of whole cloth. Second, belief in Jesus' healings and exorcisms is attested in a number of independent sources: the so-called Q tradition, Mark, Matthew's special material, Luke's special material and, with respect to healings, the Gospel of John. Third, this multiple attestation extends to a variety of literary forms: controversy, scholastic and biographical apothegms, dominical sayings (including wisdom sayings, prophetic sayings, church rules and 'I' sayings), miracles stories, legends and the Passion narrative. Fourth, Jesus' exorcisms and healings are attested in sayings of Jesus that, on independent grounds, have a strong claim to authenticity. For example, the 'divided kingdom' parable, attested by Q and Mark,[32] defends Jesus from the charge of conducting exorcisms empowered by Beelzebul (i.e. Satan). Christians hardly invented this embarrassing charge; Jesus' opponents must have admitted that Jesus cast out demons. The saying about Jesus' exorcisms (Matt. 12.28/ Luke 11.20) was probably uttered by him: it appears in Q; it lacks a post-Easter Christology; it speaks of 'the kingdom of God'; and pre-Christian Judaism was not familiar with a connection between exorcisms performed by a charismatic and the coming of the kingdom.[33]

Although it is rare for a Jesus scholar to deny that Jesus was an exorcist and a healer, there is reluctance to view specific stories of healings and exorcisms as versions of eyewitness accounts. The traditions of Q and Mark are embedded in sources that are, respectively, at least twenty and thirty-five years later than Jesus' death. One would expect that those who transmitted these stories would have heightened the miraculous, embellished them with folkloristic and novelistic details, and assimilated Jesus to miracle workers known in Jewish and pagan circles. This would especially be true if, as the form critics argued, the *Sitz im Leben* of the miracle stories was the mission to convert pagans. Some have suggested that many stories are based, not on reminiscence, but merely on the tradition that Jesus was an exorcist and that he healed people – perhaps people with certain kinds of maladies.[34]

Despite the scepticism towards the historicity of the miracle stories, certain ones have attracted defenders. After all, it strains credulity to believe that none of the sixteen healings and seven exorcisms appearing in the gospels was based on reminiscence.

John P. Meier and Graham H. Twelftree have utilized various criteria to argue that several of the accounts of healing and exorcism rest on eyewitness reports.[35] These criteria include: (1) multiple attestation in independent gospel sources (Q, Mark, M, L, John), (2) support from dominical sayings likely to be authentic, (3) features dissimilar from Judaism or early Christianity or both, (4) absence of post-Easter Christology, (5) the presence of place names, (6) the presence of names other than those of Jesus and his disciples, (7) the presence of features that deviate from the stereotypical form or content of the miracle stories, (8) the presence of concrete, vivid details unnecessary for narration, (9) signs of later additions to the core narratives, (10) the presence of features embarrassing to Christians, (11) evidence of familiarity with the topography of Palestine, especially pre-70 CE Jerusalem and (12) features that suggest an earlier Aramaic version of the tradition.

It will be instructive to look at how these criteria have been applied to two miracles stories that, according to numerous scholars, are based on reminiscence. First, the healing of Peter's mother-in-law was taken up by both Matthew and Luke from Mark (Mark 1.29–31/ Matt. 8.14–15/Luke 4.38–9). Both the location and the sufferer are identified – the former by name, the latter by kinship to Peter. Fever is not mentioned among ailments expected to be vanquished in the endtime, nor does it appear in any other miracle story. The narrative is brief and undeveloped, with no Christological titles, no mention of the miracle's effect on witnesses, and few details that could be used to edify. Moreover, the story had already circulated as a component of 'A Day in Capernaum' (Mark 1.21–34) before being incorporated into Mark's gospel.[36]

Second, the story of the healing of Bartimaeus also contains evidences suggesting it is based on memory (Mark 10.46–52/Matt. 20.29–34/ Luke 18.35–43). The location is cited (Jericho), and the name (or patronymic) of the sufferer surfaces. The story contains unnecessary details, for example Bartimaeus' begging, the use of intermediaries to summon him, and the throwing off of his mantle. In the earliest version (in Mark), Jesus asks Bartimaeus, 'What do you want me to do for you?' This information-seeking question by Jesus is unlikely to have been created by Christians. Both the Aramaic 'Bartimaeus', and the blind man's use of the Aramaic *Rabbouni* point to an earlier Aramaic version. That Bartimaeus chose a begging station along the road ascending towards Jerusalem as Jews made their way southwards to celebrate Passover accords with the topography of Palestine and the customs of first-century pilgrims. Finally, the suppliant's unusual employment of 'Son of David' could be rooted in an old tradition according to which Solomon was revered as a wonder worker.[37]

There are also other miracle traditions whose historicity has been advocated by an impressive number of scholars:

The cleansing of the leper (Mark 1.40–5/Matt. 8.1–4/Luke 5.12–16)

The healing of the paralytic (Mark 2.1–12/Matt. 9.1–8/
  Luke 5.17–26)

The man with the withered hand (Mark 3.1–6/Matt. 12.9–14/
  Luke 6.6–11)

The Gerasene demoniac (Mark 5.1–20/Matt. 8.28–34/Luke 8.26–39)

The healing of the woman with a haemorrhage (Mark 5.25–34/
  Matt. 9.20–2/Luke 8.43–8)

Jesus heals a boy possessed by a spirit (Mark 9.14–29/Matt. 17.14–21/
  Luke 9.37–43a)

The healing of the Capernaum centurion's/official's slave/son
  (Matt. 8.5–11/Luke 7.1–10/John 4.46b–54)

Jesus heals a deaf mute (Mark 7.31–7)

A blind man is healed at Bethsaida (Mark 8.22–6)

The exorcism of Mary Magdalene (Luke 8.2)

The healing of the lame man at the pool (John 5.2–47)

Jesus heals the man born blind (John 9.1–41)[38]

But did Jesus ever raise the dead or perform so-called nature miracles?[39] The verdict of scholarship is largely negative. Nevertheless, one can make a reasonably good case that Jesus did perform acts that he and others interpreted as resuscitations of the dead. Within the gospels there are three such accounts, and each evinces features that militate against a post-Easter origin.[40] Moreover, in Q (Matt. 11.2–6/Luke 7.18–23) Jesus claims that through his work 'the dead are raised'. This logion, probably authentic, should not be dismissed as a metaphor for spiritual awakening.[41]

In contrast to Jesus' revivifications, the 'nature miracles' resist a positive judgment. These miracles include five gift miracles – the marriage at Cana (John 2.1–11); the miraculous draught of fish (Luke 5.1–11; cf. John 21.1–14); 5,000 are fed (Mark 6.32–44; Matt. 14.13–21; Luke 9.10b–17; John 6.1–15); 4,000 are fed (Mark 8.1–10; Matt. 15.32–9); payment of the Temple tax (the coin in the fish's mouth, Matt. 17.24–7), a rescue miracle (stilling the storm, Mark 4.35–41/Matt. 8.23–7/ Luke 8.22–5), an epiphany (the walking on the water, Mark 6.45–52/ Matt. 14.22–33/John 6.16–21) and a punishment miracle (the cursing of the fig tree, Mark 11.12–14, 20–6/Matt. 21.18–22).

Since few of these miracles can be traced back to non-miraculous events, later misunderstood as or exaggerated into miracles, those who reject the supernatural a priori must attribute these stories to the creativity of early Christians.[42] There are Christian (and other) historians who accept the possibility that Jesus performed supernatural deeds, and yet are uneasy about affirming the historicity of the nature miracles.[43] First, only two of the eight nature miracles are attested in two independent sources;[44] the other six appear in only one. Second, the nature miracles were almost never witnessed by anyone other than Jesus' disciples, nor are there any dominical sayings (whose authenticity is widely accepted) that refer to nature miracles. This raises the suspicion that Jesus was not known to have performed such miracles. Third, these stories carry such heavy theological and Christological freight that they are easily conceivable as creations of early Christians.[45]

Let us take, for example, one of the two stories that are attested in Mark and John: 5,000 are fed. Jesus' act is reminiscent of Elisha's multiplication of loaves in 2 Kings 4.42–4. Moreover, the story seems to portray Jesus as one like, but greater than, Moses, who provided manna to Israel. The venue of this miracle (the desert), the number of loaves (five = books of Moses) and the number of baskets of leftovers (twelve = tribes) are amenable to such an interpretation. No wonder that in the Johannine account the crowd hail Jesus as 'the prophet who is to come into the world' (John 6.14), probably referring to the predicted prophet-like-Moses (Deut. 18.15–18) and then, the next day, suggest that Jesus produce manna (John 6.30–1). Jesus' feeding also adumbrates the Eucharist. This is clear in the Fourth Gospel (6.12, 51–8) and the actions of Jesus described in Mark 6.41 ('taking ... blessed ... broke ... gave') clearly anticipate the Last Supper (Mark 14.22). These considerations do not prove that none of the nature miracles is rooted in an event in Jesus' life – miraculous or otherwise[46] – but they patently demonstrate why most scholars hesitate to affirm that these narratives put us in touch with the historical Jesus.

JESUS' UNDERSTANDING OF HIS MIRACLES

If Jesus probably performed exorcisms, healings and revivifications, how did he understand their significance? Why did he undertake such actions, and what was his intention thereby?

Jesus' message fell under the rubric of 'the kingdom of God'. He announced its coming and called for repentance and faith. This preacher, however, was simultaneously a miracle worker. But why did he exorcize, heal and raise the dead? The answer is probably complex. There is good evidence to suggest that Jesus performed miracles because he believed himself to be gifted to do so through the Spirit of God. Jesus probably (1) uttered the saying of Matthew 12.28/Luke 11.20 ('[I]f it is by the Spirit ["finger" in Luke] of God that I cast out demons') and (2) employed Isaiah 61.1 ('The spirit of the Lord God is upon me') to characterize his work.

Jesus' conviction that he possessed a Spirit-given charism would explain why his practices differ sharply from those described in the *Papyri Graecae Magicae* (*PGM*).[47] Meier has demonstrated that while Jesus sometimes used means that moderns might deem magical, there is a considerable distance on the continuum between the ideal type of 'magic' as represented in the *PGM*, and the ideal 'miracle' represented by Jesus in the gospels.[48] Gerd Theissen and Annette Merz have dubbed the former as 'magical miracles' and the latter as 'charismatic miracles'.[49] This distinction undermines attempts by David E. Aune and John D. Crossan to employ the word 'magic' as a neutral sociological description of Jesus' activities.[50] On the other hand, Jesus' non-use of prayer distinguishes him from the Galilean Hasidim, such as Honi the circle-drawer and Hanina ben Dosa, to whom Geza Vermes has appealed to explain various features in the Jesus tradition.[51]

Why did Jesus make use of this charism? E. P. Sanders suggested that Jesus wanted to legitimize himself as 'a special figure in God's plan' who 'spoke for God'.[52] Yet this proposal runs against the evidence – especially that of the synoptics. Jesus refused to show a 'sign from heaven',[53] declining to heal the curious or sceptical, but giving help to those with faith.

It is more cogent to identify Jesus' motive as one materially related to his proclamation of the kingdom, especially as such is provided by the synoptic evangelists themselves as well as by several probably authentic logia used by them. Jesus likely believed himself not only to be called by God to announce the coming of the kingdom, but also to be the agent through whom God would inaugurate his reign. When accused of exorcism via sorcery, Jesus is reported to have replied, 'But if it is by the Spirit of God that I cast out demons, then the kingdom of God has come to you' (Matt. 12.28; cf. Luke 11.20). This logion appears to mean that Jesus believed that through his exorcisms God was acting against the tyranny of Satan and his demons to inaugurate his eschatological reign.

Jesus apparently believed that his healings and revivifications were fulfilling the Isaianic promises of the blessed age to come. Such an understanding is expressed in the saying of Jesus embedded in Matthew 11.2–6/Luke 7.18–23, a Q logion whose claim for authenticity is widely supported. The conviction that the miracles of Jesus were fulfilments of Old Testament prophecies underlies another Q passage: 'But blessed are your *eyes*, for they *see*, and your ears, for they hear. Truly I tell you, many prophets and righteous people longed to *see* what you *see*, but did not *see* it, and to hear what you hear, but did not hear it' (Matt. 13.16–17/ Luke 10.23–4, my emphasis). Finally, there is good reason for believing that Jesus regarded himself as the Spirit-anointed prophet of Isaiah 61.1 whose job it was 'to proclaim release to the captives and recovery of sight to the blind, to let the oppressed go free' (Luke 4.18).[54]

The synoptic evangelists closely associate Jesus' healings with his exorcisms. Two reasons might be suggested: Jesus' exorcisms sometimes resulted in bodily healing,[55] and many of Jesus' Jewish contemporaries believed that the advent of God's kingdom would spell doom for Satan and the demonic. This expectation is attested for the intertestamental period[56] and is reflected by the words of the Gadarene demoniacs, who ask Jesus, 'Have you come here to torment us *before the time*?' (Matt. 8.29, my emphasis). This expected endtime binding of Satan, crushing of the demons and rescue of their human victims constitutes the background against which Jesus uttered the parable of the binding and plundering of the strong man (Matt. 12.29/Mark 3.27/Luke 11.21–2) and the famous saying of Matthew 12.28/Luke 11.20.[57]

The foregoing invite us to believe that Jesus exorcized, healed and raised the dead because he believed that God had called him not only to announce and effect the coming of God's kingdom in words but also in deeds. Not only were sinners being forgiven and welcomed into the people of God, but God's human creation itself was being restored from the evil that had spoiled it.[58]

If, as is attested in the synoptics, Jesus believed that he was called to bring the good news of the kingdom to the poor and to encourage generosity towards the destitute, his miracles of healing and deliverance should be interpreted as embodied 'good news to the poor'. The quotation of Isaiah 61.1–2 in Luke 4.18–19 assumes this connection between illness/demon-possession and poverty. Illness interfered with income-producing work, and doctors' fees could spell ruin (cf. Mark 5.26).

It is also reasonable to accept the view of the gospels that Jesus' miracles were motivated by his compassion. 'Compassion' is explicitly attributed to Jesus in five miracle stories and in one summary, while 'mercy' surfaces in four such narratives (see n. 16 above). In the Old

Testament and other Jewish literature the ultimate redemption of Israel was predicated on God's compassion for and mercy on his people.[59]

To this point, we have assumed that Jesus regarded himself as an eschatological prophet charged with inaugurating the kingdom. But what if he regarded himself specifically as the royal scion of David, the Messiah? In a break with much of the twentieth century, scholars today are less hesitant to claim that Jesus viewed himself as such. Theissen and Merz concluded that, while Jesus did not employ 'Messiah' as a title, he nevertheless 'had a messianic consciousness'.[60] If it is correct to believe that Jesus saw himself as such, whether or not he utilized the word (and he probably did),[61] how would this affect our understanding of the significance of his miracles? There is little evidence that in Second Temple Judaism the Messiah was expected to perform miracles; however, this 'little' evidence should not be overlooked.

According to *4 Ezra* 13.50, the Davidic Messiah would show Israel 'very many wonders' after he destroyed the nations that massed against him. This apocalypse was composed seventy-five years or so after the life of Jesus, but its mixture of traditional notions concerning the Messiah with the expectation of an eschatological Moses-like prophet who would accomplish an endtime exodus complete with signs and wonders seems to reflect a synthesis visible in the Josephan sign prophets that flourished between 40 and 70 CE. True, Josephus never mentions that these would-be redeemers were called Messiah, 'the Branch' or 'the Son of David', by themselves or others. However, they did style themselves as leaders of a liberation movement against the Romans – a role expected of the Davidic Messiah.[62] Josephus' Egyptian prophet, for example, planned 'to rule over the people' (*tou dēmou turannein*) after purging Judea.[63] It might be objected that Moses' signs and wonders (and those of the sign prophets) were utterly unlike the healings, exorcisms and raisings of Jesus, and so they are, but texts such as Acts 2.22, 43; 6.8; 8.6–7, 13; 2 Corinthians 12.12 show how easy it was to apply the 'signs and wonders' terminology to the latter miracles.[64]

However, if Jesus performed miracles *because* he believed himself to be the Messiah, his reasoning may have been more circuitous than that limned in the preceding paragraph. If the Messiah was God's chief agent for giving birth to 'the age to come', and if the transition into that blessed era would be marked by the defeat of Satan and his demonic horde, along with the banishment of disease, bodily defect and death, then Jesus may have concluded that he should take the leading role in this assault against these hostile powers of 'the present age'. Such reasoning may have been facilitated by Jesus' apparent assimilation of the anointed, Spirit-empowered prophet of Isaiah 61.1 with the Davidic Messiah.[65]

Whether Jesus' messianic consciousness led to his miracle-working activity, the evidence militates against the notion that he performed these deeds to prove that he was the Messiah. It is clear enough, however, that Jesus expected people to see that in his activities – especially his miracles – God was wielding his royal power to actualize his salvific reign.[66] Thus, while Jesus did not perform his miracles *in order to legitimate* his kingdom message, they did have that effect for those who witnessed them in faith. Similarly, though Jesus may not have healed and exorcized *in order to amass* crowds, his miracles resulted in that very thing.

RECAPITULATION

The historical Jesus probably exorcized demons, healed the sick, raised the dead and, to judge from the gospels, his miracles were legion. Moreover, it is likely that several of the miracle stories of the gospels are relatively accurate reports. These judgments, of course, do not mean that Jesus performed *actual* miracles, that is to say, events incapable of being produced by natural means. The type of miracles in question can be and often are explained with recourse to natural causes.[67] On the other hand, my conclusions will be welcomed by those who believe that Jesus wrought genuine miracles. Either way, Christians who pine for a saintly teacher whose wisdom will be palatable to Christianity's cultured despisers will be disappointed. To adapt American slang – we have what we have.

And what we have is a Jesus who believed himself to be God's agent – probably specifically the royal Messiah – for inaugurating the kingdom of God and heralding its consummation. In executing this mission, Jesus exorcized demons, healed the sick and even raised a few people from the dead. Through such actions God was, in Jesus' eyes, compassionately implementing his long-awaited reign. Thus Jesus' miracles were hardly a dispensable addendum to his 'real work', but stood at its very centre. They, along with other blessings of Jesus' work, marked the beginning of the divine overthrow of the dominion of the Evil One, with all of its attendant maladies of humankind.

Although the evidence discourages the idea that Jesus performed his miracles to prove the truthfulness of his teaching or his status as the Messiah, in the end, for those who looked with the eyes of faith, these mighty deeds, in the light of Jesus' resurrection, became revelations, not only of his messiahship, but also his divine power as the Father's only and eternal Son to bestow eternal life on the world.

Notes

1 Thomas Jefferson, *The Jefferson Bible: The Life and Morals of Jesus of Nazareth* (Mineola: Dover, 2006).
2 Including the virginal conception (Matt. 1.20/Luke 1.34–5), baptism (Mark 1.9–11/Matt. 3.13–17/Luke 3.21/John 1.32–3), transfiguration (Mark 9.2–10/Matt. 17.1–9/Luke 9.28–36), resurrection (Mark 16.1–8/ Matt. 28.1–20/Luke 24.1–53/John 20.1 – 21.25), and ascension of Jesus (Luke 24.50–1/John 20.17).
3 For example, Mark 8.31–3/Matt. 16.21–3/Luke 9.22.
4 For example, John 4.16–19.
5 Matt. 28.9–10; John 20.14–18; Luke 24.13–35; 24.34; Luke 24.36–43/ John 20.19–23; John 20.24–9; Matt. 28.16–20; John 21.1–14; Luke 24.44–53.
6 For example, Mark 3.15; Matt. 10.8/Luke 9.2; Mark 6.7, 13/Matt. 10.8/ Luke 9.1–2, 6.
7 The healing of Peter's mother-in-law (Mark 1.29–31/Matt. 8.14–15/ Luke 4.38–9), the cleansing of the leper (Mark 1.40–5/Matt. 8.1–4/Luke 5.12–16), the healing of the paralytic (Mark 2.1–12/Matt. 9.1–8/ Luke 5.17–26), the man with the withered hand (Mark 3.1–6/ Matt. 12.9–14/Luke 6.6–11), stilling the storm (Mark 4.35–41/Matt. 8.23–7/Luke 8.22–5), the Gerasene demoniac (Mark 5.1–20/Matt. 8.28–34/Luke 8.26–39), Jairus' daughter and the woman with a haemorrhage (Mark 5.21–43/Matt. 9.18–26/Luke 8.40–56), 5,000 are fed (Mark 6.32–44/Matt. 14.13–21/Luke 9.10b–17), Jesus heals a boy possessed by a spirit (Mark 9.14–29/Matt. 17.14–21/Luke 9.37–43a), the healing of the blind man (Bartimaeus) or men (Mark 10.46–52/Matt. 20.29–34/ Luke 18.35–43).
8 The walking on the water (Mark 6.45–52/Matt. 14.22–33), the Syrophoenician (Canaanite) woman (Mark 7.24–30/Matt. 15.21–8), 4,000 are fed (Mark 8.1–10/Matt. 15.32–9) and the cursing of the fig tree (Mark 11.12–14, 20–6/Matt. 21.18–22).
9 The healing of the demoniac in the synagogue (Mark 1.23–8/Luke 4.33–7).
10 The centurion of Capernaum (Matt. 8.5–13/Luke 7.1–10) and on collusion with Satan (Matt. 12.22–30/Luke 11.14–23).
11 Blind men (Matt. 9.27–31), the dumb demoniac (9.32–4) and payment of the Temple tax (17.24–7).
12 Jesus heals a deaf mute and many others (Mark 7.31–7) and a blind man is healed at Bethsaida (8.22–6).
13 The miraculous draught of fish (Luke 5.1–11), the widow's son at Nain (7.11–17), exorcism of Mary Magdalene (8.1–3), the healing of the crippled woman on the Sabbath (13.10–17), the healing of the man with

dropsy (14.1–6), the cleansing of the ten lepers (17.11–19) and the healing of the ear of the High Priest's slave (22.51).

14   Also Jesus commissioned his disciples to raise the dead (Matt. 10.8).

15   Gift miracles: Luke 5.1–11 (cf. John 21.1–14); Mark 6.30–44/Matt. 14.13–21/Luke 9.10–17; Mark 8.14–21/Matt. 15.32–9; 17.24–7. Rescue miracle: Mark 4.35–41/Matt. 8.23–7/Luke 8.22–5. Epiphany miracle: Mark 6.45–52/Matt. 14.22–33. Punishment miracle: Mark 11.12–14, 20–4; Matt. 21.18–22.

16   Compassion: Mark 1.41 (in some manuscripts); 8.2/Matt. 15.32; Matt. 9.35–6; 14.14; 20.34; Luke 7.13. Mercy: Mark 10.47–8/Matt. 20.30–1/ Luke 18.38–9; Matt. 9.27; 17.15; Luke 17.13.

17   For example, Mark 8.27–8/Matt. 16.13–14/Luke 9.18–19.

18   For example, Mark 1.24/Luke 4.34; Mark 1.34/Luke 4.41; Mark 3.11–12; Mark 5.7/Matt. 8.29/Luke 8.28.

19   Mark 10.47–8/Matt. 20.30–1/Luke 18.38–9; Matt. 9.27; 15.22; cf. 12.23.

20   Mark 2.10/Matt. 9.6/Luke 5.24.

21   Mark 1.30 (perhaps)/Luke 4.38; Mark 1.40/Matt. 8.2/Luke 5.12; Mark 5.23/Matt. 9.18/Luke 8.41–2; Mark 5.28/Matt. 9.21/Luke 8.44; Mark 6.53–6/Matt. 14.34–6; Mark 7.26/Matt. 15.22; Mark 7.32; 8.22; Mark 9.17/Matt. 17.15/Luke 9.38–9; Mark 10.47–52/Matt. 20.30–3/ Luke 18.38–42; Matt. 8.5–6, 8–9/Luke 7.3, 7–8; Luke 17.13.

22   Mark 8.11–12/Matt. 12.38–42/Luke 11.16, 29–30.

23   Acclamations expressing faith appear only in Luke 5.8; 7.16; Matt. 12.23; and 14.33, but the words *pistis* ('faith') and *pisteuō* ('I believe') do not appear.

24   Mark 1.28/Luke 4.37; Mark 1.32–4/Matt. 8.16/Luke 4.40–1; Mark 1.37/ Luke 4.42; Mark 1.45/Luke 5.15; Mark 5.24, 27, 30–1/Luke 8.42, 45; Mark 6.30–4/Matt. 14.13–14/Luke 9.10–11; Mark 6.53–6/Matt. 14.34–6; Mark 7.36–7; Mark 8.1/Matt. 15.32; Mark 9.14–18/Matt. 17.14/Luke 9.37–40; Matt. 4.24–5/Luke 6.17–19; Matt. 9.26; 9.31, 33, 35–6; 12.15–16; 15.29–31; Luke 7.17.

25   John 2.1–11; 4.46–54; 5.1–18; 6.1–15 (Mark 6.32–44/Matt. 14.13–21/ Luke 9.10b–17); 6.16–21 (Mark 6.45–52/Matt. 14.22–33); 9.1–41; 11.1–53.

26   The evangelist almost certainly knew but suppressed the tradition of Jesus as an exorcist. Perhaps he wanted to place exclusive focus on the one grand exorcism of Satan himself that occurred on the cross. See John P. Meier, *A Marginal Jew: Rethinking the Historical Jesus*, 2, *Mentor, Message, and Miracles*, Anchor Bible Reference Library (New York: Doubleday, 1994), 637, n. 18.

27   John 6.1–14 with 6.35, 48; 9.1–41 with 9.5; 11.1–53 with 11.25.

28   John 5.2–47; 7.31; 9.35–8; 10.24–39; 11.4, 27; 20.30–1.

29   John 2.23; 4.45; 6.2, 22–4; 7.30–1; 10.40–2; 11.45–8; 12.9–19; cf. 3.26; 4.1.

30   John 2.11, 23; 3.2; 4.45, 48, 53; 6.14–15; 7.31; 11.45; 12.9–11, 17–19.

31   Even Rudolf Bultmann, *Jesus and the Word* (New York: Scribner's, 1934), 173, concluded: 'there can be no doubt that Jesus did the kind of deeds which were miracles to his mind and to the minds of his

contemporaries, that is, deeds which were attributed to a supernatural, divine cause; undoubtedly he healed the sick and cast out demons'.

32 Mark 3.22–7; Matt. 12.22–30/Luke 11.14–15, 17–23.

33 Graham H. Twelftree, *Jesus the Exorcist: A Contribution to the Study of the Historical Jesus*, Wissenschaftliche Untersuchungen zum Neuen Testament 2.54 (Tübingen: Mohr, 1993), 182–9, 217–20, and Gerd Theissen and Annette Merz, *The Historical Jesus: A Comprehensive Guide* (Minneapolis: Fortress, 1998), 309. Other dominical sayings related to healing and exorcism often regarded as authentic include the Q tradition Matt. 11.5–6/Luke 7.22–3 and Luke 13.32.

34 For example, Marcus Borg, *Jesus: A New Vision* (San Francisco: Harper & Row, 1987), 61.

35 Meier, *Jew*, 617–1038; Twelftree, *Jesus*, 281–330. Recently, Richard Bauckham, *Jesus and the Eyewitnesses: The Gospels as Eyewitness Testimony* (Grand Rapids: Eerdmans, 2006), has argued that the canonical gospels are based on eyewitness testimony to a much greater extent than has been normal to allow since the rise of form criticism.

36 Twelftree, *Jesus*, 315–16; Karl Kertelge, *Die Wunder Jesu im Markusevangelium*, Studien zum Alten und Neuen Testament 13 (Munich: Kösel, 1970), 61; Jürgen Roloff, *Das Kerygma und der irdische Jesus* (Göttingen: Vandenhoeck & Ruprecht, 1970), 115–16; Rudolf Pesch, *Jesu ureigene Taten? Ein Beitrag zur Wunderfrage*, Quaestiones disputatae 52 (Freiburg: Herder, 1970), 26–7; Joachim Gnilka, *Das Evangelium nach Markus*, 2 vols., Evangelisch-katholischer Kommentar zum Neuen Testament 2 (Zurich: Benziger, 1978–9), vol. I, 84–5; Theissen and Merz, *Jesus*, 312. On the 'Day in Capernaum', see Rudolf Pesch, 'Ein Tag vollmächtigen Wirkens Jesu in Kapharnaum (Mk 1,21–34, 35–49)', *Bibel und Leben* 9 (1968), 61–77, 114–28, 177–95, 261–77 (esp. 272–4).

37 Meier, *Jew*, 686–90; Twelftree, *Jesus*, 301–2. Other advocates include Roloff, *Kerygma*, 152–73; Rudolf Pesch, *Das Markusevangelium*, 2 vols., Herders theologischer Kommentar zum Neuen Testament 2 (Freiburg: Herder, 1976), vol. I, 304–5; vol. II, 174; Gnilka, *Markus*, vol. II, 111; Theissen and Merz, *Jesus*, 312; Craig A. Evans, *Mark 8:27 – 16:20*, Word Biblical Commentary 34B (Nashville: Thomas Nelson, 2001), 129.

38 Twelftree, *Jesus*, 281–330, makes a case for the probable historicity of each of these; Meier, *Jew*, 646–772, argues for the reliability of all except the cleansing of the leper, the man with a withered hand and the healing of the woman with a haemorrhage.

39 The term, 'nature miracles' represents an Enlightenment category, but usefully identifies miracles not amenable to rational explanation.

40 Jairus' daughter (Mark 5.21–43/Matt. 9.18–26/Luke 8.40–56); the widow's son at Nain (Luke 7.11–17); the raising of Lazarus (John 11.1–44). See especially Meier, *Jew*, 773–873.

41 Meier, *Jew*, 131–7, 399–401, 832–7; Twelftree, *Jesus*, 271–2, 305.

42 See, for example, David E. Aune, 'Magic in Early Christianity', *Aufstieg und Niedergang der römischen Welt* II.23.2 (1980), 1507–57 (1524).

43 For example, Twelftree, *Jesus*, 314–30, is sanguine about the historicity of a majority of the miracle stories, yet he hesitates to affirm the historicity of Jesus' stilling of a storm, his miraculous feeding of a multitude, his walking on the sea, the cursing of the fig tree and his miraculous transformation of water into wine.

44 Five thousand are fed and the walking on the water. This assumes that none of the synoptic gospels was used by the author or authors of the Fourth Gospel.

45 Theissen and Merz, *Jesus*, 301–4.

46 Twelftree, *Jesus*, 329.

47 Karl Preisendanz and Albert Henrichs, eds., *Papyri Graecae Magicae*, 2 vols. 2nd edn (Stuttgart: B. G. Teubner, 1973–4); Hans Dieter Betz, ed., *The Greek Magical Papyri in English Translation*, 2 vols. (Chicago: University of Chicago Press, 1986).

48 Meier, *Jew*, 537–52. Cf. the earlier discussion by Howard C. Kee, *Miracle in the Early Christian World* (London and New Haven: Yale University Press, 1983), 214–15, 287–8. With respect to exorcisms, see Twelftree, *Exorcist*, 173; Dieter Trunk, *Der messianische Heiler*, Herders biblische Studien 3 (Freiburg: Herder, 1994), 426.

49 Theissen and Merz, *Jesus*, 305–7.

50 Aune, 'Magic', 1515, 1522; John D. Crossan, *The Historical Jesus: The Life of a Jewish Mediterranean Peasant* (San Francisco: HarperCollins, 1991), 303–10.

51 Geza Vermes, *Jesus the Jew* (London: Collins, 1973), 58–82.

52 E. P. Sanders, *Jesus and Judaism* (Philadelphia: Fortress, 1985), 172.

53 Mark 8.11–13/Matt. 16.1–4; 12.38–9/Luke 11.16, 29.

54 The LXX not only speaks of the Spirit-filled prophet giving sight to the blind, but also as being sent to heal (*iasasthai*) those oppressed in heart. *Iasasthai* translates the Hebrew *ḥbš*, which sometimes refers to the 'binding up' or 'dressing' of wounds (for example, Ps. 147.3; Isa. 1.6; 3.7; 30.26; Ezek. 30.21). Luke's description of Jesus' healing and exorcizing activity in Luke 13.12, 16 and in Acts 10.38 suggests that he saw these as the outworking of Jesus' proclamation of release to captives and sending away the oppressed in freedom. Therefore, it would seem that Jesus could have easily understood Isa. 61.1 in terms of a ministry of healing. It is also possible that *4Q521* (*Messianic Apocalypse*) attests an expectation that the Messiah would execute the works attributed to the Spirit-empowered prophet in Isa. 61.1. On this fragmentary text, see Eric Eve, *The Jewish Context of Jesus' Miracles*, Journal for the Study of the New Testament Supplement 231 (Sheffield: Sheffield Academic, 2002), 189–96.

55 For example, Mark 9.14–29/Matt. 17.14–21/Luke 9.37–43a; Matt. 12.22–4/Luke 11.14; Matt. 9.32–4.

56 *11QMelch*; *1 En.* 54–5; *T. Mos.* 10.1. Cf. also *T. Levi* 18.12; *T. Dan* 5.10–11; *T. Sim.* 6.6; *T. Jud.* 25.3; *T. Zeb.* 9.8, although these texts may represent Christian hopes. Eve, *Jesus' Miracles*, 379: 'The hope that the demonic forces of evil would be overthrown at the eschaton is fairly well attested' in Second Temple Judaism.

57 Jesus' contemporaries may not have expected the endtime defeat of Satan to occur by means of a figure like Jesus who conducted exorcisms. Nevertheless an expectation of an eschatological overthrow of the devil and his demons is surely the background against which Jesus claimed that his exorcisms represented the actualization of God's kingdom. See Gerd Theissen, *The Miracle Stories of the Early Christian Tradition* (Philadelphia: Fortress, 1983), 277–80, and Eve, *Jesus' Miracles*, 379–81, for discussion of the creative role Jesus himself may have played in the eschatological interpretation of his healings and exorcisms.

58 See N. T. Wright, *Jesus and the Victory of God*, vol. II of *Christian Origins and the Question of God* (Minneapolis: Fortress, 1996), 186–96, and Rikk E. Watts, 'The New Exodus/New Creational Restoration of the Image of God: A Biblical-Theological Perspective on Salvation', in *What Does it Mean to be Saved?*, ed. John G. Stackhouse (Grand Rapids: Baker Academic, 2002), 15–41.

59 For example, Isa. 49.8–18; 54.8–10; Dan 9.4–19; Zech. 10.6.

60 Theissen and Merz, *Jesus*, 538.

61 See Wright, *Jesus*, 477–539.

62 Theudas (Josephus, *Antiquities of the Jews* 20.97–9; Acts 5.36); an unnamed prophet (*Antiquities of the Jews* 20.167–8; *Jewish War* 2.259); an Egyptian Jew (*Antiquities of the Jews* 20.168–72; *Jewish War* 2.261–3; Acts 21.38).

63 Josephus, *Jewish War* 2.262; cf. *Antiquities of the Jews* 20.169–71; Acts 21.38.

64 *4Q521* may attribute healing and raising the dead to the Messiah, but this fragmentary text is open to other interpretations (see n. 54 above).

65 This assimilation can be inferred from the evidence that Jesus probably viewed himself as the prophet of Isa. 61.1 and the Davidic Messiah. Such an assimilation may underlie *4Q521*. Eve, *Jesus' Miracles*, 195.

66 Matt. 11.2–6/Luke 7.18–23; Matt. 11.20–4/Luke 10.12–15.

67 Even revivifications from the dead are susceptible to this interpretation.

Further Reading

Achtemeier, Paul J., *Jesus and the Miracle Tradition* (Eugene: Cascade, 2008)

Aune, David E., 'Magic in Early Christianity', *Aufstieg und Niedergang der römischen Welt: Geschichte und Kultur Roms im Spiegel der neueren Forschung*, ed. H. Temporini and W. Haase (Berlin: de Gruyter, 1972), 12.23.2 (1980), 1507–57

Blackburn, Barry L., 'The Miracles of Jesus', in *Studying the Historical Jesus: Evaluations of the State of Current Research*, ed. Bruce Chilton and Craig A. Evans (Leiden: Brill, 1994), 353–94

Bultmann, Rudolf, *History of the Synoptic Tradition*, rev. edn (New York: Harper & Row, 1963)

Crossan, John Dominic, *The Historical Jesus: The Life of a Jewish Mediterranean Peasant* (San Francisco: HarperCollins, 1991)

Eve, Eric, *The Healer from Nazareth: Jesus' Miracles in Historical Context* (London: SPCK, 2009)

Fuller, Reginald H., *Interpreting the Miracles* (London: SCM, 1963)

Harvey, A. E., *Jesus and the Constraints of History* (London: Duckworth, 1982)

Kahl, Werner, *New Testament Miracle Stories in their Religious-Historical Setting: A Religionsgeschichtliche Comparison from a Structural Perspective*, Forschungen zur Religion und Literatur des Alten und Neuen Testaments 163 (Göttingen: Vandenhoeck & Ruprecht, 1994)

Kee, Howard C., *Miracle in the Early Christian World: A Study in Sociohistorical Method* (London and New Haven: Yale University Press, 1983)

Meier, John P., *A Marginal Jew: Rethinking the Historical Jesus*, 2, *Mentor, Message, and Miracles*, Anchor Bible Reference Library (New York: Doubleday, 1994)

Pesch, Rudolf, *Jesu ureigene Taten? Ein Beitrag zur Wunderfrage*, Quaestiones disputatae 52 (Freiburg: Herder, 1970)

Sanders, E. P., *Jesus and Judaism* (Philadelphia: Fortress, 1985)

Smith, Morton, *Jesus the Magician* (New York: Harper & Row, 1978)

Theissen, Gerd, *Miracle Stories of the Early Christian Tradition* (Philadelphia: Fortress, 1983)

Theissen, Gerd and Annette Merz, *The Historical Jesus: A Comprehensive Guide* (Minneapolis: Fortress, 1998)

Twelftree, Graham H., *Jesus the Exorcist: A Contribution to the Study of the Historical Jesus*, Wissenschaftliche Untersuchungen zum Neuen Testament 2.54 (Tübingen: Mohr, 1993)

*_Jesus the Miracle Worker: A Historical and Theological Study_ (Downers Grove: InterVarsity, 1999)

Vermes, Geza, *Jesus the Jew* (London: Collins, 1973)

Wenham, David and Craig Blomberg, eds., *Gospel Perspectives 6: The Miracles of Jesus* (Sheffield: JSOT, 1986)

Wright, N. T., *Jesus and the Victory of God*, vol. II of *Christian Origins and the Question of God* (Minneapolis: Fortress, 1986)

7 Miracles in early Christianity

JAMES CARLETON PAGET

The supernatural gifts, which even in this life were ascribed to the Christians above the rest of mankind, must have conduced to their own comfort, and very frequently to the conviction of infidels.

Edward Gibbon[1]

Christian apologetic found that appeal to miracles was by no means a trump card to play.

Geoffrey Lampe[2]

These quotations reflect two different perspectives on the importance of miracles for the Christian church in the period following the death of Jesus. For Gibbon they are one of five causes accounting for the rise of Christianity. For Lampe their importance can be overplayed for they constituted ambiguous evidence in favour of Christianity. Against such a background, this chapter will examine the character and nature of the miraculous in Christianity in the period running from the death of Jesus to the middle of the third century CE. The discussion will show that Christians moved in a world full of the miraculous. Miracles were taken for granted, although some scepticism about the phenomenon did exist, relating both to the factuality of the miracle/s described, but also to the character of the miraculous act. In this context, space will be given to the debate about magic and its definition, and the point will be made that every supposedly miraculous event could be construed, negatively, as magic. The miraculous emerges from this as something ambivalent, and it was a continuing problem for Christians to distance both their founder and other Christian miracle workers from the charge of being sorcerers. In the course of the discussion, I shall seek to show how there exist continuities between pagan discussion of magic and Christian engagement with the theme, particularly as this relates to its polemical use. The chapter will also address the question of the function of miracle. Emerging from all of this, there will be a discussion of the importance of miracle for the spread of Christianity.

MIRACLE/MAGIC IN THE NON-CHRISTIAN WORLD

Christians moved in a world where miracles were taken for granted. The messianic sect emerged from a group of people, the Jews, who were widely known for their miraculous activity, particularly exorcism. This point is illustrated in material at Qumran, in Josephus (*Antiquities* 8.46–9), in rabbinic, pagan[3] and Christian sources (see Acts 19.13–20; Justin, *Dialogue* 85). Likewise some of the magical papyri, dating from the second to the fifth centuries CE and coming from Graeco-Roman Egypt, contain formulae with the names of the Jewish God[4] and important biblical characters like Moses, Abraham and Solomon.[5] Evidence from the wider pagan environment concerning miracles is similarly plentiful.[6] While the shrines associated with the cult of Asclepius could be described as medical in that they partially functioned as hospitals, they were also centres of extra-medical practices.[7] Stories about miracle workers were common;[8] and the proliferation of magical papyri, amulets, tablets of various materials, and magical bowls, point to the commonplace character of such practices.

Ancient society was not, however, universally credulous about miracles. Extraordinary events were not always understood as supernatural intervention.[9] Cicero, in *De divinatione* 2.28.61, argued that all things had a natural cause; and historians and physicians expressed scepticism about miraculous intervention. Lucian, the second century CE author, regarded as fraudulent the miraculous events surrounding the second-century Alexander's setting up of an oracle in Abonoteichos in Paphlagonia.[10] But reactions, even amongst the educated, to Alexander, for instance, were generally positive. Even where attitudes were negative as was the case with legislation relating to magic, its efficacy was assumed otherwise charges of practising it would have been tried under laws of fraud, which they were not.[11]

Difficulties with the miraculous tended to emerge from other concerns. Did the power manifested by miracle workers have a good or bad origin? It is at this point that we have to engage in a discussion of ancient magic.

Initially the term *magos* ('magician') referred to a caste of Persian priests and so did not carry negative connotations.[12] But association with the Persians, whose religion was generally considered to be fraudulent by Greeks and Romans alike, brought negative connotations to the word. From the Hellenistic period many people, who were not Persian, started to employ the word *magos* themselves, for individuals who could be seen by others as frauds or deceivers. The sinister connotations of the word emerge in other ways. In Roman legislation 'magic' is only mentioned negatively. So Cornelius Hispallus expelled the Chaldean astrologers from Rome in 139 BCE; and in 33 BCE astrologers and magicians were expelled from Rome. In 13 BCE, in a related gesture, Augustus ordered all books on occult subjects to be burnt; and in 16 CE, or possibly a year later, all astrologers and magicians were expelled from the city, an order which was reiterated by edicts made by other emperors in 69 and 89 CE.[13] Similar measures were carried out later, especially in the reign of Septimius Severus.[14]

Despite such official policy and opinion, the presence of much 'magical' activity in Rome throughout the imperial period, as well as of travel to Egypt, the hub of such practices, to familiarize oneself with magic in general, together with the evidence provided by the magical papyri, imply a more ambivalent attitude.[15]

Determining what counted as magic in the ancient world is difficult. Specific practices, in particular divination, especially regarding the life of the emperor, were thought dangerously magical, as was the making of love potions, or potions which would induce abortion; but we struggle for a generic definition.[16] In fact most argue that all attempts at an essentialist definition are fruitless whether we seek at a general level to differentiate religion from magic, or more specifically, magic from miracle (which often involves a distinction between magic and religion), whether in terms of the attitude of the practitioner and/or recipient, the effect of the miracle, or the technique employed.[17] As Segal has noted, 'the charge of magic and its meaning depended on a complicated series of assumptions'.[18] Often these had to do with the perception of an individual or his actions, and on the perceived relationship of such a person, or indeed group, to their wider social surrounds; and, by extension, with whether they were thought to have a negative effect on their own world. The view that the second-century CE Latin author Apuleius was a magician may have had much to do with the fact that to his accusers he was a foreigner, that he had married a rich widow who had left her worldly goods to him rather than to her relatives; and that he engaged in practices regarded as peculiar. Such an essentially social view of the charge of magic, which emphasizes the alternative or alien character of the individual or group accused,[19] while vague, takes account of the types of accusations which were made in the name of magic. Such accusations were aimed either against those who were understood as subversive, considered to be doing harm by their actions or, like Apuleius, were perceived not only to be outsiders, but had experienced a considerable increase in wealth.[20] This is not to claim that those who made accusations of magic in the ancient world did not think that they were describing something real, or to denude any definition of the term of a religious aspect. It is merely to accept the subjective and socially motivated character of the charge as made.

CHRISTIAN SOURCES ABOUT MIRACLE

For the period under discussion, our sources vary considerably in their attention to the miraculous. In the New Testament (excluding the gospels), it is the Acts of the Apostles, written possibly at the end of the first century, which presents the most detailed accounts of individual miracles, often associating them with those who had a claim to being Apostles, including Paul.[21] In apparent contrast to the picture of him portrayed in Acts, reference to miracles in Paul's epistles is sparse, although where they exist they can be taken to be important. The author of the Epistle to the Hebrews seems to imply their pervasiveness (see Heb. 2.3b–4).

Outside the New Testament, relevant material is patchy. While there are allusions in the writings of the Apostolic Fathers to signs and wonders associated with Jesus (*Barnabas* 5.8) or with Satan at the endtime (*Didache* 16.4), and an attempt to differentiate a false from a true prophet (Hermas, *Mandate* 11), reference to contemporary miracle working is generally absent. Justin, Irenaeus, Theophilus of Antioch and Tertullian refer to contemporary Christian miracle workers, in particular to exorcists, but much of this lacks detail. Nearly all these writers show an awareness of the importance of miracle, and its ambivalent character, leading in some instances to piecemeal attempts to defend miracle working, especially Jesus', as not magic. By contrast more detail is found in the writings of Origen, especially his *Against Celsus*. In it Origen defends Jesus from the accusation of being a *goes* or deceiver, which constitutes an important element of the pagan Celsus' polemic. Of all these later patristic sources, the most detailed account of miracles appears in the apocryphal Acts of the Apostles.[22] These composite works of unknown authorship and date record a variety of miracles performed by the apostles, ranging from healings and exorcisms to transmutations (the changing of one thing into another), resurrections and miracles to do with animals.[23]

THE FUNCTION OF MIRACLE

What function is attributed to miracles in these writings? In some writers there is an obvious relationship between miracles and authority. On a number of occasions Paul refers to apparent miraculous manifestations when his authority is being challenged.[24] So in 1 Thessalonians 1.5, he notes that the Thessalonians' reception of the Gospel 'was not in word only' but also 'with power and the Holy Spirit', here differentiating between preaching without and with miracle; and in 1 Corinthians 2.4 Paul contrasts artful, persuasive talk (associated with his opponents) and his own preaching 'with power and the spirit'.[25] Most significantly, at 2 Corinthians 12.12, Paul writes: 'I am not lacking in any way: the signs of an apostle were performed among you with all endurance – signs and wonders and miracles'. Even if in this particular context Paul has to acknowledge that his own miraculous power appears to compare poorly with that of the so-called super-apostles, who questioned Paul's authority, he is clear about the importance of miracle for his self-understanding as an apostle.[26] For some scholars, it is Paul's desire to limit reference to his miraculous activity to contexts where his authority is being challenged which explains the limited reference to miracle in his epistles, at least when compared with Paul in Acts.[27] In this view we should assume that Paul had a richer theology of miracle than might at first seem the case;[28] and that Acts' account of Paul's miracles is not fictitious.[29]

This conviction that miracles were one way of authenticating the authority of individual figures, especially apostles, finds further support in the apocryphal acts where the authority of Peter over against the powerful figure of Simon Magus, understood as the arch-enemy of the Christian movement, is demonstrated in competitive bouts of miracle making.[30] But undercutting this idea are the places in early Christian writings where miracle is associated with non-apostolic individuals, or ordinary people. In this context we should note Paul's reference in 1 Corinthians 12.9–10 to gifts of healing and to the workings of miracles being granted to the latter, sentiments which are repeated in the longer ending of Mark (16.17–18), Justin (*Dialogue* 76) and, by implication, in Irenaeus, Tertullian and Origen.[31]

In addition miracles were used to support theological assertions. Justin, for instance, claims that Jesus 'was made man also ... having been conceived according to the will of God the Father, for the sake of believing men and for the destruction of demons'; and mentions that such a truth can be confirmed 'under your own observation. For many of our Christian men exorcise numberless demoniacs throughout the whole world and in your city' (Second Apology 6.6). More tersely, in a discussion of Jesus' identity as Messiah, Justin writes: 'You hesitate to acknowledge that Jesus is the Christ – which the Scriptures and the [miracles] wrought in his name demonstrate' (Dialogue 39.6). In these passages miracles are not the subject of discussion but support points of what we might term dogma.[32]

Such use of miracles is apologetic, that is, miracles are used in defence of an element of Christianity, especially its theology. Further evidence of such use exists. Tertullian exploits the beneficent effect of Christian exorcistic activity. At one point in his Apology, he defends Christians against the charge of being 'enemies of the human race' by pointing to the fact of Christian exorcism, here understood as an attack on a deadly foe, who affects not only individuals but society at large (see Apology 22): 'Moreover, who would deliver you from those secret foes, ever busy both destroying your souls and ruining your health? I mean from the attacks of those demons which we drive out without reward or without price?' (Apology 23; cf. also 37). For Tertullian, Christian exorcism also reveals the worthless nature of the gods for when a Christian commands a possessed person to speak, the spirit will declare itself to be a demon (Apology 23). But such apologetic use of miracle is not standard. For Christian apologists much more importance was attached to proving that Jesus and his followers were the fulfilment of Old Testament Scriptures than that they performed fantastic deeds.[33]

In this context we should note the theological difficulty that some writers expressed when discussing miracles. Origen, although he could state that Jesus 'healed the lame and blind, for which reason we regard him as Christ and Son of God' (Against Celsus 2.48), still viewed the miracles as diverting the faithful's eyes from Jesus' humanity (3.28), as being no more than a concession to those of a weaker mental disposition and therefore needful of external acts (1.38), and could imply that an appropriate interpretation of them was an allegorical one (2.48–9).[34]

Related to the role of miracles in apologetic is their importance for Christian mission.[35] This point, referred to by Gibbon, has been supported more recently by MacMullen and Brown.[36] In Acts, for instance, miracles often elicit positive, conversionary, responses (see Acts 9.35, 42; 13.12; 16.30, 33; 19.17). Eusebius, possibly reflecting his own reading of earlier sources, hints at a connection between the two at Church History 2.3.2; and Justin is clear that Simon Magus and Menander, both of whom he regards as heretics, have attracted a large following, in part through what he terms magical tricks (First Apology 26.1–2 and

56.1–2), a point also made by Hippolytus in his *Elenchos* (6.7.1, 20.1; 39.1–2; 7.32, 50).[37] Justin makes no such connection between miracle and mission when referring to the activities of the apostles or nameless Christian miracle workers of a later date (*First Apology* 50.12). Irenaeus, by contrast, hints at such a connection when he notes that those who have been successfully exorcized 'frequently both believe [in Christ] and join the church' (*Against Heresies* 2.32.4).[38] Tertullian, commenting at *Apologeticum* 23 on the fact that demons leaving the bodies of those they have invaded confess the Christian God as the true God, opines: 'Such testimonies from your so-called deities usually result in making people Christians'. Origen states that because the disciples did not possess dialectical wisdom, they must have persuaded people by miracles (*Against Celsus* 1.38); and elsewhere asserts that 'without miracles and wonders they [the apostles] would not have persuaded those who heard new doctrines ... to leave their traditional religion' (1.46). Possibly the clearest example of the conversionary power of miracles comes in the apocryphal acts. In the *Acts of John* 33–6 the apostle is explicit about his desire to convert the whole city through a miraculous spectacle; and at 37–45 the conversion of the Ephesians is brought about through the destruction of the temple of Artemis. In the *Acts of Paul*, Paul raises Anchares from the dead and the people believe; and in the *Acts of Peter* 12–13, Peter and Simon Magus compete with each other for the affections of the crowd. The latter exclaims: 'Show us another sign, that we may believe in you as the servant of God; Simon did many signs in our sight so we followed him'. Peter acquiesces by stating that he will convince the crowd not only by words but by deeds and marvellous powers.[39]

The connection between miracle and conversion should, however, be treated with circumspection. Kelhoffer, after analysing the relevant material in Justin, notes that while such a relationship is substantiated in the comments that Justin makes about Menander (see above), they are not when Justin mentions the 'orthodox'.[40] Kelhoffer does not reject the connection but thinks it unproven. Similar caution could be applied to the conclusions of MacMullen, who attributes great significance to the apocryphal acts where, as noted, conversion often results from miraculous displays. Such accounts, he believes, should be read as reflections of known historical situations; and from this he argues for the strong effect of miracles upon the pagan 'lower class'. However, others have argued that the apocryphal acts' conception of the relationship between conversion and miracle is more complex. So in the *Acts of John* the miracle which initiates conversion is a starting point for a more dramatic transformation which is seen in terms of moving from death to life. As Gallagher writes: 'Salvation depends more on commitment and action than on the passive acceptance of the miraculous'.[41] This can be read simply as a critique of a particular perception of miracle and, therefore, indirectly as evidence of the importance of miracle for conversion.

In a discussion of the function of miracle in early Christian writings importance should also be attached to the way in which miracles conveyed the ongoing presence and power of Jesus and God within the church. This is implied by the use of the phrase 'signs and wonders' in Paul, Acts and beyond to describe the miracles, which probably alludes to the Exodus tradition and God's actions on behalf of his people at that time,[42] and also by the performance of miracles 'in the name of Jesus' witnessed to in Acts, Patristic authors and the apocryphal acts.[43]

In all of this we should note that miracle stories also functioned to entertain. This is clear in the canonical Acts of the Apostles (see Acts 28), as it is in the apocryphal acts where stories of talking dogs, resurrected fish and expelled bed bugs are there to amuse as well to make theological points.

'NOT A TRUMP CARD': THE SUBSTANCE OF CHRISTIAN MIRACLES AND THE PROBLEM OF MAGIC

Much of early Christian literature concerning miracle is defensive. Two objections had to be met. One of these, less well attested, is the view that the miracles were fictitious. One of the earliest Christian apologists Quadratus, in a fragment of his mostly lost *Apology*, quoted by Eusebius at *Church History* 4.3.2, asserts that some of the beneficiaries of the miracles of Jesus were still alive at the time he was writing, implying that the validity of the reports of the miracles, in this case Jesus', were being questioned.[44] Celsus, while generally not disputing the reality of Jesus' miracles or those of contemporary Christians, questions the validity of significant miraculous events in Jesus' life, especially the Virgin Birth (*Against Celsus* 1.28), the supernatural events surrounding his baptism (1.46–7), and the Resurrection (1.55–6; 5.52–3; 6.72–3).[45] But the other, and more prominent, defence concerned the accusation that Christian miracles proved their practitioners, whether Jesus, his immediate followers or contemporary Christians, to be sorcerers.

The debate about Christianity's relationship to magic is complicated but merits discussion because it touches upon different aspects of the debate about early Christians and miracle.

Christians shared their pagan and Jewish counterparts' negative view of magic.[46] Luke portrays Peter and Paul in successful combat with those termed 'magicians' (Acts 8.9–24; 13.6–12; 19.8–20) and presents Paul's actions in Ephesus as leading to the voluntary burning of a great number of magical books (19.18–19). We read warnings against magic at *Didache* 2.2 and *Barnabas* 20.1. Justin states that Christians had left behind the magical arts (*First Apology* 14.12), or what he refers to as the enslaving power of magic (*Second Apology* 5.3); and Tertullian asserts that magic 'is the multiform plague of the human mind, the cultivator of all error' (*The Soul* 57.2). Negative interpretations of the 'wise men' of Matthew 2 (in the Greek, *magoi*) were frequent (Ignatius, *Ephesians* 19.3; Justin, *Dialogue* 78.9); and Christians were not averse to using the rhetoric of magic to blacken the reputation of those of their number they deemed heretics, including Simon Magus, Markus and Elchasai.[47]

But what then of the nature of the accusations made against Christians and their response? Much of our information comes from Origen's *Against Celsus*, which cites quotations from the *True Doctrine*, written around 170 CE. The latter, apparently repeating attacks which had been made by a non-Christian Jew, asserts that Jesus was a sorcerer who had learnt his magic in Egypt, where he had hired himself out as a labourer (*Against Celsus* 1.28). While Celsus rarely doubts the fact of Jesus' miraculous activity, he questions its inspiration. According to Origen, Celsus puts it on a level with 'the works of sorcerers who profess to do wonderful miracles, and the accomplishments of those who are taught by the Egyptians, who for a few obols make known their sacred lore in the middle of the market place and drive daemons out of men' (1.28). Similar accusations are quoted by Justin, repeating the views of non-Christian Jews (*Dialogue* 69.6–7). This negative portrayal of Jesus is repeated in Celsus' statements about Jesus' immediate followers and contemporary Christian miracle workers. 'Christians', he states, 'get the power which they seem to possess by pronouncing the names of certain daemons and incantations' (see also *Against Celsus* 6.40; 8.37). On a number of occasions Celsus is portrayed as accusing Christian 'sorcerers' of preying on the gullibility of the ignorant, and selling their wares in the market places of various cities (1.68; 3.50). Like the Jews from whom they have fled, they are no more than sorcerers and vagabonds (4.33–5). Similar accusations are found in the apocryphal acts.[48]

Christians countered this polemic in different ways. From a technical point of view they sought to draw attention to the manner in which Jesus and his followers performed miracles. So the claim, found first in Justin, and implied in accounts of miracles in Luke in Acts, that Christians were not magicians because they did not utter incantations or indulge in certain manipulations, is reflected in the claim that Jesus performed his miracles by the utterance of words (Justin, *Dialogue* 69.6–7; see 85.3 where Justin asserts that Jewish exorcizers make use of craft when they exorcize, employing 'fumigations and incantations').[49] But miracles by a word could become the basis of the accusation that Jesus was a magician (see Tertullian, *Apology* 21.17) because words could be held to be magical manipulations, just as they are in the magical papyri.[50] Related to this are Christian attempts, taking up a trope in the pagan and Jewish literature, to differentiate between spells (bad) and prayer (good). In this context Christians emphasized the fact that they performed miracles 'in the name of Jesus'.[51] But this was not a strong defence to those who took a negative view of Christianity. Curing people in the name of Jesus could appear like a spell or incantation, especially when, as seems to have been the case, Christians began to accompany their miracles in the name of Jesus with statements of varying length relating to Jesus' life.[52] Moreover, the presuppositions behind such curing 'in the name of Jesus' were the same as those held by Jews and pagans who performed cures in the name of various powerful deities, namely that to possess a name 'is to possess power over the one who bears the name',[53] a point accepted by Origen (*Against Celsus* 1.24; 4.33–4; see also 5.45). It is also important to note that such a formula could be understood as necromancy because it looked like a means of accomplishing something through the instrumentality of the dead.[54] Indeed Christian veneration of martyrs could have dangerously magical connotations because Christians appeared to be calling upon those who had died violently for help (see Tertullian, *The Soul* 57).

Other features of Christianity may have encouraged the accusation of magic. Wypustek has shown how aspects of Montanism, the late second-century prophetic heresy, gave Christianity a magic-like appearance, especially in relation to the pneumatic inspiration attributed to some, to the mediumistic enhancements, oracular utterances and prophetic trances which were associated with the movement, some of which could be likened to a 'mania' often associated with magic.

Wypustek claims that the decision of the Emperor Septimius Severus, a ruthless opponent of magicians, astrologers and prophetic dreams, to prohibit conversion to Judaism and Christianity (*Scriptores Historiae Augustae*, Severus 17.1–2) may have had more to do with the magical associations of both religions (in the case of Christianity, encouraged by the rise of Montanism), than with a desire to end Jewish and Christian proselytism as is implied by the reference in the *Historia Augusta*.[55] Tertullian notes that Christian astrologers existed (*Idolatry* 9.1–9), and Christian prophecy could look like astrology insofar as the prediction of events could appear to be as good as bringing them about. Furthermore, some have suggested that Christians used handbooks with formulae, prayers and pharmacological instructions for the purposes of exorcism and healing, a view supported by Celsus' assertion that Christian elders possessed books containing barbarian names of demons and magical formulae.[56] Finally we should mention the possibility that Christians in this period used items associated with magic like amulets or rings, even if all of the relevant evidence comes from a later period.[57]

Attempts by Christians to distance themselves from accusations of sorcery, whether relating to contemporary practice or to Jesus himself, were precarious, as demonstrated above. In the end, because Christian practice and Jesus' own practice[58] were difficult to distinguish from those which were habitually deemed 'magical', Christian writers emphasized the moral probity of Jesus or his followers, and the beneficence of their miraculous activity.[59] So Origen attacks Celsus for comparing stories about Jesus with those of magicians, stating that 'no sorcerer uses his tricks to call the spectators to moral reformation; nor does he educate by the fear of God people who were astounded by what they saw ... Nor do they even want to have anything to do with reforming men, seeing that they themselves are filled with the most infamous sin' (*Against Celsus* 1.68).[60] Similarly moral was the Christian claim that they never performed miracles for money (note the contemptuous mention by Origen in the quotation above from *Against Celsus* 1.68 of 'a few obols'), something which was a feature of pagan 'miracle workers'.[61]

However, because Celsus and others viewed the Christians as outsiders, whose presence was deleterious to the empire, they came to associate them with magic and sorcery, terms which, as noted, lacked any clear definition, and were often applied to those conceived as society's enemies. Celsus' admiration for Asclepius and the miracles associated with him (*Against Celsus* 3.3) had little to do with a clear sense of their technical or qualitative superiority over the miracles of

Jesus and his followers, but more to do with his conviction that Ascle-pius and his cult occupied an acceptable place in the religious and cultural framework of the empire, whereas Christians did not.[62]

CONCLUDING THOUGHTS

One should acknowledge the difficulty of talking about miracles and their role in the early church. This arises because of the scepticism which greets reports of such events in the present age. One scholar's call for a suspension not only of disbelief, but also of distaste, in their study, appears question-begging;[63] but it is a plea which is not based on the acceptance of the existence of miracle as such, but on an appreci-ation of the world out of which the early church emerged with its cluttered and exotic religious landscape. Against such a background, 'miracles' were less easily disbelieved or found distasteful.

Irrespective of these hermeneutical problems, the study of miracle in this period raises many questions. Did the representation of miracle change? Can we chart a clear development from the sober tones of Paul to the more flagrant and legendary cameos of Luke in Acts, to the extravagant presentations of the apocryphal gospels, and somehow hold this to be a response to a changing religious context? I doubt it. Behind Paul's sober tones, there may lie a richer and more vivid theology of miracles, and a more important role in his ministry, which letters, written to believers, only hint at. Against such a background Luke looks less extravagant; and the apocryphal acts an admittedly exuberant and novelistic extension of the same.

This last observation raises questions about the importance and frequency of miracles after Jesus. In this context number crunching (counting the amount of times miracles occur in primary sources) is not necessarily helpful. For Justin, Irenaeus, Tertullian and others miracle may not be mentioned often but where it is, it implies a role in the spread of Christianity, in the defence of certain doctrines and ideas, and in the creation of the sense of the ongoing presence of Jesus in the church. The casual mention in a letter of the third-century bishop, Cornelius, writing to a fellow bishop, Fabius of Antioch, of the presence of fifty-two exorcists in his church, amidst presbyters, janitors and readers, warns us against making judgments on this point based on the realia (Eusebius, *Church History* 6.43.11).

However, the second half of this chapter makes us wary of attrib-uting so much importance to miracle because it could too easily be seen as magic. The apocryphal acts present us with ambiguous data relevant to this issue. On the one hand, they are sensitive to the charge of sorcery, but on the other, they are extravagant in the manner and variety of miracle they depict, much more so than the apologists. Does their relative lack of sobriety speak against Lampe's judgment, referred to earlier, or does their wariness of charges of magic speak in favour of it? It seems clear that miracle was noted as an important part of Christian self-presentation, but Christian writers were aware of the fact that such practices laid them open to serious charges. This in part may explain the relative infrequency with which they were mentioned by Christian apologists and other elite authors.

Notes

1 Edward Gibbon, *The History of the Decline and Fall of the Roman Empire*, 3 vols. (1776) ed. D. Wormersley (London: Penguin, 2005), vol. I, 471.
2 G. W. H. Lampe, 'Miracles and Early Christian Apologetic', in *Miracles: Cambridge Studies in their Philosophy and History*, ed. C. F. D. Moule (London: Mowbray, 1970), 205–18 (213).
3 See Juvenal, *Satirae* 6.542–7; Lucian, *Tragodopodagra* 173; *Philopseudes* 16; *Alexander* 13; Origen, *Against Celsus* 1.26; 7.9.
4 H. D. Betz, *The Greek Magical Papyri in Translation* (Chicago: University of Chicago Press, 1992), xli. See *Papyri graecae magicae: Die griechischen Zauberpapyri*, ed. K. Preisendanz (Berlin: Teubner, 1928), IV, 1232–9, for use of names associated with the Jewish god and the patriarchs.
5 On Jewish activity in this area, see Philip S. Alexander, 'Jewish Elements in Gnosticism and Magic c. CE 70–c. CE 270', in *The Cambridge History of Judaism*, vol. III, *The Early Roman Period*, ed. William Horbury, W. D. Davies and John Sturdy (Cambridge: Cambridge University Press, 1999), 1052–78, 1210–19 (1067–78), and G. Bohak, *Ancient Jewish Magic: A History* (Cambridge: Cambridge University Press, 2007).
6 David E. Aune, 'Magic in Early Christianity', *Aufstieg und Niedergang der römischen Welt: Geschichte und Kultur Roms im Spiegel der neueren Forschung*, ed. H. Temporini and W. Haase (Berlin: de Gruyter, 1972), II.23.2 (1978), 1507–57 (1517–18), divides 'Graeco-Roman magical activities' into protective and apotropaic, aggressive and malevolent, love magic and magic aimed at the acquisition of power and control, and divination.
7 See B. Kollmann, *Jesus und die Christen als Wundertäter: Studien zu Magie, Medizin, und Schamanismus in Antike und Christentum*, Forschungen zur Religion und Literatur des Alten und Neuen Testaments 170 (Göttingen: Vandenhoeck & Ruprecht, 1996), 73–83.
8 Note Lucian's account of the activities of Alexander of Abonoteichos in his *Alexander*; and also the description in Tacitus, *History* 4.81.1–3;

Suetonius, *Vespasian* 7.2–3; and Dio Cassius, *History* 55.8.1–2, of the miracle performed by the Emperor Vespasian at Alexandria in 69 or 70 CE.

9 Harold Remus, *Pagan–Christian Conflict Over Miracle in the Second Century* (Cambridge, MA: The Philadelphia Patristic Foundation Ltd., 1983), 35–47.

10 Alexander fakes his divine ecstasy (*Alexander* 12–13), the epiphany of his oracular deity (13–17), and his wondrous feats are generally thought to be dubious (24; 28; 36; 59).

11 See James A. Francis, *Subversive Virtues: Asceticism and Authority in the Second Century Pagan World* (University Park: Pennsylvania State University Press, 1995), 92; and also A. F. Segal, 'Hellenistic Magic: Some Questions of Definition', in *Studies in Gnosticism and Hellenistic Religions*, ed. R. van den Broek and M. J. Vermaseren (Leiden: Brill, 1981), 349–75, 357.

12 Segal, 'Magic', 356.

13 See *ibid.*, 356–7; and M. W. Dickie, *Magic and Magicians in the Greco-Roman World* (London: Routledge, 2001), 192–3.

14 Septimius took a number of measures against magicians, threatening with death even those who simply possessed magical handbooks. On this, see Julius Paulus, the jurist, *Sententiae* v.xxiii.18.

15 Note how Apuleius in his *Apology* implies a positive understanding of the term (at 47 he differentiates between good and bad magic citing the XII Table) by associating it with the name of Persian priests, men, he claims, famous for their learning and sanctity. To be called such is no crime but rather a compliment (see *Apology* 25). See also Francis, *Virtues*, 92–3.

16 Francis, *Virtues*, 91–2, shows how the *Sententiae* of Julius Paulus (dating from c. 210 CE), while mentioning specific activities which are magical and punishable, does not define magic.

17 Aune, 'Magic', 1510–15, discusses the move from an almost moral approach to differentiating magic from religion, to a more sociologically/functionalist one.

18 Segal, 'Magic', 367.

19 Aune's definition of magic as 'that form of religious deviance whereby individual or social goals are sought by means alternate to those normally sanctioned by the dominant religious institution' (Aune, 'Magic', 1515), captures something of this social understanding of the term (he calls his definition 'structural-functionalist') insofar as it plays up the deviant character of what is defined as magic. Something of this is captured in the *Sententiae* of Julius Paulus, where it is stated that those who introduce new religious doctrines unknown to traditional usage are to be punished by exile or death.

20 A. B. Kolenkow, 'A Problem of Power: How Miracle Workers Counter Charges of Magic in the Hellenistic World', *Society of Biblical Literature Seminar Papers* 1 (Missoula: Scholars Press, 1976), 105–10 (107).

21 The opening chapters of Acts are filled with miracles, especially ones attributed to Peter (see, inter alia, 2.43; 3.1–2; 5.12–16). For miracles

involving Paul, see 13.4–12; 14.8–11; 16.16–18; 16.25–34; 19.11–20; 20.7–12; 28.3–6.

22 For an English translation, see J. K. Elliott, ed., *The Apocryphal New Testament: A Collection of Apocryphal Christian Literature in an English Translation Based on M. R. James* (Oxford: Oxford University Press, 1993).

23 Paul J. Achtemeier, 'Jesus and the Disciples as Miracle Workers in the Apocryphal New Testament', in *Aspects of Religious Propaganda in Early Christianity and Judaism*, ed. E. Schüssler-Fiorenza (Notre Dame: University of Notre Dame Press, 1976), 149–89 (164–8).

24 J. A. Kelhoffer, *Miracle and Mission: The Authentication of Missionaries and their Message in the Longer Ending of Mark*, Wissenschaftliche Untersuchungen zum Neuen Testament 2.112 (Tübingen: Mohr Siebeck, 2000), 271–81; and J. A. Kelhoffer, 'The Apostle Paul and Justin Martyr on the Miraculous: A Comparison of Appeals to Authority', *Greek, Roman, and Byzantine Studies* 42 (2001), 163–84 (165–75), for the points which follow.

25 On both occasions reference to 'power' and 'spirit' clearly imply miraculous activity. See especially Rom. 15.19 where Paul refers to the way in which he won obedience from the Gentiles 'by the power of signs and wonders, by the power of the spirit of God', where the latter phrase stands in apposition to the former.

26 This contrasts with Luke's understanding of an apostle in Acts which with one exception (Acts 14.4, 14) is associated with the Twelve. See Kelhoffer, *Miracle*, 277.

27 See Kelhoffer, *Miracle*.

28 Note the twice-repeated reference to 'signs and wonders' at 2 Cor. 12.12 and Rom. 15.19 where the phrase is clearly a biblical allusion, referring in particular to God's gracious acts on behalf of his people in the Exodus (see, inter alia, Deut. 13.1; 28.8, 46; 29.3), implying a rich theology of miracle.

29 On this, see John Ashton, *The Religion of Paul the Apostle* (London and New Haven: Yale University Press, 2000), 152–78.

30 See *Acts of Peter* 11–12. In the apocryphal acts, miracle working is associated exclusively with the apostles.

31 For this point, see J. A. Kelhoffer, 'Ordinary Christians as Miracle Workers in the New Testament and the Second and Third Century Christian Apologists', *Journal of the Chicago Society of Biblical Research* 44 (1999), 23–34.

32 See, inter alia, Justin, *Dialogue* 30–1; 35.7; 39.6; and 76. See also Theophilus, *To Autolycus* 2.8.7 for similar use of miracles. For discussion of these passages, see Kelhoffer, *Miracle*, 315–16.

33 See Justin, *First Apology* 30, who regards proof against the accusation that Jesus is a magician to lie in the fact he was the subject of Old Testament prophecy. See also Irenaeus, *Against Heresies* 2.32.4; and Origen, *Against Celsus* 2.48, both of whom point out that Jesus' miracles were predicted in the Old Testament.

34 See Lampe, 'Miracles', 211–12.

35 See Kelhoffer, *Miracle*, 281–2, for discussion of the relevant sources.
36 Peter Brown, *The World of Late Antiquity from Marcus Aurelius to Muhammed* (London: Thames and Hudson, 1971), 55, quoted by Ashton, *Religion of Paul*, 167.
37 References in J. A. Kelhoffer, '"Hippolytus" and Magic: An Examination of Elenchos IV 28–42 and Related Passages in Light of the Papyri Magicae', *Zetschrift für Antikes Christentum* 11 (2007–8), 517–48 (547).
38 Note also Irenaeus' comment about the heretic Markus who is 'a perfect adept at magic impostures, and by this means draws away a great number of men, and not a few women' (*Against Heresies* 1.13.1).
39 Further support for the idea that conversion and miracle are linked comes from the statistic presented by Gallagher, 'Conversion and Salvation in the Apocryphal Acts of the Apostles', *Second Century* 8 (1991), 16, that of the twenty-nine conversion stories found in the apocryphal acts, only twenty-two result from miracle. Of the seven remaining, two are tinged with the miraculous. See also S. L. Davies, *The Revolt of the Widows: The Social World of the Apocryphal Acts* (Carbondale, IL: Feffer and Simons, 1980), 44–5.
40 See Kelhoffer, *Miracle*, 321.
41 Gallagher, 'Conversion', 21. So in the *Acts of John* the cured die to their old lives which were dominated by error (33, 35, 42), shameful desires (33, 35) and idols (40, 41); and they rise into a new life marked by celibacy, purity and abstinence (53). Note should also be taken of the conversion of Stratocles in Sinai Greek Ms. 256 of the *Acts of Andrew* where Andrew's exorcizing of Stratocles' servant is followed by Stratocles being preached to by Andrew 'day and night', and only then is he thought worthy of conversion.
42 See in particular Acts 2.22, 43; 4.30; 5.12; 6.8; 7.36; 14.3; and 15.12 for the use of the phrase; and comments at n. 25 above.
43 For miracles performed in the name of Jesus, see Acts 4.10; 16.18; 19.13, 17.
44 See Lampe, 'Miracles', 209.
45 See *Against Celsus* 2.48, where Origen defends the reality of the stories of Jesus' raising people from the dead on the grounds that if they were untrue, there would be many more of them in the gospels than the three that are recorded.
46 See Remus, *Conflict*, for many of the texts cited here.
47 See Acts 8.9–24; Justin, *First Apology* 26.2; *Acts of Peter* 28; Irenaeus, *Against Heresies* 1.13; 2.31.2–3; 2.32; and Hippolytus, *Elenchos* 6.39.1 (of Marcus); 9.14.2–3 (of the Elchasaites); and 6.7.1 (of Simon Magus). These and other references are discussed by Kelhoffer, 'Hippolytus', 539–42.
48 In the *Acts of John* a praetor accuses John of being a sorcerer (31); and in the *Acts of Paul* Paul is condemned as a sorcerer by the crowds (15; 20).
49 See Irenaeus, *Against Heresies* 2.32.5 and *Sibylline Oracles* 8.272–3, where the coming one will do everything with a word. Achtemeier, 'Workers', 169–70, shows how the authors of the apocryphal acts go out of their way to perform miracles without aids. Note, for instance, how in the *Acts of John* 31–7, John is commanded to perform a miracle naked so that he may hide nothing.

50 Remus, *Conflict*, 137.
51 For earliest examples of this, see Mark 7.22; Luke 10.17; and also Acts 3.6, 16; 4.7, 10, 30; 16.18; and James 5.14. For later Christian contrasts between miracles in the name of Jesus and pagan and Jewish use of spells and other manipulations, see Justin, *Second Apology* 6; and Irenaeus, *Against Heresies* 2.32.5. On the phenomenon generally, see Aune, 'Magic', 1545–9, and Kollmann, *Jesus*, 350–1.
52 Note Origen's statement that they (the Christians) 'do not get the power which they seem to possess by any incantations but by the name of Jesus *with the recital of the histories about him*', implying the actual reading of books (*Against Celsus* 1.6, italics mine); see also *Against Celsus* 7.67, discussed by Kelhoffer, *Miracle*, 333.
53 Aune, 'Magic', 1545.
54 Aune, 'Magic', 1545, notes that when in Acts 9.34 Peter exclaims, 'Aeneas, Jesus Christ heals you!' we have a phenomenon which could be understood as necromancy for, like John the Baptist, Jesus was a 'biaiothanatos', that is, a person who had died a premature, violent death, and such spirits were available to become subject to the control of magicians. On prayer and spells more generally, see Aune, 'Magic', 1551–2; and for parallels between Christian formulae accompanying exorcisms and healings and similar formulae in the magical papyri, see Kollmann, *Jesus*, 352–3.
55 A. Wypustek, 'Magic, Montanism, Perpetua, and the Severan Persecution', *Vigiliae Christianae* 51 (1997), 276–97 (285–7). On the speculative character of this claim, see William Tabbernee, *Fake Prophecy and Polluted Sacraments: Ecclesiastical and Imperial Reactions to Montanism* (Leiden: Brill, 2007), 182–4.
56 *Against Celsus* 6.40. See Kollmann, *Jesus*, 349.
57 Clement of Alexandria, *Paidagogos* 3.11, mentions rings with images of Orpheus on them as signs of Christ. But he makes no reference to their usage.
58 See Aune, 'Magic'.
59 See E. V. Gallagher, *Divine Man or Magician? Celsus and Origen on Jesus* (Chico: Scholars Press, 1982).
60 See also Irenaeus, *Against Heresies* 2.32.4.
61 See Kollmann, *Jesus*, 362–75, who argues for the truth of the claim. See Irenaeus, *Against Heresies* 2.32.4; and Tertullian, *Apology* 37.9.
62 See Remus, *Conflict*, 105–7.
63 Ashton, *Religion*, 169.

Further reading

Achtemeier, Paul J., 'Jesus and the Disciples as Miracle Workers in the Apocryphal New Testament', in *Aspects of Religious Propaganda in Early Christianity and Judaism*, ed. E. Schüssler-Fiorenza (Notre Dame: University of Notre Dame Press, 1976), 149–89

Ashton, John, *The Religion of Paul the Apostle* (London and New Haven: Yale University Press, 2000)

Aune, David E., 'Magic in Early Christianity', *Aufstieg und Niedergang der römischen Welt* II.23.2 (1978), 1507–57

Betz, H. D., *The Greek Magical Papyri in Translation* (Chicago: University of Chicago Press, 1992)

Bovon, F., 'Miracle, Magic, and Healing in the Apocryphal Acts of the Apostles', in *Studies in Early Christianity*, ed. F. Bovon (Grand Rapids: Baker, 2003), 253–66

Davies, S. L., *The Revolt of the Widows: The Social World of the Apocryphal Acts* (Carbondale, IL: Feffer and Simons, 1980)

Dickie, M. W., *Magic and Magicians in the Greco-Roman World* (London: Routledge, 2001)

Elliott, J. K., ed., *The Apocryphal New Testament: A Collection of Apocryphal Christian Literature in an English Translation Based on M. R. James* (Oxford: Oxford University Press, 1993)

Francis, James A., *Subversive Virtues: Asceticism and Authority in the Second Century Pagan World* (University Park: Pennsylvania State University Press, 1995)

Gallagher, E. V., 'Conversion and Salvation in the Apocryphal Acts of the Apostles', *Second Century* 8 (1991), 13–29

Gibbon, E., *The History of the Decline and Fall of the Roman Empire*, vol. I, ed. D. Wormersley (London: Penguin, 2005)

Kelhoffer, J. A., 'Ordinary Christians as Miracle Workers in the New Testament and the Second and Third Century Christian Apologists', *Journal of the Chicago Society of Biblical Research* 44 (1999), 23–34

Miracle and Mission: The Authentication of Missionaries and their Message in the Longer Ending of Mark, Wissenschaftliche Untersuchungen zum Neuen Testament 2.112 (Tübingen: Mohr Siebeck, 2000)

'The Apostle Paul and Justin Martyr on the Miraculous: A Comparison of Appeals to Authority', *Greek, Roman, and Byzantine Studies* 42 (2001), 163–84

Kolenkow, A. B., 'A Problem of Power: How Miracle Workers Counter Charges of Magic in the Hellenistic World', *Society of Biblical Literature Seminar Papers* 1 (Missoula: Scholars Press, 1976), 105–10

Kollmann, B., *Jesus und die Christen als Wundertäter: Studien zu Magie, Medizin, und Schamanismus in Antike und Christentum*, Forschungen zur Religion und Literatur des Alten und Neuen Testaments 170 (Göttingen: Vandenhoeck & Ruprecht, 1996)

Lampe, G. W. H., 'Miracles and Early Christian Apologetic', in *Miracles: Cambridge Studies in their Philosophy and History*, ed. C. F. D. Moule (London: A. R. Mowbray, 1970), 205–18

MacMullen, R., *Christianizing the Roman Empire (A. D. 100–400)* (New Haven and London: Yale University Press, 1984)

*Remus, Harold, *Pagan–Christian Conflict Over Miracle in the Second Century* (Cambridge, MA: The Philadelphia Patristic Foundation Ltd., 1983)

Segal, A. F., 'Hellenistic Magic: Some Questions of Definition', in *Studies in Gnosticism and Hellenistic Religions*, ed. R. van den Broek and M. J. Vermaseren (Leiden: Brill, 1981), 349–75

8 Miracles in the Middle Ages

BENEDICTA WARD

An understanding of miracle is central to Christianity but it has always been a point of discussion and argument. At present its meaning is limited by the dictionary definition of the English word miracle: 'A marvellous event exceeding the known powers of nature and therefore supposed to be due to the special intervention of the deity or of some supernatural agency'.[1] This is to stress its etymology which derives its meaning from the Latin *mirare*, to wonder. Exclusive stress is thereby laid on that which causes wonder and amazement to us; a miracle is then seen as the subject of divine intervention, contrary to the known laws of nature.

Popular use of the word supports this meaning, which unfortunately suggests that the more that is known about the laws of nature the less room there is for intervention by God. Miracle is then seen as opposed to nature, in terms of inexplicable wonder of the ignorant, but that is not the basic understanding of miracle within the Christian church in the ancient or medieval world. The statement 'the world is full of miracles' would not then have meant 'the constant infraction of the course of this world' principally because the notion of the law of nature was not used; it would have meant 'everything created is a wonder issuing from the hand of God'; miracle was seen as *sign*, stressing theological meaning rather than psychological reaction.

For the thousand years which we call the 'Middle Ages' and in every part of the known world, there are records asserting that 'miracles' abounded, affecting every part of human life. Through the multitude of records it is clear that for the medieval church there was only one miracle, that of creation, with its corollary of re-creation by the resurrection of Christ. God, they held, created the world out of nothing in six days, and within that initial creation he planted all the possibilities for the future. All creation was, therefore, both 'natural' and 'miraculous': all natural things were filled with the miraculous. The events of every day, the birth of children, the growth of plants, rainfall, were all 'daily miracles', signs of the mysterious creative power of God at work in the universe. But they also held that human beings were so accustomed to these 'daily miracles' that they were no longer moved to awe by them and needed to be provoked to reverence by unusual manifestations of God's power. These were events within the original creation, hidden within the nature and appearance of things, which at times caused 'miracles' that seemed to be contrary to nature but were in fact inherent in it. The most usual channel for these 'hidden causes' to be made manifest was the prayers of the saints, living and dead, which was the re-creating work of Christ through them. Events happened in nature or miraculously, but both were equally the work of God.

In the Christian world, it was inevitable that miracles should be valued. Not only was the basis of faith revelation, but the biblical texts were so well known as to be internalized and known in the heart, especially the gospels, which contained accounts of *signa*, beginning with the first 'sign' wrought by Jesus at Cana (John 2.11). There was debate about whether the signs ceased with the ascension of Christ and the coming of the Spirit, but with the need for missions to convert the barbarian tribes, the signs were held to continue. The *signa* began to be called *miracula* ('wonders') or *dunameis* ('acts of power'); they were read about in the gospel and such stories of the power of God showed him to be still active today. It is not surprising that all kinds of medieval texts, not only religious writings but histories, documents, charters, laws, etc. contain references to miracles; it would be surprising if they were absent.

From the fourth century onwards, miracles had been often connected with holy places, such as the tomb of Christ, or holy events such as martyrdom, and especially with the saints, those who were thought to have most clearly embodied the love and power of God in their lives. Miracles were signs that God was able to work uniquely through them and such signs would be seen in their lives and also after their death. This is connected with the theology of Christ as the second Adam, re-creating all the world in a redeemed form, so that a new relationship is set up between humanity and all creation by God's redeeming work. This is often seen in the relationship of love and respect between the saints and the four elements, the plants, the animals and the birds, as well as in human relationships, and events relating to this were also called miracles: among the early Christian monks in Egypt, for example, Antony cured the blind cubs of a hyena, lions came to serve holy men in life and also to help bury them at death. In Anglo-Saxon England, Cuthbert was given gifts by ravens, Guthlac was always miraculously surrounded by birds, Aiden could divert fire from destroying a town.

This integral attitude to miracles as part of redeemed creation is to be found in early Greek texts which were translated into Latin and continued to exercise a profound influence on Christian life. Alongside accounts of miraculous events, there was the teaching of St Augustine on miracles, particularly in book 22 of the *City of God*. The pattern of thought had been adequately set and there was no need to rethink the subject until the twelfth and thirteenth centuries. Between Augustine and Aquinas, there was no major philosophical treatise on miracles. For Augustine, and his hearers and readers, the central miracle was redemption; contemporary miracles were seen in relation to the life of conversion of the redeemed. They were evidences of grace abounding, ways of recognizing and entering into the central miracle of Christ's redeeming work.

Miraculous events were combined with theory by Augustine when, in 416, the relics of St Stephen were brought from Jerusalem to Hippo; miracles, mainly cures, occurred, and Augustine ordered that they should be carefully recorded and publicly proclaimed (*City of God* 22.8). He wanted exact first-hand details of these events, and the collection he had made was the first miracle book of the Middle Ages; he insisted that a permanent record should be kept for the future, but he also wanted the miracles known about, there and then, in order to edify his own Christian congregation. These were miracles which were related to the bones of the first martyr, Stephen, a biblical person from the apostolic age, and Augustine had no hesitation about accepting them and using them. Miracles performed by saintly living men were respected but those connected with the bodies of dead saints known in the Bible proved especially congenial to the newly converted barbarians in the West.

Following Augustine's example, another influential writer used the same method of examining the miracles of living and dead saints and presenting them for the purpose of preaching. This can be seen in the works of the Venerable Bede (673–735 CE). Bede's most usual word for miracle is not *miracula* but *signa*. He was interested in establishing the external details of events in the same way in which he was concerned with the grammatical text of the Scriptures: the words needed to be exact in order for the reader to pass safely through to their inner significance. It was not marvellous phenomena as such that he looked for but the significance of these and of all events. He agreed with

Gregory the Great that it was a greater miracle to save a sinner than to raise the dead. Bede used accounts of miracles of the living and the dead in a particularly interior way; his question was always, 'why?', 'what does this signify for me?'. This was in line with his view of the Bible; he understood the Scriptures as a letter written by God to mankind which needed continual exploration to understand its full and present meaning. The literal sense needed to be established, but the real interest lay in the inner spiritual meaning for the hearer. Likewise the world was to Bede and his contemporaries a back-drop to a great panorama where man was both audience and actor; events in contemporary life were first to be established, *literaliter*, but then the true interest lay in their significance, *spiritualiter*. When a miracle-working girdle vanished mysteriously from a nunnery the question for Bede was not how did this happen, but why.[2] The answer was that it happened in order that the nuns might not become superstitious or contentious about the girdle as a relic. When lightning rolled around the heavens, it was both to show the good the power of God and to terrify the ungodly.[3] Layer after layer of meaning and significance could be uncovered in miracles; and it was the effect they had on recipients that was central. Bede looked to present and future significance rather than to the past of events.

From the eleventh and twelfth centuries, however, it seems that thought about miracles underwent some changes. Perhaps 'change' is too strong a word; it was more that the traditional approach to miracles continued and deepened especially in monastic circles, until it emerged as so interior that it could quite easily be divorced from external reality altogether. Meanwhile, a secondary theme, the mechanics of events, always there but rarely emerging, became more prominent until it took over altogether later as science.

The great figure of the period is Bernard of Clairvaux and he is an example of both the interior theme of signs and exterior events called miracles. For Bernard, as for Augustine and Bede, the great miracle was salvation: 'there are three miracles', he wrote, 'the union of God and man, of mother and virgin, and of faith and the human heart'.[4] For his monks he consistently urged the interior view of miracles: in his sermon on St Martin he urged his hearers to distinguish between miracles which were to be wondered at, and virtues which were to be imitated. Wonder at the works of the Almighty, whether the creation of children, the fall of rain, the beauty of a flower or an unlooked-for cure was excellent, but more than wonder was needed on the Christian path. In a sermon on St Victor, Bernard presented the saint's miracles for the wonder of hearers, but stressed rather the miracle of his good works, which were to be imitated.[5] When his friend, Malachy of Armagh, died Bernard instituted a miracle of healing with the body of Malachy at his funeral, saying that his goodness was such a wonder that no one would believe it except for miracles that surrounded him; but he concluded, 'Malachy's miracle was himself'.[6] In this he was following, of course, St Paul, 'though I speak with the tongues of men and of angels and have not charity I am become as sounding brass or a tinkling cymbal'(I Cor. 13.1). However, as will be shown later, alongside his spiritual, interior view of miracles, Bernard was also a protagonist of cures as exterior events.

This double approach to miracles in Bernard was reflected in miracles inside and outside the Cistercian cloister. Within the Order, the Cistercians produced large miracle collections, book after book of miracles, recorded most of all about Cistercians, by Cistercians, for Cistercians. These miracles were predominantly about that most interior of all miracles, visions. The monks saw angels in choir and cloister, helping their work and prayer, saints walked beside them as they goaded home tired cattle, the Virgin Mary wiped the sweat from the brows of Cistercian reapers. An old lay brother, jealous of the attentions of an angel who supported another brother in choir when he was sick, tried to catch the angel for himself and rushed after him down the choir. These were above all authenticating miracles, a kind of propaganda internal to the Order, to urge the brethren to continue in what must have seemed at times an uncongenial if not intolerable way of life. Visions of future glory in store for the faithful Cistercian and the perils awaiting him if he left the Order were particularly forceful. In this plethora of miracles, it could be said that the monks had taken the interiorizing attitude to miracles to its extreme, and rejected the actuality of miracles as events altogether. In the record of practical miracles of judgment, or of favour, the cures of illness, events happening to people who could be identified and known by name, place, occupation, such details became less and less necessary in the cloister and could be changed at will. The emphasis in these stories was entirely on what was edifying, on what was interior, on what would strengthen and convert.

It was a short step from such interiorization to the collections of miracles as *exempla*, for use in sermons. It is possible to see this result in the thirteenth century in the *Exordium Magnum Cisterciense*,[7] the miracle book of Conrad, a thirteenth-century Cistercian abbot of Eberbach. After five books of miracles about individual Cistercians, the miraculous rewards of their praiseworthy behaviour and their visions, the last two books are simply stories illustrating certain dangers, certain themes; the need for facts had reached its lowest level and all that mattered was that the stories should illustrate a theme, usually didactic, aimed at moral improvement.

The greatest number of miracles of interiority was the huge number of stories told about the Virgin Mary.[8] According to the New Testament, the person closest to Christ in his earthly life was his mother, Mary. All that is known of her life is written in the discreet pages of the gospels and Acts; later some material was added from the romance of the *Proto Evangelion of St James*. Everything that is known about miracles during her lifetime can be summed up in one phrase: 'Mary kept all these things and pondered them in her heart' (Luke 2.19). In her, the greatest of miracles took place; God became man, the virgin became a mother, the Word became flesh. Mary was entirely absorbed by her Son, and any other account of marvels in her life would have seemed impertinent.

This was not the case, however, with thought in the later Middle Ages about Mary. Both theological reflection and devout meditation were confident that one so near to Christ must share especially closely in His redeeming work, and moreover be compassionately ready to use her intimate relationship with her son to plead for sinners. The immense increase in devotion to Mary in the later Middle Ages was part of a new concern with the human person of Jesus Christ. As well as traditional devotion to the redeeming Saviour, increasingly attention focused on the poor man of Galilee, his birth and childhood and his sufferings on the cross, along with Mary as a human mother who suckled the child and suffered with him at the foot of the cross. She was seen, therefore, as a loving woman who would always be available to show mercy to suppliants. Innumerable miracles were attributed to her and became the centre of the most important pilgrimages of the later Middle Ages. Her miracles were associated with shrines in her honour or with special devotions to her, but they were also focused on physical remains connected with her. These relics were unexpected, since Mary, like her Son, was held to have been taken straight into heaven at her death. Like the Holy Sepulchre of Christ, the tomb in which the Virgin's dead body was laid was found to be empty. No body, no relics, and therefore no bones of the Virgin Mary have ever been invented; but even more than in the case of Christ, devout imagination demanded physical, tangible relics, most often of an intimate kind. Some are connected with her part in the infancy of Christ, some with her place during his death, and a few simply with her own person.

Her shift, her slipper, her hair, drops of milk from her breast, provided the emotional focus for the building of great cathedrals and drew pilgrims in their thousands. With no warrant whatsoever in Scripture, miracles connected with the relics of the Virgin became an essential part of medieval life. Miracles of the Virgin were often connected with her protection in times of danger, especially the ultimate danger of death and judgment. Throughout the thirteenth century, she was exalted increasingly as a loving woman, concerned above all with mercy and pity towards the poor, the sinful, the needy.

Miracles as interior conversion and exterior cure were held together throughout the Middle Ages, but a new attitude which challenged this understanding was the approach which asked the question 'how' instead of providing the reason 'why' miracles took place: looking at the past mechanics of an event rather than its then-current meaning. It was to become a scientific approach with a great future; it raised new questions about biblical miracles. Augustine had, to some extent, been interested in the 'how' question, and devoted a chapter of the *City of God* to a discussion of the natural causes of wonders in nature. But for him to understand how something had been performed enhanced rather than destroyed its wonder: they were still works of God for our benefit. But in the twelfth century, a new interest in secondary causes pointed the way towards scepticism, towards the impression that because certain causes had been discerned, the miracle could be explained. Here the criticism of Guibert of Nogent (c. 1055–1124) about the validity of a relic which its owner claimed was a tooth of Christ was symptomatic of a new interest in the causes of miracles. For Augustine, exploring the mechanics of events had added to their credibility, but in the twelfth century it was otherwise. Simon of Tournai, for instance, asked how the raising of Lazarus happened.[9] Was his breath suspended and then restored? Could he eat? Was he able to live, though still dead? Could he marry, beget children and, if so, how? Would he die? He asked similar questions about the miracle of the loaves and fishes: how were they multiplied? Did the loaves grow larger or were there many small loaves from the original five? In the thirteenth century, an Irish commentary on the Scriptures, *De Mirabilibus Sacrae Scripturae*, asked the same 'how' question: how, for instance, did Christ and Peter walk on water: 'It is possible to ask whether the bodies of the Lord and St Peter grew lighter in their nature so that the water held them up or if the water solidified so that it could support human bodies'.[10] These seemed to many to be strange questions, but they were ones that related to a new interest in the mechanics of events. The concept of an 'order of nature' which presupposed also an order of super-nature was emerging, which was to become increasingly significant in relation to miracles.

This pondering of the mechanics of events of miracles was one way of thinking, but there was also, as has been seen, a divorce of miracles from any actual event so that they could be changed at will, which led also to a use similarly separated from edification in the new world of romance and entertainment. Chroniclers, for instance, described miraculous events, but their interest was not in their meaning or in their mechanics but in entertainment: by presenting exciting, marvellous, new and wonderful details of events, as just that. William of Newburgh, for example, described the fate of three men mysteriously dead in a pit not as an instance of divine judgment or as a warning against bad behaviour, but as a strange accident caused by the presence of quick-lime.[11] He dwelt at length on ghosts, vampires, and the strange and terrible hauntings of graveyards in the countryside; he even described the visit of the first Martians in his story of the green children who suddenly appeared in a village. William of Malmesbury mixed his stories of miracles connected with saints with stories about Siamese twins, a witch carried off by demons, and the extraordinary tale of a man bitten by a leopard.[12] When mice came, as was their due, to eat him, the man jumped into the sea to escape them and swam out towards a ship; the mice swam after him, sailing on the rinds of pomegranates. These stories were all recounted as 'marvels', they were not about actual cures and they were far-removed from the interiority of Augustine, Bede and Bernard.

It was all very well to assert that all that mattered was salvation, revealed by sign or wonder, but there were many who simply wanted results from miracles, here and now and for them; there were sick to be cured, dangers to be averted, justice to be bestowed, judgments to be changed for the better. For most people, what they looked for were events to help in this world and, in a situation which was virtually without access to medicine or to justice for the majority, appeal to the intervention of the saints, especially by prayer at the places where they were buried, increased. When stories of actual cures by the saints' miracles were recounted, symbolism was there but there were also practical details. The following story told in the great collection of posthumous miracles of Thomas Becket is typical; in it, there is a propaganda theme but also an insistence on fact:

> On the next day the light of a fourth miracle shone in Canterbury. A poor woman of our city, called Brithiva, had become blind. She held darkness to be the same as light. Although royalty remained

silent, Brithiva, simple, illiterate and physically blind, believed Thomas to be a martyr. She sought a hospice where she asked if anything was there that had been in contact with the martyr. She asked to borrow anything of that sort and a woman there offered her a garment stained with the martyr's blood. Believing, she rubbed the cloth over her eyes and in so doing rubbed away the darkness of her malady. Others had guided her there but she went away needing the help of no one.[13]

In the miracles attributed to Frideswide of Oxford, the story of a north-country clerk, Stephen, was certainly geared to show the power of the saint, but the events themselves were carefully recorded about this early instance of a student with Oxford influenza:

A zealous clerk called Stephen, from Yorkshire, came and lived in Oxford at that time. He was clever for his age and outstandingly beautiful, but a daily fever afflicted him and made him seek the help of doctors. He spent all his money on them in vain, and he grew worse each day. When human assistance failed, he fled to heavenly help. He was so wasted that he could hardly stand, his eyes were sunk, and his face pale; he went and prayed the virgin Frideswide to help him and after he had drunk the water at her shrine and rested from the exhaustion caused by the fever, he recovered and his full strength gradually returned.[14]

The care for salvation through signs and wonders did not, then, exclude a practical approach to events. During the lives of saints as well as after their death, miraculous cures were recorded, though the saint in question may well have taken a highly symbolic stance about such matters. For instance, while Bernard, as has been discussed earlier, influenced the interiorization of miracle in his writings, in the eyes of those who knew him he was seen as a practical wonder-worker. He performed hundreds, if not thousands, of miracles, most of which were curative. He did them while he was alive, and he did them willingly. He asserted the profound truth that love was the only miracle, but found that others wanted to experience this in practice. Bernard provides an excellent picture of the two main themes about miracles in the Middle Ages – the interiority which asks why the miracle happens and the external demand for cures. Bernard was in no way concerned with the approach which wants to know 'how'; everything happened by the will of God, that was the answer to any question about mechanics. But in spite of Bernard's interior spiritual understanding of miracle as sign, he was deeply involved in miracles as events, especially in Geoffrey of Auxerre's account of Bernard's preaching of the Second Crusade in Germany.[15] It seems to be a unique record of its kind and it is difficult to know quite how to interpret it. It is predominantly about a group which accompanied Bernard, recording miracles as they happened. The account falls into three parts, each covering a different section of the journey, and the people involved in making the record were well known and trustworthy. They are about Bernard the saint and inter-iorizer, but they provide an excellent example of miracles performed as a living saint, recorded in meticulous detail by well-informed, astute and reputable observers:

> As they travelled, the companions saw Bernard acting as another Christ and they wrote down every day what each of them had seen. The pattern was simplicity itself:

> EBERHARD: On that day I saw him cure three others who were lame.
> FRANCO: You all saw the blind woman who came into church and received her sight before the people.
> GUADRIC: And we saw that a girl whose hand was withered had it healed, while the chant at the offertory was being sung.
> GERARD: On the same day I saw a boy receive his sight.
> BISHOP HERMAN: The priest of the town of Herenheim, for so it was called, showed me a man who had been blind for ten years who came from his home on the first Sunday of Advent, and was blessed by Bernard as he passed and he returned to his home seeing. I had heard of this before and everyone in that area confirmed it.
> EBERHARD: I heard from two honest men, one a priest the other a monk, about two people in the town of Lapenheim who on that same day were blessed and received sight.
> PHILIP: On Monday in my presence a blind man was led into the church and after the saint had laid his hand on him, just as you have heard from everyone, the people proclaimed that he could see.
> ABBOT FROWIN: I myself with brother Godfrey saw that man coming in.
> FRANCO: On Tuesday, in Frieburg the mother of a blind boy brought him in the morning to our lodging; and when the Father was told that after he had touched him he could see, he ordered inquiries to be made about him; and I myself did this. I interrogated the boy and he replied that he could see clearly and proved it with many actions.

This uniquely practical account formed a part of the *Vita Prima*, a record of Bernard's public life; while it showed that Bernard worked miracles and cured many, it also claimed that when Bernard went home or visited another Cistercian house, he ceased his miracles, partly to spare the monks the disturbances created by crowds asking for cures, but also because he recognized that within the cloister the interest of the monks was in a different kind of wonder: the inner miracles of prayer and salvation. This theme of the 'monastic' Bernard prevailed in the account of his posthumous cult. After his death a cure was reported during his funeral and the brothers were dismayed by the excitement it caused. It was said that the abbot ordered Bernard to stop performing miracles, 'He asked him by virtue of obedience not to perform any more miracles' and Conrad of Eberbach adds, 'from that day until now he has never been seen to do any miracles in public'.[16] This may be a pious invention to cover a lack of actual miracles, but it is also indicative of one of the main elements in the image of Bernard as *vir Dei*. What did Bernard himself think about his own signs and wonders? In a letter to the Cistercian pope, Eugenius, he wrote:

> But perhaps they say, how shall we know if this word comes from the Lord? What signs have you given that we may believe in you? I do not reply to that; spare my modesty. Reply on my behalf and for yourself also, according to that which you have heard and seen or according as God inspires you to answer.[17]

Bernard had no doubts about the miracles, and his unswerving belief in the cause of God overflowed in his preaching, drawing crowds to hear him, most of whom would have had no Latin. For this very reason, for many the impact of the experience of his presence rather than his words was foremost and led to physical healing. Others, including some of those cured, were inwardly inspired, and took the cross; some joined Bernard and returned with him to the novitiate at Clairvaux. Geoffrey mentions thirty such men, including Archdeacon Philip of Liège, Alexander of Cologne and Volkmar, chaplain to the Bishop of Constance.

The details given of the journey and of those present were not in question; it was clear where they went and who they were. What, then, did they see? They affirm that they saw and heard Bernard being asked to cure the sick and him doing so. Can these first-hand records of such miraculous cures be considered as events, taking place visibly during the three months of the tour of Germany? It seems that they could: they were events which were seen and recorded by well-known monks and clerics. Bernard himself took an active and even eager part in the cures. He would make the sign of the cross and pray for a cure in the name of Christ, or the Trinity or just himself. On several occasions he was interested in the outcome of events and sent his companions to see if the person concerned was really cured. There was an overwhelming demand from crowds for his power and a confident expectation of cures. Often, he was lost in the crowds so that his companions could not observe his actions. Emotion similar to that at the shrines of the saints accompanied these scenes, with shouts of 'Christ is risen', the ringing of bells, weeping, repentance and public jubilation.

The number of cures performed must have been considerably more than those recorded, but the records note the healing of 235 cripples, 172 blind as well as cures of the deaf and dumb, demoniacs and those afflicted with other illnesses. People came to Bernard as a healer, and in their veneration of him they treated him very much as they would treat the relics of a dead saint at his tomb. These miracles are close to shrine miracles, both in their nature and in their number. Respected witnesses wrote down what they saw. Why, then, was this type of account of Bernard not used by later writers, such as Herbert of Clairvaux, Caesarius or Conrad? Why was this form of record not used again? Above all, why was it not acceptable for his canonization?

I think the record-takers provided the wrong information. The records provide almost no details about the recipients of these miraculous cures: 'a boy', 'a woman of the town', 'a man' are usually all that is given, unless the one cured was already known to the party, as in the case of Anselm of Havelberg. This vagueness may point to the authenticity of the record. The party was among crowds of unknown non-latinate people, and the difficulty of communication and also of note-taking must have been considerable. Moreover, the link between virtue and miracle was assumed and not specifically made. The observers stressed their own probity and the goodness of Bernard, but did not give the first-hand details about those cured which was what was increasingly required.

Official canonization was evolving and the witness of good men to miracles was not sufficient: Innocent III demanded detailed accounts, that is, first-hand experiences, not only of what was seen by *vires auctorabiles*, but the evidence of those actually cured. Canonization was now beginning to be seen as a papal perquisite,[18] with clear expectations about what evidence was required. Alexander III canonized Bernard on 18 January 1174. Eleven years earlier he had been asked to canonize him at the Council of Tours, but this was postponed as there were too many applications for papal canonization for them to be considered during the council. By the time application was made again, expectations about miracles had changed. Bad men and heretics could carry out miracles, so it was not simply evidence of exterior miracle that was required, but marks of interior virtue in the proponent of the cure. There was no doubt about the virtues of Bernard, but the elaborate evidence from Germany was not quite what was wanted on another count: first-hand evidence had now to be given by the subjects of the miracles themselves. The classic and acceptable account of miracles for canonization at this time was the dossier of miracles attributed to Gilbert of Sempringham, one of the few canonizations by Innocent III. Name, place, status, condition of the one cured and the manner of cure were recorded, as well as details about the witnesses and also the reputation for virtue of the saint. 'Reliable witnesses' were being supplemented by those who had experienced cures physically, in a literal sense.

The new concern for evidence of virtue in the lives of those committing miracles was an attitude which ruled out local miracle workers like St Guinefort and fair Rosamund. Bernard was too well known to be kept out of the canon of the saints for that reason, but the account of Bernard in Germany, dependent as no other on the *vidi* of eye-witnesses, was already out of date when it was recorded. A misunderstanding of the new requirements for canonization meant that it was not repeated elsewhere. Certainly to Bernard's companions and, indeed, to Bernard himself, such events revealed the power of God acting in the world; they were recorded precisely to show the glory of God in a living man. But simply saying what you had seen was not enough for the new process of canonization. The new rules stressed two things: miracles were on the one hand *signa*, signs of redemption linked to virtue in the exponents, and they were also events for which was demanded detailed evidence from those who were cured.

How, then, were miracles actually seen? When we talk about 'seeing miracles', sight and seeing are always double sided, and that is the way we use 'to see' in normal conversation. 'I see' or 'I see' means two things: to see with the eyes, or to see with understanding. There is a change here between modern times and the Middle Ages: we think we have not 'seen' until our physical eyes have looked; they thought one cannot 'see' physically until one understands. For them, what was foremost was not the eyes of the body, but the 'eyes' of the heart. The eyes and their sight might be a way to inner understanding; sight was important, but never final. 'To see' mattered when it led to understanding which could not be reached in any other way. There is a poetic dimension to medieval discussions of reality, especially with regard to miracles, and inner sight was what mattered. To see in itself with the eyes was not enough; physical vision was flawed – the end that was sought was the vision of God: wonders and signs were nothing in themselves but pointed towards the end of a restored creation, whether for Augustine or for Bernard. And even then, inner seeing is not the end:

> We shall rest and we shall see; we shall see and we shall love; we shall love and we shall praise; behold what shall be in the end without end.[19]

To conclude: miracles abounded in the Middle Ages and were recorded in the accounts of saints, shrines, pilgrimages, liturgy and daily life. Their ultimate literary source was the Bible, where *miracula* was not the word used but *signa*, not wonder, but meaning. But the signs were always recounted in detail as events attesting the reality of God-with-man on earth. The pattern for these medieval accounts of cures is biblical; gospel cures were the familiar pattern. However many details might be altered according to social situation, the need of the recipients was the same. Medieval miracles had the same message as those in the gospels: God is among us, God is for us and God is in us. There was also, then, as always, the same human need for cures of the same types of sickness, a kind of *koinonia* of suffering, which reached out to God-in-Christ for not only salvation but earthly help in ultimate and personal need. Miracles in the Middle Ages were seen as facts: they were spiritualized, theologized and criticized, but they continued to be recorded as events about people in detail.

Notes

1 C. T. Onions *et al.*, eds., *The Shorter Oxford English Dictionary*, 2 vols. (Oxford: Clarendon Press, 1973), vol. II, 1331 ('miracle').
2 Bede, 'The Life of St Cuthbert', ch. 23, in Bede, *Two Lives of Saint Cuthbert: A Life by an Anonymous Monk of Lindisfarne and Bede's Prose Life*, texts, translation and notes by Bertram Colgrave (Cambridge: Cambridge University Press, 1940, 1985), 231–5.
3 *Bede's Ecclesiastical History of the English People*, ed. Bertram Colgrave and R. A. B. Mynors, Oxford Medieval Texts (Oxford: Clarendon Press, 1969), 343–4 (4.3). For a discussion of Bede and miracles, see Benedicta Ward, 'Miracles and History: A Reconsideration of the Miracle Stories used by Bede', in *Famulus Christi: Essays in Commemoration of the Thirteenth Centenary of the Birth of the Venerable Bede*, ed. Gerald Bonner (London: SPCK, 1976), 70–7, and William D. McCready, *Miracles*

and the Venerable Bede (Toronto: Pontifical Institute of Mediaeval Studies, 1994).

4 Bernard of Clairvaux, 'In Vigilia Nativitatis: Sermo Tertius' ('Third Sermon for the Vigil of the Nativity of the Lord'), in Sancti Bernardi, *Opera*, 8 vols., vol. IV (Rome: Editiones Cistercienses, 1966), 216–17.

5 Bernard of Clairvaux, 'In Natali Sancti Victoris: Sermo Primus' ('On the Anniversary of St Victor: First Sermon'), in Sancti Bernardi, *Opera*, 8 vols., vol. VI.1 (Rome: Editiones Cistercienses, 1970), 30–1.

6 Bernard of Clairvaux, 'Vita Sancti Malachiae' ('The Life of St Malachy'), in Sancti Bernardi, *Opera*, 8 vols., vol. III (Rome: Editiones Cistercienses, 1970), 370.

7 Conrad, Abbot of Eberbach and Bruno Griesser, *Exordium magnum Cisterciense, sive, Narratio de initio Cisterciensis Ordinis*, Series scriptorum S. Ordinis Cisterciensis 2 (Rome: Editiones Cistercienses, 1961); English trans. Benedicta Ward and Paul Savage, *Great Beginnings of Citeaux: The Exordium Magnum of Conrad of Eberbach* (Collegeville: Cistercian Publications, 2009).

8 For an introduction to the miracles of the Virgin, see Richard W. Southern, *The Making of the Middle Ages* (London: Cresset Library, 1953), ch. 5, 'From Epic to Romance' (219–59).

9 Simon of Tournai and Joseph Warichez, *Les Disputationes de Simon de Tournai*, Spicilegium sacrum lovaniense, études et documents 12 (Louvain: 'Spicilegium sacrum lovaniense', bureaux, 1932), 210–11.

10 *De Mirabilibus Sacrae Scripturae, Patrologia latina*, Patrologiae cursus completus: Series latina, ed. J.-P. Migne, 217 vols. (Paris, 1844–64), vol. XXXV, col. 2197.

11 William of Newburgh, *Historia Rerum Anglicarum*, in *Chronicles of the Reigns of Stephen, Henry II, and Richard I*, 2 vols., Rerum Britannicarum Medii Aevi Scriptores, Rolls Series 82, 2 vols., ed. Richard Howlett (London: Longman, 1884–9), vol. I, 85.

12 William of Malmesbury, *Gesta Regum*, 2 vols., Rerum Britannicarum Medii Aevi Scriptores, Rolls Series 90, ed. William Stubbs (London: HMSO, 1886), vol. II, 344.

13 James C. Robinson *et al.*, eds., *Materials for the History of Thomas Becket*, Rerum Britannicarum Medii Aevi Scriptores, Rolls Series 67, 7 vols. (London: Longman, 1875–85), vol. II, 41.

14 *Miracles of St Frideswide, Patrologia latina*, Patrologiae cursus completus: Series latina, ed. J.-P. Migne, 217 vols. (Paris, 1844–64), vol. CLXXXV, no. 51 col. 579E.

15 *De miraculis per beatum Bernardum facis Fribergi Basileae, locisque vicinis, Patrologia latina*, vol. CLXXXV, cols. 469–524. The third part of the *Historia* differs from the first two sections; it records cures performed by Bernard as he returned from Liège to Clairvaux, followed by notes of more miracles on his journey a few days later to a Council and then back to Clairvaux; some details were also added of the journey to Frankfurt. The material was collected by Geoffrey – probably after the return to Clairvaux and sent by him to the Bishop of Constance at his request. The party left Liège in January 1147 and reached Clairvaux on

6 February, going by Gembloux, Cambrai and Chalons and staying at monasteries on the way.

16 Ward and Savage, *Great Beginnings of Citeaux*, Bk 2, cap. 20.

17 Bernard of Clairvaux, 'De Consideratione', in Sancti Bernardi, *Opera*, 8 vols., vol. III (Rome: Editiones Cistercienses, 1963), 412–13.

18 For a discussion of miracles and canonization, see E. W. Kemp, *Canonization and Authority in the Western Church* (London: Oxford University Press, 1948).

19 Augustine, *City of God* 22.30.

Further reading

Brewer, Ebenezer Cobham, *A Dictionary of Miracles, Imitative, Realistic, and Dogmatic* (London: Chatto and Windus, 1884)

Chenu, Marie-Dominique Nature, *Man, and Society in the Twelfth Century: Essays on New Theological Perspectives in the Latin West* (Chicago: University of Chicago Press, 1968)

Colgrave, Bertram, 'Bede's Miracle Stories', in *Bede, his Life, Times, and Writings: Essays in Commemoration of the Twelfth Centenary of his Death*, ed. A. H. Thompson (Oxford: Clarendon, 1935), ch. vii

Finucane, Ronald C., *Miracles and Pilgrims: Popular Beliefs in Medieval England* (London: J. M. Dent, 1977)

Goodich, Michael, *Miracles and Wonders: The Development of the Concept of Miracle, 1150–1350* (Aldershot: Ashgate, 2007)

Grant, Robert M., *Miracle and Natural Law in Graeco-Roman and Early Christian Thought* (Amsterdam: North Holland, 1952)

Guibert of Nogent, 'On Saints and their Relics', in *Medieval Hagiography: An Anthology*, ed. Thomas Head (New York: Routledge, 2001), 399–427

Kemp, E. W., *Canonization and Authority in the Western Church* (London: Oxford University Press, 1948)

McCready, William D., *Miracles and the Venerable Bede* (Toronto: Pontifical Institute of Mediaeval Studies, 1994)

Turner, V. W. and E. L. B. Turner, *Image and Pilgrimage in Christian Culture: Anthropological Perspectives*, Lectures on the History of Religions, new series 11 (Oxford: Blackwell, 1978)

Vauchez, André, *Sainthood in the Later Middle Ages* (Cambridge: Cambridge University Press, 1997)

*Ward, Benedicta, *Miracles and the Medieval Mind: Theory, Record and Event, 1000–1215* (London: Scolar, 1982)

'Miracles and History: A Reconsideration of the Miracle Stories used by Bede', in *Famulus Christi: Essays in Commemoration of the Thirteenth Centenary of the Birth of the Venerable Bede*, ed. Gerald Bonner (London: SPCK, 1976), 70–6

Part III

Miracles and major religions

9 Miracles in traditional religions

FIONA BOWIE

On his first fieldwork trip to the Dowayo of Northern Cameroon in West
Africa, Nigel Barley took great trouble to cultivate his relationship with
the Old Man of Kpan, a renowned rainmaker. Through assiduous questioning and observation, Barley had confirmed his hunch that for the
Dowayo, skulls, pots and stones are related in a single complex: the
rainchiefs' skulls cause rain, and can be replaced with water jars for
festivals. The mountain on which the all-important rain stones were
kept was known as 'the crown of the boy's head', and the rainchiefs were
the cross-over point between these conceptual domains. Before leaving
Cameroon, Barley was keen to see the most powerful and sacred spot on
the mountain for himself, a large white rock below the summit, 'the
ultimate defence of the Dowayos' which, if removed by the rainmaker,
would flood the whole world destroying all its inhabitants. At the end of
his stay Barley was rewarded with a trip to the mountain to see the rain
stones, but asked for one final thing – he had not actually seen the Old
Man make rain, so would he grant him that wish? The Old Man pointed
out that Barley had already seen him splash the rain stones so the party
should hurry down the mountain before dark as it would rain on the way
home. Barley continues the story:

> The storm hit us at the very worst point of the descent where we
> were executing goat-like leaps across the fissures. Granite becomes
> very slippery when wet. At one point I was reduced to crawling on all
> fours. The Old Man was sniggering and pointing to the sky. Had
> I now seen? We were shouting above the storm to be heard. 'That's
> enough', I cried, 'you can make it stop'. He looked at me with a
> twinkle in his eye. 'A man does not take a wife to divorce her the
> same day', he replied.[1]

In the self-deprecating style of his narrative, Barley neatly sums up the
reaction of most anthropologists and other Western observers when
faced with seemingly impossible 'miraculous' events. While the Old

Man and his Dowayo companion were 'cock-a-hoop' about the tempest, Barley maintained:

> I, of course, would never believe anything so against the grain of my own culture without much better evidence than this. I – like they – see what I expect to see. The anthropologist in the field is seldom troubled by 'false' beliefs of those about him; he simply puts them in brackets, sees how they all fit together and learns to live with them on a day-to-day basis.[2]

This gulf between the world view of the Western observer, even one who participates extensively in local life, and the cosmology of many non-Western peoples, is pertinent to our discussion of miracles in traditional religions. Those who have studied the religions of non-Western ('traditional') peoples, particularly anthropologists – who made this intellectual domain their speciality – attempt by and large to be 'objective', even scientific, in their phenomenological bracketing out of questions of truth and validity. Wendy James has outlined the trajectory of this intellectual dilemma. Although focusing on the 'primitive' religions of 'tribal' or small-scale societies, anthropologists, whatever their personal persuasion or nationality, are by virtue of their education generally looking through a Judaeo-Christian lens: 'Here were the peoples and "beliefs" perceived as historically prior, closer to nature, culturally simple, peoples and beliefs for whom and for which Western civilizations already had a broad range of terms to hand, even in their sacred texts'.[3]

We have, therefore, two areas that first need to be addressed before we can explore the nature and function of miracles in traditional religions – first, the notion of miracle beyond the context of the Judaeo-Christian tradition and, second, the boundaries of the category 'traditional religion'. Are we looking for some kind of 'authentic', 'primitive'/'prior' form of religiosity unaffected ('untainted'?) by Western concepts, or by the so-called World Religions, or are we concerned rather with what certain peoples (if so which peoples and where?) actually believe, their religious practice and performance? What, indeed, can we make of the concept 'religion' within this journey of exploration?

One might add a third dimension to our study – what if we discover that the 'Other' of traditional religion is no different from 'Us'? The ethnographic record illustrates the ways in which an 'enchanted' view of the world is never far away, whether we look at beliefs in the Evil Eye in Europe and elsewhere, at folk beliefs in spirits, at the Western

Spiritualist tradition, the resurgence of interest in mediumship, various forms of Neo-Paganism and earth-healing in popular media and contemporary Western culture. There is considerable convergence and continuity between many different traditions. The polarity between Western 'rational/scientific' and Judaeo-Christian cosmology appears as an academic construct rather than ethnographic fact. If supraordinary, scientifically inexplicable events ('miracles') do occur it is at least probable that it is not so much their occurrence that varies as their interpretation and relationship to cultural expectations. Our study becomes one of identifying common themes that are more prominent in but not exclusive to 'traditional religions'.

DEFINING THE MIRACULOUS

A miracle in the 'strong' sense in which it is used in English today may be defined as an event that exceeds expectations. It may be something fortuitous that appears to contravene the laws of nature, or which is considered impossible from the perspective of the physical and human sciences. An otherwise inexplicable random event may be regarded as miraculous when the direct intervention of Divinity in human affairs is recognized. Miracles therefore are positive in their manifestation and implications for human beings, outside the scope of the mundane, and go beyond current scientific understandings of the natural world. A miracle is a bending of the structure of the universe in our favour. We can approach the concept of natural law in an open inclusive manner – taking the long view that our knowledge is as yet partial and evolving, and that what seems inexplicable today may become a common-place tomorrow – or we can invoke a range of unseen forces to account for many of the apparently miraculous events that grace our lives. In non-Western societies unseen beings and forces generally form part of an indigenous cosmology, and are regarded as part of nature. For the Western materialist raised in a post-Enlightenment world of rational laws, with faith in the scientific method, the significant portions of human experience that involve unusual events or evident anomalies that escape our scientific framework are problematic. Do we dismiss them, ignore them, ridicule them (or those who point them out), try to eliminate them or seek to accommodate them?

If, for the moment, we accept that one of the dividing lines between Western post-Enlightenment and 'traditional' peoples is a limited, materialist as opposed to an expansive, personalized view of the world (although this is of course much too simple an equation as it leaves aside the role of religious belief and practice), we have an immediate problem in delimiting the natural in a consistent way. How are we to recognize the boundary between the natural and super-nature – between what is expected and what might be termed miraculous? A miracle must, to rephrase Mary Douglas' description of dirt, 'have two conditions: a set of ordered relations and a contravention of that order ... where there is [a miracle] there is a system'.[4] Whether something might be properly described as miraculous (accepting that no such equivalent term exists in many languages) depends on the set of ordered relations in question. For many peoples in the world the universe is not impersonal and inanimate, waiting only to be used (or abused) by human actions. It is a dynamic system in which human beings are one interconnected part. Human actions, thoughts, wishes and ritual performances are part of a moral complex, concerned with the harmony or disharmony of the whole created order. Citing numerous examples, Douglas sums up a traditional world view that,

> looks out on a universe which is personal in several different senses.
> Physical forces are thought of as interwoven with the lives of
> persons. Things are not completely distinguished from persons
> and persons are not completely distinguished from their external
> environment. The universe responds to speech and mime. It discerns
> the social order and intervenes to uphold it.[5]

What the Westerner might see as miraculous, or often attempt to 'bracket out' (dismiss) as coincidence, despite evidence to the contrary (Nigel Barley, for instance, had witnessed other examples of the rain-maker's prowess), is for most people within such 'traditional' cultures simply a demonstration of a personalized relationship with the universe in action.[6]

Mary Douglas, in an article entitled 'Magic and Miracle',[7] sought to distance herself from the views of Sir James Frazer, and his enthusiastic disciple and founding father of the ethnographic method, Bronislaw Malinowski. Like most observers they were content to sneer at the fallacious childishness of the magician or sorcerer, who believed that the magical rite had external efficacy. Douglas, rather, reads 'primitive magic' as miracle, analogous to the 'miracle-believing ages of Christianity'. A miracle is not dependent on a rite but 'could be expected to erupt anywhere at any time in response to virtuous need or the demands of justice ... The power of miraculous intervention was believed to exist, but there was no certain way of harnessing it.'[8]

This discomfort with the literalism apparent in the rainmaker's art might, however, say more about Western unease with the notion of a personalized universe than about the nature of belief and practice in the societies in question. Societies in which thought and action interact with the powers of nature, with spirits, gods, demons, and other universal persons and forces. This embarrassment is projected onto the non-Western Other in their 'traditional societies', who cannot possibly hold such illogical beliefs if they are really as logical and civilized as Us? Such a view does not fit easily with the words and actions of the Old Man of Kpan. He had splashed remedies on the stones and as a direct consequence it rained. A world in which the power of thought accompanied by appropriate ritual words and actions effects actual change is the personalized, integrated, dynamic universe of most 'traditional' peoples, whether the sympathetic Durkheimian or determined sceptical positivist likes it or not.

The differences between Western and 'traditional' ways of seeing and understanding are in practice continually undermined. In a discussion of spiritual landscapes two geographers, J. D. Dewsbury and Paul Cloke, describe the tension or 'crash' between a 'technical-scientific *view* of language' and 'the speculative-hermeneutical *experience* of language' stating that the former 'unhelpfully holds sway despite hinging on that non-essential distinction, set forth in an unqualified manner long ago, between the rational and irrational'.[9] Looking back to Heidegger's observation that 'in modern times' what he terms 'the intrinsic flow of the "life-stream"' has been 'solidified' and 'objectified' through a view of language as object rather than presence, they ask rhetorically:

> It is irrational, is it not, to believe in spirits? Or is it? If the technical-scientific view becomes increasingly understood by the multiple and fragile practices that underwrite it, the validation of knowledge equally shifts. It is not the human subject position that objectifies the world and sees it without mediation but the technologies of the world ... that disclose us in the seeing.[10]

They are making a similar point to one attributed to Georges Bataille, whom they also cite: 'The tool changes nature and man at the same time: it subjugates nature to man, who makes and uses it, but it ties man to subjugated nature'.[11]

The importance of experience as a means of interpretation is one that many anthropologists have tried to come to terms with epistemologically. Edith Turner grappled with the surprise and discomfort of actually seeing a nebulous spirit form extracted from a patient when taking part in a healing ritual among the Ndembu of Central Africa.[12] Although a practising Catholic for many years, it was for Edith Turner a conversion to the reality of spirits, and she realized that hitherto her understanding of unseen forces had been primarily metaphorical and symbolic, not actual, present and 'material'. The notion of miracle is embedded within a particular language and cosmology. In dealing with the miraculous, the contravention of the rules of science or the break-through of unseen powers into the material world, we need to recognize that there might indeed be nothing 'miraculous', nothing unexpected or anomalous. The Durkheimian dichotomy of sacred and profane sets up, according to Georges Bataille, a distinction between the invaluable, alluring but 'vertiginously dangerous' world of the sacred and that 'clear and profane world where mankind situates its privileged domain'.[13] It is the apparent privileging of the 'profane' material world that distinguishes a dominant Western from a 'traditional' cosmology. What happens to the concept of miracle in a society in which nature is neither sacred nor profane, and in which it is taken for granted that gods, spirits and elemental forces are known and called upon by those with the skill and inclination to understand and manipulate their power?

TRADITIONAL PEOPLES AND TRADITIONAL RELIGIONS: A CAVEAT

The term 'tradition' is widely used but comes with an awkward pedigree, often standing as a cipher for the earlier terms 'primitive' and 'savage' in the ethnographic and theological literature. More recently the term 'indigenous' has come into favour, with movements associated with indigenous rights, or the study of indigenous knowledge, for example. There are several problems with knowing who or what we are talking about, and in dealing with the neo-colonial premises behind whatever terms we choose. The base-line is that each of these designations is a form of shorthand for 'the Other', people not like Us – the assumed point of reference being a Euro-American Westerner, or at least Western-educated or elite member of a technologically more advanced culture. Nineteenth-century anthropologists and sociologists were fascinated with the peoples and cultures of Australasia, Amazonia and the tribal areas of Southeast Asia, as these peoples were thought to be exemplars of a pre-industrial way of living and thinking – a kind of living fossil or example of a stage in humanity's evolutionary path from hunter-gatherer to modern cosmopolitan farmer and industrialist. While oral cultures may be conservative and technologically simple, it is now recognized that we are all a product of a particular history, and share a similar evolutionary path. The marginal peoples of the world (such as the Khoisan of Southern Africa, or the peoples of the Amazon Basin) are marginal in many cases because of earlier expansionist movements that displaced them from more fertile lands or more central locations. What we see are the remnants of earlier civilizations and not primitive timeless noble savages. Terms such as 'traditional' or 'indigenous' are also inevitably anachronistic – all peoples have some sort of 'tradition' if by this we mean language, social structures, beliefs and practices, technologies and so forth, which are passed down from one generation to another. These may be more or less dynamic and open to outside influences. They may be syncretic or anti-syncretic, but just as everyone is an indigene somewhere, so we all have various established ways of doing things. A more descriptive term such as 'small-scale' or 'pre-literate', or perhaps 'tribal' society – focusing on aspects of social structure, language use and political organization, can serve as alternatives, but each term has its drawbacks if we are looking for an inclusive, value-free nomenclature. In what sense, for instance, could the Iroquois Federation, which united disparate peoples over a wide area of North America, be described as small scale? Does a term such as 'pre-literate' impose an inappropriate evolutionary or historical framework? Literacy is unevenly distributed within most of the world's literate cultures, being an elite skill in many. Cultures which oppose literacy as a matter of principle, such as the Kogi of the Sierra Nevada de Santa Marta in Colombia, would not see themselves as set on a path to mass literacy; they are not pre-literate but, like Socrates, pro-oral.

If the notion of a traditional people is problematic the same is true of a traditional religion. Are we in fact looking for some sort of imagined authenticity? How many influences can be absorbed for a religion to remain 'traditional'? Is it what people in 'traditional' societies believe and practice or are we forced to imagine a prior state that is superior or truer, 'more traditional', than the one we actually find? Mircea Eliade in his classic work on shamanism saw 'the ecstasy induced by [the shaman's] ascent to the sky or descent to the underworld' as the key feature of this particular religious complex.[14] He therefore stated that shamanism as described by scholars such as Shirokogoroff, who described the shamanic complex of the Siberian Tungus (Evenk) peoples in the 1930s, was 'aberrant' or 'degenerate', as the Tungus emphasized spirit possession and the taming of spirits rather than ecstasy. This search for authenticity or purity is not confined to scholars of religion; it may also play a part in the self-understanding of the practitioners themselves. In her study of a Yoruba-inspired community in the United States, Kamari Maxine Clarke describes the way in which Oyotunji villagers in South Carolina react to the dismissal of their ancestral pretentions by Nigerian Yoruba with the counter-claim that, by adopting Western clothing and foreign religious practices, the Nigerians have forfeited their status as authentic Yoruba Orisa worshippers. The baton of authenticity has passed to those in the United States who make a self-conscious effort to eradicate non-traditional influences in all aspects of their daily life, as well as in their religious beliefs and practices, irrespective of genealogy or ethnic origins.[15]

If rather than search for an authentic religious tradition we decide to look at what people actually do and think, how they perform their rituals and tell their mythic narratives, we find a complex and confusing picture. Christianity or Islam, Hinduism or Buddhism, often sit alongside a 'traditional religion', their elements intertwined. While there may be nostalgia in some quarters for a pure, traditional form of religion uncontaminated by outside forces, others are more at ease with a mixed, hybrid heritage.

Our search, then, for a miracle in traditional religions is compromised by the difficulties we face in seeking to define a concept (miracle) that is so critically dependent upon a particular religious and cultural discourse, and by the impossibility of identifying a 'traditional religion' that is not also influenced by a world religion. Those who practise traditional religions are also citizens of a global culture. The boundaries of that 'tradition' are conceptual and metaphoric. We could follow the lead of the African-American Orisa-Voodoo worshippers in South Carolina and declare that here we have traditional, authentic, Yoruba religion, or we could explore the specifically Yoruba forms of Christian healing in African-led churches in Nigeria. Which of the two is to be regarded as 'traditional religion'? It will depend on how we wish to draw the boundaries around these terms, and whether geography or self-ascription, religious conservatism or hybridization, are important qualifiers or disqualifiers in our quest for a miracle in 'traditional religions'.

HEALING MIRACLES

One place to start in our search for the miraculous in traditional religions is in healing, described by Turner as 'Of all religious acts ... the most innocent, the most often miraculous, the most often desired'.[16] Health, balance and harmony within the body of the individual and within the body politic, are constant human preoccupations. Whether someone who looks for healing regards it as a miracle in the 'strong' Judaeo-Christian sense of direct intervention of God (or gods), or as super-abundant nature will, as discussed above, depend upon one's notion of the natural order and its boundaries, and on the perceived legitimacy of a particular interpretation of an event.

As a result of her research over many years in both Western and non-Western societies, Turner groups healing under three main headings: healing with energy, healing with power and healing with spirits. Healing *energy* is often felt in the hands as heat, with disease as a spiritual substance that has to be extracted, often with great effort on the part of the healer and patient. *Power* is described as something bigger than energy, a force that can overtake the healer, superimposing itself on his or her will. It may come unexpectedly and often occurs where human interconnectedness (*communitas*) is strongly experienced. *Spirits*, by contrast, tend to be insistent and take the initiative. They may possess the healer and demand entrance into his or her body in order to accomplish their healing work.[17] These three forces are sometimes combined in one person or one healing episode, or may remain distinct. They appear to be universal, and where not culturally recognized may take both healer and patient by surprise. Healing powers may be welcomed as miraculous gifts, rejected or utilized sparingly. They may be sought, learnt or inherited, and may of course fail as well as succeed. While there are various explanations for spiritual healing, often well articulated, as with the vital force or *chi* energy utilized in Chinese acupuncture, they remain beyond scientific medical models of healing.

We shall start by looking at shamanic healing in a number of different 'traditional' cultures, a class of healing that would be seen as miraculous (or treated as trickery) from a Western scientific perspective, if it were not so often simply ignored or bracketed out. We will need to be flexible with our boundaries. As Ronald Hutton notes, Siberian peoples are often taken as exemplars of 'classical' shamanism, but their cultures are 'mobile and dynamic, and shared a continent with some of the world's most elaborate and expansionist religious systems'.[18] Even the most geographically remote, isolated ethnic groups may incorporate elements from neighbouring peoples of both Turkic and Mongolian origin, and be influenced by various strands of Christianity, Buddhism and Islam. The same is equally true in Africa, the Americas or Southeast Asia, where 'traditional' beliefs are in fact an amalgamation of many ideas and practices over time and from different sources.

Common to societies that may be considered to hold shamanic beliefs is an assumption that human beings have (at least) two forms of life energy that can become separated. One is tied to the biological organism and its physiological processes. The other, also essential to the life of the organism, can travel outside the body during sleep, or can be sent out while in a trance or altered state of consciousness. This separable spirit or soul can communicate with other spirits or souls of those still living and with discarnate spirits – both human and other once-embodied entities. A shaman will typically undergo an initiatory calling that involves sickness and subsequent curing, effected only when the vocational calling by the spirits to work as a shaman is heeded. A shaman must learn to work with other guardian spirits or tutelary helpers, which may be the spirits of ancestors, animals or other spirit creatures or people. Healing is an important aspect of their work, and although diagnosis and cure take many forms, the diagnosis is often either soul loss or the intrusion of an unwanted spirit or object into a patient.

Stories of soul loss and retrieval can be found in many different continents. There are various methods used by the shaman to enter a trance state and send the soul or life force out of his or her body. Common among these is the use of hallucinogens, music and dance, drumming, meditation or self-hypnosis. The dramatic tales of action taking place at a level of reality invisible to the ordinary eye are often remarkably similar to one another across both time and culture, and commonly involve a journey in which the shaman locates and restores the missing soul or soul-portion to the patient.

Among the Shoshoni Plains Indians, children were advised not to play near a tent where a healer was working lest they come between the patient's soul and that of the healer, preventing the soul's safe return. Soul retrieval is even reported where the patient has apparently died, as the following account illustrates:

> A Crow Indian mother had lost her little girl, who was three or four years of age. Morgan Moon's sister said, 'The child is dead; there is nothing to do.' But her brother retorted, 'No, the soul has just temporarily left the body. I shall bring it back.' He touched the top of the child's head, stroking it round the crown. The child opened her eyes and looked at him. Her soul was close to the body and entered it through the top of the head. The next day the girl was playing again. She was quite well.[19]

Some of the most vivid and dramatic accounts of 'miracle' healing involving mediumship are those recounted by Sidney Greenfield, an anthropologist who has worked for many years with a variety of spirit healers in Brazil. The difficulty of distinguishing between healing miracles in a 'traditional' religion and in a non-traditional one is starkly brought to the fore by the nature of Brazilian religious hybridism, and by the similarity of accounts of healing that cut across or combine elements from Amazonian shamanic rituals, African cults, Christianity – both Catholic and Protestant – and Kardicist Spiritism, with its roots in Eastern religions via nineteenth-century America and the writings of Allan Kardec in France. In a striking summary of Brazilian healing and the cosmological understanding that lies behind it, Greenfield invites the reader to join him,

> on an adventure to a land where spirits, incorporated in mediums, cut into patients with scalpels, kitchen knives, and even electric saws to remove, at times with unwashed fingers, infected materials and growths. Yet the patients are given no anaesthetic, feel little if any pain, and develop no infections. They recover without complications. People suffering from physical and emotional symptoms participate in rituals in which specialists enter into trances, incorporating antagonists from patients' previous lifetimes. The antagonists are talked into stopping whatever they are doing that is causing the problem. When they do, the suffering party recovers ... Alternatively, a patient, after being mysteriously cured of symptoms that a doctor may not have been able to diagnose, thanks a deity from Africa, embodied in a host, or the spirit of a deceased rogue, prostitute, or slave, becomes an initiate in a religion whose origins go back to villages in West Africa from which the ancestors of slaves were taken centuries ago. Some people accept Jesus and join a Pentecostal church after being inexplicably cured of their symptoms by the Holy Ghost following prayer by a pastor speaking in tongues.[20]

The surgical procedures Greenfield observed would be regarded as miraculous from the perspective of known medical science (his many hours of video recordings and participation in healings convinced him and others that the surgeries he witnessed could not be dismissed as mere trickery). Those conducting the surgeries and most of the patients accept the supernatural explanations offered, and in a Christian (or Kardicist) setting this may well include the notion of a miracle – albeit an eagerly anticipated and even predictable one. Greenfield himself is less sure, and looks to research on trance and hypnosis to explain the power of the mind to heal the body under autosuggestion. How untrained healers diagnose and treat patients successfully is, however, not easy to explain (away?) by any known scientific theories.

MIRACULOUS INTERVENTION

Equally common in 'traditional' societies, and equally implausible from a rational point of view, are the tales of natural phenomena and material objects changing shape, acquiring new powers, or gaining an intentionality normally reserved for human agents. Edith Turner tells the story of just such a miraculous intervention involving an Inupiat whaling captain and healer, Robert Nashanik, in Alaska. Robert and a friend, Greg, had been hunting on the ice when Robert met a polar bear. He shot at and injured the animal, but the gun jammed and he had to run for his life. After half a mile he stopped and looked for his friend on the flat ice, but couldn't see him. He climbed a ridge and saw a black dot in the distance, and went towards it. The dot turned out to be Greg, *swimming.* His snowmobile had driven onto thin ice and he had fallen in. Robert told Greg to break the ice and make his way towards him. All Robert had with him was a piece of rope about five feet long.

> 'I lay down on the ice ... with my rope. What could I do? The rope was so short. I prayed and threw it to him. It stretched', said Robert softly, looking puzzled. 'Like elastic. It became long. Greg took the end and I pulled him out. It was hard to do because he was wearing a jacket with a lambskin lining, and it was soaked and very heavy. He still had his gun looped around his body. So he never lost his gun.'[21]

Turner comments that, 'Here, Robert, like the others, didn't seem to claim strange powers for himself; he was just surprised at how things happened'. There are 'miracles' that rely on the coincidence of otherwise natural occurrences, such as when something prayed for comes to pass, and those which appear to defy the laws of nature – as when Jesus turned water into wine, or Robert's rope in a moment of crisis exceeded its normal length. As in the examples of spiritual healing in Brazil observed by Sidney Greenfield, with their mixture of African, Native American and Christian input, the Inupiat of Alaska often combine a traditional shamanic view of the world with deeply held Christian faith. The Christian God joined forces with rather than replaced the healers' helping spirits.

Miraculous intervention need not be attributed to God or Divinity. It might involve a shaman, clairvoyant or diviner finding missing people or objects, or pointing to the cause of misfortune (be it witchcraft, ancestors, the evil eye, or simply coincidence or fate). In the 1920s J. H. Hutton mentioned that the Angami in northern India consult seers to find stolen property or to identify a thief, a practice that led to conflict with the British authorities, who feared that innocent people were being identified.[22] In Africa recourse to witchfinders was denounced for similar reasons.

When it comes to clairvoyance we may be in the realms of the apparently miraculous, but it is another ability that appears to cross all cultural and religious boundaries (as any fan of 'psychic detective' programmes on television will be well aware). What separates such practices in 'traditional' religions from their occurrence in contemporary Western societies is the acceptance in the former of such abilities as normative. Not all Western scholars have Einstein's 'utter humility toward the unattainable secrets of the harmony of the cosmos' and are consequently unable to see or seek value in 'native' or non-Western explanations. Ronald Hutton makes this point when he gently chides Shirokogoroff for declaring that a shaman's spirits 'were in reality altered states of mind' or Piers Vitebski, 'who has suggested that shamanic spirits can be viewed as the practitioner's own alter ego or projections'.[23] Hutton admits that such interpretations 'make sense of many of the phenomena concerned' and that they are phrased in a terminology that 'westerners are likely to find both meaningful and sympathetic'. He notes, however, two significant drawbacks. One is that the people so described do not interpret the facts that way. Spirits in Siberian cosmologies are not just in the mind, but out there, in nature, part of their natural and human environment. The second objection Hutton raises is that, despite our faith in rationalism, science and Enlightenment thinking, 'ultimately the psychologising of Siberian spirits is itself a statement of faith, resting upon no ultimate proof'. We become so used to explaining away or bracketing out the emic (insider) perspectives of non-Western peoples that we can become blind to the relativity of our own essentializing discourses. As Hutton puts it, 'It makes sense to modern westerners of otherwise uncanny or repugnant phenomena; but in its different way the native explanation made equal sense, and with as much claim to objective demonstration of evidence'.[24]

EXPLANATIONS AND COSMOLOGIES: MIRACLES AS PART OF THE NATURAL ORDER

Malidoma Patrice Somé is a member of the Dagara people from Burkina Faso in West Africa. His name means 'he who makes friends with the stranger/enemy', and he walks the line between the spirit

world of his own people, Roman Catholicism brought by French missionaries, and the life of a Western-educated intellectual and writer.
The Dagara, Somé tells us,

> are well known throughout West Africa for beliefs and practices
> that outsiders find both fascinating and frightening. The Dagara
> connection with beings from the Spirit World has resulted in the
> accumulation of firsthand knowledge of subjects regarded in the
> West as paranormal, magical, or spiritual. Dagara 'science', in this
> sense, is the investigation of the Spirit World more than the world of
> matter. What in the West might be regarded as fiction, among the
> Dagara is believed as fact, for we have seen it with our eyes, heard
> it with our ears, or felt it with our own hands.[25]

The world of the Spirit permeates the everyday order, so that work, for
instance, is described as 'an intensification of the work that Spirit does in
nature'.[26] What Somé describes as 'Spirit' is the same or very similar to
the universal breath or energy known in Japan as *ki*. It is the intelligent
and animating force behind and within all visible life forms. 'Spirit
administers nature, the complex interweaving of life forms and cycles
of time that we experience as the natural world. Nature, in fact, is such a
complex organism that only the intelligence of Spirit can manage it.'[27]
The healing work of the shaman or traditional doctor, the miraculous
interventions that can lengthen a rope to save a life, can conjure strange
creatures and open doors to invisible worlds, are all part of an understanding of the relationship between this life force or Spirit and matter.
Just as an animal with a keen sense of smell lives in a different sensory
world to a human being, so the Dagara in West Africa, Inupiat in Alaska
or indeed anyone whose culture keeps open the doors to such a world –
lives with an awareness of presence (or of its potential). The spirits of
ancestors, of nature and of a host of other creatures are not mere psychic
phantasmagoria but are as real as the person next to one.[28]

The Inupiat whaling captain Clem Jackson takes anthropologists to
task for 'discovering' or inventing meanings and analyses that bear no
relationship to what people themselves say about their culture,[29] and
this inability to be believed is perceived as yet another form of neo-
colonialism, one against which it can be hard to argue, backed up as it is
with the force of 'progress' and modernity. The apparently more sophisticated cultures of the Far East or India earned a greater degree of
respect from missionaries, travellers, anthropologists and Western
intellectuals than some of the so-called tribal peoples, although their
underlying cosmologies often bear a strong resemblance to those of

traditional or shamanic cultures. Within Shinto, for instance, 'human-kind is understood as living in a shared cosmos which is both sacred and mysterious, and the religion expresses a profound spiritual awareness of the divine power of which all natural phenomena are manifestations'.[30] *Kami* (god/spirit/deity) can be both manifest in nature (which includes the human) or be a bridge to it. Within the Shugendo or shamanic Buddhist tradition, healing power, like that of the Inupiat described by Edith Turner, involves learning to direct energy electromagnetically and to project an intention to effect healing at a distance.[31]

Where does this leave our exploration of miracles in traditional religions? What we can say is that there is a way of perceiving the world that is ubiquitous in non-Western societies (although not shared by everyone), and present within Euro-American culture (as a minority viewpoint) in which the 'miraculous' is part of the natural order. This viewpoint is not dependent upon a particular religious affiliation, but is usually accompanied by an awareness of the spiritual unity of human beings with one another and with the rest of the cosmos. It is a view that sees the world as alive, interconnected, responsive and dynamic. It is directed towards the good but capable of evil. Whether we are looking for miracles in a traditional or Western context, Edith Turner suggests that we should apply Occam's razor, the rule of parsimony, and should not, therefore, 'go out of our way to invent complicated explanations so as to avoid accepting the possibility of the existence of spirit being and powers', rather than learning 'simply to listen to what those adept at these matters are saying and begin to take them seriously'.[32] That would indeed be a miracle.

Notes

1 Nigel Barley, *The Innocent Anthropologist: Notes from a Mud Hut* (London: British Museum Publications, 1983), 159–60.
2 *Ibid.*, 60.
3 Wendy James, *The Ceremonial Animal: A New Portrait of Anthropology* (Oxford: Oxford University Press, 2003), 119.
4 Mary Douglas, *Purity and Danger: An Analysis of Concepts of Pollution and Taboo* (London and Henley: Routledge and Keegan Paul, 1976), 35.
5 Douglas, *Purity and Danger*, 88.
6 The phenomenological move of 'bracketing' is a way of prioritizing subjectivity over experience of the world. Faced with data that cannot be accommodated the observer narrows the range of vision to that which allows for a semblance of control, thus restoring authority to the self.
7 Douglas, 'Magic and Miracle', in *Purity and Danger*, 58–72.

8   Douglas, *Purity and Danger*, 59.

9   J. D. Dewsbury and Paul Cloke, 'Spiritual Landscapes: Existence, Performance and Immanence', *Social and Cultural Geography* 10 (2009), 695–711 (703).

10 *Ibid.*, 703.

11 Georges Bataille, *A Theory of Religion* (New York: Zone, 1992), 41, cited by Dewsbury and Cloke, 'Spiritual Landscapes', 709.

12 Edith Turner with William Blodgett, Singleton Kahona and Fideli Benwa, *Experiencing Ritual: A New Interpretation of African Healing* (Philadelphia: University of Pennsylvania Press, 1992), and Edith Turner, *Among the Healers: Stories of Spiritual and Ritual Healing around the World* (Santa Barbara: Praeger, 2006).

13 Bataille, *A Theory of Religion*, 36, cited by Dewsbury and Cloke, 'Spiritual Landscapes', 704.

14 Mircea Eliade, *Shamanism: Archaic Techniques of Ecstasy* (1964) (London: Arkana, Penguin, 1988), 499.

15 Kamari Maxine Clarke, *Mapping Yoruba Networks: Power and Agency in the Making of Transnational Communities* (Durham, NC, and London: Duke University Press, 2004), 14–16, 66.

16 Turner, *Among the Healers*, xx.

17 *Ibid.*, xxii–xxiii.

18 Ronald Hutton, *Shamans: Siberian Spirituality and the Western Imagination* (London: Hambledon, and New York: Continuum, 2001), 61–2.

19 Ake Hultkrantz, *Shamanic Healing and Ritual Drama: Health and Medicine in Native North American Religious Traditions* (New York: Crossroad, 1992), 93.

20 Sidney M. Greenfield, *Spirits with Scalpels: The Culturalbiology of Religious Healing in Brazil* (Walnut Creek: Left Coast, 2008), 9.

21 Edith Turner, *The Hands Feel It: Healing and Spirit Presence among a North Alaskan People* (DeKalb: Northern Illinois University Press, 1996), 176.

22 J. H. Hutton, *The Angami Nagas* (London: Macmillan, 1921), 245, cited by Vibha Joshi, 'Human and Spiritual Agency in Angami Healing', *Anthropology and Medicine* 11 (2004), 269–91 (274).

23 Hutton, *Shamans*, 67.

24 *Ibid.*, 67.

25 Malidoma Patrice Somé, *The Healing Wisdom of Africa: Finding Life Purpose Through Nature, Ritual, and Community* (New York: Penguin, 1999), 2.

26 *Ibid.*, 66.

27 *Ibid.*, 2.

28 This is not to say that all individuals in 'traditional' cultures are equally sensitive to or interested in the world of spirits, but to be a 'sceptic' or materialist in a culture in which such views are normative would be consciously to reject the world view or cosmological underpinnings of one's own culture.

29 Turner, *The Hands Feel It*, 67.

30 Ikuko Osumi and Malcolm Ritchie, *The Shamanic Healer: The Healing World of Ikuko Osumi and the Traditional Art of Seiki-Jutsu* (London: Century, 1987), 16.
31 *Ibid.*, 13; Turner, *The Hands Feel It*, 74–5.
32 Edith Turner, 'The Soul and Communication between Souls', in *Ontology of Consciousness: Percipient Action*, ed. Helmut Wautischer (Cambridge, MA, and London: MIT Press, 2008), 79–98 (93).

Further reading

Barley, Nigel, *The Innocent Anthropologist: Notes from a Mud Hut* (London: British Museum, 1983)
Bataille, Georges, *A Theory of Religion* (New York: Zone, 1992)
Clarke, Kamari Maxine, *Mapping Yoruba Networks: Power and Agency in the Making of Transnational Communities* (Durham, NC, and London: Duke University Press, 2004)
Dewsbury, J.D. and Paul Cloke, 'Spiritual Landscapes: Existence, Performance and Immanence', *Social and Cultural Geography* 10 (2009), 695–711
Douglas, Mary, *Purity and Danger: An Analysis of Concepts of Pollution and Taboo* (London and Henley: Routledge and Keegan Paul, 1976)
Eliade, Mircea, *Shamanism: Archaic Techniques of Ecstasy* (1964) (London: Arkana, 1989)
Greenfield, Sidney M., *Spirits with Scalpels: The Culturalbiology of Religious Healing in Brazil* (Walnut Creek, CA: Left Coast, 2008)
Hultkrantz, Ake, *Shamanic Healing and Ritual Drama: Health and Medicine in Native North American Religious Traditions* (New York: Crossroad, 1992)
Hutton, J.H., *The Angami Nagas* (London: Macmillan, 1921)
Hutton, Ronald, *Shamans: Siberian Spirituality and the Western Imagination* (London: Hambledon, and New York: Continuum, 2001)
James, Wendy, *The Ceremonial Animal: A New Portrait of Anthropology* (Oxford: Oxford University Press, 2003)
Joshi, Vibha, 'Human and Spiritual Agency in Angami Healing', *Anthropology and Medicine* 11 (2004), 269–91
Osumi, Ikuko and Malcolm Ritchie, *The Shamanic Healer: The Healing World of Ikuko Osumi and the Traditional Art of Seiki-Jutsu* (London: Century, 1987)
Somé, Malidoma Patrice, *The Healing Wisdom of Africa: Finding Life Purpose through Nature, Ritual, and Community* (New York: Penguin, 1999)
Turner, Edith, *The Hands Feel It: Healing and Spirit Presence among a North Alaskan People* (DeKalb: Northern Illinois University Press, 1996)
  Among the Healers: Stories of Spiritual and Ritual Healing around the World (Santa Barbara: Praeger, 2006)
  'The Soul and Communication between Souls', in *Ontology of Consciousness: Percipient Action*, ed. Helmut Wautischer (Cambridge, MA, and London: MIT Press, 2008), 79–98
Turner, Edith, with William Blodgett, Singleton Kahona and Fideli Benwa, *Experiencing Ritual: A New Interpretation of African Healing* (Philadelphia: University of Pennsylvania Press, 1992)

10 Miracles in Hinduism

GAVIN FLOOD

Transposing a category such as 'miracle' that developed in the context of one tradition, namely Christianity, to the traditions of India is not an easy task. We need to ask questions such as what is served by such transposition, are there analogous categories in the traditions of India and, if there are, do they serve a similar function as the category 'miracle' in the West? We need therefore to read carefully across traditions in the service of comparison. Within Christianity and Western philosophy there are a number of understandings of what a miracle is. Hume defines miracle as 'a violation of the laws of nature'[1] but in earlier centuries Aquinas defined it as a change in the natural order, something 'sometimes done by God outside the usual order assigned to things ... because we are astonished ... when we see an effect without knowing the cause'.[2] That is, a miracle is an event without a natural cause, whose cause is God and his ability and desire to disrupt the usual order of things. The concept of miracle therefore entails the concept of a law of nature. Transplanting this definition into India, it is not clear that Indian religions developed any concept directly akin to this although the Indian conception of astonishing or wondrous events is close to Thomas. There is an understanding in Indian religions from ancient times that the usual patterns of material causation can be changed. While at one level this is a disruption of natural causation, at another level it is in accord with natural law, with the law of the universe. Indeed, one of the signs of spiritual progress was understood precisely in these terms as an apparent disruption of material causation in the possession of supernormal powers. There are, then, two contexts which offer analogues to the Western category, namely the development of power in yoga that leads to various supernormal powers or accomplishments (siddhi), and the perception of the disruption of material causation in popular piety characterized by wonder (adbhuta). In the former case the power to go against the usual patterns of material causation is believed to be from a human agent who has gained such powers through dedicated effort and who understands the order of the universe or *dharma*. In the latter case the change in material causation is from God or a higher power that acts directly on the world usually through a human teacher or guru. Thus there is power in the sacred image or icon which symbolizes the deity and similarly there is power in the holy person who, like the icon, also symbolizes the deity. In both cases there is cause of wonder or astonishment among the wider population.

Both the cultivation of supernormal powers in the context of yoga and asceticism and the idea of wondrous events that disrupt material causation, have occurred in a world view in which the cosmos is filled with beings and powers beyond the physical. We might say that these are signs of an enchanted world that is generally now gone, having declined with the rise of modernity over the last 300 years. Certainly the worlds of medieval Europe and medieval India are parallel insofar as both could be described as sharing a view of enchantment that, to use Charles Taylor's description, 'is the world of spirits, demons, and moral forces'.[3] We can surely generalize about this world shared in both civilizations that the veil between the community and some other supernatural reality is thin and that forces outside of material causation were constantly interacting with and impinging upon our world. People were in danger of being possessed by supernatural forces perhaps through a moral or ritual failure and conversely people could benefit from the power imbued in certain material objects set aside as sacred, such as a saint's relic or the icon (*mūrti*) of a deity. The dead were near at hand as ancestors with whom one interacted through funerary rites which lasted up to a year (the *antyeṣṭhi* or 'last sacrifice' in Hinduism) and whom one feared lingering on as a ghost. People in both medieval European and South Asian civilizations inhabited an enchanted world in which human agency was linked to divine or supernatural agency and where people were part of a cosmos and found meaning in life through being located within a hierarchical, cosmic order.[4] Thus in Orthodox angelology we have the Holy Trinity at the top of the universe with ranks of angels arranged beneath this, with the human world beneath this and the demonic realms below. Similarly in the Tantras we read of multiple worlds with purer, powerful supernatural beings at the top of the hierarchy and grosser, more solidified or dense beings located below this. A person as a soul (*jīva*) could be reincarnated into any of these levels and as any of these types of beings depending on its past actions (*karma*). It was the location in the cosmos and therefore the kind of body that determined a soul's experience and defined its meaning in the scheme of things.[5]

We must, therefore, understand the category of miracle and any Indian equivalent in the general context of this world view that is cosmological and hierarchical. This 'enchanted' view understood action in the world as being linked to a greater cosmic field. Although the details differ, this general understanding is shared across Indian religions from ancient times to the early modern period. Thus Buddhism, Jainism and Hinduism have ornate cosmologies within the context of which the idea of a miracle must be understood.

One of the key ideas is that the world can be affected 'miraculously' through the will of a spiritually accomplished person (that is, someone with a higher realization) or through the impinging of supernatural agency. Supernormal powers can be attained through effort and the application of spiritual technologies, specifically yoga or meditation. The Indian traditions shared a common sacred language of Sanskrit, although Buddhism and Jainism articulated their ideas in different Prakrits as well. What, then, are the nearest semantic equivalents to the term 'miracle' in Indian religious literature? The contexts in which events analogous to miracles occur are supernormal powers attained in yoga and meditation through an act of will and supernatural events associated with saints and icons. Various terms are associated with these contexts. For the first context we have a number of terms. In the Pali canon of Theravāda Buddhism we have a developed system in which magical powers appear as the result of reaching the fourth level of meditation (*jhāna*). These are called *iddhi* whose Sanskrit equivalent is *siddhi*, a term that can be rendered not simply as 'supernormal power' but also as 'accomplishment' or even in certain circumstances 'perfection'. For the second context we have a number of Sanskrit terms such as *āścarya, adbhuta, atimānuṣa, vismaya* and *camatkāra*[6] all of which can be rendered as 'wonder', 'astonishment', 'spectacle' or 'miracle' which generally occur in the context of mythological and hagiographical literature, although *camatkāra* occurs in the context of aesthetics and religious experience in the Śaivism of Kashmir.

THE HIERARCHICAL UNIVERSE

But before we explicate these ideas we need to describe a more basic level of assumptions about our life and the universe in general. The law that governs both the natural and social order is called *dharma*, which can be variously rendered as 'law', 'duty', 'truth' or even 'religion'. Miracles in Hindu traditions are not so much the disruption of *dharma* but are in accordance with *dharma*, but what appears to be miraculous at this level has an explanation in the context of a higher level. That is, we need to understand the Hindu equivalent of 'miracle' in a cosmological context. India developed complex and ornate cosmologies although the fundamental ideas behind them are clear. There are two principles that operate in these cosmologies, the first is that the lower levels of the universe are emanations of higher levels and are within the control of forces that operate at that higher level. Second, the mind takes the forms of its objects and so the object of focus transforms the mind. Let us look at both of these principles.

In these hierarchical universes there are powerful beings high up in the hierarchy who control a realm, world or group of worlds. Forms in the material world might be connected with these higher supernatural forces. Thus snakes are within the realm of command of the supernatural beings called Nāgas. Similarly, control or access to a particular level of the universe will allow one to affect lower levels. The medieval Hindu world is replete with examples of these hierarchical cosmologies. A group of texts that developed in the early medieval period from about the eighth century, called Tantras or Āgamas, were regarded as revelation by their followers. These texts were composed within the three great traditions that comprised most of medieval Hinduism focused on Śiva, the Goddess (Śakti) or Viṣṇu. To take one example from Śaivism, in the cosmical hierarchy the lower levels of the universe are emanations or coagulations of the higher. Furthermore, supernatural beings which exist at a higher cosmic level have control over lower realms. Thus, for example, a class of beings called Vidyeśvaras have their own domains and rule those worlds within their sphere.[7] Furthermore, these higher beings are expressed as sounds: their bodies are sound bodies articulated in the lower realm of this world as mantras or verses from the Scriptures. The sound formulas in the world expressed in 'gross' speech are manifestations of the more subtle sound of the deities they express. This leads us on to the second principle of these hierarchical cosmologies that the mind takes on the form of its objects.

Generally in Indian models of consciousness, the objects of consciousness determine its quality and form (an idea not dissimilar to Aristotle). Thus 'pure' objects of consciousness such as deities, sacred persons and mantras purify consciousness, whereas the objects of selfish desires and vices have a polluting effect. This idea is fundamental to the soteriology of Indian religions as we see with the doctrine of mantras. Mantras are verses from sacred texts repeated in a ritual. It is believed that the mantra embodies a deity and through repeating the mantra the mind of the practitioner is transformed to a higher level.[8] The control or power of the mantra allows power or control over the world. Through repeating the mantra the mind of the practitioner is transformed to the level of its origin: a divine agency, as it were, takes over from a human one. Both contexts of the 'miraculous' in Hinduism, that of supernormal power and supernatural events, must be located in this hierarchical, cosmological context.

YOGA

One of the earliest texts which presents an analysis of human consciousness and its potential is Patañjali's *Yoga Sūtras*, probably composed during the early centuries of the common era. In this text the philosopher of yoga presents an account of the human mind and its persistent habits driven by desires which must be disrupted in order to achieve spiritual insight and liberation. Patañjali assumes the basic metaphysics of the dualistic system of philosophy called Sāṃkhya in which the soul (*puruṣa*) is eternally distinct from matter (*prakṛti*) but apparently entangled by it. For Patañjali the goal of life is liberation which is the separation or isolation (*kaivalya*) of the soul from matter, of the *puruṣa* from *prakṛti*. To achieve this state we need to control the mind which is constantly flowing out from the body into the world according to its desire. Indeed, he famously defines yoga as 'the cessation of mental fluctuations'.[9] Once the mind is stilled and focused on a single point (*ekāgrata*) then the practitioner experiences higher states of awareness (*samādhi*) in a graded sequence which eventually leads to liberation, the ultimate human fulfilment. A consequence of developing these states of awareness is 'supernatural' power. The term Patañjali uses to describe these phenomena is *vibhūti*, great power, might, splendour or glory and he takes us through the stages of its development.

First, the mind takes on the form of its object in *samādhi* and becomes absorbed. Patañjali's pithy Sanskrit is:

Tad evārthamātranirbhāsaṃ svarūpaśūnyam iva samādhiḥ[10]

We can render this literally as 'concentration is simply the appearance of the object of consciousness only, as if empty of one's own nature'. In a more explicatory translation Hariharananda Aranya renders the passage:

> When the object of meditation only shines forth in the mind as though devoid of the thought of even the self (who is meditating), that state is called Samadhi or concentration.[11]

The idea is clear that the practitioner becomes completely absorbed in the object of meditation such that he is no longer aware of his own nature as distinct from the object. Through mastery of these states of higher consciousness there arises the illumination of wisdom (*prajñāloka*).[12] Patañjali describes a complex system of different *samādhi*s, but the basic point is clear that the practitioner becomes absorbed in the object of meditation which is an internal, mental object such that awareness of the external world ceases while awareness of the consequences of this concentration increases. Thus having become absorbed in *samādhi* the yogin acquires knowledge of his previous births and achieves an insight that all these births were characterized by suffering. Even the pleasures of life are suffering compared to the blissful state of liberation. The practitioner also acquires knowledge of other minds (*paricittajñāna*), the power of invisibility, foreknowledge of one's death, superhuman strength, knowledge of distant objects, and significantly knowledge of cosmic regions (*bhuvanajñāna*).[13] Vyāsa in his commentary lists the eight attainments (*siddhi*s), namely ability to become as minute as an atom (*aṇimā*); extreme lightness (*laghimā*); the ability to increase one's size (*mahimā*); attaining or reaching anything (*prāpti*) such as touching the moon with the tip of the finger; irresistible will (*prākāmya*) by which the yogin can go through solid earth; control over the elements (*vaśitva*), mastery over the elements (*īśitṛtva*); and resolution to determine the nature of the elements (*yatrakāmāvasāyitva*).[14] The commentary further illustrates these powers. For the yogin with powers, the hardness of the earth is unable to stop the functions of the yogin's body and so he can pass through stone and he is not made wet by the liquidity of water. Fire cannot burn him, the wind cannot move him, and space cannot show him for he disappears from view and hides himself.

These are strange lists of accomplishments at first reading. The eight *siddhi*s present abilities that accomplished yogins possess although the context for their use or why the yogin would wish to use such powers is left vague. The commentary does say that yogins do not use these powers to go against the stability of nature (*bhūtaprakṛtināmavasthānam*) and do not go against the will of a previous master who brought about a particular disposition of things. This is a somewhat enigmatic passage, but it seems to indicate that the previous master (*pūrvasiddha*) refers to the Lord who creates, maintains and destroys the cosmos. The yogin, then, does not go against the natural order ordained by God.

These lists of supernatural accomplishments clearly illustrate the idea of a cosmic order and the ways in which the yogin can change lower levels through mastery of higher. Supernatural accomplishments illustrate the fundamental cosmological idea that the lower levels of the universe are controlled by higher; that to access the source of lower manifestation is to have power over it. The gross elements (*bhūta*), namely earth, air, fire, water and space (*ākāśa*) have their origin in a higher level of the universe from which they emerge. Control over the elements (*bhūtajaya*) is reflected in the above lists of accomplishments and is one of the stated goals of the yogin.[15] Each of the elements has a particular characteristic or property: hardness is a feature of earth, liquidity of water, heat of fire, mobility of wind, and all pervasiveness of space. Control over the subtle level from which they emanate, called the level of the *tanmātras*, means control over the gross elements and so subtle and gross elements follow the will (*saṇkalpa*) of the yogin as a cow follows its calf. Thus the subtle element of smell is the essential character of the earth element and control over this subtle element means control over the earth; the properties of the elements can be changed at the yogin's will with knowledge of the subtle elements.

What appear to be miraculous phenomena manifested by the yogin, such as his amazing powers, are completely in accord with the yogic understanding of natural law. The powers of the yogin are not a miracle in the sense of an event that goes against material causation, but are understood as using the natural order to effect change in the world in accordance with the yogin's will. The extent to which the yogin penetrates higher levels of the cosmos is the extent to which he has control over the lower levels and so can perform supernormal accomplishments. What appears to be a miracle in this world is the yogin's ability to control structurally higher principles. Later texts make this clear. The tantric Śaiva text the *Māliniviyaottara tantra* composed before the ninth century CE delineates two paths for the yogin to take: on one path he attains liberation as well as enjoying powers along the way, on the other path he wishes to attain a specific power and should direct his efforts towards the world ruler who governs the level where the desired power is accessible.[16] This view of yoga as the means of attaining power in also found in Vaiṣṇava texts, such as the *Jayākhya-Saṃhitā*.[17]

The yogin achieves all this by developing an inwardness which is also conceptualized as a journey through the cosmos. The journey inwards is simultaneously a journey upwards towards the source of the universe. The text speaks of the sun, moon and pole star as lights which appear in the inner vision of the yogin and through his concentration on them, take him out of this world and the physical body into higher cosmic regions. By developing fixed concentration on the inner sun the yogin experiences higher worlds; the inner sun is a gateway into other dimensions of the universe. Thus the text reads: 'through concentration on the sun there is cognition of higher worlds' (*bhuvanajñānaṃ sūrye saṃyamāt*).[18] Through this inner journey into the self and thereby into the cosmos, the yogin achieves higher levels of awareness and thereby control over the lower levels. The commentary lists seven cosmic regions from the lowest hell (*avīchi*) up to the 'true world' (*satya loka*) occupied by different kinds of celestial beings. One group, for example, who dwell in a particular region (the Prājopatya), have mastery over the gross elements (and so the lower regions) and meditation is their food. Journeying up through these regions the yogin must not be distracted as beings who dwell in those higher regions will tempt him to stay, saying that 'this is a pleasant place, here is a lovely woman' and so on.[19] But the yogin must not be distracted from his goal of liberation at the top of the cosmos and so cultivates detachment from even these pleasures. This theme of disparaging the yogic miracles became standard, particularly in the nineteenth-century Hindu renaissance. Ramakrishna, for example, speaks in derogatory terms about yogic powers regarding them as hindrances and temptations on the spiritual path. He cites a story of an ascetic who could walk on water after fourteen years of practising asceticism in the forest. The ascetic told his guru of his great mastery who replied that what he had accomplished after fourteen years of great effort is achieved everyday by ordinary men paying a penny to the boatman.[20]

The ultimate miracle is, of course, the conquest of death. This is a trope that we find throughout the literature of yoga. The yogin can conquer death even in the body and attain immortality. Indeed, in medieval yogic literature the elixir of immorality (*amṛta*) is thought to be contained within the body, stored in the cranium, and through yogic practice this nectar that sits at the crown of the head constantly dripping down, can be arrested and the body made pure, strong and immortal.[21] There is even one practice, the *khecārī mūdrā*, in which the yogin rolls the tongue to the back of the throat in the belief that this will arrest the dripping of the nectar of immortality. This idea of the perfect body is ancient. The *Śvetāśvatara Upaniṣad* speaks of the body attained through the fire of yoga[22] and later texts of the Haṭha yoga school and the Nātha yogins are centrally concerned with immortality and longevity. That yogins can live a very long time is attested in some literature (for example, Shiva Puri Baba who may have lived for 120 years or so)[23] but this is not regarded so much as a miracle as the consequences of dedicated effort and yogic attainment. There is much emphasis on the body, especially in later texts, but even in Patañjali we find the idea that yoga perfects the body. He writes that the perfection of body (*kāyasampat*) is attained through yoga which means that the yogin attains beauty, grace, strength and the hardness of diamond.[24] These ideas persist into the present. Indeed the eluding of death is a strong theme in yoga literature and practice and one further power needs to be mentioned and that is 'yogic suicide' or *utkrānti*. This is the ability, attested in the *Yoga Sūtras* and later Śaiva scriptures, of the yogin to exit his body at will having become weary of the world (*nirveda*). His vital energy is gathered together and rises up through the body, exiting via the cranial aperture and thence to the world of Śiva where he remains liberated, a final conclusion to the yogin's career.[25]

We have in this material the idea that cosmology is closely linked to a psychology of meditation in which state of mind and world of experience are coterminous. This view is fundamental to understanding the idea of supernatural power in Indian religions. The lower levels of the universe, as we have said, are governed by the higher and the yogin who has mastery of the higher levels can control and manipulate the elements that comprise the lower levels and so is able to perform what appear to be miraculous feats. These powers, however, are discouraged as a distraction from the ultimate goal of liberation and there is a rhetoric of disparaging such worldly powers as distractions at best and as dangerous at worst in creating stronger desires in the yogin. If the goal of liberation is detachment from the world of the senses and from human desires – the desire for power and sex – then cultivating supernatural powers might take the yogin away from that goal. Nevertheless, in spite of the anti-powers rhetoric, yogic texts are concerned with supernatural power and a complete book of the *Yoga Sūtras* comprising fifty-five verses is dedicated to them by Patañjali.[26]

The idea of miracle maps on to the idea of supernatural power achieved through yoga and categorized in some detail in key texts such as the *Yoga Sūtras*. There is also another context in which the term 'miracle' is apposite, and that is with regard to saints or holy persons; the gurus, monks and nuns who are so revered in popular Hinduism and to whom are attributed various supernatural occurrences and healing. Such occurrences are within the category of *adbhuta*, a wonder or marvel, indicating a seeming disruption of normal, material causation.

MIRACLES AND HOLY PERSONS

Literature in Sanskrit and vernacular languages is replete with supernatural occurrences. Indeed, the very concept of 'myth' entails an element of the 'miraculous'. Stories of the gods and wonders that occur around them are attested not only in ancient literature but are the life blood of popular stories narrated at village level. 'Wonder' (*adbhuta*) is a mode of reception of texts and stories which bear witness to the truths of the supernatural world and the ways in which that world impinges upon this world governed by material causation. The *Rāmāyana* speaks of the god Hanuman like a monkey, the story of Nala tells of talking geese and gods who have the power to change their form, and so on. In the Purānas we have many stories depicting wondrous events and also in hagiographies. Thus, for example, in the *Bhāgavatga Purāna* which extols the miraculous actions of Krishna, we have the circle dance (*rāsamandala*) in which Krishna manifests copies of himself in order to dance with 16,000 cow girls or *gopīs*; each girl thinks that he dances exclusively with her.[27] While this might seem to transgress law (*dharma*), it does not actually do so because Krishna is the Lord: as fire consumes everything without being polluted, the text says, so blatant transgressions of law done by the more powerful are not faults. Indeed, they are causes of wonder and spiritual absorption signified by trance-like states, horripilation and ecstasy.[28]

Hagiographies also bear witness to miracles. There are many examples here from the life of the monistic philosopher Śankara (788–820 CE) to the life of the theist Caitanya (1486–1533 CE). Let us take an example from the latter. Caitanya, the founder of the Bengali Vaisnava tradition (part of which has become Hare Krishna devotion) was believed to be an incarnation of both Krishna and his consort Rādhā. In his hagiography the *Caitanya Caritāmrtā*, Krsnadāsa Kavirāja documents a number of miraculous events associated with his life. For example, the text tells the story of a Brahmin called Vāsudeva who had leprosy. He heard that Caitanya was visiting his village and went to the house where he was staying where the master embraced him. At the touch of Caitanya 'the leprosy fled away with his sorrow, and now full of joy his body became beautiful. Witnessing the grace of Prabhu [Caitanya], his heart was astonished.'[29] As is generally the case, the occurrence of the miracle here has a teaching function. The cure of Vāsudeva, a 'bad brahmin' by virtue of having his disease from the sins of a past life, shows the mercy, power and greatness of Caitanya. Those who hear this story with faith and reverence, the text continues, will be joined to the feet of Caitanya and so achieve salvation.

Such narratives are not, however, restricted to 'great literature' of the epics and Purānas (*itihāsa*), but are common in vernacular languages as well up to the present time. For example, a Bengali story narrated to Kirin Narayan tells of how a low-caste girl became transformed into the Tulsī plant. The Tulsī is a basil shrub worshipped throughout India as a goddess related to Krishna. In this story, a low-caste cobbler girl desires to marry Krishna who is already married to Rukmani. She ends up marrying Krishna as a second wife and is transformed into the Tulsī plant.[30] Miraculous stories also accrue around the lives of holy men and women and it is common for devotees to narrate the miraculous events that surround a particular holy person. Hindu traditions regard holy persons and teachers in very high regard. This is not simply a respect for learning but also awe in the face of their charisma or the supernatural power they are thought to possess. The sight or *darśana* of the holy person is auspicious and thought to convey merit. Indeed, a guru or holy person could be regarded as akin to the image of a deity in the temple. Both deity and guru possess sacred power and embody a transcendent energy. As the power of the deity is ritually brought down into the image and thereby empowered, so the guru is thought to be empowered and miraculous happenings are often associated with gurus.

There are many examples of such 'marvellous' happenings. Perhaps the most famous contemporary guru associated with the miraculous is Sathya Sai Baba. Sai Baba was born in 1926 to a poor family in Andhra Pradesh and his life is surrounded by devotees bearing witness to his miraculous powers. He claims to be a reincarnation of the saint Sai Baba of Shirdi (d. 1918) and also to be an incarnation (*avatāra*) of Shiva and Shakti. His career has been of increasing claims to divinity supported by a large organization and thousands of devoted followers. At the heart of his teachings is the idea that we are all God and that the difference between him and others is that he has realized this. He advocates what he regards as the universal human values of truth (*satya*), right conduct (*dharma*), non-violence (*ahimsā*), love of God and world (*prema*) and peace (*śanti*). He also teaches the unity of world religions and service to humanity.[31] These teachings, which are typical of Hinduism after the nineteenth century, are accompanied by miraculous events and Sai Baba demonstrating miraculous powers. The most important of these is materializations of objects such as watches, necklaces, rings and gold ornaments. Of particular importance is the manifestation of ash (*vibhuti*) from his finger tips, although other substances are also said to be produced such as red powder for tilak marks, turmeric powder, sweets, fruit, holy water and Śiva *liṇgas*. Ash is sacred to Śiva and, significantly, the term *vibhuti* is used synonymously with *siddhi*. He is also attributed with powers of clairvoyance, levitation and appearing in two places at once, or bilocation. One of the most recent claims to a miracle by Sai Baba was in 2006 when he told his devotees that he would appear in the moon. The large crowd that gathered were disappointed because of the overcast weather.[32] Sai Baba does not appear to perform healing miracles.

The important point is that Sai Baba is said to perform miracles as a sign of his divinity. These manifestations are taken to be evidence for his claims by devotees and evidence of his fraudulence by his critics and rationalists. There is much controversy surrounding Sai Baba. On the one hand there is good work funded by the Sai Baba centre or ashram and many positive claims have been made about the transformative effect of the guru on people's lives; yet on the other he has borne the brunt of negative criticism that his 'miracles' are in fact sleight-of-hand[33] and accusations of sexual abuse and even complicity in murder.[34] With Sai Baba we have a curious mix of a traditional yogic understanding of powers, as attested in yoga literature, in a very modern context with a Western understanding of miracles. Sai Baba himself would seem to be aware of this context and speaks to both Hindu tradition and Western belief in miracles as the disruption of material causation.

There are other, less controversial gurus who are also said to manifest 'miracles' in a less overt way, such as the miracle of transforming life itself. The 'hugging guru' from Kerala, Mata Amritananadamayi Devi sits for long hours simply hugging devotees who line up to receive her blessing and claim to come away transformed. Other, local 'miracles' in India are common, associated with particular persons and places revered as possessing divine power. Indeed, possession by a deity in a ritual context is common in many parts of India and might be seen as a kind of miracle. The *teyyam* tradition of Kerala studied by Rich Freeman describes how selected members of a low-caste group become possessed by deities of local shrines and dance through the compound area blessing devotees by being seen, giving *darshanam*. These *teyyams* might also offer predictions and give advice.[35]

CONCLUDING REMARKS

The primary semantic equivalent to miracle is found in the yogic traditions of Hinduism where supernormal powers are seen as a consequence of a particular level of attainment (*siddhi*). Rather than a disruption of natural law, these powers are regarded as the ability to use natural law, to change causation in the material world. Not only is the idea of *siddhi* a theme in yoga literature in Sanskrit, it is also attested in people's experience. What is interesting in the contemporary context is that traditional understandings of yogic accomplishment have fused with Western understandings of the miracle as the disruption of natural law in gurus such as Sai Baba. In this context we must lastly mention the 'miracles' associated with icons of the gods. In September 1995, a 'miracle' occurred in a Delhi temple when the elephant-headed god, Ganesha, drank milk offered during worship. Due to mass communication this phenomenon spread and icons of Ganesha were drinking milk throughout the world within a few days. This was attested from Malaysia to London and 60 per cent of Delhi's population visited a Ganesha temple at this time.[36] The phenomenon died down in due course and was explained by 'rationalists' in India as the porous stone of the image absorbing the liquid. Clearly we are within the traditional category of 'amazement' and 'wonder', but set in a very modern context with mass communication ensuring that the miracle became a global phenomenon. Depending upon how we define or understand them, we might say that miracles do exist in Hindu traditions as accomplishment due to the efforts of yoga and as amazement at supernatural agency in the world. In Christianity we might say that the significance of miracles lies in their bearing witness to the supreme power of God and, originally, of Jesus through apparently going against natural law. In Hindu conceptualization miracles in the sense we have described do not go against natural law but rather use a higher understanding of natural law to express the eternal truth of the universe, to express *dharma*.

Notes

1   David Hume, 'Of Miracles', in *Enquiries Concerning Human Understanding*, 3rd edn, ed. L. A. Selby-Bigge, rev. and notes P. H. Nidditch (Oxford: Oxford University Press, 1975), 109–31 (114–15).

2   Thomas Aquinas, *Summa contra Gentiles*, trans. Anton Pegis *et al.* (Notre Dame: Notre Dame University Press, 1975), vol. III, 101.

3   Charles Taylor, *A Secular Age* (Cambridge, MA: Belknap, 2008), 16.

4   For a good account of this world view in Europe that could equally apply to India, see C. S. Lewis, *The Discarded Image: An Introduction to Medieval and Renaissance Literature* (Cambridge: Canto, 1994).

5   Gavin Flood, *The Tantric Body* (London: Tauris, 2006), 101–6.

6   Monier Monier-Williams, *A Dictionary, English and Sanskrit* (1851) (Delhi: Motilal Banarsidass, 1976), 504.

7   Flood, *The Tantric Body*, 123–4.

8   Jan Gonda, 'The Indian Mantra', *Oriens* 16 (1963), 244–97.

9   *Yoga-sūtras* 1.2: *yogaś cittavṛttinirodha*.

10   *Ibid.*, 3.3.

11   Hariharananda Aranya, *The Yoga Philosophy of Patañjali* (Albany: SUNY Press, 1983), 252.

12   *Yoga-sūtras* 3.5.

13 *Ibid.*, 3.18–25.

14 *Ibid.*, 3.45 commentary.

15 *Ibid.*, 3.44.

16 Somdeva Vasudeva, *The Yoga of the Māliniviyaottara tantra* (Pondichery: Institut française, 2004), 253.

17 *Jayākhya-saṃhitā* 33.1ab. Reference from Vasudeva, *The Yoga of the Māliniviyaottara tantra*, 253 n.18.

18 *Yoga-sūtras* 3.26.

19 *Ibid.*, 3.51 commentary.

20 Max Muller, *Ramakrishna: His Life and Sayings* (London: Longmans, Green and Co., 1900), 154.

21 See James Malinson, *The Khecarimudra of Adinatha* (London: Routledge, 2005).

22 *Śvetāśvatara Upanisad* 2.12. Olivelle Patrick, *The Early Upanisads: Annotated Text and Translation* (New York: Oxford University Press, 1998), 419.

23 J. G. Bennett, *The Long Pilgrimage: Life and Teachings of Shiva Puri Baba* (London: Thorsons, 1975).

24 *Yoga-sūtras* 3.46.

25 Vasudeva, *The Yoga of the Mālinīvijayottara tantra*, 437–45.

26 David White, 'Early Understandings of Yoga in the Light of Three Aphorisms from the Yoga Sūtras of Patañjali', in *Du corps humain, au carrefour de plusieurs savoirs en Inde*, ed. Oscar Botto *et al.* (Bucharest and Paris: de Boccard, 2004), 611–27, argues that seeking after supernatural power was the main focus of early yogic practice.

27 *Bhāgavata Purāṇa* 10.33.3.

28 *Ibid.*, 10.32.4–9.

29 Kṛṣṇadāsa, *Caitanya Caritāmṛta* 2.7.33–9.

30 Kirin Narayan, 'How a Girl Became A Sacred Plant', in *Religions of India in Practice*, Princeton Readings in Religions, ed. Donald S. Lopez (Princeton: Princeton University Press, 1995), 487–94.

31 See Lawrence A. Babb, 'Sathya Sai Baba's Magic', *Anthropological Quarterly* 56 (1983), 116–24. Also *idem*, *Redemptive Encounters: Three Modern Styles in the Hindu Tradition* (Berkeley: University of California Press, 1986). For a general survey of his life see http://en.wikipedia.org/wiki/Sathya_Sai_Baba

32 http://en.wikipedia.org/wiki/Sathya_Sai_Baba

33 Erlendur Haraldsson, *Modern Miracles: An Investigative Report on Psychic Phenomena Associated with Sathya Sai Baba* (New York: Fawcett, 1997).

34 David Bailey, *A Journey to Love* (Prasanthi Nilayam: Sri Sathya Sai Towers Hotels Pvt. Ltd, 1997).

35 Rich Freeman, 'The Teyyam Tradition of Kerala', in *The Blackwell Companion to Hinduism*, ed. Gavin Flood (Oxford: Blackwell, 2003), 307–26.

36 Axel Michaels and Barbara Harshav, *Hinduism: Past and Present* (Princeton: Princeton University Press, 2004), 222–3.

Further reading

Babb, Lawrence A., *Redemptive Encounters: Three Modern Styles in the Hindu Tradition* (Berkeley: University of California Press, 1986)

Flood, Gavin D., *The Tantric Body: The Secret Tradition of Hindu Religion* (London: I. B. Tauris, 2006)

*Flood, Gavin D., ed., *The Blackwell Companion to Hinduism* (Blackwell: Oxford, 2003)

Freeman, Rich, 'The Teyyam Tradition of Kerala', in *The Blackwell Companion to Hinduism*, ed. Gavin D. Flood (Oxford: Blackwell, 2003), 307–26

Gonda, Jan, 'The Indian Mantra', *Oriens* 16 (1963), 244–97

Goswami, C. L. and M. A. Shastri (trans.), *Srimad Bhagavata-Mahapurana*, 2 vols. (Gorakhpur: Gita, 2005)

Haraldsson, Erlendur, *Modern Miracles: An Investigative Report on Psychic Phenomena Associated with Sathya Sai Baba* (New York: Fawcett Books, 1997)

Kṛṣṇadāsa Kavirāja Gosvāmi, Edward C. Dimock and Tony Kevin Stewart, *Caitanya Caritāmṛta of Kṛṇadāsa Kavirāja: A Translation and Commentary* (Cambridge, MA: Harvard University Press, 1999)

Malinson, James, *The Khecarimudra of Adinatha* (London: Routledge, 2005)

Michaels, Axel, and Barbara Harshav, *Hinduism: Past and Present* (Princeton: Princeton University Press, 2004)

Müller, F. Max, *Râmakrishna: His Life and Sayings* (London: Longmans, Green, and Co., 1900)

Narayan, Kirin, 'How a Girl Became a Sacred Plant', in *Religions of India in Practice*, Princeton Readings in Religions, ed. Donald S. Lopez (Princeton: Princeton University Press, 1995), 487–94

Olivelle, Patrick, *The Early Upanisads: Annotated Text and Translation* (New York: Oxford University Press, 1998)

Patañjali, Hariharānanda Āraṇya, Paresh Nath Mukerji and Vyāsa, *Yoga Philosophy of Patañjali Containing his Yoga Aphorisms with Vyāsa's Commentary in Sanskrit and a Translation with Annotations Including Many Suggestions for the Practice of Yoga* (Albany: State University of New York Press, 1983)

Vasudeva, Somdeva, *The Yoga of the Māliniviyaottara tantra* (Pondichery: Institut française, 2004)

White, David, 'Early Understandings of Yoga in the Light of Three Aphorisms from the Yoga Sūtras of Patañjali', in *Du corps humain, au carrefour de plusieurs savoirs en Inde*, ed. Oscar Botto *et al.* (Bucharest and Paris: de Boccard, 2004), 611–27

11 Miracles in Islam

DAVID THOMAS

The nearness of God as a force and influence in the world is fundamental in Islam. In the Qur'ān-based disciplines, God is understood as the direct cause of all events, so much so that issues of secondary causality have been strenuously debated and questioned among Muslim theologians. God's overwhelming closeness makes it easy for Muslims to admit the miraculous in the world; in fact, there has often been more difficulty in deciding what is not miraculous.

The environment in which Islam originated and developed in western Arabia in its early years was, as far as can be told, one of belief in a pantheon of local gods, goddesses and spiritual beings, whose influence ran through all aspects of individual and community life, and also of awareness of great figures of past religious history, many of them familiar to readers of the Hebrew Bible and the gospels, who had represented the creator God's power in the world. It was the genius of Muḥammad or, in traditional terms, it was given to him, to see the many forms of belief adhered to in the seventh-century world as parts of one whole, and to proclaim the existence and activity of the one God, from whom everything came and to whom everything that happened in history and in society could be ascribed. His proclamations that celebrated the existence and presence of the one God, and denied any power apart from him, formed the starting point of distinctive visions of the world and the way in which things happened, and they provide the context of continuing reflections among Muslims about the nature of the ordinary and the extraordinary.

MIRACLES IN THE QUR'ĀN

According to traditional accounts, the Qur'ān was revealed to Muḥammad between 610 and 632 CE by the angel Gabriel from God himself. In Muslim belief and theological reflection this is God's own utterance that has been with him from eternity. It is, therefore, a source of authority and information that is not to be questioned or doubted. If there is one central theme that unites all the diverse and, for some, divergent parts of the revelation, this is that God is absolute unity, and that there is no rival beside him in divinity or power.

Among the many consequences of this emphatic teaching – it is summed up in the term *tawḥīd*, 'the declaration that God is one' – is the insistence that in his omnipotence and omniscience God presides over everything. Thus, not only is he Creator but he continues in control of all events, from sending rain and forming the foetus in the womb (Q 3.6; 23.14; 96.2), to delivering judgment at the end of time (1.4). For this reason, the Qur'ān constantly calls people to notice the wonders of God, and to realize that they are signs of his existence and active presence.

The Qur'ān makes clear that God is the Lord of history. Thus, for example, in verses from an early stage of the revelations it recalls how God saved Mecca from attack in the year 570 CE, in which Muḥammad is generally said to have been born: 'Seest thou not [Muḥammad] how thy Lord dealt with the Companions of the elephant? Did he not make their treacherous plan go astray? And he sent against them flights of birds, striking them with stones of baked clay' (105.1–4).[1] Commentators interpreted this event as a miracle in which God caused birds to pick up stones and then drop them on the army of the Abyssinian governor of Yemen, as it advanced with its battle elephants. The stones brought out sores on the warriors' bodies, and they abandoned their expedition.

Even more spectacularly, God was with the army of the young Muslim community as they fought their first battle from their base at Medina against their still-pagan Meccan opponents. The engagement took place at the wells of Badr in 624 CE, and the Muslim army was reputedly outnumbered by three to one. But according to what the Qur'ān recounts, God sent angels 'ranks on ranks' (8.10) to fight with the Muslims, and even more miraculously caused the two sides to see each other as fewer than they really were: 'And remember when ye met, he showed them to you as few in your eyes, and he made you appear as contemptible in their eyes: that Allah might accomplish a matter already enacted' (8.44).

The pagan Meccans were made to feel overconfident, and the badly equipped Muslims were given heart, all in accordance with a preordained plan. So the Qur'ān is justified in saying that the victory was won by God, but even more that he was actually present in the whole affair in the most direct manner, even performing the actions of the Muslims as they fought, and of the Prophet when he threw dust to blind the pagans (a miracle ascribed to Muḥammad in later times): 'It was not ye [Muslims] who slew them; it was Allah: when thou [Muḥammad] threwest [a handful of dust], it was not thy act, but Allah's: in order that he might test the Believers by a gracious trial from himself' (8.17). God is immediately behind and in every event, giving it a miraculous character and loading it with moral significance. Therefore, the whole world is charged with meaning, and everything can potentially be a miraculous sign that points evidentially to God.

A term that appears frequently in the Qur'ān to denote miracle is *āya* (pl. *āyāt, āy*). It serves a range of meanings, from token or indication – the sun and moon are tokens of day and night (7.12) – to sign of God's creative activity – marriage partners and the love between them, the variations in human languages and skin colours, sleep at night and activity by day (30.21–3) – to demonstrations of God's power that constitute proofs irrefutable to the rational and condemnatory to the heedless – the people drowned in the flood in which Noah was saved ignored God's signs (10.73). The term frequently carries a moral or educative load, and so easily comes to denote the accounts of God's activity in the lives of the prophets by which people may learn (2.87; 6.124), and also the verses of the Qur'ān itself, whose chapters, *sūras*, comprise different numbers of *āyāt*.

Cognate terms in the Qur'ān serve similar functions. The adjective *bayyina*, 'clear', 'manifest', appears as a modifier of *āya*: 'We have sent down to thee [Muḥammad] manifest signs [*āyāt bayyināt*]' (2.99); but it also appears alone as a substantive to denote the clear indications of God and his ways: 'Be not like those who are divided amongst themselves and fell into disputations after receiving clear signs [*bayyināt*]' (3.105). It suggests evidence so obvious that no responsible, straight-thinking individual would deny it. Derivations of the verb *'ajaba*, 'to wonder', 'to be astonished', which are less frequent, denote human reactions to divine actions, or the miraculous nature of the actions and their results (10.2, 38.5).

These terms suggest initiatives from God that seek to evoke a response on the part of humans which consists primarily of acknowledging his existence and power, and then of recognizing the relationship they have with him. The fact that these actions or events are miraculous is intentionally to evoke this response and the belief expressed in appropriate conduct that issues from it. Thus, they are elements within God's overall will to give guidance to created humanity, and they function as the first step in arousing awareness of him by provoking humankind to think about the character of what can be seen around.

In addition to the miraculous character of the order of the world, the Qur'ān refers to what may more readily be recognized as miracles in relation to the prophetic messengers who came from God to bring the detailed utterances of his will. It refers to at least twenty-five of these messengers, all of them human but chosen specifically by God, and it speaks of miraculous feats associated with them. Thus, when Abraham (Ibrāhīm) is thrown by his idolatrous people into a fire, 'We said, "O fire! Be thou cool and [a means of] safety for Abraham"' (21.69), when he obeys the command to sacrifice his own son, 'This was obviously a trial – and we ransomed him with a momentous sacrifice' (37.106–7), and when Moses (Mūsā) at the burning bush throws down his staff, 'He saw it moving [of its own accord] as if it had been a snake' (28.31). Similarly, in the case of David (Dāwūd), 'It was our power that made the hills and the birds celebrate our praises with David, it was we who did [all these things]', and Solomon (Sulaymān), 'We subjected the wind to his power, to flow gently to his order, withersoever he willed' (38.36).

What is either implied or stated in these examples is given clear expression in two accounts of a miracle of Jesus ('Īsā), who in one of them says, 'I have come to you [people] with a sign [āya] from your Lord, in that I make for you out of clay, as it were, the figure of a bird, and breathe into it, and it becomes a bird by Allah's leave [bi-idhn Allāh] (3.49). Here the miracle of clay birds becoming real birds that fly when Jesus breathes on them happens through the permission or help of God. It is not because of any power that Jesus has within himself, just like the other prophetic messengers, but because of a feat performed by God for him. This is emphatically attested in the other version of this miracle account: 'And behold! Thou [Jesus] makest out of clay, as it were, the figure of a bird, by my leave [bi-idhnī], and thou breathest into it, and it becometh a bird by my leave, and thou healest those born blind, and the lepers by my leave. And behold! Thou bringest forth the dead by my leave' (5.110). There is no room for doubt that God is immediately present as these miracles occur, and if he is not alone the one who performs them he is certainly the agent who acts through the prophetic instruments to make them occur. Their purpose is evidently to attest in a particular way to the messenger who has appeared, sometimes, as with Moses, to realize that he has been chosen as messenger, but often to prove in public that this is an extraordinary individual, and more importantly that he has been sent in order to point to the reality of God, and in the case of Abraham, Moses, David and Jesus to alert people to the divinely revealed Scriptures they have been given to proclaim to their communities (3.48; 4.163; 87.18–19). Again, the final intention is to evoke a response in the form of changed beliefs and changed morality.

THE QUR'ĀN AS MIRACLE

The world depicted in the Qur'ān is one in which miracles are part of the ongoing course of events, because everything that takes place does so through God's action and, as an evidential sign, points to him. But there are also unusual and miraculous events associated with prophetic messengers as proofs of their special position.

The Qur'ān contains stories of a series of messengers that later Muslim authors compiled together into what can be called an Islamic salvation history. This begins with Adam, whose creation without parents (3.59) is alluded to as proof of his status, continues with figures many of whom are familiar from the Bible such as Noah, Abraham, Moses, David, Solomon, John the Baptist and Jesus, each sent to a particular community with a proclamation from God and usually accompanied by evidential miracles, and ends with Muḥammad. The Qur'ān depicts Muḥammad very much in the same terms as other messengers, who were sent with revealed messages containing saving guidance for their communities, except that it declares him as the culmination of this line (in 33.40 he is called 'Seal of the prophets', *khātam al-nabiyyīn*, which is normally interpreted to mean the last of them).

It should follow from this that Muḥammad is given evidential miracles like the prophetic messengers before him. But here the Qur'ānic teaching is not straightforward. On the one hand it appears to suggest that his opponents demanded a miracle from him but did not witness one: 'They say, "Why is not a sign [*āya*] sent down to him from his Lord?" Say, "Allah hath certainly power to send down a sign, but most of them understand not"' (6.37). The implication in such utterances is that a miracle, no matter how impressive, will never stand as final proof for people who are convinced against the Prophet and will not be forthcoming. In this respect, his experience echoes that of his prophetic predecessors, who despite the wonders attending their coming were often rejected and dismissed by the very people to whom they were sent: 'Mocked were [many] messengers before thee; but their scoffers were hemmed in by the thing that they mocked' (6.10). So their miracles never overcame the reservations and stubbornness of their opponents, and sometimes of their own people.

But on the other hand, there are indications that miraculous events involving the Prophet did take place to provide the evidence of his status, like his predecessors. The reference in 94.1–4 – 'Have we not expanded thee thy breast? And removed from thee thy burden, the which did gall thy back? And raised high the esteem [in which] thou [art held]?' – was understood by some interpreters to mean that Muḥammad's chest had physically been opened by angels and his insides cleansed, and is generally taken to mean that he was purified in a unique way. The reference in 54.1–2 – 'The hour [of judgement] is nigh, and the moon is cleft asunder. But if they see a sign, they turn away, and say, "This is [but] transient magic"' – was interpreted as a physical occurrence in the heavens witnessed by Muḥammad and people around the world. And the reference in 17.1 formed the basis of a tradition that became a whole genre of literature in itself: 'Glory to [Allah] who did take his servant for a journey by night from the Sacred Mosque [al-masjid al-ḥarām] to the Farthest Mosque [al-masjid al-aqṣā], whose precincts we did bless – in order that we might show some of our signs'.

Apart from saying that the servant, obviously Muḥammad, was taken through the night by God from one mosque (masjid, 'place of prostration in prayer') to another, this is elegantly enigmatic. But in commentaries and the biographical literature it was taken to refer to a journey in which Muḥammad travelled on a miraculous beast called the Burāq from the mosque in Mecca (al-masjid al-ḥarām) to the mosque in Jerusalem (al-masjid al-aqṣā, the name of the mosque on the Temple Mount which, mainly as a result of this reference, is widely regarded as the third holiest place in Islam), and from there up to heaven into the presence of God himself.

The story of this event was greatly elaborated as time went on. The point from which Muḥammad on the Burāq ascended to heaven (the whole account is often called the mi'rāj, 'ascent') was identified as the rock on the Temple Mount which at an early point in the Islamic era was enclosed in the Dome of the Rock; before he went up he was joined by all the previous prophetic messengers and led them in prayer (symbolizing his precedence over them); he was conducted on his journey by the angel Gabriel (the angel who brought revelations to him and his predecessors, as well as announcing in the Qur'ān the birth of Jesus to Mary), and ascended through a succession of heavens; and in later accounts he went through a succession of hells and saw the fate of sinners in a manner that anticipated and, it has been plausibly argued, influenced Dante's lurid descriptions in the *Inferno*.

These later amplifications of references in the Qur'ān that at best hint at miracles associated with Muḥammad boost his status to that of at least the equal of the greatest of his predecessors. But they do not substitute for what is taken as the greatest of his miracles, the Qur'ān itself.

The Arabic of the Qur'ān is a tight rhyming prose that approaches poetry though is formally distinct from it. Its economy and elegance has stirred admiration in both Muslims and non-Muslims when they hear it recited (the word *Qur'ān* actually means 'recitation'). And it appears that even in Muḥammad's lifetime it was recognized as a phenomenon quite different from parallel instances. Individuals who set themselves up as rival prophets to Muḥammad delivered utterances in the same style, particularly the 'false prophet' Musaylima, in an evident attempt to emulate this genius. And its qualities were claimed as inimitable, and therefore indications of its divine origins. As though in response to taunts from critics, it lays out a challenge: 'Say, "If the whole of mankind and jinns were to gather together to produce the like of this Qur'ān they could not produce the like thereof, even if they backed up each other with help and support"' (17.88), and 'If ye are in doubt as to what we have revealed from time to time to our servant, then produce a *sūra* like thereunto; and call your witnesses or helpers (if there are any) besides Allah, if your doubts are true' (2.23). While the background of such verses cannot be known for sure, they clearly appear to imply that while opponents rejected the proclamations delivered by Muḥammad, the actual literary form of these proclamations was accepted as evidence of its authenticity. It was guaranteed by the fact that it could not be imitated, not even a single chapter (*sūra* is the Arabic term for each of the 114 formal divisions of the Qur'ān). The fact that none of Muḥammad's contemporaries successfully met this challenge (and in later times none of the few Muslims who tried) was taken as proof that such style could not have been fashioned by a human mind and must therefore point to its divine origins with God as author.

Thus, the Qur'ān is for Muḥammad a miracle that parallels the miracles of earlier prophetic messengers, an event that is not produced by him but for him through God's action. Just as Moses' staff and Jesus' clay birds are transformed by God as evidential signs, so the Qur'ān, as it is brought in portions from God by the angel Gabriel for Muḥammad to recite, is provided as a sign of his prophetic status. And it is made all the more miraculous by the fact that he himself was supposed to have been illiterate (based on the references in 7.157 and 158 to *al-nabī al-ummī*, 'the unlettered prophet').

The conviction that the Qur'ān with its uniquely sublime Arabic style was a miracle became a principle of doctrine at an early stage in Islamic history, expressed as *i'jāz al-Qur'ān*, 'the rendering incapable by the Qur'ān', or the inimitability of the Qur'ān; this gave rise to the term used to designate a prophetic miracle, *mu'jiza*, 'a thing that renders others incapable of doing the same or of repeating it'. Although the evidence for the precise nature of the theological discussions that took place in the important early centuries of Islam is sparse, it appears that at this time Muslim theological experts often held that the actual literary qualities of the Qur'ān were proof of its status simply because they could not be imitated. The arguments of a detractor such as the free-thinking monotheist Abū 'Īsā al-Warrāq (*fl.* 850 CE), who jibed that the challenge issued in verses that called opponents to produce a comparable *sūra* was calculatedly artificial because these people were too taken up with warfare to respond,[2] hollow as it sounds, serves to show the gathering strength of the doctrine at this time. And the reservation expressed by the slightly earlier rationalist theologian Ibrāhīm al-Naẓẓām (d. *c.* 845 CE) that the inimitability resided not in any intrinsic qualities of the Qur'ān, because Arabs in earlier times had achieved comparable feats of stylistic eloquence and linguistic purity, but in the time of the Prophet this ability was miraculously removed from them,[3] attests to the prevalence of the alternative view that the *i'jāz* was located in the actual text of the Qur'ān itself.

MIRACLES IN THE THEOLOGICAL MILIEU

From its origins in early seventh-century Arabia, Islam quickly spread through the Middle East and North Africa. In these regions Christianity, Judaism and Zoroastrianism were deeply rooted, and there remained within the Islamic world huge populations of non-Muslims for some centuries. In these centuries, particularly the mid-eighth to the eleventh centuries, Islamic religious thought developed into characteristic systematic forms. Its main exponents frequently engaged in debates and confrontations with representatives of Christianity and other faiths, and in consequence they often thought out their theological positions in response to questions posed by followers of other faiths or in the light of issues that were debated within other faiths.

Clearly, Christians would find it overwhelmingly difficult to accept Muslim claims about the prophetic status of Muḥammad and the revealed status of the Qur'ān. Surviving polemical texts show that Christian theologians living under Muslim rule at best accepted him as a prophet for the Arabs alone with a scripture that approximated to the Bible, and more frequently dismissed him as a self-seeking charlatan and the Qur'ān as a pastiche of biblical truth. In response to such criticisms there developed within Islam a genre that came to be identified as *dalā'il al-nubuwwa*, 'proofs of prophethood'. Few early examples survive, but from those that do it can be seen that it was characterized by accounts of the excellent personal qualities possessed by the Prophet, predictions of his coming contained in the gospels and Hebrew Bible (as was confirmed by such verses as Q 61.6, where Jesus gives 'glad tidings of a messenger to come after me'), and references to the miracles he performed.

One of the best-known early examples of this genre is the *Kitāb al-dīn wa-al-dawla*, 'The Book of Religion and Empire', by 'Alī ibn Rabban al-Ṭabarī (d. *c.* 860 CE), who worked at the caliphal court in Baghdad for many years as a Christian but then converted to Islam at the age of seventy. In this book he performs an almost unique and prodigious feat of identifying more than 130 biblical references to the coming of Muḥammad and Islam. And he also discusses the miracles associated with the Prophet.

Among these miracles, as might be expected, 'Alī mentions the Qur'ān, and what he says about the superior quality of its contents is worth quoting at length:

> It has, indeed, become a miracle of meanings, which no writer of books on this subject has tried to explain without recognizing his incompetence and renouncing his discourse and his claim to such an explanation. When I was a Christian, I did not cease to say in accordance with an uncle of mine who was one of the eloquent and learned men among Christians, that rhetoric was not a sign of prophetic office on account of its being common to all nations. But when I waived tradition and customs, and broke with the promptings of habit and education, and examined the meanings of the Qur'ān, then I found that the question was not as its holders believed it to be. I have never met with a book written by an Arab, or a Persian, or an Indian, or a Greek, which contained, like the Qur'ān, unity, praise, and glorification of the most high God; belief in his Apostles and Prophets; incitement to good and permanent works; injunction of good things, and prohibition of evil things; exhortation to heaven and restraining from hell. Who has ever written, since the creation of the world, a book with such prerogatives and qualities, with such influence, sweetness and charm upon the heart, and with such attraction, felicity and success, while its producer, the man to whom it was revealed, was unlettered, not even knowing how to write, and having no eloquence whatever? This is without doubt and hesitation a mark of prophetic office.[4]

The zeal of the convert is not difficult to detect here, though this fulsome praise nevertheless shows how striking the literary qualities of the Qur'ān could appear to be. And for 'Alī this is all the more awesome because Muḥammad was unlettered and unlearned.

In addition to this evidence, 'Alī also adduces examples of miraculous events that are immediately recognizable as works of wonder. They include the Night Journey, which here Muḥammad proves when he returns home by giving the sceptical Meccans details about a caravan approaching the town that he could not have known about without seeing it, the sudden and painful deaths of five of his most vehement critics in Mecca, his diverting a storm that threatened to damage some dwellings, turning a plant stem into a sword and understanding what a bird was communicating, a calf that was about to be slaughtered proclaiming his advent, a wolf doing the same, his withholding rain, increasing food and providing water for his companions on a journey: 'We hurried towards him, and there was with him a drinking vessel in which there was water. He put his hand in it, and caused the water to jet out of his fingers, as if there were springs. We drank and quenched our thirst, and made our ablutions; and we were four hundred men.'[5]

'Alī goes on to list events foretold by Muḥammad that were realized in the Prophet's own day, and events foretold by him that were realized after his death,[6] things that in 'Alī's own consideration the Prophet could never have known about by unaided human means. The net result is that for this convert Muḥammad emerges as exhibiting the characteristics that a true messenger of God would have, supernatural power and knowledge, and above all literary accomplishments that so surpass those of others they render them incapable.

'Alī does not show in this work any awareness of the need to authenticate these miracles for a possible hostile audience who might not accept the authority of his biographical sources or of the Qur'ān, even though he is writing with Christians and Jews in the forefront of his mind. But miracles were very much part of the arguments that were used between Muslims and Christians in particular, and one form of proof involving them became a regular feature of Muslim anti-Christian polemical works.

Clearly, Christians persistently questioned Muslim claims about the prophetic, divinely authenticated status of Muḥammad, provoking responses of the kind instanced in 'Alī al-Ṭabarī's *Kitāb al-dīn wa-al-dawla* and other, maybe less extravagant examples of *dalā'il al-nubuwwa* literature. But Muslims, on their side, questioned Christian claims about the divine sonship of Jesus, invoking the Qur'ānic declaration that he was no more than a human prophet sent as part of the line of messengers to bring a revealed scripture to his own people. They produced many arguments to prove this, and a favourite was the comparison of miracles performed by Jesus, and supposedly upheld by Christians as indicative proofs of his divinity, with equivalent miracles performed by other prophets.

This polemical feature of Muslim works against Christianity can be traced from the late eighth century onwards, and one of the most elaborate examples of it occurs in another work of 'Alī al-Ṭabarī, which he wrote just after his conversion to Islam. It continues for many centuries, showing how convincing it appeared to Muslims. The form presented by the early tenth-century theological master Abū Manṣūr al-Māturīdī (d. 944 CE) in his *Kitāb al-tawḥīd*, 'Divine Unity', shows it in its typical and uncompromisingly hostile form.

Al-Māturīdī begins by arguing that if, as the Christian opponents maintain, the manifestation of miracles by God through Jesus proves that he was God's Son, then the same must apply to Moses, and it is no defence to say that Moses' miracles were only made manifest when he prayed for God's help, because Jesus too prayed and implored God, as in the Garden of Gethsemane. And again, it cannot be claimed that Jesus only prayed to God in order to instruct others how to do this, because the same can be claimed for Moses. There is no intrinsic qualitative difference between the two prophetic figures.

Furthermore, it cannot be claimed that Jesus' miraculous actions single him out as divine. Just as he revived a dead man, so did Ezekiel, while more impressively Moses turned a lifeless staff into a snake; just as Jesus provided food for many, so Muḥammad provided flour for his followers to make bread; just as Jesus turned water into wine, so Elisha turned water into oil; just as he walked on water, ascended into heaven, and healed the sick, so Elijah and Elisha did the same; and while Jesus' insignificance is proved by his allowing himself to be mocked and crucified, Elijah's strength of purpose is demonstrated by his calling fire down on the soldiers who were pursuing him.[7]

On the face of it, this is an effective argument. It takes miracles as a given, but it contests their probative quality, for while they certainly come from God and are manifested by him on or around a prophet, they do not constitute proof that the status of the prophetic individual is any more than human. Their purpose is to attest to God's mysterious gracefulness in calling people's attention to the human channels of his revealed guidance and the scriptural teachings they bring, and their purpose is to evoke a response to the teachings and to produce transformations in human lives. It is not to stir up extravagant adulation for the human individuals themselves.

THE NATURE OF THE MIRACLE

This polemical motif went through a change as it was incorporated into the structure of Islamic theology and made part of the systematic treatises that covered all aspects of religious thinking, from the reasoned presentation of Islamic theological issues to the refutation of Christianity and other faiths. As it appears in the works of two later tenth-century theologians, it becomes clear that there is less interest in the vivid comparisons between the miraculous actions of Jesus and other prophets and more in the nature of the miracles themselves as occurrences within the physical world.

The Ash'arite theologian Abū Bakr al-Bāqillānī (d. 1013) raises this issue of the probative character of Jesus' miracles in his refutation of Christianity as part of his treatise the *Kitāb al-tamhīd*, 'The Introduction'. At this point he may have been drawing on the source that was used by al-Māturīdī, though he is more interested in what actually happened on the physical level when Jesus' miracles were performed than in the similarity between his miracles and those of other prophets.

> Say to them [the Christians]: Why do you say that the Word of God united with the body of Christ but not with the body of Moses or Abraham or any of the other prophets?
>
> If they say: Because of the signs performed and miracles made through Jesus the like of which humans are not capable of, such as raising the dead, healing the blind and the leper, making what is little a lot, turning water into wine, walking on the water, his ascension into heaven, healing the sick, making the crippled walk, and other miraculous signs – so he must have been divine, and the Word must have united with him; say to them: Why do you claim that Jesus was the performer and originator of the signs you describe? Why do you deny that he was incapable of a small or great part of this, and that God almighty was the one who performed all this that appeared through him [*an yakūnu Allāh ta'ālā huwa alladhī fa'ala jamī' mā zahara 'alā yadihi min dhālika*], and his position in this was the same as the other prophets when signs appeared through them?[8]

The actual process of the miraculous action need not have involved any power or responsibility from Jesus himself, but only action from

God, who could have made the miracle appear 'at the hands of Jesus' or 'through him' (*alā yadihi*) without Jesus effecting any part of it. Al-Bāqillānī gives point to what he contends by going on to say that should his Christian opponents insist that if a prophet such as Moses cannot rank as divine, while Jesus can, because Moses was not the originator of his miracles but prayed for them to be made manifest through him, then since Jesus is also recorded as praying there is no valid distinction between them.

In these compressed arguments this Muslim theologian is beginning to analyse the nature of the miracle, locating its origin solely within God's power and identifying the prophet as no more than its channel. The only part played by the prophet is in requesting God to perform the miraculous action or, in the terminology used, to cause it to be manifest – just as in the Qur'ān Jesus made the clay birds fly *bi-idhn Allāh*, by the permission or help or authorization of God, not by any capability of his own.

The slightly later rationalist Mu'tazilite theologian 'Abd al-Jabbār al-Hamadhānī (d. 1025) takes this further in the equivalent section against Christian doctrines of his theological compendium *Al-mughnī fī abwāb al-taḥwīd wa-al-'adl*, 'The *summa* on divine unity and justice'. He shows even less interest in actual comparisons between prophets than al-Bāqillānī, and instead focuses on the central point that the actual appearance of miracles is no different in the case of Jesus and in other prophets. Furthermore, despite what Christians maintain, God can cause miracles without being in immediate contact with things that are changed, and he therefore need not have been incarnate in Christ for the miraculous actions to occur. And even more than this, if some Christians persist in saying that there must have been contact between the divine and created for Christ's miracles to have occurred, then logically this contact would have been between God and the actual physical being or thing affected by the miraculous actions rather than with Jesus himself, 'because this was the location of the action and not Jesus' (*li-anna dhālika huwa maḥall al-fi'l dūna 'Īsā*).[9] In this analysis, the precise chain of physical action is examined in order to show that if the power for the miracle lies with God alone, human agency is removed and the occurrence of the miracle involves only God's direct action on the object of the miracle without any need for the involvement of a secondary human agent. Here the prophets, of whom Jesus is of course one, are reduced to nothing more than channels of God's power and will.

At the same time as these theological and physical analyses of the miraculous actions associated with prophets were being conducted according to the precise logical principles of Islamic theology, the question of miracles associated with prophets and the wonderful actions of saintly people such as the Shīʿī Imāms and Ṣūfī saints was also being explored. The issue that presented the greatest challenge was how to draw a distinction between the wonders (*karāmāt*, sing. *karāma*, also meaning 'mark of honour', 'esteem'; it may have been coined because of its phonetic similarity to the Greek *charisma*) that were ascribed to holy individuals, such as the Ṣūfī saints, and the miraculous actions, *muʿjizāt*, that were claimed as evidence for the specifically designated line of prophetic messengers which had reached its end with Muḥammad. Since God was the immediate agent of the actions that came from all created beings, was there any real distinction, and could saintly people be distinguished from prophetic messengers?

Some theologians, particularly among the rationalist Muʿtazila, denied that the wonders ascribed to saintly individuals were anything more than tricks intended to attract a following. But most Muslims came to accept that while God does indeed confer wonders upon such individuals, these are signs of personal distinction which are meant for them alone, unlike prophetic miracles, which are intended to draw public attention to the authenticity of a human who has been sent to deliver a revealed message to a community. And thus the saintly individual is inferior to the prophet, and the *karāma* inferior to the *muʿjiza*. But this distinction, which was uneasily maintained by theologians, had little effect among the mystical followers of saintly individuals. It is usually observed in Ṣūfī manuals, but biographies of Ṣūfī masters are often full of accounts of the wonders they performed, and it is clear that their effect is to instil awe and often veneration that went beyond the boundaries set for maintaining the distinction between worship of God and the human.

In defence of *karāmāt*, it was explained that as the initiate progressed along the path of holiness to the ultimate goal of unity with God, and passed through various stages of self-abandonment, he became so aware of nothing other than God that this awareness became visible through him and his actions took on the marvellous quality of a being who is motivated and activated only by its proximity to God. But the danger of seeing the marvellous actions as ends in themselves and as sources of spiritual pride was also acknowledged. It was rather earthily summed up in the maxim: 'Marvels are the menstruation of men': they could become obstacles to full union with God by rendering the saint impure.

Just as saintly Muslims were looked upon as virtual sources of divine power, so the person of Muḥammad attracted increasing veneration in Ṣūfī thought. He was hailed as the primordial light according to which God created the world, and he was regarded as the summation of the whole of human nature and the reflection of the divine reality, the *Insān al-kāmil*, the Perfect Man. The fourteenth-century mystic 'Abd al-Karīm al-Jīlī addresses him in a poem as follows:

O Centre of the compass! O inmost ground of the truth!
O Pivot of necessity and contingency!
O Eye of the entire circle of existence![10]

It was natural in such circumstances to regard everything associated with Muḥammad as possessing miraculous powers, even single hairs and his sandals, which were preserved in parts of the Islamic world.

One of the most impressive extensions of this regard for things associated with the Prophet as miraculous is the thirteenth-century poem known as the *Burda*, 'The Mantle Poem', after the cloak that Muḥammad used to wear. The poet al-Būṣīrī told how he had dreamt when he was ill that the Prophet had come to him and thrown his cloak over him and healed him, and then he wrote this poem in celebration of the Prophet's unsurpassed character. The poem itself gradually became an object of piety, and the act of copying it is still thought particularly virtuous, while to recite certain verses from it is thought to ensure miraculous cures for physical and mental illnesses.

CONCLUSION

The story is told of how Muḥammad ibn Ya'qūb, a ninth-century Ṣūfī adept, was rescued in the desert by two Christian monks. They had nothing with them to eat or drink as they travelled, but on the first night one monk miraculously produced food and water for them by praying and then scratching in the sand, on the second night the other monk did the same, and on the third night the Muslim did the same. This continued night after night until finally a voice was heard declaring that God willed to show through the Muslim 'the superiority we have granted the Prophet Muḥammad over all other prophets and apostles. And this is the sign, in order to honour you and the community of my Prophet!' This voice speaking directly from heaven made the two monks convert, acknowledging the superiority of Islam.[11] Of course, the story is part of commonplace legend, and its reference to miracles is by no means unique to Islam. But what is distinctive is the appearance of God's voice in vindication of the Muslim and his faith. It makes the story an instance of the principle that miracles in Islam in both their pre-eminent and popular form are always manifestations of the divine, and therefore whether *mu'jizāt* or *karāmāt* they are always *āyāt*, signs to arrest the mind and cause it to recall the miraculous nature of everything that occurs because it comes from God and witnesses to him. This instrumental character is at the heart of all forms of understanding miracles in Islam.

Notes

1   All quotations from the Qur'ān are taken from the translation by 'Abdallāh Yūsuf 'Alī, *The Meaning of the Holy Qur'ān* (Beltsville: Amana, 1989).

2   See David Thomas, *Anti-Christian Polemic in Early Islam: Abū 'Īsā al-Warrāq's 'Against the Trinity'* (Cambridge: Cambridge University Press, 1992), 26–9.

3   Referred to by Abū al-Ḥusayn al-Khayyāṭ, *Kitāb al-intiṣār*, ed. and trans. A. Nader (Beirut: Imprimerie catholique, 1957), 23 (Arabic text), 25 (French trans.).

4   'Alī al-Ṭabarī, *The Book of Religion and Empire*, trans. A. Mingana (Manchester: Manchester University Press, 1923), 50–1.

5   *Ibid.*, 30–6.

6   *Ibid.*, 37–49.

7   See David Thomas, *Christian Doctrines in Islamic Theology*, History of Christian–Muslim Relations 10 (Leiden: Brill, 2008), 100–5.

8   Translation from *ibid.*, 193.

9   *Ibid.*, 318–21.

10   Quoted in Annemarie Schimmel, *And Muhammad is his Messenger: The Veneration of the Prophet in Islamic Piety* (Chapel Hill: University of North Carolina Press, 1985), 137–8.

11   From Abū Nu'aym al-Iṣfahānī, *Ḥilyat al-awliyā'*, trans. Carl-A. Keller, 'Perceptions of Other Religions in Sufism', in Jean Jacques Waardenburg, *Muslim Perceptions of Other Religions: A Historical Survey* (New York: Oxford University Press, 1999), 182–3.

Further reading

Aigle, Denise, ed., *Miracle et karāma*, Hagiographies médiévales comparées 2 (Turnhout: Brepols, 2000)

Bāqillānī, Muḥammad ibn al-Ṭayyib, trans. Gustave E. von Grunebaum, *A Tenth-Century Document of Arabic Literary Theory and Criticism* (Chicago: University of Chicago Press, 1950)

Chodkiewicz, Michel, *Seal of the Saints: Prophethood and Sainthood in the Doctrine of Ibn 'Arabī*, Golden palm series (Cambridge: Islamic Texts Society, 1993)

Cruise O'Brien, Donal B. and Christian Coulon, *Charisma and Brotherhood in African Islam*, Oxford Studies in African Affairs (Oxford: Clarendon Press, 1988)

Ess, Josef van, *The Flowering of Muslim Theology* (Cambridge, MA: Harvard University Press, 2006)

Gwynne, R. W., *Logic, Rhetoric and Legal Reasoning in the Qur'ān: God's Arguments* (London: Routledge, 2004)

Larkin, Margaret, 'The Inimitability of the Qur'ān: Two Perspectives', *Religion and Literature* 20 (1988), 31–47

Martin, Richard C., 'The Role of the Basrah Mu'tazilah in Formulating the Doctrine of the Apologetic Miracle', *Journal of Near Eastern Studies* 39 (1980), 175–89

Renard, John, *Seven Doors to Islam: Spirituality and the Religious Life of Muslims* (Berkeley: University of California Press, 1996)

Windows on the House of Islam: Muslim Sources on Spirituality and Religious Life (Berkeley: University of California Press, 1998)

*Schimmel, Annemarie, *Deciphering the Signs of God: A Phenomenological Approach to Islam* (Albany: State University of New York Press, 1994)

And Muhammad is his Messenger: The Veneration of the Prophet in Islamic Piety (Chapel Hill: University of North Carolina Press, 1985)

Smith, Grace Martin and Carl W. Ernst, *Manifestations of Sainthood in Islam* (Istanbul: Isis, 1993)

Thomas, David, *Christian Doctrines in Islamic Theology*, History of Christian-Muslim Relations 10 (Leiden: Brill, 2008)

'The Miracles of Jesus in Early Islamic Polemic', *Journal of Semitic Studies* 39 (1994), 221–43

12 Tales of miraculous teachings: miracles in early Indian Buddhism

RUPERT GETHIN

From its beginnings in the fourth or third century BCE, Buddhist literature abounds in tales of miracles (Sanskrit *prātihārya*; Pali *pāṭihāriya*). From the early centuries BCE these miracles are depicted in the stone reliefs on Buddhist monuments across India. For the Chinese pilgrims Faxian and Xuanzang, visiting India in the fifth and seventh centuries CE respectively, stories of the miracles performed by the Buddha and his disciples informed the very landscape of Buddhist pilgrimage sites as well as the imaginations of Buddhist pilgrims.[1]

The present chapter does not attempt to survey miracle across the Buddhist world and throughout Buddhist history, but rather to highlight some of the themes that characterize the Buddhist approach to the miraculous by focusing on Indian sources that exercised considerable influence as Buddhism spread beyond the India and across Asia. While such an approach has the disadvantage of leaving in the shadows much that is colourful and distinctive in the tales of the miraculous in the Buddhist traditions of East and Southeast Asia, it has the advantage of mapping out a common ground that these diverse traditions might recognize.

The earliest phase of Buddhist literature (fourth to first centuries BCE) takes the form of two sets of texts: (1) the collections (*nikāya*, *āgama*) of the Buddha's sayings (*sutta*, *sūtra*) and (2) monastic rules (*vinaya*). Both sets are 'canonical' in that they are regarded as the authoritative 'Word of the Buddha' (*buddha-vacana*). They have come down to us in part or in full in various recensions in ancient Indian languages and in Chinese and Tibetan translation. A second phase of Indian Buddhist literature involved the production of the Abhidharma texts and Mahāyāna sūtras (second century BCE to fourth centuries CE) as well as, from the second century CE onwards, exegetical works of the various Indian schools of Buddhist thought, including the Mahāyāna. While the precise status of the Abhidharma texts and Mahāyāna sūtras was disputed in India, they too were regarded as 'the Word of the

Buddha' by their ancient advocates. Important Buddhist texts were also composed beyond India in the various countries to which Buddhism spread (the kingdoms of Southeast Asia, China, Korea, Japan, Tibet and Mongolia) during the first millennium of the Christian era, but the present discussion draws primarily on Indian sources composed before the sixth century CE.

For the earliest phase of Buddhist literature I shall refer to the sayings contained in the Pali Nikāyas. For the exegetical traditions I shall refer to three sources in particular: (1) Chapter 12 of 'The Path of Purification' (*Visuddhimagga*), a Pali text composed in Ceylon probably in the early fifth century CE by a monk of the Theravāda school named Buddhaghosa;[2] (2) Chapter 7 of the 'The Treasury of Abhidharma' (*Abhidharmakośa*), a Sanskrit text composed in northern India in the fourth or fifth century by a monk named Vasubandhu which provides an account of the positions of the Sarvāstivāda school as well as some of its critics;[3] (3) Chapter 43 of the *Da zhi du lun* (*Mahāprajñāpāramitāśāstra*), a Mahāyāna treatise on the practice of a bodhisattva on his way to buddhahood which was composed in Sanskrit but survives only in a Chinese translation made at the beginning of the fifth century.[4] All three of these texts represent ways of thinking that have had and continue to have currency beyond India – the *Visuddhimagga* in Sri Lanka and Southeast Asia, the *Abhidharmakośa* and the *Da zhi du lun* in Tibet and East Asia.

THE SIX HIGHER KNOWLEDGES

Western discussions tend to assume an understanding of miracle as 'an unusual event that is the result of direct divine circumvention or modification of the natural order'.[5] The Buddhist notion of 'miracle' (*prātihārya*) does not conform to this understanding. Extraordinary and wondrous though the feats of the Buddha and his disciples may be, they are nevertheless perfectly 'natural' insofar as they are achieved by mental training. The 'miracles' most commonly encountered in Buddhist texts are regarded as natural expressions of the extraordinary power of the mind of the accomplished holy man (*sādhu*).

In common with texts of other Indian religious traditions, such as Patañjali's *Yoga Sūtras* (c. fourth century CE), Buddhist texts understand that as a consequence of the mastery of contemplative techniques leading to states of deep concentration (*samādhi*) the practitioner of yoga can acquire the ability to manipulate his or her mind and thereby accomplish certain extraordinary feats, both of mind and body, that are beyond the capacity of ordinary humans. In the earliest Buddhist sources these abilities are most commonly presented integrated with a series of 'higher knowledges' (Sanskrit *abhijñā*; Pali *abhiññā*) that culminate in the knowledge that is final 'enlightenment' or, more literally, 'awakening' (*bodhi*) itself. Later Indian Buddhist scholastic literature thus routinely refers to 'six higher knowledges' each of which has a standard definition in the early sources that comes down to us with only minor variations:

1. Knowledge that consists in the realization of the fruits of success (Sanskrit *ṛddhi*; Pali *iddhi*) in meditation: (i) being one, he becomes many; (ii) he appears then vanishes; (iii) he passes unhindered through walls and mountains as if through air; (iv) he rises up out of the earth and sinks down into it as if it were water; (v) he walks on water as if it were solid like earth; (vi) he travels through the sky cross-legged like a bird; (vii) he touches and strokes with his hand things of such power as the sun and moon; (viii) he has mastery with his body as far as the world of Brahmā.

2. Knowledge that consists in godlike hearing: he hears sounds both divine and human, far and near.

3. Knowledge of others' states of mind: he knows whether or not another's mind is affected by desire, hate or delusion, is dull, distracted, inferior, superior, concentrated, freed.

4. Knowledge that consists in the recollection of previous lives: he remembers his previous lives – from one birth to 100,000 births, over many periods of expansion and contraction of the universe he remembers his name, family and class, what food he ate, his experience of unhappiness and happiness.

5. Knowledge of the death and rebirth of beings: with purified godlike vision, he sees beings dying and being born; he understands how beings are inferior or superior, fair or ugly, fortunate or unfortunate according to their actions; how beings who behave badly in body, speech and thought are after death born in a hell; how beings who behave well in body, speech and thought are after death born in a heaven.

6. Knowledge of the destruction of taints: he truly understands suffering, its origin, its cessation, the way leading to its cessation; he truly understands the taints, their origin, their cessation, the way leading to their cessation; in understanding this, his mind is freed from the taints of desire, becoming and ignorance; freed, he understands that birth is destroyed, and the spiritual life fulfilled.

The last three of these six are sometimes given as the 'three knowledges' (Sanskrit *vidyā*; Pali *vijjā*) said to have been attained successively by the Buddha on the night he finally achieved full awakening.

In the canonical texts these six or three knowledges most commonly occur preceded by a description of the Buddhist practitioner's attainment of four progressive meditative 'absorptions' (Sanskrit *dhyāna*; Pali *jhāna*). The mind concentrated in these 'absorptions' is not merely temporarily cleansed of the defilements that ordinarily plague it, it is extremely 'sensitive and workable', and thus can be directed towards the attainment of these higher knowledges.

Insofar as the ability to practise the various 'miraculous' powers is presented in early Buddhist literature as encompassed by the higher knowledges, the performance of 'miracles' is fully integrated with the practices that lead directly to awakening. The ability to perform miracles results from the very same adeptness in the practice of the *dhyāna*s that facilitates progress along the path towards awakening. And since the ability to perform miracles is an extension of the practice of *dhyāna*s rather than a consequence of awakening, it follows that miracles can be performed prior to awakening; and since the practice of *dhyāna*s is not seen as exclusive to the followers of the Buddha, it follows that miraculous powers may be displayed by non-Buddhists as well. So, for example, the Sri Lankan Buddhist monk, the late Hammalava Saddhatissa, in his book *The Buddha's Way* straightforwardly takes the view that Jesus and his miracles are to be understood in such terms: Jesus was in some sense an accomplished yogin.[6] So, in sum, according to Buddhist theory the first five of the six higher knowledges can be attained and practised prior to awakening and by non-Buddhists.

HOW TO DEVELOP MIRACULOUS POWERS

The early texts frequently refer to four *iddhi-pāda*s or four 'foundations for [the realization of the fruits of] success [in meditation]': deep concentration achieved by way of the application of the wish to practice, energy, state of mind and investigation. These are suggestive of developing the capacity to concentrate the mind using a variety of contemplative objects and techniques.[7]

The later exegetical literature agrees on presenting the 'miraculous' powers as based on accomplishment in the practice of deep concentration. Buddhaghosa explains that in order to develop the ability to practise the first five higher knowledges, the meditator must have mastery of eight levels of concentration using eight objects of contemplation known as *kasiṇas*: earth, water, fire, air, blue, yellow, red, white. This practice begins with concentrating on an actual instance of the object and progresses to absorption in the abstract notion of 'the totality of earthness', and so forth. Such mastery is extremely difficult and only accomplished by very few (Vism XII 2–9).[8] The Mahāyāna *Da zhi du lun* also emphasizes the importance of concentration using the same objects of contemplation mentioned in the *Visuddhimagga*.[9] What seems to be assumed in all sources is the practice of a kind of mental gymnastics. The effect on the mind is likened to making gold pure and workable (Vism XII 12).

Having acquired this facility in controlling the mind, the meditator uses the perfect concentration of the fourth absorption as the basis for the various miraculous powers. Should he want to walk on water, say, he focuses his mind on the idea of earth until he achieves the fourth absorption; then after withdrawing his mind from this perfect mental absorption, he resolves that water should become earth, allowing him (and others) to walk on it (Vism XII 95–7).

FURTHER TYPES OF MIRACLE AND THEIR CLASSIFICATION IN BUDDHIST LITERATURE

It was recognized in Indian Buddhist exegetical literature that the list of six higher knowledges did not explicitly cover all instances of the miraculous; additional types are sometimes said to be implicit in the six, or alternative schemes are proposed for classifying types of miracle. Thus having 'mastery with the body as far as the world of Brahmā' is interpreted as including, among others, the abilities 'to make what is far near and what is near far, and to make what is much little and what is little much'. By way of illustration, we are told how, when he was offered too many cakes, Mahākassapa, one of the chief disciples of the Buddha, managed to make just one bowl of them, and how on another occasion he returned from his alms round with just one bowl of rice gruel offered by a poor man's wife which the Buddha by his resolve made sufficient for the whole community of monks; the story adds that seven days later the poor man became rich (Vism XII 126–7).

The 'godlike vision' which accomplishes the knowledge of the death and rebirth of beings is explained as encompassing knowledge of the future (*anāgataṃsa-ñāṇa*), exemplified in the Buddha's vision of the decline and rise of human fortunes culminating in the appearance of the future Buddha Metteyya (Sanskrit Maitreya) in the *Cakkavatti-sīhanāda-sutta* (D III 71–79; Vibh-a 373). The second of the eight miraculous abilities that are the fruits of success in meditation – appearing then vanishing – is understood to include not only making oneself appear and vanish, but also making external objects appear and vanish (Vism XII 84).

Providing a simple twofold classification for kinds of *ṛddhi* or power that come from accomplishment in deep concentration, the *Abhidharmakośa* (VII 48–51) and *Da zhi du lun* divide them into powers that consist of movement (*gamana*) and those that consist of creation (*nirmāṇa*).[10]

The term used for the 'powers' here, namely Pali *iddhi* and Sanskrit *ṛddhi*, has the general meaning of 'success' or 'accomplishment' and is not restricted in meaning to the power to perform miracles. In its exposition of *iddhi/ṛddhi* the exegetical literature gives lists of types of success and accomplishment that may arise from various causes (Vism XII 23–44, Abhidh-k VII 53–6). Thus a bird's ability to fly is still a type of *ṛddhi/iddhi*, although it is not the result of success in meditation; it is an accomplishment that arises as a result of actions (*karma*) done in a previous life and which certain beings are born with. On the other hand, certain types of wonder can be worked not only as a result of success in meditation, but through mastery of certain magical arts. Other miracles, while having their basis in accomplishments in meditation, arise spontaneously rather than as a result of specific resolve (Sanskrit *adhiṣṭhāna*; Pali *adhiṭṭhāna*): a monk sitting in deep concentration is taken for dead by a group of cowherds who then bring firewood and set fire to him, yet not even a corner of his robe is burnt; a lay woman, because she is absorbed in meditation on kindness (Sanskrit *maitrī*; Pali *mettā*), is protected from injury when a jealous rival pours hot oil over her head (Mp I 451–2).

THE PERFORMANCE OF MIRACLES BY THE BUDDHA AND HIS DISCIPLES

In the earliest texts, the Buddha himself is routinely portrayed as exercising his ability to perform miracles: he makes someone sitting near him invisible to another (Vin I 16); he overpowers fiery dragons (*nāga*) by himself bursting into flames (Vin I 25); he disappears from one shore of the Ganges and reappears together with the community of monks on the far shore (D II 89); when the great god Brahmā fails in his own attempt to make himself invisible, the Buddha makes himself invisible (M I 330); he prevents the murderer Aṅgulimāla, who is walking as fast as he can, from catching up with him (an example of making what is near far) (M II 99; Vism XII 125); by the power of his mind he compels a group of monks to come into his presence (S III 92).

While many of the Buddha's monastic disciples are also routinely credited with miraculous powers in the earliest literature, it is Maudgalyāyana (Pali Moggallāna) who is considered chief in this respect (A I 23). One of his specialities is stirring sloppy monks into action by shaking their dwelling with his big toe (S v 269–71). He is also described as communicating with the Buddha across great distances by means of the godlike vision and hearing (S II 275–6). On another occasion, having read a fellow monk's mind, Maudgalyāyana immediately appears in front of him (S v 294–7).

*

All surviving versions of the Buddhist monastic rule (*vinaya*) recount a version of the story of Piṇḍola Bhāradvaja. It is said that one day a sceptical merchant, seeking proof of the extraordinary powers of holy men, suspended a sandalwood alms bowl from the top of a bamboo pole with the challenge that if there were any holy man with the ability, he should fly up and take the bowl. No one rose to the challenge until two of the Buddha's disciples came by: Piṇḍola and Maudgalyāyana. Eventually it was Piṇḍola who flew up and took the bowl. The excitement this caused alerted the Buddha, who arrived and suggested that such an exhibition should be likened to a woman exposing herself for a few coins. Adding that it neither aroused faith in those lacking faith nor strengthened faith in those with faith, he pronounced a monastic rule: 'a display of miraculous power beyond the capacity of ordinary men should not be exhibited to the laity' (Vin II 112).

One might read this rule as rather convenient: if anyone who is not a Buddhist monk or nun should come and request a demonstration of flying through the air, say, there is a ready-made response: 'Such a demonstration is against the rules of our order'. Indeed, in one version of this story the non-Buddhist ascetics who declined to fly up and claim the bowl respond that their reasons for not doing so were similar to the Buddha's and if only he would demonstrate a miracle they would too. In this version of the story the Buddha responds that he will indeed perform a miracle, and the story of Piṇḍola becomes the prelude to the Buddha's performance of the 'Great Miracle' or 'Miracle of the Pairs' (*yamaka-pāṭihāriya/-prātihārya*) at Śrāvastī (Pali Sāvatthī). When the non-Buddhist ascetics protest that he has just laid down a rule forbidding such public displays he answers that the rule does not apply to him: a king may forbid others from taking fruit from trees in his garden, but that does not mean that he cannot take it himself.

The tradition of the Buddha's performance of the 'Miracle of the Pairs' at Śrāvastī is part of Buddhism's common heritage. This miracle can only be performed by a buddha and involves sending forth streams of fire and water from his body (an example of making things appear and vanish). After performing this miracle the Buddha ascended to the Heaven of the Thirty-Three where he spent the three months of the rainy season teaching the assembly of gods.[11]

The stories of the establishment of the monastic rule prohibiting public performance of miracles and of the Buddha's performance of the Miracle of the Pairs illustrate a tension in the attitude towards miracles in early Buddhist literature: they are but a cheap trick beneath a monk's dignity, yet with the Miracle of the Pairs the Buddha himself is portrayed as performing the ultimate miracle. There is, thus, on the one hand a readiness to embrace fully the performance of miracles, and on the other a more sober and even sceptical assessment of their appropriateness. Yet such scepticism takes a specific form and should not be misconstrued as a general questioning of the value of the ability to perform miracles for a monk's progress along the Buddhist path. The attempt to marginalize the practice of miraculous powers in the earliest Buddhist texts must be considered a feature of Buddhist modernism, and related to the late nineteenth- and early twentieth-century preoccupation with recovering a historical Buddha congenial to the rationalist and ethical sensitivities of certain Buddhist apologists.

The suggestion that we find in early Buddhist literature instances of a straightforward rejection of the practice of miracles, and that this rejection represents the attitude of the historical Buddha probably goes back to Rhys Davids' 1899 translation of the *Kevaddha-sutta* (D I 211–23).[12] Such a reading of this important sutta (other versions of which are preserved in Sanskrit and Chinese translation) is problematic. The *Kevaddha-sutta* begins with the householder Kevaddha requesting the Buddha to invite a monk to give a display of miraculous powers (*iddhi-pāṭihāriya*) in order to increase people's faith. The Buddha responds that this is not his custom. There are, he says, three kinds of 'miracle': of accomplishment in meditation (*iddhi*), of revealing another's thoughts (*ādesanā*) and of instruction (*anusāsanī*). Of the first (which comprises the eight abilities associated with the first of the six higher knowledges, i.e. becoming many, appearing and vanishing, etc.), the Buddha comments that a person with faith in the Buddha might witness a Buddhist monk demonstrating these eight kinds of accomplishment in meditation, and might then tell someone lacking such faith. The former, inspired by his faith, would exclaim, 'Wonderful! This ascetic has great power. I saw him demonstrating these miraculous powers.' But the latter, remaining unimpressed, might respond, 'There is a magical art called *gandhārī* – it is by means of this that this monk enjoys various kinds of miraculous accomplishment.' The Buddha concludes: 'Seeing *this* danger in miracles of accomplishment in meditation, I am troubled by them, ashamed of them, and shun them.' The Buddha goes on to suggest that the same might happen in the case of the miracle of revealing another's thoughts: the faithful are impressed, but the sceptical attribute the feat to a magical art called *maṇika*. So once more the Buddha expresses his strong reservations. Finally the Buddha explains the miracle of instruction by giving a full account of the progressive stages of the Buddhist path. This account culminates in the description of the higher knowledges (*abhiññā*) ending in awakening. Significantly the first of these higher knowledges involves the realization of *precisely* the eight miraculous abilities involved in the display of miraculous powers (*iddhi-pāṭihāriya*) and that the Buddha has just refused to instruct a monk to display. Nevertheless, about this third miracle, the miracle of instruction, the Buddha is represented as expressing no reservations.

This text does not, then, present a simple rejection of miracles. Like the monastic rule, it questions the appropriateness of their public performance as a means of attracting followers. Miracles may impress the faithful, but for the wrong reasons: they are in awe of the wonder-worker flying through the air, forgetting what is truly impressive, the saint who is awakened and has rooted out all greed, hatred and delusion. The sceptics, on the other hand, remain unimpressed: mistrusting the 'miracle', they put it down to some trick.

Following this exchange, the Buddha tells Kevaddha of a monk who had mastered the ability to enter into a deep concentration (*samādhi*) in which the path leading to the heavens of the gods appeared; this is in effect the eighth of the various powers that follow success in meditation, namely 'mastery with the body as far as the world of Brahmā'. The monk's quest is to ask the gods who dwell in these heavens where it is that the elements of earth, water, fire and air cease. Eventually he comes into the presence of Brahmā himself, who despite declaring himself the all-powerful creator cannot satisfy the monk with an answer. The monk is forced to return to his teacher, the Buddha, who explains that it is with the mind that achieves enlightenment that the four elements finally cease.

So while the monk who journeys to the heavens fails to find the answer he is seeking, his 'mastery with the body as far as the world of

Brahmā' is nonetheless a step on the path towards enlightenment. Moreover, insofar as the instruction the Buddha gives Kevaddha by way of explanation of 'the miracle of instruction' includes instruction in the eight miracles of accomplishment in meditation (*iddhi*), this whole dialogue expresses the paradoxical nature of the Buddhist attitude towards the working of miracles. The ability to perform miracles may not be a necessary or sufficient condition for awakening, yet in the course of following the path to awakening a monk or nun may well acquire that ability, and it may well contribute to progress towards the goal.

In another early discussion of the same three miracles – of accomplishment in meditation, of revealing another's thoughts and of instruction – while it is again emphasized that the miracle of instruction is superior, it is nevertheless made clear that the Buddha and many hundreds of his disciples possess proficiency in the performance of *all three* types of miracle (A 1 168–73). The efficacy of the practice of all three miracles is similarly emphasized in the Mūlasarvāstivādin *Mahāvadāna-sūtra* with regard to previous buddhas and their disciples.[13]

MIRACLES AS TEACHING

The story in the *Kevaddha-sutta* of a monk with the ability to visit different realms is an early instance of what became a common narrative theme in Buddhist literature. Another is the tale of Maudgalyāyana's visits to various hells and heavens recounted at the beginning of the *Mahāvastu*;[14] after each visit Maudgalyāyana returns to an assembly of monks, nuns and laity to recount what he has seen and warn of the suffering of the hells and the ultimate impermanence of the lives of even the gods. Elsewhere we are told how when Maudgalyāyana descends into hell he creates a lotus flower on which to sit and teach the inhabitants of hell (Mp 1 133, As 277). The ability to visit other realms – an aspect of mastery with the body as far as the world of Brahmā[15] – thus becomes closely associated with spiritual progress, both one's own and others'. A revelation of the realms of hell and heaven (classified as an example of making something appear and then vanish) is also the culmination of the narrative of the Miracle of the Pairs. Having performed this miracle in Śrāvastī and ascended to the Heaven of the Thirty-Three to teach the assembly of the gods, the Buddha descended far away to the west in Sāṃkāśya (Pali Saṃkassa) on a jewelled staircase accompanied by various gods: at that moment the realms of heaven and hell were revealed.[16] Thus Sāṃkāsya along with Śrāvastī becomes one of eight principal places of Buddhist pilgrimage.[17]

When we consider Buddhist tales of the miraculous more generally, we find that miracles are often presented as some sort of teaching aid: the Buddha's overpowering of fiery dragons by bursting into flames is followed by other miracles that culminate in the conversion of a group of matted-hair ascetics. The trick which prevents the serial killer Aṅgulimāla from catching up with the Buddha turns out not to be his method of escape, but a way of bringing Aṅgulimāla to a realization after he shouts after the Buddha to stop; the Buddha's response ('I have stopped. Why don't you?') provokes Aṅgulimāla to question his way of life. And Maudgalyāyana's ability to shake a building with his big toe is precisely put to use to return lax monks to their spiritual practice.

When the working of miracles is illustrated in later literature, the examples once more highlight their usefulness as teaching aids. To return to the homiletic use of accounts of other realms, a number of stories are told recounting how the skill in making things appear and vanish is used to afford an audience a vision of both hell and heaven: for example, some centuries after the death of the Buddha, a monk of Ceylon named Dhammadinna began a sermon by turning his fan face downwards to reveal an opening right down to Avīci, the worst of hells, and then face upwards to reveal an opening up to the heaven world of Brahmā: having provoked in his audience the fear of hell and a longing for the world of Brahmā he proceeded to teach with the result that some in his audience reached awakening there and then (Vism XII 80).

In an interesting twist another tale tells how this same Dhammadinna skilfully uses another monk's abilities in making things appear and vanish to reveal to the latter his spiritual shortcomings. A certain Mahānāga mistakenly considered himself to have attained awakening sixty years earlier. Realizing Mahānāga's mistake, Dhammadinna flies through the air to meet him and persuades Mahānāga to use his own accomplishments in meditation to conjure up an angry elephant. Mahānāga does so but with the result that he himself jumps up in fear at the vision he has created, whereupon Dhammadinna asks him whether those whose defilements are destroyed have fear. At this Mahānāga realizes that he has not reached awakening as he thought and that he still has spiritual work to do (Vism XX 110–13; Vibh-a 489–90).

That the primary purpose of the ability to perform miracles is its usefulness for teaching the path to awakening is made explicit in the Mahāyāna *Da zhi du lun*:

The bodhisattva, detached from the objects of the five senses, accomplished in the attainment of absorption in meditation [*dhyāna*], possessed with kindness [*maitrī*] and compassion [*karuṇā*] achieves higher knowledge in the interest of beings and displays extraordinary and wonderful things in order to purify beings' minds. Why? If he did not do extraordinary things he would not be able to lead so many beings to find escape [from suffering].[18]

In his influential *Abhidharmakośa*, Vasubandhu equates the knowledge that consists in the realization of the fruits of success in meditation, the knowledge of others' states of mind, and the knowledge of the destruction of taints (the first, third and sixth of the higher knowledges) with the miracles of accomplishment in meditation, revealing another's thoughts, and instruction respectively. Playing on the Sanskrit etymology of *prātihārya* or 'miracle', he comments that the first, third and sixth higher knowledges are called miracles 'because they captivate the minds of those whose minds need training' and 'because by their means one brings back the minds of those who are disaffected and indifferent'. He emphasizes that the miracle of instruction is the highest since the other two can be produced by means of magical arts, while the third cannot be separated from the higher knowledge of awakening (Abhidh-k vii 47).

*

One of the eight powers that constitute the first of the six higher knowledges is the ability 'to become many'. This involves the creation of a mind-made body that is an exact copy of its original, endowed with all faculties and senses. Thus we are told that when the Buddha spent three months in the Heaven of the Thirty-Three teaching the assembled gods, he would create such a mind-made body to carry on teaching while he went to the mythical Lake Anavatapta (Pali *Anotatta*) to collect alms and to convey to his disciple Śāriputra (Pali *Sāriputta*) what he had been teaching to the gods.

The idea of creating another body that will perform the task of teaching is developed in the Mahāyāna notion of the three bodies of a buddha. Early Buddhist literature describes the Buddha as having a body with the thirty-two marks of 'the great man' (*mahāpuruṣa*). These marks are not marks that we can normally see; they are the marks on a body gradually developed over many lifetimes of spiritual practice. For the bodhisattva on the path to buddhahood the end point of the development of this other body is the 'enjoyment body' (*sambhoga-kāya*) of a Buddha, teaching in a cosmic 'buddha-field' (*buddha-kṣetra*).

But this 'enjoyment body' is not the one routinely seen here in this world. What we ordinarily see is the *nirmāṇa-kāya* or magically created body of a buddha. From this perspective the historical Buddha Gautama was not the real Buddha at all, but rather the creation of a cosmic buddha, an expression of a buddha's compassion and skill in helping beings to find an escape from suffering. What a Buddha is in himself is the *dharma-kāya*, the 'body' (*kāya*) or sum of perfect qualities (*dharma*), the eternal, unchanging truth of the way things are.

Perhaps the ultimate expression of the performance of miracles as a way of Buddhist teaching is to be found in the vast Mahāyāna *Avataṃsaka-sūtra*. Here, in the process of following the path to buddhahood, the bodhisattva perfects the ability to magically transform himself and the world around him for the benefit of beings. His abilities in this respect become extraordinary:

> At will he displays the array of the realms of all the buddhas at the end of a single hair; at will he displays untold arrays of the realms of the buddhas of all kinds; at will in the twinkling of an eye he creates as many individuals as there are particles in untold world-systems ... In the arising of a thought he embraces the ten directions; in a moment of thought he controls the manifestation of innumerable processes of complete awakening and final nirvāṇa ... In his own body he controls countless manifestations of the qualities of the buddha-fields of innumerable lord buddhas.[19]

The *Avataṃsaka-sūtra* culminates in the *Gaṇḍavyūha-sūtra* which, as Luis Gómez has discussed, plays on the theme of 'wonder-working as a metaphor for perfect Buddhahood and magic deception as an image for the true nature of things'. But the bodhisattva is no ordinary wonder-worker: 'his magical creations are not merely apparitions within the "reality" of our everyday world, rather they are that reality as manifested to the enlightened'; moreover, 'his creations, though conforming to the delusion of his audience, are presented in order to reveal the true nature of the delusion, unlike the magician who rests content with his deception'.[20]

BEYOND WONDER-WORKING

This discussion of 'miracle' in Buddhism has highlighted wonder-working in order to reflect a particular focus of the tradition itself, yet Buddhist literature contains many examples of other types of miracle. In the first place it is not only those who are accomplished in the attainment of meditation that are instrumental in miraculous happenings. A story of a boy whose mother fell seriously ill illustrates the miraculous power of 'the statement of truth' (Sanskrit *satyakriyā*; Pali *saccakiriyā*): when Cakkana's mother fell ill and the doctor said that she needed fresh hare's meat, Cakkana's brother sent him off to catch a hare. Cakkana was about to kill a hare when he reflected that it would not be right to take the life of another for the sake of his mother's life, and so let the hare go. Scolded by his brother, Cakkana went to his mother and affirmed a truth: 'Since I was born I am not aware that I have intentionally taken the life of a living creature'. Immediately his mother recovered from her illness (Ps I 203–4 = Spk II 149–50 = As 103). The boy's commitment to not harming a living creature provides the basis for an affirmation of truth which has the effect of curing his mother. The power of kindness or friendliness (Sanskrit *maitrī*; Pali *mettā*) to ward off dangers and protect one from harm is a common theme and is not restricted to human beings: a spear flung at a cow giving milk to her calf bounces off not because of the power of the cow's meditation, 'but simply because the cow's state of mind was one of strong love – such is the great power of kindness' (Vism IX 72).

Other miraculous events occur which are not the acts of individual wonder-workers such as the Buddha or his disciples. For example, various miraculous portents that occur in connection with the career of a buddha: when the being who will become the Buddha is conceived radiance spreads throughout the universe; when he is born two showers of water come from the sky and bathe him and his mother; earthquakes accompany his awakening, his first teaching, his decision to renounce life, and his death (D II 14–15, 107–9). But such events are once again not seen as divine purpose intervening in the natural order of things, they are rather part of the profound cosmic order of things (*dhamma-niyāma*) (As 274). Certainly sometimes other beings – gods – appear to participate in this cosmic order, helping events unfold as they should: gods persuade the Buddha-to-be not to undertake a full fast by saying that they will feed him if he does; or when the Buddha hesitates to teach, the great god Brahmā intervenes to request him to teach. Yet the Buddhist tradition's own explanations of such events – the Buddha deliberately waited for Brahmā to make his request because it would provide an example to others (Ps II 177) – tend to shift the emphasis back to the Buddha's own deliberate miraculous control of the unfolding of events which nevertheless remain part of a pattern that is the expression of the profoundest truth about the universe.

The final and ultimate wondrous cosmic event associated with the Buddha Gotama in the Theravāda sources is the disappearance of his relics (*dhātu-parinibbāna*). Marking the disappearance of the Buddha's teaching from the world, his relics, which have been dispersed around the world, will spontaneously gather together at the place of the Buddha's awakening. There they will become one single mass of gold emitting rays of six colours. Finally they will spontaneously burst into flames and disappear without trace.[21] Yet the disappearance of the relics is only the prelude to the coming of the next buddha. To quote the words of a text from a different Buddhist school describing the coming of the future Buddha, Maitreya:

Then the perfectly awakened Maitreya, with a following of 800 million monks, will approach Mount Gurupādaka . . . where the skeleton of Kāśyapa remains undisturbed. Mount Gurupādaka will open itself up for the perfectly awakened Maitreya, whereupon the perfectly awakened Maitreya will take the undisturbed skeleton of the monk Kāśyapa with his right hand, put it into his left hand, and thus teach dharma to the disciples of the Buddha: 'Monks', he will say, 'when people lived for one hundred years, there arose in the world a teacher named Śākyamuni, who declared the disciple named Kāśyapa to be the best of those who preach . . . the virtues of the purified'.[22]

How is it that the relics of the Buddha come together to mark the end of his dispensation? How is it that the bones of Kāśyapa endure until the coming of the Buddha Maitreya? The answer in both cases seems to be by the power of 'resolve' (Sanskrit *adhiṣṭhāna*; Pali *adhiṭṭhāna*); certainly this is explicit in the case of the Buddha (Mp I 91), but the case of Kāśyapa's enduring bones becomes a point of controversy among the teachers whose views Vasubandhu outlines in his *Abhidharmakośa*: some say that it is possible to make a resolve that is efficacious beyond death; others argue that this is impossible and that Kāśyapa's bones are preserved not by his determination but as a result of the power of gods (Abhidh-k VII 52).

While the miraculous exploits of individual thaumaturges – the Buddha and his disciples – may have the power to impress and occasion awe, they are at the same time woven into a grander narrative, the cosmic and transcendent (Sanskrit *lokottara*; Pali *lokuttara*) narrative that encompasses the buddhas of the past, present and future and gives these tales of the miraculous their true meaning.

But this grand narrative does not end with the death of the Buddha and his immediate disciples, it is continued in the tales of the miraculous feats worked by the Buddhist saints whom legend credits with facilitating the spread of Buddhism across India, such as Upagupta, Moggaliputtatissa and Mahinda, and whose names and deeds become associated with the Emperor Aśoka as the great patron of Buddhism in the third century BCE.[23] Such tales of wonder-working saints continue with figures such as Padmasambhava (eighth century)[24] and Milarepa (Mi-la Ras-pa) (1040–1123) in Tibet,[25] and in the medieval biographies of eminent Chinese monks,[26] and in the tradition of Burmese wizards (*weikzas*), who prolong their lives until the coming of the next Buddha, Metteyya.[27]

Thus despite recording a formal prohibition on performing miracles before laity, despite telling us of the Buddha's reluctance to instruct a monk to perform a miracle in order to inspire faith, Buddhist tradition is not shy of recounting tales of the miraculous powers of the Buddha and his disciples in order to inspire and encourage us. The 'miracle of instruction' turns out in the end to subsume all other types of miracle. Even if we cannot witness the miracles of the Buddha and his disciples directly, we can hear of them, visit the places where they occurred, and see them carved in stone and depicted in paintings.

Notes

Abbreviations: A = *Aṅguttara Nikāya*; Abhidh-k-bh = *Abhidharma-kośa-bhāṣya*, ed. P. Pradhan (Patna: Kashi Prasad Jayaswal Research Institute, 1967); As = *Atthasālinī*; D = *Dīgha Nikāya*; Dhp-a = *Dhammapada-aṭṭhakathā*; M = *Majjhima Nikāya*; Mp = *Manorathapūraṇī*; Paṭis = *Paṭisambhidāmagga*; S = *Saṃyutta Nikāya*; Spk = *Sāratthappakāsinī*; Vibh-a = *Vibhaṅga-aṭṭhakathā*; Vism = *Visuddhimagga*, ed. H. C. Warren and D. Kosambi (Cambridge, MA: Harvard University Press, 1950). Unless otherwise stated editions are those of the Pali Text Society.

1 See James Legge, *A Record of the Buddhistic Kingdoms Being an Account by the Chinese Monk Fâ-Hien of His Travels in India and Ceylon* (Oxford: Clarendon Press, 1886); Samuel Beal, *Si-Yu-Ki: Buddhist Records of the Western World*, 2 vols. (London: Trübner & Co., 1884).

2 Vism XII; Ñāṇamoli, *The Path of Purification (Visuddhimagga) by Bhadantācariya Buddhaghosa* (Colombo: Semage, 1964), 409–78.

3 Abhidh-k-bh VII; Louis de La Vallée Poussin, *Abhidharmakośabhāṣyam*, 4 vols., trans. L. Pruden (Berkeley: Asian Humanities, 1988–90), vol. IV, 1155–213.

4 *Da zhi du lun* 28, Taishō no. 1509, vol. 25.264b–269b; E. Lamotte, *Le traité de la grande vertu de sagesse*, 5 vols. (Louvain: Institut Orientaliste, 1940–80), vol. IV, 1809–77.

5   David Basinger, 'Miracles', in *Routledge Encyclopedia of Philosophy*, ed. Edward Craig (London: Routledge, 1998), vol. vi, 411–16 (412).

6   H. Saddhatissa, *The Buddha's Way* (London: George Allen & Unwin, 1971), 79–80.

7   Rupert M. L. Gethin, *The Buddhist Path to Awakening: A Study of the Bodhipakkhiyā Dhammā* (Leiden: Brill, 1992), 81–103.

8   Cf. *Da zhi du lun* 28, *T.* 25.264b–c; Lamotte, *Le traité*, vol. iv, 1820–1.

9   *Da zhi du lun* 28, *T.* 25.264b–c; Lamotte, *Le traité*, vol. iv, 1820–1.

10 *Da zhi du lun* 28, *T.* 25.264b; Lamotte, *Le traité*, vol. iv, 1819–20.

11 Dhp-a III 199–230; E. W. Burlingame, *Buddhist Legends Translated from the Original Pali Text of the Dhammapada Commentary*, 3 vols. (Cambridge, MA: Harvard University Press, 1921), vol. III, 35–56; Divyāvadāna 155–61; Andy Rotman, *Divine Stories*, Part 1 (Boston: Wisdom, 2008), 270–7.

12 T. W. Rhys Davids, *Dialogues of the Buddha* (London: Oxford University Press, 1899), vol. i, 272.

13 *The Mahāvadānasūtra: A New Edition Based on Manuscripts Discovered in Northern Turkestan*, ed. Takamichi Fukita (Göttingen: Vandenhoeck & Ruprecht, 1989), 150–1.

14 E. Sénart, ed., *Le Mahāvastu: texte sanscrit*, 3 vols. (Paris: Imprimerie Nationale, 1882–97), vol. i, 5–33; J. J. Jones, *The Mahāvastu*, 3 vols. (London: Luzac & Co., 1949–56), vol. iv, 6–29.

15 See Paṭis II 209, Vism XII 119.

16 Dhp-a III 225; Burlingame, *Buddhist Legends*, vol. III, 53; Vism XII 72–9.

17 The other six are Lumbinī (where the Buddha was born), Bodhgayā (where he achieved awakening), Sārnāth (where he first taught), Rājagrha (where he subdued an angry elephant through kindness), Vaiśālī (where he received an offering of honey from a monkey) and Kuśinagarī (where he died). For accounts of Faxian's and Xuanzang's visits to Sāṃkāśya in the fifth and seventh centuries, see Legge, *Buddhistic Kingdoms*, 47–55, and Beal, *Buddhist Records of the Western World*, vol. i, 203.

18 *Da zhi du lun* 28, *T.* 25.264b; Lamotte, *Le traité*, vol. iv, 1819–20.

19 J. Rahder, ed., *Daśabhūmikasūtra* (Leuven: J. B. Istas, 1926), 91; Thomas Cleary, *The Flower Ornament Scripture*, 3 vols. (Boston: Shambhala, 1984–7), vol. II, 108.

20 Luis O. Gómez, 'The Bodhisattva as Wonder Worker', in *Prajñāpāramitā and Related Systems: Studies in Honor of Edward Conze*, ed. Lewis Lancaster (Berkeley: University of California Press, 1977), 221–61 (235–6, 229).

21 Sv 899–900 = Vibh-a 433; a slightly different version is given at Mp I 91; the literature of other Buddhist schools gives yet another version; see John S. Strong, *Relics of the Buddha* (Princeton: Princeton University Press, 2004), 226.

22 Edward B. Cowell and Robert Alexander Neil, eds., *The Divyāvadāna: A Collection of Early Buddhist Legends* (Cambridge: Cambridge University Press, 1886), 61; Rotman, *Divine Stories*, 126.

23 See John S. Strong, *The Legend and Cult of Upagupta: Sanskrit Buddhism in North India and Southeast Asia* (Princeton: Princeton University Press, 1992); N. A. Jayawickrama, *The Inception of Discipline and the Vinaya Nidāna* (London: Pali Text Society, 1986); John S. Strong, *The Legend of King Aśoka: A Study and Translation of the Aśokāvadāna* (Princeton: Princeton University Press, 1983).

24 Kenneth Douglas and Gwendolyn Bays, *The Life and Liberation of Padmasambhava*, 2 vols. (Emeryville: Dharma Publications, 1978).

25 Lobsang P. Lhalungpa, *The Life of Milarepa* (New York: Dutton, 1977).

26 See John Kieschnick, *The Eminent Monk Buddhist Ideals in Medieval Chinese Hagiography* (Honolulu: University of Hawai'i Press, 1997), 67–111; John Kieschnick, *The Impact of Buddhism on Chinese Material Culture* (Princeton: Princeton University Press, 2003), 24–82.

27 Strong, *The Legend and Cult of Upagupta*, 245–7; Patrick Pranke, 'On Becoming a Buddhist Wizard', in *Buddhism in Practice*, Princeton Readings in Religions, ed. Donald S. Lopez (Princeton: Princeton University Press, 1995), 343–58.

Further reading

Beal, Samuel, *Si-Yu-Ki: Buddhist Records of the Western World*, 2 vols. (London: Trübner & Co., 1884)

Burlingame, E. W., *Buddhist Legends Translated from the Original Pali Text of the Dhammapada Commentary*, 3 vols. (Cambridge, MA: Harvard University Press, 1921)

Gethin, Rupert M. L., *The Buddhist Path to Awakening: A Study of the Bodhi-Pakkhiyā Dhammā* (Leiden: Brill, 1992), 81–103

'The Resurrection and Buddhism', in *Resurrection Reconsidered*, ed. Gavin D'Costa (Oxford: One World, 1996), 201–16

The Foundations of Buddhism (Oxford: Oxford University Press, 1998)

Gombrich, Richard, 'The Buddhist Attitude to Thaumaturgy', in *Bauddhavidyā-suddhākaraḥ: Studies in Honour of Heinz Bechert on the Occasion of his 65th Birthday*, ed. Petra Kieffer-Pülz and Jens-Uwe Hartmann (Swisttal-Odendorf: Indica et Tibetica Verlag, 1997), 165–84

*Gómez, Luis O., 'The Bodhisattva as Wonder Worker', in *Prajñāpāramitā and Related Systems: Studies in Honor of Edward Conze*, ed. Lewis Lancaster (Berkeley: University of California Press, 1977), 221–61

Jaini, P. S., 'Buddha's Prolongation of Life', *Bulletin of the School of Oriental and African Studies* 21 (1958), 546–52

Kieschnick, John, *The Eminent Monk: Buddhist Ideals in Medieval Chinese Hagiography* (Honolulu: University of Hawai'i Press, 1997)

Lamotte, E., *Le traité de la grande vertu de sagesse*, 5 vols. (Louvain: Institut Orientaliste, 1940–80)

La Vallée Poussin, Louis de, *Abhidharmakośabhāṣyam of Vasubandhu*, 4 vols., trans. Leo M. Pruden (Berkeley: Asian Humanities, 1988–90)

Legge, James, *A Record of the Buddhistic Kingdoms Being an Account by the Chinese Monk Fâ-Hien of His Travels in India and Ceylon* (Oxford: Clarendon Press, 1886)

Lévi, Sylvain and Edouard Chavannes, 'Les seize arhat protecteurs de la loi', *Journal Asiatique* 8 (1916), 5–48, 189–304

Lhalungpa, Lobsang P., *The Life of Milarepa* (New York: Dutton, 1977)

Ñāṇamoli, *The Path of Purification (Visuddhimagga) by Bhadantācariya Buddhaghosa* (Colombo: Semage, 1964)

Pranke, Patrick, 'On Becoming a Buddhist Wizard', in *Buddhism in Practice*, Princeton Readings in Religions, ed. Donald S. Lopez (Princeton: Princeton University Press, 1995), 343–58

Schmithausen, Lambert, *Maitrī and Magic: Aspects of the Buddhist Attitude Toward the Dangerous in Nature* (Vienna: Verlag Österreichischen Akademie der Wissenschaften, 1997)

Strong, John S., 'The Legend of the Lion-Roarer: A Study of the Buddhist Arhat Piṇḍola Bhāradvāja', *Numen* 26 (1979), 50–88

The Legend and Cult of Upagupta: Sanskrit Buddhism in North India and Southeast Asia (Princeton: Princeton University Press, 1992)

13 Miracles in Christianity

RALPH DEL COLLE

The testimony to miracles has never been absent from Christianity although the theological and philosophical understanding of them has varied over the centuries. Whether they have been significant or marginal to the life of the church has in part been determined by popular piety, religious aspirations and expectations, and the judgment rendered about them in teaching, preaching and theology. There is a considerable difference at these levels, for example, between a Presbyterian parish schooled in the cessationist theology of certain forms of Calvinism and that of a Pentecostal congregation whose very existence is informed by the conviction that the extraordinary events of Pentecost continue in the life of the church. Here we may distinguish between affirmations of the miraculous in the witness of Holy Scripture to which both congregations would assent, and the belief that miracles have ceased or indeed still occur. Add to this the additional challenge that with the emergence of modernity in Western culture the former would come under scrutiny as well, it becomes clear that to speak of miracles is a complicated matter for many a Christian.

An important distinction is also in order. Miracles fit into the category of the extraordinary course of religious events. How this differs from ordinary religious events is also a matter of some debate, especially if religious experiences are considered as operations of divine grace. Therefore, the healing story of Jesus and the paralytic in the synoptic gospels (Matt. 9.1–8; Mark 2.1–12; Luke 5.17–26) poses the perennial question to faith, in the words of Jesus following his declaration of the forgiveness of sins: 'Which is easier to say to the paralytic, "Your sins are forgiven", or to say, "Rise, take up your pallet and walk"?' (Mark 2.9). Both ostensibly are works of God's grace. Or, in the language of what came to prevail in Latin Christianity, both are supernatural, although in common usage it is the healing that is considered extraordinary. Surely, it is an act of grace when God forgives sins and regenerates the sinner. Although not defined as a miracle per se

St Augustine can speak of the 'justification of the wicked [as] ... a greater work than the creation of heaven and earth'.[1] This distinction between the ordinary workings of grace and extraordinary miracles in the Christian theological account of divine agency is important. Both faith itself and its extraordinary manifestations require an apologetic. In the case of miracles, the apologetic will be more demanding. In the ordinary life of a believer faith may be present without miracles but not without grace. That the paralytic's sins were actually forgiven is clearly a matter of faith, which the sceptic can easily dismiss. That he rose up and walked was evident to all. Even the sceptic must offer an explanation of what happened. Nevertheless, faith cannot be separated from miracles. Jesus' miracles were often a response to faith (Matt. 8.10; 9.29). Conversely, not many mighty works occurred in his hometown of Nazareth due to their lack of faith (13.58). Therefore, the witness to miracles and faith will be similar. Miracles, then, are a subset of the understanding of faith and its theological explanation of God's general and special action in the world. We may distinguish between miracles, the theology of miracles and the apologetic offered on their behalf.

THE HISTORY OF MIRACLES IN CHRISTIANITY

Patristic era

Some of the Church Fathers were rather circumspect about miracles. The main issue was how to relate the criteria of discernment to the witness of miracles. The biblical testimony already demonstrated that wonders can be performed by those who oppose God as in the case of the Egyptian magicians who could change their staffs into snakes as Aaron did (Exod. 7.10–12) at the Lord's command and the Egyptians by their magic arts. Or, that New Testament apocalyptic prophesies that false messiahs and prophets may even mislead the elect (if that were possible) through their signs and wonders (Mark 13.22). Indeed this is a dimension of the deceiving power (2 Thess. 2.11–12) that God sends in the last days and that culminates in the appearance of the two beasts who possess the authority and power of the dragon (Satan), the second of which will perform great signs to deceive the inhabitants of the earth (Rev. 13.13–14). No wonder that with reference to another group, false disciples as distinct from the antichrist, Jesus could say only those who do the will of the Father will enter the kingdom of heaven rather than those who without this witness perform prophecies, exorcisms and mighty works in his name (Matt. 7.21–3).

Eusebius was aware of this and therefore counted it no argument in favour of the Montanists that, analogous to the witness of miracles, they could boast of many martyrs (*Church History* 5.16), a view consistent with Paul who argued that without love, tongues, prophecies, extraordinary faith, evangelical poverty and martyrdom count for nothing (1 Cor. 13.1–3). In another place, recalling such sub-apostolic fathers as Clement of Rome, Polycarp and Ignatius of Antioch, he also mentions one Quadratus blessed with a prophetic gift and others who 'with the grace and cooperation of God ... even at that late date many miraculous powers of the divine Spirit worked through them, so that at the first hearing whole crowds in a body embraced with whole-hearted eagerness the worship of the universal Creator' (*Church History* 3.37). Their veracity was in evidence because of the message of faith being preached, that word of God proclaimed as a foundation by the apostles and delivered in faithful preaching and transmitted through the 'inspired gospels in writing'.

The same dilemma concerning authenticity occupied the considerations of Origen (*c*. 185–254 CE) and Augustine (*c*. 354–430 CE). In his treatise *Against Celsus*, Origen replied to this pagan critic's charge that the miracles of Jesus were no different than those performed by 'dealers in magical arts'. Quite to the contrary, Origen remonstrates. Rather than performing them for show as Celsus charges, the miracles of Jesus along with his instruction induce his hearers to 'undertake the reformation of their characters' (*Against Celsus* 1.68). The same argument is made against the benefits bestowed by the legendary Greek poet and miracle worker Aristeas as compared to Jesus. In addition to the criterion of character, Origen also brings into play the doctrine of the incarnation, prophesied beforehand, and bearing fruit in communion with God by which humans who follow the precepts of Jesus are raised to the divine (3.26–8).

Augustine articulates similar concerns. Initially, he adopted what appears to be a cessationist position, namely, that miracles ceased after the establishment of Christianity or, in his words, the founding of the Catholic Church. His reasons have to do with the integrity of faith: 'lest the mind should always seek visible things, and the human race should grow cold by becoming accustomed to things which when they were novelties kindled its faith' (*True Religion* 47). Later he would partially retract this position by observing that miracles do still take place but not with the same frequency and greatness as at the beginning (*Retractions* 1.12.7; 1.13.5). In the *City of God*, Augustine enumerates many miracles of his own day, some of which he witnessed, yet insists that those in Scripture are more widely known as compared to the limited particularity of those that are contemporary (*City of God* 22.8).

The cessationist understanding was not uncommon among the Church Fathers although not necessarily a majority view. If the early Augustine was representative of the West, in the East one of no less stature than John Chrysostom (347–407 CE) articulated similar concerns. For him, one should not expect miracles for if one practises the virtues, especially love, one is not in need of signs and such signs gain nothing for the Christian where virtue is absent (*Homilies on Matthew* 44.4 (on Matt. 13.24–30)). It also comprises the integrity of faith. Quoting the risen Christ's words to Thomas – 'Blessed are they who have not seen and have believed' (John 20.29) – Chrysostom argues that the overpowering course of events that miracles generate make for an abridgement of faith (*Homily on the First Letter to the Corinthians* 6.5). Within the broader framework of the Spirit's activity and the bestowal of gifts or charisms, Chrysostom underscores the difference between the apostolic age and the church in his own day. He does not disown charisms, such as tongues and prophecy, but internalizes and spiritualizes them,[2] a view consistent with his understanding of faith. This does not discount the fact that the experience of the charisms, including miracles, decreased in the life of the church, although many Church Fathers still bear witness to them in Christian antiquity.

More to the point there is sufficient witness that miracles played a part in evangelization and missions. As Kenneth Scott Latourette has remarked: 'It was not only to miracles of moral rebirth to which Christians could point. Pagans were also attracted by the miracles of healing wrought in the name of Christ.'[3]

Additionally, one should not underestimate the role of holiness combined with spiritual power. Such power could manifest itself in conversion, healings and exorcisms, not unlike the healing of the woman with a haemorrhage where Jesus perceived power (*dunamis*) had gone out from him (Mark 5.21–34). Spiritual power was associated not only with holy men and women but also with testimonies of martyrdom, relics, icons and the intercession of the saints. Already in place by late antiquity, many of these practices would shape the development of medieval Christianity. The important point is that such spiritual power appeared greater than that embedded in the surrounding culture. The testimony of Sozomen (*c*. 435) about the conversion of his friend Alaphion is typical:

> Alaphion it appears was possessed of a devil; and neither the pagans nor the Jews could by any enchantments deliver him from this affliction, but Hilarion, by simply calling on the name of Christ,

expelled the demon and Alaphion and his whole family immediately embraced the faith.

(Sozomen, Church History 5.15.14–17)

Even as signs and wonders were factors in conversion to the faith, so too, they figured in the ongoing life of faith. This was clearly evident in the monastic culture that developed in both East and West. The same concern about discernment and authenticity weighed heavily in the religious experiences of the monks since the very nature of their calling was the pursuit of holiness. It was not uncommon for various supernatural experiences to be rejected as temptations since the devil could appear as an angel of light (2 Cor. 11.14) as is related, for example, in the following story:

> The devil appeared to a monk disguised as an angel of light and said to him, 'I am the angel Gabriel and I have been sent to you'. But the monk said, 'See if you have not been sent to someone else; I am not worthy to have an angel sent to me'. And at once the devil vanished.[4]

In this case, as with many others, humility is the true sign of monastic holiness and supernatural experiences are in service of that virtue.

As Benedicta Ward has observed, various interpretations of miracles are involved, all to the benefit of faith, the two most significant being: 'either as a wonder to be marvelled at or as sign to be explored and understood'.[5] Authenticity connects the wonder with the true interiority of faith and holiness. Indeed miraculous wonders can lead to faith as in the instance of conversion but they can also lead to a more intimate union with God for those on the continuing pilgrimage of Christian life. Miracles can also be a sign of orthodoxy as the Eastern monks testified when confronted by various Christological heresies in the ancient church.

Medieval era

One must remember that from late antiquity through the medieval era the notion of miracle is not primarily an interventionist one in which God sets aside the laws of nature. In a world understood as God's creation, coming forth from the hand of God, miracles are signs of God's marvellous presence and activity. Again in Ward's words, miracles are 'not *contra naturam* but *praeter* [beyond] or *supra* [above] *naturam*'.[6] Thus the words of the eleventh-century Benedictine abbot, Desiderius of Montecassino (1058–87):

> Almighty God sometimes shows his miracles not only in great things but also in minor matters, so that the faith of believers shall be more and more increased and thus it causes all creatures to break out in

praise of their Creator, since he is seen to have a care with fatherly piety in all those things that are granted to human endeavour.[7]

Or, those of Sicard, Bishop of Cremona (1185–1215):

> Wonderful is God who works wonderfully in all things, and more wonderfully in those beyond the course of nature ... confirming these things by miracles, that is, works unfamiliar to men, happening not contrary to nature which is always obedient to its Creator, but beyond nature, which does not usually work in such a way by its own force.[8]

This does not mean that the extraordinary was not noticed and even promoted. Apparitions of the Virgin Mary and the saints in visions and dreams, relics with curative powers, healings, and miraculous crucifixes were all reported as well as the pious sensibility that various sacramentals such as holy water and blessed candles provide spiritual and even material protection. The most famous of one of these phenomena is the story of St Francis of Assisi at the Church of San Damiano where Christ speaks to him from the cross to repair his house that has fallen into ruins. Within the framework of God's ever-present activity, the extraordinary blends with the ordinary within the world view of this era. *Miracula exteriora* and *miracula interiora* are both expected with the former in service of the latter. Authentic works of power, whether exterior or interior, are intended to increase sanctity.

Overall, the claim to the miraculous was broad, resident in the realm of popular devotional cults and piety to the elevated religious experiences of saints and mystics. St Ignatius Loyola (1491–1556), the founder of the Jesuits, testified in his autobiography to a number of mystical experiences, usually visionary, that were formative for his early spiritual growth. It was precisely these experiences that led him to develop his 'rules for discernment of spirits' in his *Spiritual Exercises*, a manual for retreat directors. This presumes a level of expectancy in the realm of experimental religion, and although the more common experience would be interior to the person praying, they could also be used to discern the more extraordinarily miraculous as well.

Reformation and Counter-Reformation

With the advent of the Reformation a critique of the miraculous emerged from among the magisterial Protestant Reformers. Most influential was that of John Calvin (1509–1564), the Geneva Reformer. In his discussion of anointing with oil he admits that the anointing signified for the early church the Holy Spirit and the gifts he bestowed including healing, but only as a symbol of such grace and not as its instrument. But in regard to his own day he adopted a cessationist position not dissimilar to some of the Church Fathers:

> But that gift of healing, like the rest of the miracles, which the Lord willed to be brought forth for a time, has vanished away in order to make the new preaching of the gospel marvellous forever.

And,

> The Lord is indeed present with his people in every age; and he heals their weaknesses as often as necessary, no less than of old; still he does not put forth these manifest powers, nor dispense miracles through the apostles' hands. For that was a temporary gift, and also quickly perished partly on account of men's ungratefulness.[9]

Similar sentiments had already been expressed by Martin Luther (1483–1546); not only in regard to the passing of miracles ('the days of miracles is past'),[10] but to their reconfiguration in reference to the spiritual work of God in the soul. Common to both Reformers are those words of Calvin implicating that miracles are no longer needed due to the true preaching of the gospel and according to the logic of the magisterial Reformation, the proper administration of the sacraments. Not only did this position assist the Reformers in their polemic against the Catholic Church with its so-called miraculous excesses in the arena of popular piety, but also held in check any similar tendencies in the Radical Reformation where religious enthusiasm in their judgment took root. The Reformers' criterion of discernment in meeting this challenge was not the authority of the church but the soundness of the gospel preached.

Yet the testimony of miracles did not entirely cease among the diverse and splintered Protestant movement. Connections of piety and expectation to pre-Reformation sensibilities were not entirely erased despite the 'stripping of the altars'. Traces of continuity between radical Reformers and medieval heretical sects such as the 'Spiritual Franciscans' has been noted by many. It was the appeal to the experience of the Holy Spirit by the 'spiritualist' wing of the Radical Reformation, as distinct from the Anabaptist wing, that set the context for religious enthusiasm and the possibility of miracles.

However, signs and wonders were not entirely absent in the Reformed stream of the magisterial Reformation, specifically, among some Puritans in England. An emphasis on interior miracles (mystical and spiritual) as taught, for example, in Luther's delineation of 'works which are done with the power of God ... In the first place, Christians have the Gospel, Baptism, and the Sacrament',[11] could be correlated with a Calvinist emphasis on divine providence. This nurtured a testimony to the miraculous (physical and exterior) or, at least, to wonders and marvels (*miranda*); the latter suggesting the discernment by faith of the works of God. Alexandra Walsham comments: 'such occurrences only appeared miraculous in the eye of the beholder: their actual natural causes remained cloaked and hidden from the view of imperfect human beings'.[12] The Puritan divine William Ames (1576–1633) understood that when God works in his extraordinary providence, it is above 'the usual and appointed order'. In an interesting turn of phrase Ames elaborates: that '[w]hatever is effected is, by metonymy of the effect, called a miracle'.[13] Such events included preservation in disasters, deliverance from dangers (the 1588 defeat of the Spanish Armada!), recovery from illness and other apparent supernatural occurrences; a host of events that could be classified if not miraculous outright then as 'special and extraordinary providences'. Additionally, the resurgence of the enthusiastic impulse, seldom absent from the Christian story, focused attention on miracles as the object of more direct witness wherever it flourished.

The Counter-Reformation Catholic Church did not neglect the promotion of the miraculous. It continued throughout the Baroque period and into the modern era appearing in a variety of forms. Not that the ecclesiastical hierarchy always and immediately assented to these events. The healing cult that built up after the apparition of Mary at Lourdes, France in the mid-nineteenth century is one example of a cautious hierarchy gradually affirming the supernatural events that took place – it took four years. Also, a close guard was kept up against those heterodox groups within the church that did not measure up to either doctrinal orthodoxy or pastoral supervision. An exemplary case was that of the Jansenists in France in the seventeenth century.

Hyper-Augustinian in their theology, the Jansenists also laid claim to numerous miraculous occurrences. This is quite instructive considering that their conflict with church authorities and religious orders that opposed them such as the Jesuits had more to do with the theology of grace they espoused than it did with the miraculous that neither the church nor the Jesuits were in principle opposed to. It was not so much a question of exterior versus interior life, but how supernatural grace is operative in the interior life to which miracles may or may not be of assistance. One thing miracles could not resolve, however, was the orthodoxy of their doctrine, at least from the perspective of the church's magisterium.

On the Protestant side a contemporary, although very different, movement was that of the Quakers, the Society of Friends. As its nomenclature suggests, they earned their name from the physical manifestations that attended their religious experience. George Fox (1624–91), their main founder, was known not only for his religious enthusiasm and his willingness to suffer for it but for his miracles as well. His lost 'Book of Miracles' (only reconstructed in the twentieth century from his writings) records 150 miracles of which healings constitute the majority.[14] Although not the first, for example Montanism, early Quakerism was a charismatic movement, a distinction that renders an account of religious experience that is somewhat different than that espoused by traditional mysticism.

Recall the thesis that miracles in Christian theology are best understood within the pneumatological and charismatic framework of the Christian life. The work of the Holy Spirit (pneumatology) and the gifts the Spirit bestows (charisms or *charismata*) constitute the larger framework within which the working of miracles takes place. Healing is one of these charismatic manifestations. Contrast this with infused contemplation characteristic of classical mysticism. While both entail an experiential immediacy in relation to the divine, classical mysticism focuses on the union with God associated with progress in holiness. Charismatic gifts, in contrast, are directed to the edification of others. In this regard early Quakerism was an experiential religious movement with charismatic manifestations before settling into more sober forms of Quaker silence and expectant waiting.

Other movements emerged with various degrees of religious enthusiasm coincident with expectations of the miraculous. All of them to one extent or the other were familiar with the power of God descending upon their adherents accomplishing any number of works of grace from conversion and repentance to assurance of salvation, and prophecy and healing in some quarters. Among these were the French Prophets of Cevennes and the Camisards, seventeenth-century groups connected with the Huguenots, and the Convulsionaries of St Medard with Jansenist roots in the eighteenth century. Also in the eighteenth century the German Moravians and the English Methodists expected the power of God to effect graced transformations among its members, with the former more quietist than the latter. But it is the spiritual descendants of the Anglican priest John Wesley (1703–91), whose heart was 'strangely warmed' under Moravian influence in 1738, who prepared the way for a more robust emergence of the supernatural and the miraculous. Wesley himself, the founder of the Methodists, took issue with cessationism and witnessed 'several things' that he judged could not 'be accounted for by the ordinary course of natural causes, and which I therefore believe ought to be "ascribed to the extraordinary interposition of God". If any man can choose to style them *miracles*, I reclaim not.'[15]

The significance of Wesley and the Methodists was not just that they were at the fountainhead of the 'revivalism' that would greatly influence Evangelical Protestantism. The First Great Awakening in North America and subsequent awakenings were all heavily experiential with the power of God evident in physical manifestations as well as in interior conversion. By the early nineteenth century, this pattern of revivals was systematized in the evangelistic work of Charles Finney (1792–1875). The relevant influence of these movements was that expectation of the power of God or the outpouring of the Holy Spirit were integrated into the Christian doctrinal schema. The power of God, or a baptism with the Holy Spirit, was taught as a second work of grace after the first work of conversion and regeneration. This second work was identified initially as a work of sanctification, to free the believer from the power of sin in one's life. The Wesleyan emphasis on 'entire sanctification' was the predominant one, but non-Wesleyan versions also appeared which spanned denominational boundaries among Anglo-Saxon Protestants. By the latter half of the nineteenth century, the 'Holiness Movement' was in full force out of which (along with other movements) the expectation of divine healing also emerged. This set the stage for the advent of an explicit signs and wonders movement with the birth of Pentecostalism at the turn of the twentieth century.

Modern era

It was the proto-Pentecostal movement of the Irvingites in England that signalled the two-fold emphasis on the gift of tongues (*glossolalia*) and prophecy as signs of God's power. Edward Irving (1792–1834), a Presbyterian pastor, encouraged both baptism with the Holy Spirit and the exercise of spiritual gifts in the new church he founded, the Catholic Apostolic Church. Likewise, John Alexander Dowie (1847–1907), founder of the Christian Catholic Church, conducted a healing ministry and founded an intentional Christian community at Zion City, north of Chicago. Both of these signs of the Spirit – 'inspired speaking' and healing – came together along with the doctrine of Spirit baptism, a subsequent work of grace following conversion that empowered the Christian for witness and mission, as the signature elements of the Pentecostal movement. Combined with strong eschatological sensibilities, the belief in an imminent second coming of Christ, early Pentecostals understood their movement as the restoration of signs and wonders in the Last Days before the coming of the Lord.

Although there are many aspects to Pentecostalism and while it cannot be considered the exclusive provenance of Christian expectation for the supernatural and miraculous, its explicit signification of signs and wonders as evidence of the outpouring of the Holy Spirit elevated both the visibility and status of miracles. More importantly Pentecostalism has been the direct or indirect source of numerous offshoots and charismatic movements within global Christianity in the twentieth century and beyond, all of which retain a normative belief in signs and wonders. Classical Pentecostal churches, those denominations established after an initial phase of revival in the first quarter of the twentieth century, have influenced the healings revivals of the 1950s, the charismatic movements within the historic churches of the 1960s and 1970s, the third wave of Evangelical neo-charismatics of the 1980s, various and sundry independent neo-Pentecostal churches worldwide, and non-white Indigenous Churches. Even more dramatically, the miraculous has been the explicit subject of healing ministries throughout the history of Pentecostalism. Healing evangelists developed international reputations as signs and wonders accompanied their preaching, and as many flocked to their campaigns specifically to find healing for their maladies. Such figures as Aimee Semple McPherson, William Branham, Oral Roberts, Kathryn Kuhlman, T. L. Osborn, John Wimber, Francis McNutt and Reinhard Bonnke are among those notaries who possessed these healing gifts and that identifies a type of religious figure that still distinguishes the Pentecostal and Charismatic movements.

In addition to being the fastest growing sector of Christianity, Pentecostal and charismatic movements, which have occurred in nearly all Christian communions, have reintroduced into the realm of the normal Christian life and lay Christian spirituality a dynamic sense of divine presence and action. This is not confined to the interior work of grace, although the pursuit of holiness and the close association with perfectionist tendencies in the Holiness Movement are still very much a part of Pentecostal and charismatic intentionality. The latter does not necessarily resolve all the excesses within the various movements, especially where signs and wonders function not so much as a sign of the gospel as they do of a consumerist prosperity incentive.

Nevertheless, Pentecostals have cultivated discernment and pastoral judgment to identify and wean out excess and error. Needless to say, Pentecostal and Charismatic theologians have been quick to refute cessationist theological positions. One such theologian, Jon Ruthven, has argued, for example, that the eschatological dimensions of pneumatology, the Holy Spirit's work as a harbinger of the kingdom of God to come, is inimical to cessationism. As expected, what is at stake is the underlying theology of miracles, to which we now turn.

THEOLOGY OF MIRACLES

The understanding of miracles has traditionally had two foci. The first has been the causal explanation of miracles relative to theological accounts of divine agency and providence. The second has to do with the apologetic dimension both in defending the authenticity and integrity of miracles and how they function as credible signs of the faith. The latter has been of particular concern to Western Christianity as it passed through the European Enlightenment and into modernity. The first, even in the pre-scientific age, required considerable theological and philosophical examination in order to render a coherent account of the relationship between the action of God and the doctrine of creation. We begin with this first concern.

Miracles and divine agency

Thomas Aquinas (1225–74) best captures a mature account of how God acts in miracles. Drawing on definitions set forth by St Augustine he expands on them and counters objections. One definition is as follows:

> Where God does anything against that order of nature which we know and are accustomed to observe, we call it a miracle.
>
> (*Against Faustus* 26.3)

Interestingly, in his explication Thomas does not elaborate on how God works against nature but simply identifies God as the cause of miracles that are performed outside causes accessible to human knowledge. Thomas further argues that miracles surpass the powers of nature, happen outside the natural course of things, and are above nature 'not only by reason of the substance of the thing done, but also on account of the manner and order in which it is done' (*Summa Theologiae*, 1a, q. 105, a. 7). Presupposed in these comments is an entire metaphysics of creation in which Thomas articulates the relation between God and the created order in terms of causality. Creation is dependent on God as its first cause. The primary divine causality of creation does not, however, eliminate secondary created causes as instrumental in the existence and conservation of created reality. All created things participate in the divine act of existence for their very being. In the course of the usual ordering and operations of creation the latter is still dependent on God for its own act of existence in which God is present and active in creation as its principal cause. Thus God acts through intermediate or secondary causes, that is, created causalities, without ever denying that God is always the first cause. In this respect divine agency is interior to the workings of creation. This, in fact, allows created entities to actualize other created realities by their participation in God's act of being. It also refers to the traditional Thomistic axiom that only for God are essence and existence identical. Created entities indeed have their act of being (*esse*) but they are not their own act of being.

Because creation is subject to God as its creator and participates in God's act of being it is possible to affirm that in the case of miracles divine agency can function in such a manner that God can do something outside, beyond or above the created order. God can so act that 'by producing the effects of secondary causes without them, or by producing certain effects to which secondary causes do not extend', a miracle can occur (*Summa Theologiae*, 1a, q. 105, a. 6). Since all created things by virtue of their participated act of being exist in a state of obediential potency to God, when God acts miraculously the divine agency surpasses but does not violate the created order. As Thomas explains, it indeed exceeds the hope of nature but not the hope of grace (1a, q. 105, a. 7). Therefore, the classical Thomistic axiom that 'grace does not destroy nature but perfects it' (1a, q. 1, a. 8), informs the understanding of miracles as well as ordinary acts of grace.

Needless to say, this explanation of miracles in concert with a metaphysical explanation of the doctrine of creation did not always prevail in the history of Christian thought. The impact of the Enlightenment challenged the Christian witness to miracles, both those recorded in Sacred Scripture and to contemporary testimony as well. Initially, Enlightenment sensibilities favoured natural religion over revealed religion and thus measured the biblical witness by what was considered possible according to the new scientific world view. These were important developments and evoked debate and significant theological and philosophical responses covered elsewhere in this book.

Our concern is to trace the variety of theological understanding of miracles that informs the life of the church. Our concentration will not be on the credibility of miracles in the Bible, which entails not only the theological understanding of miracles but questions of literary genre, historical-critical method, apologetics, the doctrine of revelation, and the authority and inspiration of Scripture. In other words, a vast array of issues emerged from the Enlightenment and what followed in its wake, especially the critical awareness of historical consciousness and its application to the ancient texts of the Christian Scriptures.

More relevant to the theological understanding of miracles was the emergence of a new world view in which the relationship between the supernatural, understood as the divine agency in grace, and the natural or the order of creation were driven apart. If the laws of nature no longer reflected a participation in the divine act of being and the action of God that is concurrent with creaturely agency, then miracles could be understood as a violation of what God or nature constituted as the order of creation, for example Baruch Spinoza (1632–77). Or, miracles were simply irrelevant to reason's grasp of moral and religious truth. Granted that this did not all happen at once; there were laudable attempts at identifying the continuities between faith and reason, between natural religion and revealed religion in the work of, for example, John Locke (1632–1704) and Bishop Joseph Butler (1692–1752). However, after the assaults of David Hume (1711–66) on the credibility of miracles and testimony to them, and the delimitation of speculative reason by Immanuel Kant (1724–1804), the realm of nature no longer required active divine agency. Likewise, the theology of miracles could not be (in this view) expounded with any degree of reasonableness that did not violate nature and its rational workings.

One important theological response was to reduce the scope of miracles not only in their quantity – perhaps not every wondrous event recorded in Scripture is a miracle – but in their theological import as well. Friedrich Schleiermacher (1768–1834) exemplified this strategy. Within a Newtonian scientific world view of mechanistic cause and effect as background, Schleiermacher, a one-time pietist elevated by romanticism, sought a continuity of nature and grace in which the distinction between natural and supernatural disappears. Within this hermeneutic all is miracle without distinguishing particular events as supernatural in origin for, as he stated in *On Religion: Speeches to its Cultured Despisers*, 'Every finite thing, however, is a sign of the Infinite ... Miracle is simply the religious name for event.'[16] Schleiermacher tried simultaneously to preserve both the scientific account of nature and an omnipresent divine agency. The miraculous then may be reduced to religious feeling, the greatest of which is the feeling of redemption in Christ. In this respect the metaphysical account of miracles has been deferred to the significance of religious feeling and consciousness. This was quite in harmony with a strong tradition that emphasized the *miracula interiora*, almost to the exclusion or insignificance of the *miracula exteriora* apart from interior faith.

Miracles and apologetic witness

In the face of emerging modernity, however, not all were willing to sacrifice the *miracula exteriora* as a point of Christian apologetics regarding the integrity of Scripture and for some the continued present possibility of miracles. One could easily defend the authenticity of biblical miracles – that they are historical and supernatural acts of God – and remain a cessationist. Benjamin Warfield (1851–1921) of Princeton Seminary typified this approach thus mounting polemics against both modernist tendencies in theology and religious enthusiasm among Protestant evangelicals. His definition of miracle is noteworthy for the ground it seeks to defend as the basis of Christian apologetics:

A miracle then is specifically an effect in the external world, produced by the immediate efficiency of God. Its *differentiae* are: (1) that it occurs in the external world, and thus is objectively real and not merely a mental phenomenon; and (2) that its cause is a new super-natural force, intruded into the complex of nature, and not a natural force under whatever wise and powerful manipulation.[17]

On both counts this differs from Schleiermacher. In terms of manifestation, miracles are exterior and the distinction between natural and supernatural is preserved.

Such intra-theological debates would continue and the subject of miracles became part of a larger landscape of issues that divided modernists and theological conservatives with some of these battles being waged at levels of ecclesiastical leadership and doctrinal orthodoxy. The First Vatican Council (1869–70) in its dogmatic constitution *Dei Filius* affirmed that 'God willed that external proofs of His revelation, viz. divine facts, especially miracles and prophecies, should be joined to the interior helps of the Holy Spirit' in order to demonstrate that the obedience of faith is in harmony with reason (Chapter 3) and it precluded in the canons (no. 3) any denial of miracles or that they 'can never be recognized with certainty'. Catholic and Protestant apologetic versions of the *miracula exteriora* were thus advanced with the theology of miracles still being debated into the twentieth century. Two representative versions of these theologies, while by no means comprehensive, illustrate the issues that are at stake.

C. S. Lewis (1898–1963), Anglican layman and apologist, on the one hand, recognized the necessity of coming to terms with the relationship between the natural and the supernatural. Naturalism, a term that excludes God and the supernatural – 'nothing can come into Nature from the outside because there is nothing outside to come into, Nature being everything'[18] – is indicative of the present world view characteristic of modernity. The first task, therefore, is to make the case for supernaturalism, for that which is beyond nature, 'exists on its own, and has produced the framework of space and time and the procession of systematically connected events which fill them', that is, Nature.[19] It is an attempt to recapture the metaphysical ground for miracles defined as 'an interference with Nature by supernatural power'.[20] The case he argued appealed to 'Reason' as that aspect of creaturely existence that is supernatural, meaning that it is derived from 'an eternal, self-existent, rational Being, whom we call God', thereby establishing each mind as 'an offshoot, or spearhead, or incursion of that Supernatural reality into Nature'.[21] It is an argument for supernatural theism exemplified in the grand miracle of the Incarnation. Nature itself is open to supernatural divine agency because God is its creator.

Paul Tillich (1886–1965), on the other hand, and in ways reminiscent of Schleiermacher, sought to move beyond what he termed 'naturalism and supranaturalism'. Naturalism cannot account for the infinite distance between 'finite things and their infinite ground'.[22] Supranaturalism, on the other hand, reduces God to a being among other beings even if the highest being. Rather, he argues, the finite world points beyond itself to its self-transcendent ground, namely, God who stands against the world and for it. Miracles then are those sign-events, unusual and astonishing, that point to the mystery of being and are received in ecstatic experience. In an intriguing turn of phrase, Tillich states 'that ecstasy is the miracle of the mind, and that miracle is the ecstasy of reality'.[23] Tillich's attempted 'third way' was intended to avoid separation between the finite and the infinite, and to retain the sign value of miracles as constitutive of their meaning and explanation. Miracles are possible because the very ground of creation manifests in finite realities its self-transcendence in the infinite.

Despite their different tacks both of these approaches see the necessity of a speculative/constructive account of the God–world relation in order to retain the theological credibility of miracles. Both avoid the sharp language of contradiction between miracles and the natural order. And both, in very different ways, also agree that miracles are such because of what they signify. Although there are many other recent explications of miracles these two are illustrative of two fruitful accounts from different sides of the theological spectrum.

To return to Thomas Aquinas, the ontological aspect ('something that transcends the powers of nature') and the intentional aspect (what they signify) of miracles are determinative for their authenticity as portents and wonders in human religious experience.[24] This psychological aspect of miracles bespeaks the veridicality of miracles only if the first two conditions are fulfilled. In sum, this becomes a matter of faith and discernment, whether it is applied in the canonization process of the Roman Curia of the Catholic Church (for which evidence of miracles is required), or a Pentecostal assembly's receptivity to the ministry of a healing evangelist. To some degree miracles in the life of the Christian Church will continue to echo the gospel accounts that many follow Jesus because they saw the signs he did (John 6.2) while the risen Lord also commends those 'who have not seen and yet believe' (20.29).

Notes

1 Augustine, *Tractates on the Gospel of John* 72.3 (*Patrologia latina*, Patrologiae cursus completus: Series latina, ed. J.-P. Migne, 217 vols. (Paris, 1844–64), vol. xxxv, col. 1823), quoted in the *Catechism of the Catholic Church* (Liguori: Liguori Publications, 1994), 537.

2 Kilian McDonnell and George T. Montague, *Christian Initiation and Baptism in the Holy Spirit: Evidence from the First Eight Centuries* (Collegeville: Liturgical, 1994), 291.

3 Kenneth Scott Latourette, *A History of Christianity*, 2 vols. (New York: Harper & Row, 1975), vol. i, 107.

4 Cited by Benedicta Ward, 'Monks and Miracle', in *Miracles in Jewish and Christian Antiquity: Imagining Truth*, ed. John C. Cavadini, Notre Dame Studies in Theology 3 (Notre Dame: University of Notre Dame Press, 1999), 130, and in *The Wisdom of the Desert Fathers: Apophthegmata Patrum, from the Anonymous Series*, trans. Benedicta Ward (Oxford: SLG, 1975), 50 (no. 178).

5 Ward, 'Monks and Miracle', 128.

6 *Ibid.*, 133.

7 *Patrologia latina*, Patrologiae cursus completus: Series latina, ed. J.-P. Migne, 217 vols. (Paris, 1844–64), vol. cxlix, cols. 0997D–8A; trans. G. A. Loud, 'Monastic Miracles in Southern Italy c. 1040–1140', in *Signs, Wonders, Miracles: Representations of Divine Power in the Life of the Church: Papers Read at the 2003 Summer Meeting and the 2004 Winter Meeting of the Ecclesiastical History Society*, ed. Kate Cooper

and Jeremy Gregory (Woodbridge and Rochester: Boydell Press for the Ecclesiastical History Society, 2005), 109.

8 Daniele Piazzi, *Omobono di Cremona: Biografie dal XIII al XVI secolo: edizione, traduzione e commento* (Cremona: Diocesi di Cremona, 1991), 36–7, trans. Brenda Bolton, 'Signs, Wonders, Miracles: Supporting the Faith in Medieval Rome', in *Signs, Wonders, Miracles*, ed. Cooper and Gregory, 162.

9 John Calvin, *Institutes of the Christian Religion*, 2 vols., ed. John T. McNeill, trans. Ford Lewis Battles (Philadelphia: Westminster, 1960), vol. II, 1467 (4.19.18–19).

10 Martin Luther, *Luther's Works*, 55 vols., ed. Jaroslav Pelikan and Helmut T. Lehman (St Louis: Concordia, 1955), vol. XXIV, 79.

11 *Ibid.*

12 Alexander Walsham, 'Miracles in Post-Reformation England', in *Signs, Wonders, Miracles*, ed. Cooper and Gregory, 285.

13 William Ames, *The Marrow of Theology*, IX, 11–12, in William Ames, *The Marrow of Theology*, ed. and trans. John Dykstra Eusden (Boston: Pilgrim, 1968), 108.

14 Rosemary Moore, 'Late Seventeenth-Century Quakerism and the Miraculous: A New Look at George Fox's "Book of Miracles"', in *Signs, Wonders, Miracles*, ed. Cooper and Gregory, 335–44.

15 John Wesley, second letter to Dr Church, 17 June 1746, *The Works of John Wesley: Third Edition, Complete and Unabridged*, vol. VIII: *Addresses, Essays, Letters* (1872) (Grand Rapids: Baker, 1991), 414–81 (460).

16 Friedrich Schleiermacher, *On Religion: Speeches to its Cultured Despisers* (New York: Harper, 1958), 88.

17 Benjamin B. Warfield, 'The Question of Miracle', *The Bible Student* (March 1903), 121–6, reprinted in John E. Meeter, ed., *Selected Shorter Writings of Benjamin B. Warfield*, 2 vols. (Phillipsburg: Presbyterian and Reformed, 1973), vol. II, 167–204 (170).

18 C. S. Lewis, *Miracles: A Preliminary Study* (New York: Macmillan, 1947), 21.

19 *Ibid.*, 20.

20 *Ibid.*, 15.

21 *Ibid.*, 37.

22 Paul Tillich, *Systematic Theology*, 3 vols. (Chicago: University of Chicago Press, 1951–63), vol. II, 7.

23 *Ibid.*, vol. I, 117.

24 Rene Latourelle, *The Miracles of Jesus and the Theology of Miracles* (New York: Paulist, 1988), 269; *Summa Theologiae*, IIA IIAE, q 178, a.1.

Further reading

*Brown, Colin, *Miracles and the Critical Mind* (Grand Rapids: Eerdmans, 1984)
Cavadini, John C., ed., *Miracles in Jewish and Christian Antiquity: Imagining Truth*, Notre Dame Studies in Theology 3 (Notre Dame: University of Notre Dame Press, 1999)

Cooper, Kate and Jeremy Gregory, eds., *Signs, Wonders, Miracles: Representations of Divine Power in the Life of the Church: Papers Read at the 2003 Summer Meeting and the 2004 Winter Meeting of the Ecclesiastical History Society* (Woodbridge and Rochester: Boydell for the Ecclesiastical History Society, 2005)

Geivett, Douglas R. and Gary R. Habermas, eds., *In Defense of Miracles: A Comprehensive Case for God's Action in History* (Downers Grove: Inter-Varsity, 1997)

Knox, Ronald, *Enthusiasm: A Chapter in the History of Religion* (Oxford: Oxford University Press, 1950; repr. Westminster: Christian Classics, 1983)

Larmer, Robert A., *Questions of Miracle* (Montreal and Buffalo: McGill-Queen's University Press, 1996)

Latourelle, Rene, *The Miracles of Jesus and the Theology of Miracles* (New York: Paulist, 1988)

Latourette, Kenneth Scott, *A History of Christianity*, vol. I (New York: Harper & Row, 1953, 1975)

Lewis, C. S., *Miracles: A Preliminary Study* (New York: Macmillan, 1947)

McInerny, Ralph, *Miracles: A Catholic View* (Huntington: Our Sunday Visitor, 1986)

Mullin, Robert Bruce, *Miracles and the Modern Religious Imagination* (New Haven and London: Yale University Press, 1996)

Newman, John Henry, *Two Essays on Biblical and Ecclesiastical Miracles* (London: Longmann, Green and Co., 1918)

Porterfield, Amanda, *Healing in the History of Christianity* (Oxford: Oxford University Press, 2005)

Ruthven, Jon, *In the Cessation of the Charismata: The Protestant Polemic on Postbiblical Miracles* (Sheffield: Sheffield Academic, 1993)

Schleiermacher, Friedrich, *The Christian Faith*, ed. H. R. Macintosh and J. S. Stewart (Philadelphia: Fortress, 1928)

On Religion: Speeches to its Cultured Despisers (New York: Harper, 1958)

Springer, Kevin, ed., *Power Encounters: Among Christians in the Western World* (San Francisco: Harper & Row, 1988)

Tillich, Paul, *Systematic Theology*, 3 vols. (Chicago: University of Chicago Press, 1951–63)

Ward, Benedicta, *Signs and Wonders: Saints, Miracles, and Prayer from the 4th Century to the 14th*, Collected Studies 361 (Aldershot: Variorum, 1992)

Williams, J., Rodman, *Renewal Theology 1: God, the World & Redemption* (Grand Rapids: Zondervan, 1988)

14 Miracles in Jewish philosophy

KENNETH SEESKIN

BIBLICAL AND RABBINIC ROOTS

We can begin with the obvious fact that most of the Hebrew Bible is organized in chronological fashion and that many of the events it narrates appear to be supernatural, for example creation, the flood, the exodus from Egypt, revelation at Sinai. But we should be wary of attributing a modern view of miracles to an ancient text. For a modern theist, nature is an impersonal system of causes and effects that God oversees and interferes with when circumstances warrant. Thus a miracle is often defined as a *violation* of the natural order. It is noteworthy, however, that there is no word in biblical Hebrew that corresponds to what we call *nature* and therefore no way to say that nature has been violated. Rather everything that happens has a single explanation: God willed it. Sometimes that will follow a normal pattern, sometimes not.

Despite the prevalence of wondrous or unanticipated events in the Bible, Judaism has always regarded miracles with ambivalence. As Maimonides (1138–1204) indicates in *Guide of the Perplexed* 2.22, to deny the possibility of miracles is to say, in effect, that having created the world, God cannot introduce any changes in it.[1] This certainly seems wrong. On the other hand, Judaism worships a God who does not act in a capricious fashion, and to cite miracles as proof of religious doctrines is to run the risk that the people will be seduced by charlatans. In regard to the second point, Deuteronomy 13.2–4 tells us that if a prophet or dreamer promises signs or omens, and those signs or omens come true, but the prophet bids one to follow other gods, the prophet should be disregarded. In fact, the passage goes on to say that God may send false prophets in order to test the people's resolve.

The rabbinic sages faced a similar issue. To deny the possibility of miracles is to deny the saving power of God; but to accept them uncritically is to court chaos. There are of course many stories of individual miracle workers in rabbinic literature, the question is: what

larger significance do these miracles have? In a ground-breaking passage
(*b. Bava Metzi'a* 59b), the rabbis respond by saying none. The issue
concerns a legal dispute between two rabbis about the cleanness of an
oven. God sides with one rabbi and produces a series of miracles to
show that this rabbi is right. But the opposition responds by quoting
Deuteronomy 30.12, which says that the Law is not in heaven. The
rabbis conclude that rather than look to miracles, they will listen to
arguments and follow majority rule.

Another rabbinic doctrine expresses the same ambivalence. Midrashic literature (*Genesis Rabbah* 5.5; *Exodus Rabbah* 21.6) suggests
that during the first six days of creation, God made an arrangement with
the sea so that it would divide to allow the Israelites to pass through
unharmed, with the sun and moon so they would stand still for Joshua,
with the ravens so they would feed Elijah, with fire so that it would not
harm Hananiah, Mishael and Azariah, with the lions so that they would
not devour Daniel, and with the fish so that it would swallow Jonah. In a
similar way, the Mishnaic tractate *Chapters of the Fathers* maintains:

> Ten things were created on the eve of the Sabbath at twilight,
> namely: The mouth of the earth [that swallowed Korach], the mouth
> of the well [which furnished water in the desert], the mouth of the
> ass [that spoke to Balaam], the rainbow [which appeared after the
> flood], the manna, the shamir [used to cut the stones that were used
> to build the Temple], the shape of the written characters, the
> engraving instrument, and the tablets of stone.
>
> (*m. Pirqê Avôth* 5.8)[2]

Again we have an attempt at compromise. If none of these things
happened, history would not contain evidence of a saving God. On
the other hand, a God who must constantly intervene in creation to
avoid disaster is unacceptable. Therefore the only reasonable thing to
say is that extraordinary events were woven into the fabric of history
from the beginning. Creation is a unique event that reflects divine
freedom. Once the work of creation is finished, history proceeds
according to a preordained plan.

Although this doctrine still leaves questions unanswered, versions
of it can be found in Philo, Judah Halevi, Maimonides, Gersonides, and
Rosenzweig.[3] The idea is that the created order contains both normal
forces, which are evident to the average person, and hidden or extraordinary forces, which are not. To the prophet, whose knowledge of the
created order surpasses that of ordinary people, the manifestation of
hidden forces is known and can be predicted. Thus Moses knew the sea

had the potential to split. Empirical objections aside, the Midrashic view tries to preserve the idea of a faithful God and an orderly world by saying the true order goes beyond the realm of what science can explain.

THE MEDIEVAL SYNTHESIS OF FAITH AND REASON

Because much of the thrust of medieval philosophy was to show there is no conflict between reason and revelation, the role of miracles had to be justified. One such attempt was that of Saadia Gaon (882–942 CE). If reason and revelation cannot conflict, any prophet who uses a miracle to establish something repugnant to reason is bogus.[4] Why then did God not rely on reason alone? Saadia has two answers. The first is that not everyone is capable of grasping the impact or details of rational argument. The second is that the scope of reason is limited.[5] Though reason can prove the existence of God, it cannot tell us how to praise God. By the same token, reason dictates that stealing is wrong but cannot tell us everything we need to know about the laws of property and inheritance. To fill in the gaps, God must appoint a messenger. The way to identify such a messenger is to have him predict a sign or wonder. In this way, miracles are public events that serve a rational purpose.

More broadly, the issue of miracles was tied up with the controversy over the creation or eternity of the world. If God created the world, it would seem he is free to do with it what he wants.[6] If the world is eternal, and has always existed in the form it has now, it would seem God enjoys no such freedom: history has always and will always follow its normal course. How can we decide whether the world was created? One strategy is to say there is empirical confirmation for the existence of miracles and therefore eternity is false. This strategy is taken by Judah Halevi (1075–1141), who argues that if we had to rely on reason alone, we would end up with an abstract conception of God as first cause of the world. Not only would this leave us guessing how God wants to be worshipped, it would not give us what we really want: the living God of Abraham, Isaac and Jacob. Thus:

> I [the Rabbi] believe in the God of Abraham, Isaac and Israel, who led the Israelites out of Egypt with signs and miracles ...[7]

How do we know these signs and miracles occurred? Halevi answers that because there were 600,000 witnesses (Exod. 12.37) to these events, and an unbroken tradition to preserve their memory, their authenticity is unimpeachable.[8]

For a modern thinker trained to regard the biblical narrative with suspicion, this argument is inadequate. How can we use a revealed text to authenticate the claims of revelation? We should understand, however, that for Halevi, it is philosophical argument, which is prone to doubt and uncertainty, that is inadequate.[9] Simply put: no argument can compare to the immediacy of direct observation, a fact which, we shall see, is borne out by the hesitant tone of Maimonidean philosophy.

Although he does not mention Halevi, Maimonides rejected his approach. Faced with the extremes of Aristotelian naturalism, which does not allow for the possibility of spontaneous action in God, and the voluntarism of the Asharites, who reject all causal connection and view everything as a miracle, Maimonides sought to steer a middle course.[10] Against the Aristotelians, he argues not that there is evidence miracles have occurred but that it is possible they could occur. Against the Asharites, he argues that Aristotle's account of the earthly realm is accurate and typically seeks naturalistic explanations of biblical narratives. For example, Maimonides argues that with the exception of Moses, all prophetic experiences take place in a dream or vision whether the text says so explicitly or not.[11] Thus Abraham's hospitality to the three visitors, Jacob's wrestling with the angel, and Balaam's speaking to his donkey are taken as visions rather than reports of actual events.[12]

With respect to Moses' encounter with God, Maimonides argues that one can believe *either* that the whole episode was an intellectual apprehension involving no sensory input *or* that the vision of a created object is implied, but there is no question that the latter represents a concession rather than his considered view.[13] Earlier, in the *Mishneh Torah*, he tells us: 'The Jews did not believe in Moses, our teacher, because of the wonders he performed. Whenever anyone's belief is based on wonders, he has misgivings, because it is possible to perform a wonder through magic or sorcery.'[14]

Maimonides' rationalism is also apparent in his view of the messiah. Although he was firmly convinced in the coming of a messiah, he was equally convinced that the messiah will not be expected to perform miracles. In fact, at *Mishneh Torah* 14, *Kings and Wars*, 11.3, 12.1–2, he cites with obvious satisfaction a rabbinic dictum that during the days of the messiah, nature will still follow its normal course.[15] The claim (Isa. 11.6) that the wolf shall lie down with the lamb is to be taken as a figurative way of saying that Israel will be at peace with the other nations. It follows that historical progress will come by natural means so that people will have to rely on the development of their own talents rather than an act of God.

Having conceded part of the naturalist argument, Maimonides hesitates when it comes to God. If natural causation were all we have, Aristotle would be right in holding that the world is eternal. Although eternity is logically possible, by which Maimonides means that no demonstration can prove creation, he argues that the best explanation of the phenomena we observe is that it was created.[16] Once we admit it was created, we have admitted that God can accomplish something nature alone cannot. This leaves the question of how to explain any purported case of a miracle undecided. In general Maimonides' approach is open-minded: if there is a good reason to accept one, we should; if not, no religious principle is violated by seeking another explanation.

We saw that in his earlier writing, Maimonides adopts the rabbinic view according to which all miracles were provided for during the first six days of creation. By the time he gets to the *Guide of the Perplexed*, however, he modifies his position. Though he cites the rabbinic view and does not openly criticize it, neither does he say he accepts it.[17] On the one hand, he wants to retain the view that God does not will things serially. If all miracles were provided for during creation, God does not have to make a new decision every time an anomaly is needed. Rather there is one decision that holds for all time. On the other hand, he wants to abandon the idea of an essential nature that contains strange or unpredictable qualities.[18]

He therefore argues that if a miracle occurs, it is only a temporary change in the way things behave and leaves their customary natures intact:

> I have said that a thing does not change its nature in such a way that the change is permanent merely in order to be cautious with regard to the miracles. For although the rod was turned into a serpent, the water into blood, and the pure and noble hand became white without a natural cause that necessitated this, these and similar things were not permanent and did not become another nature.
>
> (*Guide* 2.29, 345)

It is not part of the nature of a rod to turn into a serpent. When Moses performed the miracle, a genuine anomaly occurred. Because the anomaly was short lived, the nature of the rod is exactly as described by natural science. A miracle cannot go on forever. If it did, what was once viewed as an anomaly would now be seen as a customary occurrence forcing us to revise our conception of the original nature, and people would begin to take the miracle for granted so that it would no longer command attention. On this point, it would be helpful to recall that ancient and medieval science did not have a Newtonian conception of natural law. The world science investigates is a composite of matter and form. By its very nature, matter is unruly and occasionally refuses to accept form. So it is not surprising that anomalies occur. Along these lines, Aristotle distinguishes the exactness demanded by the mathematician from that demanded by the natural philosopher on the grounds that the former applies only to immaterial things (*Metaphysics* 995a15–20). As far as the earthly realm is concerned, a natural law is a generalization that holds 'always or for the most part', which means it can admit exceptions without being overturned (*Physics* 196b10–15).[19]

Again it is misleading to say that miracles *violate* nature. Because it demands generality, Aristotelian science does not take up the question of anomalies or singularities. That is why Maimonides thinks that however much attention they grab, miracles leave the natural order intact. The difference between Maimonides and Aristotle is that the latter thought exceptions to natural laws were the result of chance while the former allows for the possibility that they are the result of design.[20] The fact that God has the power to change or annihilate the natural order implies that it is neither necessary in itself nor necessary with respect to its cause. Rather, its existence follows from a free choice so that extraordinary events can occur if God deems them appropriate.

As is often the case, a strong movement in one direction creates an opposite movement in another. This is certainly the case with Nachmanides (1194–1270), a kabbalist and biblical commentator who returned to the view that miracles are an established fact supported by the testimony of an entire nation. From this fact, he infers the truth of creation *ex nihilo*, divine knowledge of individuals, divine providence and, when the miracle is foretold by a prophet, the existence of prophecy.[21] Nachmanides therefore calls into question the existence of a natural order that operates apart from God: 'No one can have a part in the Torah of Moses our teacher unless he believes that all our words and our events [as described in the Torah] are miraculous in scope, there being no natural or customary way of the world in them'.[22]

Nachmanides' argument is that the Torah constantly promises rewards for good deeds and punishment for evil ones. Because there is no natural connection between human behaviour and weather, crops or good health, there must be hidden miracles in what we take to be the course of nature.[23]

Beyond the hidden miracles are the public ones such as the parting of the Red Sea. As if to confirm Halevi's criticism of philosophy, the certainty with which Nachmanides reaches his conclusions about creation, divine knowledge and providence contrasts sharply with the studied scepticism of Maimonides, who argued that such doctrines, though true, could not be known with complete confidence. It is worth noting, however, that in both Halevi and Nachmanides, divine providence is partial and applies first and foremost to the Jewish People.

Gersonides (1288–1344) takes us back in the direction of rationalism. Like Maimonides, he argues that once one accepts creation, the possibility of miracles follows immediately (*Wars*, 6.2.9, 470).[24] According to the biblical text, some miracles are revealed to a prophet before they occur, for example the Ten Plagues visited on Egypt, while others are not revealed. Of the latter type, there are also two kinds: those in which a prophet prays for a miracle, for example Elisha's request that those pursuing him be blinded, and those in which a miracle follows a prophetic decree, for example Elisha's miracle of the oil. In general, miracles are ascribed to a prophet and undertaken for the good of the people.

This raises the question of the identity of the agent who performs the miracles. Although one might think the answer has to be God, Gersonides maintains otherwise (*Wars* 6.2.10, 474–86).[25] If God were the proximate cause of miracles, the Agent Intellect (the celestial intelligence responsible for the order of the sublunar realm) would be superior to God because it would be responsible for what can be known scientifically while God would be responsible for anomalies. To see this another way, the activity of the Agent Intellect would be continuous while that of God would be intermittent. Moreover, if God were the proximate cause of miracles, the prophet, whose knowledge comes from the Agent Intellect, could not be involved in them. Nor could the prophet himself be the proximate cause of a miracle because no person has the knowledge needed to perform them. Gersonides concludes that the proximate cause is the Agent Intellect, while God is the remote or indirect cause.

We saw that Gersonides also subscribes to the view that miracles were woven into the fabric of history during the first six days of creation. Commenting on *m. Avôth* 5.6, he argues that it is significant that the miracles were arranged at twilight.[26] During the day, God was free to create the world as he wanted. Once nightfall came, creative activity ceased, and the order God established began to play itself out. By saying the miracles were arranged at twilight, the rabbis implied they share in both the freedom of divine activity and the orderliness of the world after creation. How can this be? Gersonides' suggestion is that we think of miracles as hypothetical. The normal order dictates that water is heavier than air and seeks a common level. Although God did not necessitate Pharaoh's attempt to pursue the Israelites at the sea, given that Pharaoh did pursue them, God arranged for the waters to part. Had Pharaoh been more generous, nothing out of the ordinary would have happened.

In general the philosophers of the medieval period tried to reconcile divine freedom, which implies the possibility of extraordinary action, with metaphysical perfection, which implies immutability. Their argument is that the creation of natural processes is not itself a natural process. Since the history of the world involves both, it is not surprising that it involves both normal and unexpected events.

THE RISE OF MODERNITY

The medieval attempt at reconciliation came under sharp criticism from Baruch Spinoza (1632–77). In Chapter 6 of the *Theological-Political Treatise*, he begins with the tendency to ascribe to God anything that falls outside the limits of human understanding.[27] According to the common view, God's providence is most clearly revealed by extraordinary events rather than normal ones. As noted earlier, this implies there are two powers at work: God and nature. It also implies there are two faculties in God: will and wisdom. From a wide range of possible scenarios considered by his wisdom, God is supposed to will the one in which his providence can best be shown to humans. Were this scenario to include only natural events, we are told, humans would not be able to see the hand of God at work and would soon fall into disbelief.

But, Spinoza protests, this account makes no sense. Since most theologians hold that God is one and simple, will and wisdom cannot be distinct. It follows that if God understands everything as it is, he must will everything as it is. Because nothing can be true apart from God's will, the laws of nature follow from the necessity and perfection of the divine nature. Thus anything that contravened these laws would also contravene God's will. So far from establishing the existence of God, a miracle would establish the fallibility of God because it would show that his will is not ultimate. To the suggestion that there are two orders, one natural and the other supernatural, Spinoza replies that the efficacy and power of nature are identical with the efficacy and power of God; thus any limitation on one would be a limitation on the other. He concludes that a miracle is simply an event whose explanation according to natural causes is unknown. If its causes are unknown, it can teach us nothing about God. On the contrary, the way to learn about God is to study those things whose causes are known, which is to say those things which follow the order and necessity of nature. In effect, Spinoza's criticism is to say that if God is truly immutable, it will not do to say that one set of principles applies to creation, another set to what happens afterwards. Not surprisingly, Spinoza believed in an eternal world.

It would be one thing if, like Hume, Spinoza wrote to undermine Scripture, but interestingly enough, he claims to find support in Scripture. He cites the passage from Deuteronomy 13 mentioned above to show that according to Scripture, even false prophets could work miracles so that unless people are endowed with knowledge and love of God, miracles can mislead them.[28] Indeed, the story of the exodus shows that despite witnessing the ten plagues and the parting of the Red Sea, the people were so ignorant of the true nature of God they could worship a golden calf. This is not to deny that the Israelites *believed* they could acquire knowledge of God by witnessing miracles but that such knowledge was actually forthcoming.

In other respects, Spinoza follows the medieval rationalists in arguing that Scripture often uses symbolic or metaphorical language to describe natural events. When it says that God hardened Pharaoh's heart, all that is meant is that Pharaoh was obstinate; when it says that God opened the windows of heaven, all that is meant is that it rained very hard.

The cogency of Spinoza's position rests on the identification of God with nature. In the *Theological-Political Treatise*, he describes natural laws as decrees of God. In the *Ethics* he is more explicit and uses the phrase 'deus sive natura' (God or nature), where the disjunction is inclusive.[29] The traditional Jewish view is that God is not to be found *in* nature but above or beyond it. It is true of course that Spinoza's view of nature is not the standard one. According to him, nature is infinite, all-powerful, self-caused and self-sustaining. In short, he endowed nature with many of the properties typically reserved for God.

By the same token, he denies that God deliberates or chooses between alternatives. Rather God acts from the same necessity by which he exists. It is therefore absurd to suppose that God could do anything different from what his nature dictates.

From a medieval perspective, this is Aristotelianism all over again: the God who cannot act in a spontaneous fashion. The difference is that what the medievals who believed in creation see as a limitation on God, Spinoza sees as a mark of perfection. Whether we are talking about God or the course of events, Spinoza argues that contingency (the ability to choose between X and Y without being necessitated) is nothing but a reflection of human ignorance.

Although few people in Jewish philosophy adopted Spinoza's naturalism, many followed him in other respects. Against the medievals, Spinoza argued that the prophets were not educated in scientific or philosophical subjects. Instead, their teachings concern matters of behaviour: singleness of heart and the practice of justice and charity.[30] That is why it has little to contribute to our understanding of what causes the things we see. Spinoza also argued that we have to approach the Bible historically. This means that our chief goal is not to validate its truth but to understand its meaning.[31] If the prophets held views of God or nature different from ours, rather than project our views onto a text composed thousands of years ago, we should get clear on what they believed even if we are convinced it is false. If, for example, the prophets thought the sun revolved around the earth, that is what the text means despite the fact that modern science has established the opposite.

Two consequences follow. The first is that one cannot use Scripture to validate the occurrence of miracles. The fact that people in a pre-scientific age described their experience a certain way has no tendency to show that things happened exactly as they said. The second is that if religion is concerned with practical rather than theoretical questions, miracles are no longer critical. As Spinoza sees it, the ultimate end of all human action is to love God not from fear of punishment or the pursuit of pleasure but simply for what God is.[32] The law that bids us to love God is divine in the sense that (1) it is common to all people, (2) it does not depend on the truth of a historical narrative, and (3) it does not require the performance of ceremonies. For our purposes, the most important feature of divine law is (2) because it says that the validity of the law has nothing to do with miracles. It is valid simply because it can be known by the light of reason.

Although Spinoza was put in *cherem* (excommunicated) by the rabbinic court of Amsterdam in 1656, his influence is clearly visible in the thought of Moses Mendelssohn (1729–86), a key figure in the German Enlightenment who remained an orthodox Jew. Mendelssohn's account of Judaism begins with the modernist contention that God is impartial: a just God would never reveal truths necessary for human salvation to one people but deny them to others. Accordingly:

> I therefore do not believe that the powers of human reason are insufficient to persuade men of the eternal truths which are indispensable to human felicity, and that God had to reveal them in a supernatural manner.[33]

There is then no need for God to produce a miracle to convince people that he exists, that virtue is its own reward or that the soul is immortal.

If so, what becomes of the miracle at Mount Sinai? Here Mendelssohn takes a more traditional view. If the eternal truths necessary for human salvation derive from reason, the specific legislation given to the Jewish people derive from historical events founded on faith and confirmed by miracles.[34] That legislation is binding on all Jews until God again speaks to the entire nation and rescinds it. Mendelssohn's position succeeds to the extent that it paved the way for Jews to take their place in an increasingly tolerant and cosmopolitan society. The legislation binding on Jews is consistent with the eternal truths of reason and therefore poses no threat to Christianity. But it failed to answer one of the central questions it set for itself. If the eternal truths are all that is needed for human salvation, why did God burden the Jews with extra legislation? Alternatively, if such legislation helps people to remember and reflect on the eternal truths, why did God not distribute them more broadly?

FROM THE NINETEENTH TO THE TWENTIETH CENTURY

The problems associated with Mendelssohn's view made it necessary to look for an alternative. The most significant was the Neo-Kantianism of Hermann Cohen (1842–1918). Immanuel Kant (1724–1804) argued that the truths of religion, in particular the existence of God and the immortality of the soul, could not be demonstrated by theoretical reason but were necessary postulates of practical reason. In other words, they are needed to help us make sense of our obligations as rational agents. Like Mendelssohn, Kant insisted these truths are not historical in nature and can be discovered by reason a priori. To the degree that one accepts them on the basis of miracles, his acceptance would be conditioned on a particular reading of history and therefore less secure than acceptance based on reason alone.

Kant's conception of a rational religion is spelled out in *Religion within the Limits of Reason Alone*. Although it claimed to be universal in scope, his religious philosophy was in fact an idealized version of Christianity that relegated Judaism to the status of a national cult. As if in reply, Cohen's masterpiece was entitled *Religion of Reason out of the Sources of Judaism* and tried to show that an idealized version of Judaism that met all the demands laid down by Kant could be constructed from biblical and rabbinic sources.[35] As such, it has no need of miracles and sees them as a throwback to mythology.

We can better understand Cohen's project by saying his conception of a religion of reason stands to historical religion in the same way that the ideal of a perfect democracy stands to the day-to-day workings at city hall. Instead of a God who acts *in* history, Cohen offers the idea of a perfect moral agent who stands *above* it.[36] Instead of a historical encounter between God and Moses, Cohen offers a correlation between the essence of humanity and the essence of divinity.[37] What matters in revelation is not the fact of its occurrence but the moral necessity of its content. Not only is there no need for miracles in an idealized religion, they would interfere with everything Cohen is trying to do. As he points out, miracles are anomalies, cases where reason is stymied.[38] By contrast, revelation is for Cohen a metaphorical way of talking about the origin of reason.[39] To make revelation dependent on the receipt of sensory evidence would undermine the validity of reason rather than support it.

Although he would not normally be classified as a Neo-Kantian, Emmanuel Levinas (1906–95) also distrusted miracles or what he called the numinous aspect of religion. 'Judaism', as he proudly proclaims, 'has decharmed the world'.[40] Properly understood, it rejects the idea of a supernatural God whose actions inspire wonder and who enters into an exchange relationship with human beings. Rather than a miracle worker, God presents himself as an issuer of commandments, in particular the commandment to respect the dignity of human life. Nothing in this experience requires the miraculous; in fact, the miraculous would just be a distraction because it would divert attention from the imperative force of the commandment. We do not need thunder and lightning to recognize the dignity of human life; for Levinas, all we have to do is look at the face of another person and see its vulnerability.

A more sympathetic position on miracles can be found in the works of Franz Rosenzweig (1886–1929) and Martin Buber (1878–1965). The crux of their view is to suggest that we abandon the distinction between natural and supernatural upon which most accounts of miracles rely. Although Rosenzweig follows the traditional view according to which miracles were planned during creation, he gives it a new twist.

The important feature of a miracle is not its unusual character but the fact that a prophet is able to see it coming and interpret it correctly. Thus: 'Miracle and prophecy hang together. Whether a magic effect is operative in miracle at the same time may be left open and is left open.'[41] Crucial to Rosenzweig's point is a distinction between a prophet and a sorcerer. If the former appeals to divine providence, the latter appeals to mysterious forces that conform to his own will.

According to Rosenzweig, what the prophet sees is not a chaotic world with constant interruptions but the opposite: the lawfulness of the world as it unfolds according to God's plan. In fact, Rosenzweig notes, the idea of natural law originally cohered with that of miracle[42] because both are based on the assumption of an underlying order in things. With the development of natural science, however, natural law came to designate the inner connection of events rather than their content. But, Rosenzweig maintains, it is the content that matters. Rather than a metaphysical anomaly, a miracle is therefore a sign of God's presence to or involvement with the world.

In a similar way, Buber argues there is not one realm of spirit and another of nature; there is only the realm of God.[43] Thus revelation is not a historical event involving thunder and lightning but the meaning we ascribe to a natural event: 'for natural events are the carriers of revelation, and revelation occurs when he who witnesses the event and sustains it experiences the revelation it contains'.[44] To experience revelation one must be open to the depth of the experience and the possibility of transformation. God's presence is eternal. In principle, any event, no matter how ordinary, can be the occasion for someone to feel the presence of God. The question then is how we respond to the event not the mechanics of its causation. The advantage of Buber's account is that the empirical question, 'Did this actually happen?', is no longer relevant. Rather than argue about the accuracy of the biblical narrative, we should be asking what message it is attempting to convey.

CONCLUSION

Spinoza to the contrary not withstanding, the overall thrust of Judaism is the transcendence of God. The Bible sought to show that God is not limited in the way that kings, armies or meteorological phenomena are. To accomplish this, it narrates events that inspire awe and wonder. The philosophers of the medieval period attempted to generalize from the biblical narrative and argued that God is not limited by the principles that govern natural causation. For Spinoza, this line of argument is mistaken because nature is infinite and thus has no limits. With the influence of Kant, the question was no longer one of God's overpowering nature but of God's doing something nature alone cannot: commanding certain forms of behaviour and prohibiting others. Whether we experience these commands as following from reason alone or as issuing from a personal encounter, literal interpretation of biblical miracles is beside the point. We saw that the Bible itself is suspicious of miracles and asks us to think twice before following someone who works them.

My own conviction is that the rabbis were right: a miracle neither confirms nor refutes a religious doctrine. If a theist and a naturalist both witnessed the same event, the theist would see the hand of God while the naturalist would only see a series of physical interactions. Even if one is convinced the hand of God is involved, one would immediately have to confront a series of questions: what kind of God is responsible for this event? Is it the God of Israel? Is a message being communicated? If so, what? No matter how extraordinary, the event would raise as many questions as it answers.

Beyond the question what message is communicated, there is the question of what happens to belief in God when the miracles stop. People are inclined to see the hand of God in events that bring good fortune, especially if it is unanticipated. But what happens when fortune turns the other way. According to David Hartman: 'If one's whole sense of faith depends upon a miracle-based conception of the biblical promises of reward and punishment, then one risks exchanging God for alternative sources of well-being and security'.[45]

The issue of bad fortune is particularly relevant to a people who have experienced centuries of persecution, culminating in the horrors of Nazi genocide. If God saw fit to save the Israelites from Pharaoh, why was an equally impressive miracle not forthcoming during the time of Hitler? Put in such stark terms, the question has no answer except to say that true faith has nothing to do with fortune. In this respect, Hartman is right. A person who claims to see the hand of God in events that go his way is not looking for God but the equivalent of a genie in a bottle. If there is a lesson to be learned, it is that a miracle can be effective only against a background of prior doctrines and convictions. Rather than short-circuiting the deliberative process, it should be a way of stimulating it. While awe and wonder are part of religious experience, they cannot be allowed to exhaust it.

Notes

1 Moses Maimonides, *Guide of the Perplexed*, trans. Shlomo Pines (Chicago and London: University of Chicago Press, 1963), 319.
2 *Daily Prayer Book: Ha-Siddur Ha-Shalem*, trans. and ed. Philip Birnbaum (New York: Hebrew Publishing Co., 1977), 516.
3 Philo, *Mos.* 1.33, 38, 158, 210–11; Judah Halevi, *Kuzari*, trans. Isaac Heineman (Oxford: East and West Library, 1947); Maimonides, 'Eight Chapters', in *A Maimonides Reader*, ed. Isadore Twersky (West Orange: Behrman House, 1972), 382–3, and *Guide*, 2.29, 344–5; Levi ben Gersonides, *Wars of the Lord*, vol. III, trans. Seymour Feldman (Philadelphia: Jewish Publication Society of America, 1999), 6.2.10, 479–86; Franz Rosenzweig, *The Star of Redemption*, trans. William H. Hallo (Notre Dame: University of Notre Dame Press, 1970), 94–6.
4 Saadia Gaon, *The Book of Beliefs and Opinions*, trans. Samuel Rosenblatt (New Haven: Yale University Press, 1948), 164 (on 3.8). For an overview of the status of miracles in medieval Jewish Philosophy, see Howard Kreisel, 'Miracles in Medieval Jewish Philosophy', *Jewish Quarterly Review*, new series 75 (1984), 99–133.
5 Saadia, *Beliefs and Opinions*, 3.3, 145–7.
6 See *ibid.*, 7.1, 411, and Maimonides, *Guide*, 2.25, 328.
7 Halevi, *Kuzari*, 33.
8 *Ibid.*, 42–3. For a medieval precedent for this argument, see Saadia, *Beliefs and Opinions*, Introduction, 6, 29–30. For a modern account, see Rosenzweig, *Star*, 96–7.
9 For more on this point, and a comparison between Halevi and Maimonides, see David Hartman, *Israelis and the Jewish Tradition* (New Haven: Yale University Press, 2000), 38–43. The thrust of Hartman's argument is to defend Maimonides against the miracle or 'event-based' theology of Halevi.
10 Maimonides, *Guide*, 1.73, 202; 2.22, 317–20.
11 *Ibid.*, 2.41, 385–6.
12 *Ibid.*, 2.42, 388–9.
13 *Ibid.*, 1.21, 50–1.
14 Maimonides (Rambam), *Mishneh Torah* (Laws of the Foundation of the Torah), trans. Eliyahu Touger (New York and Jerusalem: Moznaim, 1989), 262 (1, Basic Principles, 1–2).
15 See *A Maimonides Reader*, 223–4. The dictum in *Sanhedrin* 91b reads: 'The sole difference between the present and the days of the messiah is delivery from servitude to foreign powers'.
16 Maimonides, *Guide*, 2.24, 323–7.
17 *Ibid.*, 2.29
18 For further discussion of Maimonides' view of miracles and his desire to steer a middle course, see Kreisel, 'Miracles', 106–8; Hannah Kasher, 'Biblical Miracles and the Universality of Natural Laws: Maimonides' Three Methods of Harmonization', *Journal of Jewish Thought and Philosophy* 8 (1998), 25–52.

19 Cf. Maimonides, *Guide*, 2.20, 312.
20 *Ibid.*, 2.29, 346.
21 Ramban (Nachmanides), *Commentary on the Torah*, 5 vols., trans. Charles B. Chavel (New York: Shilo, 1971–6), vol. II, 172–3 (on Exod. 13.16). For an overview of Nachmanides' position, see David Berger, 'Miracles and the Natural Order in Nachmanides', in *Rabbi Moses Naḥmanides (Ramban): Explorations in his Religious and Literary Virtuosity*, ed. Isadore Twersky (Cambridge, MA: Harvard University Press, 1983), 107–28.
22 Ramban (Nachmanides), *Commentary*, 2.172–3 (on Exod. 13.16).
23 *Ibid.*, 2.65 (on Exod. 6.2); cf. 1.215–16 (on Gen. 17.1).
24 Gersonides, *Wars*, 6.2.9, 470.
25 *Ibid.*, 6.2.10, 474–86.
26 *Ibid.*, 6.2.10, 484–6.
27 Spinoza, *Theological-Political Treatise*, 2nd edn, trans. Samuel Shirley (Indianapolis: Hackett, 2001), 71–3.
28 *Ibid.*, 76–7.
29 Benedict de Spinoza, *A Spinoza Reader: The Ethics and Other Works*, ed. Edwin M. Curley (Princeton: Princeton University Press, 1994), 98; cf. 16, 59, 198, 202–3.
30 Spinoza, *Treatise*, 6.
31 *Ibid.*, 88–9.
32 *Ibid.*, 50–1.
33 Moses Mendelssohn, *Jerusalem*, trans. Allan Arkush (Hanover: University Press of America, 1983), 94.
34 *Ibid.*, 127.
35 Hermann Cohen, *Religion of Reason out of the Sources of Judaism*, trans. Simon Kaplan (Atlanta: Scholars Press, 1995).
36 *Ibid.*, 94–9.
37 *Ibid.*, 79.
38 *Ibid.*, 72.
39 *Ibid.*, 72.
40 Emmanuel Levinas, *Difficult Freedom*, trans. Sean Hand (Baltimore: Johns Hopkins University Press, 1990), 14.
41 Franz Rosenzweig, *The Star of Redemption*, trans. William W. Hallo (Notre Dame: University of Notre Dame Press, 1970), 95.
42 *Ibid.*, 95.
43 Martin Buber, *Israel and the World* (New York: Schocken, 1948), 131.
44 *Ibid.*, 98.
45 Hartman, *Israelis*, 85.

Further reading

Cohen, Hermann, *Religion of Reason out of the Sources of Judaism*, trans. Simon Kaplan (Atlanta: Scholars Press, 1995)
*Frank, Daniel H., Oliver Leaman and Charles H. Manekin, *The Jewish Philosophy Reader* (London and New York: Routledge, 2000)

Halevi, Judah, *Kuzari*, trans. Isaak Heinemann (Oxford: East and West Library, 1947)

Hartman, David, *Israelis and the Jewish Tradition* (New Haven: Yale University Press, 2000), 38–43

Kaufmann, Yehezkel, *The Religion of Ancient Israel*, trans. Moshe Greenberg (New York: Schocken, 1972), ch. 3

Kellner, Menachem, *Maimonides Confrontation with Mysticism* (Oxford: Littman Library of Jewish Civilization, 2006)

Kreisel, Howard, 'Miracles in Medieval Jewish Philosophy', *Jewish Quarterly Review*, new series 75 (1984), 99–133

Prophecy: The History of an Idea in Medieval Jewish Philosophy (Dordrecht: Kluwer, 2001)

Levinas, Emmanuel, 'A Religion for Adults', in *Difficult Freedom*, trans. Sean Hand (Baltimore: Johns Hopkins University Press, 1990), 11–23

Maimonides, Moses, *A Maimonides Reader*, ed. Isadore Twersky (West Orange: Behrman House, 1972), 222–7, 382–3, 402–23

The Guide of the Perplexed, trans. Shlomo Pines (Chicago and London: University of Chicago Press, 1963)

Rosenzweig, Franz, *The Star of Redemption*, trans. William H. Hallo (Notre Dame: University of Notre Dame Press, 1970), 93–7

Spinoza, Baruch, *Theological-Political Treatise*, 2nd edn, trans. Samuel Shirley (Indianapolis: Hackett, 2001), ch. 6

Urbach, Ephraim E., *The Sages*, trans. Israel Abrahams (Jerusalem: Magnes, 1979), ch. 6

Part IV
Miracle today

15 Issues in the history of the debates on miracles

COLIN BROWN

Christian appeals to 'mighty works', 'wonders' and 'signs', though not demonstrative proofs, date from the New Testament. At Pentecost, Acts 2.22 represents Peter as saying: 'You that are Israelites, listen to what I have to say: Jesus of Nazareth, a man attested to you by God with deeds of power, wonders and signs that God did through him among you, as you yourselves know'. A similar statement is made in Acts 10.38.

Three comments may be made. First, Peter and his hearers shared a common world view, which was shaped by the Hebrew Bible, and which provided the context for discourse regarding divine action. Second, the claims made on behalf of Jesus state rather less than those made by later apologists. Neither passage says that Jesus demonstrated personal divinity as Son of God incarnate by performing miracles. Acts 2.22 refers to what God 'did through him'. Acts 10.38 attributes Jesus' power to 'the Holy Spirit ... for God was with him'. Third, these passages represent the other side of the coin to charges that Jesus was a false prophet who performed the capital offence of using signs and wonders in order to lead astray (Deut. 13.1–5). The charges surfaced in the accusation that Jesus was casting out demons by Beelzebul, 'the ruler of the demons'.[1] They were based on the Torah (or 'Law' in English Bibles). The Christian response was to protest Jesus' righteousness, and to appeal to the Law *and* the Prophets (for example, Matt. 5.17–18; Luke 4.18–19; Isa. 61.1–2). The controversy was ultimately a question of *hermeneutics* – whether Jesus fitted the profile of the prophet who performed signs and wonders in order to lead astray, or that of the Spirit-anointed servant. In this chapter we shall note critical issues from the fourth to the twentieth centuries.

THE FOURTH AND FIFTH CENTURIES

The power of Christ to heal, drive out demons and put magicians to flight was a potent factor in the growth of Christianity.[2] Nevertheless, miracles were not without problems. Eusebius of Caesarea, Gregory of Nyssa and Augustine of Hippo represent three responses.

Eusebius of Caesarea

Eusebius (c. 260–c. 340 CE) addressed challenges against Jesus as a miracle worker. The first was that Jesus practised magic.[3] It came from two quarters: adherents to Graeco-Roman religions and orthodox Jews. Eusebius' *Demonstration of the Gospel* followed the tradition of Justin Martyr and Origen.[4] Jesus fulfilled the prophecies of the Hebrew Scriptures. His meekness, reasonableness and purity were not marks of a 'deceiver'. His followers would hardly have faced martyrdom, had they believed otherwise.

The second challenge centred on Apollonius of Tyana, a Neo-Pythagorean sage of the first century. The principal source is *The Life of Apollonius* by Philostratus who belonged to the circle around the emperor Septimius Severus and his wife Julia Domna.[5] Philostratus' *Life* is widely regarded as a philosophical romance. Scholars debate whether it was intended as pagan propaganda, depicting Apollonius as a rival to Jesus. Some have suggested that both Jesus and Apollonius belonged to the generic category of the 'divine man', while others have protested that the 'divine man' is a synthetic concept invented by modern scholarship.[6]

Philostratus made only implicit contrasts with Jesus, including the resuscitation of a bride on her wedding day, and the ascension of Apollonius on his death. But *Truth-loving Words to Christians* by the Roman governor of Bithynia, Sossianos Hierocles, drew direct comparisons. Eusebius replied with *Against Hierocles*, remarking that Hierocles stood alone in comparing Apollonius with Jesus. Hierocles argued that both were 'pleasing to the gods', but it was wrong to rank Jesus higher. To Eusebius, the issue was whether to rank Apollonius 'among divine and philosophic men or among wizards'. Since only Jesus belonged to the former category, Apollonius must belong to the latter.

Gregory of Nyssa

Gregory (329/30–c. 395 CE) was a Cappadocian father who staunchly defended the Council of Nicea (325 CE), that Jesus' divinity was *homo-ousios* (of the same substance) as the Father's. Gregory's view reflects a shift from the time when the primary question was whether Jesus was possessed by Satan or anointed by the Spirit of God. In Gregory's day the crucial issue was the relationship of Jesus' humanity to his divinity. Gregory saw Jesus' sufferings as tokens of his humanity. 'The evidence of his divinity comes through the miracles' (*Catechetical Oration* 34).

St Augustine of Hippo

The issues that Augustine (354–430 CE) wrestled with were of a different order. How should one think of miracles? Augustine defined miracles as, 'whatever appears that is difficult or unusual above the hope and power of them who wonder' (*The Usefulness of Believing* 34). Miracles fell into two classes: those that 'cause only wonder' and those that 'procure great favour and good will'. To see a person flying would provoke only wonder, but the healings and nature miracles of Jesus brought benefit.

This distinction lay behind Augustine's belief that the age of miracles had largely ceased. Miracles were important in the founding of the church, but they 'were not allowed to continue till our time, lest the mind should always seek visible things' (*True Religion* 47).

Augustine rejected the idea that miracles broke the laws of nature. God does not act contrary to nature, 'when it is contrary to what we know of nature' (*Against Faustus* 26.3). Elsewhere Augustine entertained the conjecture that God had implanted seeds in creation that lay dormant until the time was ripe (*The Trinity* 3.9.16).

Augustine returned to miracles in *The City of God* (416–22 CE), which was written in vindication of Christianity against charges that abandonment of the old gods was responsible for the sack of Rome (410 CE). Augustine now argued that miracles, wrought so that the world might believe, have not ceased even when the world has come to belief (*City of God* 22.8). He himself had witnessed the restoration of sight to a blind man at Milan in the presence of the emperor. Miracles demonstrate God's sovereignty.

AQUINAS AND MIRACLES

For the medieval mind, miracles were in the main unproblematic, and the age was rife with miracle stories. Intellectual thought largely followed Augustine.[7] Thomas Aquinas (*c.* 1225–74), the greatest of the medieval theologians and the most formative thinker for subsequent Catholicism, treated Augustine's ideas as fixed points. Where he differed, he did so to express the same ideas in terms of the Aristotelian philosophy that provided his conceptual framework.

This point is exemplified by the way in which Aquinas recast Augustine's argument in terms of God as the first cause and creatures as secondary causes:

> Thus if we look to the world's order as it depends on the first cause, God cannot act against it, because then he would be doing something contrary to his foreknowledge, his will or his goodness. But if we take the order in things as it depends on any of the secondary causes, then God can act apart from it; he is not subject to that order but rather it is subject to him, as issuing from him not out of a necessity of nature, but by decision of his will.
>
> (*Summa Theologiae* 1.105.6)

In two respects Aquinas differed from Augustine – in his refusal to speculate on how miracles came about, and in his insistence that God alone works miracles. It is astonishing only to the ignorant that a magnet attracts iron.

REFORMATION AND COUNTER-REFORMATION APOLOGETICS

In the age of the Reformation two attitudes to miracles stand out – one theological and pastoral, the other apologetic and polemical.

Martin Luther

The theological and pastoral attitude is illustrated by a sermon of Luther (1483–1546) on John 14.10–11: the works of Jesus are 'not only divine works, but they are witnesses of God the Father. Therefore he who sees and hears these sees God the Father in them; and he is not only persuaded that God is in Christ and that Christ is in God; but from them he can also be comforted with the assurance of God's fatherly love and grace towards us.'[8]

John Calvin

Calvin (1509–64) shared the theological and pastoral view of miracles, even seeing them as *sacramental* signs (*Institutes* 4.14.18). The apologetic and polemical use of miracles appears in Calvin's 'Prefatory Address to King Francis', *Institutes* (1536). Catholic opponents had pointed to miracles in the Catholic Church as proof that God had not deserted it. They invited Calvin to show what miracles authenticated his church. Calvin replied that his teaching was attested by the gospel miracles, and counter-attacked by saying that those 'miracles' which our adversaries point to are delusions of Satan, drawing people away from true worship of God (cf. Deut. 13.2–4). From this time onwards, miracles were used increasingly in legitimating belief systems.

RATIONALISM AND THE AGE OF ENLIGHTENMENT

Pyrrhonism

The eighteenth-century Age of Enlightenment marked the culmination of the rise of scepticism, which began in the Renaissance with the discovery of ancient scepticism known as Pyrrhonism.[9] The term derives from the Greek sceptic, Pyrrho of Elis (*c.* 365–275 BCE) whose ideas are known through the writings of Cicero, Diogenes Laertius' *Lives of the Eminent Philosophers* and Sextus Empiricus' *Outlines of Pyrrhonism*. Sextus stressed the importance of careful observation over theory and dogma in medicine. The Pyrrhonists took from him scepticism about uncritical reliance on the senses and the inability of reason to discover ultimate truth. Catholic apologists saw in Pyrrhonism a weapon against Calvinism. Protestant apologists responded that the Catholic Church's claim to be guardian of theological truth rested on the Church's own word.

Baruch (or Benedictus de) Spinoza

The rationalism of René Descartes (1596–1650) was an attempt to defend science from the scepticism of Pyrrhonism.[10] The pantheistic rationalism of Baruch Spinoza (1632–77) demonstrated *Descartes' Principles of Philosophy* (1663) in a geometric manner. It was followed in 1670 by a treatise on politics and religion, *Tractatus Theologico-Politicus*, which among other things pioneered biblical criticism. Spinoza's chief work was his posthumously published *Ethics* (1677). Spinoza was born to Jewish parents, but was ejected from the synagogue on account of his unorthodox views. He saw reality as *deus sive natura* – 'God or Nature', a single entity that was the ground of its own being. Spinoza's *Tractatus* described 'the universal laws of nature [as] decrees of God following from the necessity and perfection of the Divine nature. Hence, any event happening in nature which contravened nature's universal laws would necessarily contravene the Divine decree, nature, and understanding.' Consequently, 'we cannot gain knowledge of the existence and providence of God by means of miracles' (ch. 6). Either an event had a natural explanation, which would mean that it was not a miracle, or it was a pseudo-miracle performed by a false prophet (Deut. 13).

In seventeenth-century Britain two conflicting lines of thought emerged. One was Deism with its dismissal of miracles. The other was early modern science, which found a place for miracles in its world view.

Deism

The word 'deist' appears to have been first used by Calvin's disciple Pierre Viret to describe an unidentified group who professed belief in God, but rejected Jesus. The first major figure in Deism was Lord Herbert of Cherbury (1583–1648), who served as British ambassador to the French court and joined the circle surrounding Descartes. While in Paris Lord Herbert published a Latin treatise *On Truth* (1624, 2nd edn 1645), which was in part a reply to Pyrrhonian scepticism and in part an alternative to Catholic and Protestant orthodoxy, based on innate ideas.

The scepticism of Thomas Hobbes (1588–1679) dates from his exile in France where he encountered Pyrrhonism. Hobbes' *Leviathan* (1651) presented a theory of church and state, which urged liberty of thought in private on such matters as miracles, but in public one must submit to the sovereign as 'God's lieutenant'.

Before examining the Deists' attacks on miracles, we should note Hugo Grotius (1583–1645), the Dutch jurist and statesman. Grotius had been imprisoned for life for his Arminian convictions, but escaped to Paris in 1621. He served as Swedish ambassador in Paris, but was never called to service in Holland. In 1627 he published in Latin *The Truth of the Christian Religion*, a title that echoed Lord Herbert's. It defended Christianity as the true religion, in harmony with God's rationally ordered world, and was written to assist sailors and merchants, when confronted by other religions. Books 5 and 6 defended Christianity against Judaism and Islam. The miracles of Jesus were proved to be Divine, because Jesus taught 'the Worship of one God, the Maker of the World' (5.5). Grotius was perhaps the first modern scholar to entertain the thought that Deuteronomy 13 might be applied to Jesus. However, he promptly dismissed it on the grounds that Jesus taught reverence for the writings of Moses and the prophets.

Charles Blount (1654–93) was a follower of Lord Herbert and Hobbes. In 1680 he published a collection of Hobbes' sayings criticizing religion, and an annotated version of *The Two First Books of Philostratus Concerning the Life of Apollonius Tyanaeus*. It was followed by a tract ascribed to Blount, *Miracles No Violations of the Laws of Nature*, which was a paraphrase of the chapter on miracles in Spinoza's *Tractatus*.

In what follows I shall omit major figures like John Toland (1670–1722) and Matthew Tindal (1655–1733) in order to focus on the deist critique of prophecy and miracles. The assault on prophecy (which was widely held to be a form of miracle) was led by Anthony Collins (1676–1729), a friend and trustee of John Locke. It came in the form of two books, published long after Locke's death – *Discourse on the Grounds and Reasons of the Christian Religion* (1724) and its sequel *The Scheme of Literal Prophecy Consider'd* (1726). Collins argued that prophecies like 'a virgin shall conceive and bear a son' (Isa. 7.14/Matt. 1.23) and 'Out of Egypt have I called my son' (Hos. 11.1/Matt. 2.15) were not supernatural predictions of the birth and childhood of Jesus. Both had fulfilment within the lifetime of the prophets who made them, and therefore they could not be used to legitimate Christian belief. Christian use of such prophecies was based on rabbinic allegorical interpretation. What both Collins and the apologists of his day overlooked was that Matthew's use of Old Testament prophecy was not predictive in the simplistic sense, but typological in the sense of history repeating itself.

Having disposed of predictive prophecy, Collins planned to turn to miracles as the other pillar of apologetics, but was pre-empted by the erratic former Cambridge don and cleric, Thomas Woolston (1670–1731), with his six *Discourses on the Miracles of our Saviour* (1727–9). Each of Woolston's pamphlets was ironically dedicated to a bishop of the Church of England. The miracle stories of the gospels should not be treated as historical events, but as allegories comparable with those detected by Collins in Christian use of prophecy. The star of Bethlehem (Matt. 2.1–12) was a will-o'-the-wisp. Woolston complained that if Apollonius of Tyana had turned water into wine (John 2.1–11), people would have reproached his memory. Woolston's sharpest criticisms were reserved for Jesus' resurrection, which was the most barefaced imposture 'ever put upon the world'. Jesus' disciples had bribed the soldiers guarding the tomb, and had stolen the body.

Woolston was tried for blasphemy, and sentenced to a year's imprisonment and a fine of £100. Because of crowded prison conditions, Woolston was permitted to live in his own home under a form of house arrest. However, he continued to defend his views, and sales of his pamphlets afforded him a living.

Both deists and orthodox divines appealed for clemency. Among the latter was Thomas Sherlock (1678–1761), who emerged as an eighteenth-century C. S. Lewis. Sherlock was successively Bishop of Bangor, Salisbury and London, and the bishop to whom Woolston dedicated his fifth *Discourse.* Sherlock's *The Tryal of the Witnesses* (1729) went through many editions in England and Europe. The book opened with a discussion of Woolston's trial among gentlemen of the Inns of Court, who decided to carry out a mock trial. But this time it was the disciples who were in the dock. It was agreed that the witnesses were sincere, but was their testimony credible? In his summing up the judge turned to Locke's analogy of water freezing (see below). In normal experience the dead do not return to life. But this fact cannot rule out the possibility of what God can do. Logically we are not entitled to say that resurrection is impossible. The jury duly acquitted the disciples.

Early modern science

We now turn to seventeenth-century scientists who wrote in defence of miracles. Among them were members of The Royal Society of London for Improving Natural Knowledge, which received its charter in 1662 from King Charles II. An early member was Joseph Glanvill (1636–80), of Bath Abbey and chaplain to the king. Like other members, Glanvill adopted a moderate empiricist approach, which steered a middle course between the rationalism of Spinoza and the scepticism of Pyrrhonism. He was prepared to recognize realities (including witchcraft) beyond the scope of reason, when he believed that empirical evidence warranted it.

Miracles were distinguished from natural events by transcending 'all the powers of mere nature'. Because some miracle stories were fraudulent, it did not mean that all were. Glanvill emphasized what Robert M. Burns calls 'the principle of context'. It was not merely the wonders of Jesus and his teaching, but their conjunction of other circumstances, including his holy life, that strengthened 'the conclusion, that he could be no other than the Son of God, and Saviour of the world'.[11]

A similar view was advanced by Sir Robert Boyle (1627–91), a founding member of the Royal Society and 'the father of chemistry'. Boyle agreed with Glanvill over witchcraft, and held a similar approach to miracles. If an alleged miracle contradicted reason and religion, Boyle would reject it. 'But if the revelation backed by a miracle proposes nothing that contradicts any of these truths ... [but accords with them] I then think myself obliged to admit both the miracle, and the religion that it attests'.[12] A devout Bible student, Boyle left in his will the sum of £50 a year for the annual 'Boyle Lectures' to refute 'infidels'.

John Locke

The terms empiricist and empiricism have a murky history. Today they are used of philosophy from Locke to Hume, which stressed the importance of sense experience and critical reflection in acquiring knowledge. But neither Locke nor Hume called themselves empiricists.[13] The early history of the term suggested a charlatan or quack, which was how Sextus Empiricus was viewed in some quarters. John Locke (1632–1704) followed in the tradition of Glanvill and Boyle. He studied at Oxford and was an MD, but did not practise medicine. In the last days of the Stuart monarchy he lived in Holland, where he enjoyed the company of Dutch Arminian theologians and scholars, and where he completed *An Essay Concerning Human Understanding* (1690) and various political tracts.

Locke rejected the innate ideas of Descartes and Lord Herbert. Knowledge was founded on experience, observation and the mind's reflections on them. Locke's philosophy combined respect for both science and religion. Whereas reason led to the discovery of truths which the mind deduced from sense experience, faith was assent to propositions, 'based upon the credit of the proposer, as coming from God'. The thought was further developed in the posthumous *Discourse of Miracles* (1706).

Revelation was concerned with truths that were 'above reason', but not 'contrary to reason'. Miracles were contrary to normal experience, but our limited experience could not rule them out. Locke illustrated the point by the story of the Dutch ambassador and the King of Siam. The ambassador told the king that in his country it was possible for an elephant to walk on water. The king replied that he had always believed the ambassador, but now he knew that he was lying. But the ambassador was referring to conditions of which the king had no experience – when ice freezes so hard that it can support the weight of an elephant. Locke's illustration continued to exercise philosophers for years to come. Thomas Sherlock thought that it settled the matter, but Hume insisted that the prince 'reasoned justly'.

Locke made further stipulations. No miracle that detracted from the honour of God or was inconsistent with morality could be regarded as divine. God could not be expected to perform miracles to inform people of things that they could discover for themselves. Genuine miracles were never trivial. What is clear from Locke's discussion is that miracles were important primarily in order to legitimate revelation. In this regard prophecy of future events was a form of miraculous legitimation.

David Hume

Hume (1711–76) is widely regarded as the greatest British philosopher. Shortly before he died of cancer he composed an account of

'My Own Life'. Remarking on the events of 1749, when he returned from a diplomatic mission to Italy, Hume experienced 'mortification' to find 'all England in a ferment' over Conyers Middleton, while his own 'performance was entirely overlooked and neglected'. Middleton's *A Free Enquiry into the Miraculous Powers which are Supposed to have Subsisted in the Christian, from the Earliest Ages through Successive Centuries* (1748) crowned a career in polemics. It provoked a monograph-length letter in reply from John Wesley, who complained that Middleton had 'contrived to overthrow the whole Christian system'. Middleton's subject matter – post-biblical miracle stories in the early church – was different from Hume's. But the style of argumentation was similar. Today the situation is reversed. Middleton's work is read only by professional scholars, while Hume's continues to occupy centre stage.

Hume's 'Of Miracles' appeared as §10 in his *Enquiry Concerning Human Understanding* (1748). He had intended to include it in his *Treatise of Human Nature* (1739), but friends persuaded Hume to delay.[14] Scholars have wondered about the appropriateness of including a discussion of miracles in an *Enquiry Concerning Human Understanding*. But in light of the role played by miracles in seventeenth- and eighteenth-century discussions of truth-claims, Hume's inclusion of the essay – given his convictions – was appropriate.

Hume's argument was about *analogy*, proportioning one's beliefs to the evidence, and judging evidence in light of our understanding of the world. His discussion was in two parts. In the first Hume gave a definition of miracles, which was also a proof of their impossibility. 'A miracle is a violation of the laws of nature; and as a firm and unalterable experience has established these laws, the proof against a miracle, from the very nature of the fact, is as entire as any argument from experience can possibly be imagined.' In a footnote Hume gave a second definition, which – whether he realized it or not – included the kinds of conditions which theists stipulate concerning the possibility of miracles: a miracle was '*a transgression of a law of nature by a particular volition of the Deity, or by the interposition of some invisible agent*'.

In Part II of his discussion, Hume advanced four arguments designed to show that testimony to miracles was never strong enough to outweigh everyday experience. First, witnesses must be 'of such unquestioned good sense, education and learning as to secure us against all delusion in themselves'. The attested facts must be performed 'in such a public manner and in so celebrated a part of the world, as to render detection unavoidable'. Second, Hume drew attention to human fondness of gossip and exaggeration. Third, 'miracles are observed chiefly to abound among ignorant and barbarous nations'. Fourth, Hume argued that miracles of rival religions cancel each other out, and thus cannot be deployed to support truth-claims.

While Hume avoided direct reference to gospel narratives, they were nevertheless the target of his stipulations. So too were his concluding remarks about the veracity of Tacitus' account of miracles associated with Vespasian, reports about recent miracles in Spain and Paris, and the hypothetical return from the dead of Queen Elizabeth I. In words that echoed Hebrews 12.1, Hume concluded, 'And what have we to oppose to such a cloud of witnesses, but the absolute impossibility or miraculous nature of the events, which they relate? And this surely, in the eyes of all reasonable people, will alone be regarded as a sufficient refutation.'

Critics have noted something disingenuous about Hume's appeal to the 'laws of nature', when in his *Treatise of Human Nature* and *Enquiry* he had insisted causal connection is something that 'we *feel* in the mind'. Hume's emphasis on miracles as *violations* overlooks the possibility of divine immanent activity in the ordering of events. Was Hume's argument an exercise in applying Bayes' probability theory?[15] Hume's stipulations about testimony seem framed to preclude the gospel narratives. The claim that miracles of rival religions cancel each other out is flawed on two counts. First, religions generally do not appeal to miracles to establish their truth. Second, one would have to find *similar* miracles in different religions to make the comparison effective. What Hume had done was not to demonstrate the impossibility of miracles, but to raise questions about appealing to miracles in order to establish the veracity of a particular religion.

NINETEENTH-CENTURY INTERPRETATIONS

H. E. G. Paulus

H. E. G. Paulus (1761–1851), the German editor of Spinoza's *Works* and author of *The Life of Jesus as the Basis for a Purely Historical Account of Early Christianity* (2 vols., 1828), proposed natural explanations. Jesus' healings resulted either from spiritual power or from skilful use of medications. Jesus did not walk on the water, but was standing on the shore, his features and location obscured by mist. The feeding stories involved people sharing their food. Jesus did not die on the cross, and was revived by the cool atmosphere of the tomb.

David Friedrich Strauss

The second way of treating miracles was the mythical interpretation of Strauss (1808–74). Strauss sneered at the 'vulgar rationalism' of Paulus, and was disillusioned by reading Schleiermacher's lectures on the life of Jesus. Strauss' *The Life of Jesus Critically Examined* (2 vols., 1835–6) deprived Strauss of an academic career and secured his place in the history of scholarship.

Strauss' approach had two aspects. Negatively it rejected both the supernaturalism of the gospels and the explanations of the rationalists. Positively it embraced a thoroughgoing mythological reading of the texts. His use of analogy was twofold. On the one hand, to qualify as historical, reported events of the past should bear analogy to events in contemporary experience. On the other hand, biblical narratives were judged to bear analogy to myths of antiquity.

The miracle stories of the gospels were shaped by popular messianic expectation – not only that the Messiah should perform miracles (John 7.31), but also the *kinds* of miracles that the Messiah should perform. The latter included supernatural dispensation of food (Exod. 16), opening the eyes of the blind (2 Kgs. 6) and raising the dead (1 Kgs. 17; 2 Kgs. 4). Jesus was made to fulfil the prophecy of Isaiah 35.5–6. Strauss observed: 'it is always incomparably more probable that histories of cures of the lame and the paralytics in accordance with messianic expectation, should be formed by legend, than that they really should have happened'.[16] In attacking miracles, Hume sought to undermine the Christian belief-system; Strauss sought to undermine supernatural Christology. Strauss invoked a Hegelian Christology which celebrated not the union of God with a particular individual, but the outworking of the cosmic spirit through humanity in history.

Friedrich Schleiermacher and Ernest Renan

The third approach, exemplified by F. D. E. Schleiermacher's *The Christian Faith* (1821; 2nd edn 1830–1) and *Life of Jesus* (1864), and J. E. Renan's *Life of Jesus* (1863), focused on the spiritual achievements of Jesus. The physical marvel was superseded by the spiritual miracle.[17] When Schleiermacher's lectures on *The Life of Jesus* were published a generation after his death, Strauss commented, 'Schleiermacher, we can say, is a supernaturalist in Christology but in criticism and exegesis a rationalist. His Christ, however many of the miraculous attributes of the old confession may have been removed, still remains essentially a superhuman, supernatural being.'[18]

The History of Religions School

The fourth way of treating miracles was that of the History of Religions School of the late nineteenth and early twentieth centuries. The School sought to situate the history and literature of Judaism and early Christianity in the context of ancient religion and culture, and to identify what was of enduring value. Richard Reitzenstein examined Hellenistic miracle stories. Otto Weinreich explored Graeco-Roman stories of miraculous healing. Paul Fiebig edited a collection of miracle texts and an anthology of rabbinic miracles.

The stories were factored into the work of Wilhelm Bousset (1865–1920) and Rudolf Bultmann (1884–1976) who represented the continuation of the History of Religions approach in the twentieth century. It found expression in Bultmann's programme of demythologization, which held that the entire thought-world of the New Testament was the mythical product of Jewish apocalyptic and Gnostic myth. The Christian message must be demythologized and presented in existential terms in order to speak to the modern world.

TWENTIETH-CENTURY ISSUES

B. B. Warfield

The work of B. B. Warfield (1851–1921) of Princeton Theological Seminary (long a bastion of Calvinistic orthodoxy) was in a class of its own. *Counterfeit Miracles* (1918), later titled *Miracles: Yesterday and Today, True and False* (1954), leaned heavily on Conyers Middleton's rejection of post-apostolic miracles. It was an incomparable inventory of objections to the miraculous – apart from biblical miracles. Miracles played a necessary part in the founding of the church. Thereafter, reports of miracles were inadequately grounded, or the kind of miracles attested in Deuteronomy 13.1–5, which led people astray.

C. S. Lewis

Lewis' bestselling *Miracles: A Preliminary Study* (1947) was a study in popular apologetics. Lewis (1893–1963) spent much of his career at Magdalen College, Oxford, teaching English. He saw two basic ways of looking at the world – naturalism and supernaturalism. Lewis equated naturalism with determinism – all effects are determined by antecedent physical causes. If so, we have no control over our thinking, and there can be no question of miracles. In a manner reminiscent of the Idealism taught at Oxford around World War I, Lewis argued that the human mind and moral values were 'supernatural', insofar as they transcended the physical. Once we acknowledge the transcendent God of Christian faith, we must acknowledge that such a God may perform miracles. In saying this, Lewis had inverted the traditional apologetic argument that miracles legitimated the Christian belief system. With Lewis the belief system legitimated the possibility of miracles.

Lewis distinguished between 'Miracles of the Old Creation' (the multiplication of loaves and fishes) and 'Miracles of the New Creation' (the Resurrection). In the former, the processes of nature were accelerated. In the latter, the New Creation had broken into the world of nature, giving us a glimpse of the world to come. Two observations may be made. It is one thing for corn to be multiplied in the field and fish in the sea, but it is something else for corn to be harvested and baked, and fish to be caught and cooked. The second observation is that Lewis took the gospel miracle stories at face value. Admittedly, his book was intended to be *A Preliminary Study*. As such, it relieved Lewis from paying attention to the literary form and function of the gospel miracle stories, and from studying their religious and social setting in Second Temple Judaism and the Graeco-Roman world.

Richard Swinburne

A more sophisticated approach was Swinburne's *The Concept of Miracle* (1970), which addressed head-on 'the Humean tradition'. Swinburne saw miracles in terms of non-repeatable counter-instances of laws based on statistical evidence. He conceded Hume's point that we should accept the historical evidence – apparent memory and the testimony of others – only if the falsity of the latter would be 'more miraculous', that is more improbable than the related events.[19] On the other hand, in weighing evidence 'we would need only slender historical evidence of certain miracles to have reasonable grounds to believe in their occurrence, just as we need only slender historical evidence to have reasonable grounds for belief in the occurrence of events whose occurrence is rendered probable by natural laws'. If, on other grounds, we had evidence of a God of such a character as to be able to intervene in the natural order, a higher probability should be given to the evidence.[20]

Magic

Swinburne's work was a philosophical answer to Hume, but it did not address biblical interpretation, or the question of magic, which was made acute by the publication by Karl Preisendanz of the Greek

Magical Papryri.[21] The papyri raise the question of the relationship of miracles to magic. Morton Smith used the papyri to revive the ancient charges that Jesus was in fact a magician.[22]

In *The Historical Jesus: The Life of a Mediterranean Peasant* (1991), John Dominic Crossan depicted Jesus as a Jewish Cynic who sought to undermine the authority of Rome and its Jewish clients by 'magic and meal'. Although he used the term 'magic', Crossan distanced himself from Morton Smith. He used the word partly to shock readers, and partly to set Jesus in the tradition of Elijah and Elisha who healed outside the official priestly system. Crossan's work was not unproblematic. There were no known Jewish Cynics in Galilee in the time of Jesus. Cynics were not magicians, and magicians were not Cynics. Despite his elaborate methodology, Crossan paid scant attention to Jewish sources and the Jewishness of Jesus. His subsequent work calls in question whether Jesus healed people physically, as distinct from pronouncing them whole.[23]

Further developments

My own study of the history of the debates and of the miracle stories of the gospels has forced the conclusion that we need greater integration of disciplines, and a new strategy for reading the gospels. We need to read them critically, but also with what Paul Riceoeur called *a second naivety* – reading them on their own terms, each one separately, in order to discover what each evangelist is saying. We need also to read them as *ancient biography*,[24] which in the case of religious biography served the function of defending its subject from misplaced zeal on the part of followers and misplaced criticism on the part of enemies.

We need to read the gospels 'with the grain' and 'against the grain'. By 'with the grain' I mean reading the gospels with a view to discerning what their authors want us to see (Thesis A). By 'against the grain' I mean trying to see how the opponents of Jesus viewed him (Thesis B). In fact, we can only properly understand Thesis A, if we also understand Thesis B. I have attempted to do this in a preliminary way.[25] But fuller working out of this project is a work in progress.

Notes

1 Matt. 12.22–37; Mark 3.20–30; Luke 11.14–23; 12.10; cf. John 7.12; 8.48; 11.47–8.
2 Athanasius, *On the Incarnation* 45–50; Ramsay MacMullen, *Christianizing the Roman Empire (A.D. 100–400)* (New Haven and London: Yale University Press, 1984).

3   In his account of Nero's horrendous treatment of Christians, whom
    Nero blamed for the fire of Rome, Tacitus traced the origin of the
    'pernicious superstition [*exitiabilis superstitio*]' to 'Christus' who
    had undergone the death penalty under Pontius Pilate (*Annals*
    15.44). The terminology suggests magic for which the penalty
    was death. See Ramsay MacMullen, *Enemies of the Roman Order*
    (Cambridge, MA: Harvard University Press, 1966), 125. On Jewish
    views of Jesus, see Justin, *Dialogue* 69, 102, 106–7; *First Apology* 30;
    Origen, *Against Celsus* 1.38, 68; *b. Sanhedrin* 43a. On Jewish atti-
    tudes to magic, see Philo, *Special Laws* 1.65, 315–17; 11Q19 54; Cairo
    Genizah copy of the *Damascus Document* 12 12.2–3; *m. Sanhedrin*
    7.4, 10.
4   Harold W. Attridge and Gōhei Hata, eds., *Eusebius, Christianity, and
    Judaism* (Detroit: Wayne State University Press, 1992), 510–22;
    Graham N. Stanton, 'Jesus of Nazareth: A Magician and a Prophet
    Who Deceived God's People?', in *Jesus of Nazareth: Lord and Christ*,
    ed. Joel B. Green and Max Turner (Grand Rapids: Eerdmans, and
    Carlisle: Paternoster, 1994), 164–80.
5   Philostratus, *Life of Apollonius* 1.3; Attridge and Hata, eds., *Eusebius,
    Christianity, and Judaism*, 510–22.
6   Apollonius figured in the writings of Charles Blount, Thomas Wool-
    ston, F. C. Baur, John Henry Newman and, in modern times, G. Petzke.
    The leading advocate of the 'divine man' theory was Ludwig Bieler.
    See the discussion by Barry L. Blackburn, *Theios Anēr and the Markan
    Miracle Stories*, Wissenschaftliche Untersuchungen zum Neuen
    Testament 2.40 (Tübingen: J. C. B. Mohr [P. Siebeck], 1991).
7   Benedicta Ward, *Miracles and the Medieval Mind*, rev. edn
    (Philadelphia: University of Philadelphia Press, 1987).
8   Martin Luther, *Luther's Works*, 55 vols., ed. Jaroslav Pelikan and Hel-
    mut T. Lehman (St Louis: Concordia, 1955), vol. xxiv, 73.
9   Richard Henry Popkin, *The History of Scepticism: From Savonarola to
    Bayle* (Oxford: Oxford University Press, 2003).
10 Descartes received his education at the Jesuit seminary at La Flèche,
    where some of his teachers had embraced Pyrrhonism. His famous
    cogito ergo sum ('I am thinking therefore I am'), which was first used
    by Augustine against the sceptics of his day, was an attempt to play the
    Pyrrhonists at their own game of systematic doubt. There is at least
    one thing that the doubter cannot doubt – the fact that he is doubting
    and thus that he exists as a thinking being.
11 Robert M. Burns, *The Great Debate on Miracles: From Joseph Glan-
    ville to David Hume* (Lewisburg: Bucknell University Press, 1981), 50.
12 *Ibid.*, 55.
13 David Hume, 'Of the Academical or Sceptical Philosophy', in *Enquiries
    Concerning Human Understanding*, 3rd edn, ed. L. A. Selby-Bigge, rev.
    and notes P. H. Nidditch (Oxford: Oxford University Press, 1975), 149–
    65, rejected the '*excessive* scepticism' of Pyrrhonism as self-defeating,
    but concluded that 'a more *mitigated* scepticism' 'may be both durable
    and useful' (161, Hume's emphasis).

14 Hume's correspondence indicates that he conceived the argument while at La Flèche, where a learned Jesuit told him of a miracle that had occurred there. On hearing Hume's objections the Jesuit replied that they would equally undermine the Gospel miracles. Hume agreed.

15 Richard Swinburne, ed., *Miracles* (New York: Macmillan, and London: Collier Macmillan, 1989).

16 David Friedrich Strauss, *The Life of Jesus Critically Examined*, trans. George Eliot 1846, new edn, ed. Peter C. Hodgson (London: SCM, 1973), 457.

17 Friedrich Schleiermacher, *The Christian Faith*, ed. H. R. Mackintosh and James Stuart Stewart (Edinburgh: T&T Clark, 1999), §103.

18 David Friedrich Strauss, *The Christ of Faith and the Jesus of History: A Critique of Schleiermacher's Life of Jesus*, trans. Leander E. Keck (Philadelphia: Fortress, 1977), 160.

19 Richard Swinburne, *The Concept of Miracle* (London: Macmillan, 1970), 51.

20 *Ibid.*, 68–9.

21 Karl Preisendanz and Albert Henrichs, eds., *Papyri Graecae Magicae: Die griechischen Zauberpapyri*, 2 vols. (1928), 2nd edn (Stuttgart: Teubner, 1973 and 1974); Hans Dieter Betz, *The Greek Magical Papyri in Translation Including the Demotic Spells*, vol. 1: *Texts*, 2nd edn (Chicago and London: University of Chicago Press, 1992).

22 Morton Smith, *Jesus the Magician* (San Francisco: Harper and Row, 1978). For a more balanced assessment, see David E. Aune, 'Magic in Early Christianity', *Aufstieg und Niedergang der römischen Welt* II.23.2 (1980), 1507–57.

23 John Dominic Crossan, *Jesus: A Revolutionary Biography* (San Francisco: HarperSanfrancisco, 1994).

24 Richard A. Burridge, *What Are the Gospels? A Comparison with Graeco-Roman Biography*, 2nd edn (Grand Rapids: Eerdmans, 2004).

25 Colin Brown, 'Synoptic Miracle Stories: A Jewish Religious and Social Setting', *Foundations and Facets Forum* 2.4 (1986), 55–76; Colin Brown, 'The Jesus of Mark's Gospel', in *Jesus Then & Now: Images of Jesus in History and Theology*, ed. Marvin Meyer and Charles Hughes (Harrisburg: Trinity Press International, 2001), 26–53.

Further reading

Aune, David E., 'Magic in Early Christianity', *Aufstieg und Niedergang der römischen Welt* ii.23.2 (1980), 1507–57

Blackburn, Barry L., *Theios Anēr and the Markan Miracle Traditions*, Wissenschaftliche Untersuchungen zum Neuen Testament 2.40 (Tübingen: Mohr-Siebeck, 1991)

*Brown, Colin, *Miracles and the Critical Mind* (Grand Rapids: Eerdmans, 1984; repr. Pasadena: Fuller Seminary Press, 2006)

Jesus in European Protestant Thought 1778–1860, Studies in Historical Theology 1 (Durham: Labyrinth, 1985; repr. Pasadena: Fuller Seminary Press, 2008)

'The Jesus of Mark's Gospel', in *Jesus Then & Now: Images of Jesus in History and Theology*, ed. Marvin Meyer and Charles Hughes (Harrisburg: Trinity Press International, 2001), 26–53

Burns, Robert M., *The Great Debate on Miracles: From Joseph Glanville to David Hume* (Lewisburg: Bucknell University Press, 1981)

Burridge, Richard A., *What Are the Gospels? A Comparison with Graeco-Roman Biography*, 2nd edn (Grand Rapids: Eerdmans, 2004)

Collins, Derek, *Magic in the Ancient Greek World*, Blackwell Ancient Religions (Malden, MA: Blackwell Publishing, 2008)

Crossan, John Dominic, *The Historical Jesus: The Life of a Mediterranean Peasant* (San Francisco: HarperSanfrancisco, 1991)

du Toit, David S., *Theios Anthropos*, Wissenschaftliche Untersuchungen zum Neuen Testament 2.91 (Tübingen: Mohr-Siebeck, 1997)

Israel, Jonathan I., *Radical Enlightenment: Philosophy and the Making of Modernity 1650–1750* (Oxford: Oxford University Press, 2001)

Kee, Howard C., *Miracle in the Early Christian World: A Study in Sociohistorical Method* (New Haven and London: Yale University Press, 1983)

MacMullen, Ramsay, *Enemies of the Roman Order: Treason, Unrest, and Alienation in the Empire* (Cambridge, MA: Harvard University Press, 1966)

Meier, John P., *A Marginal Jew: Rethinking the Historical Jesus*, 2: *Mentor, Message, and Miracles*, Anchor Bible Reference Library (New York: Doubleday, 1994)

Philostratus, *The Life of Apollonius of Tyana*, 2 vols., Loeb Classical Library, ed. and trans. Christopher P. Jones (Cambridge, MA: Harvard University Press, 1912)

Popkin, Richard H., *The History of Scepticism: From Savonarola to Bayle* (Oxford: Oxford University Press, 2003)

Reventlow, Henning Graf, *The Authority of the Bible and the Rise of the Modern World* (Philadelphia: Fortress, 1985)

Stanton, Graham N., 'Jesus of Nazareth: A Magician and a Prophet Who Deceived God's People?', in *Jesus of Nazareth: Lord and Christ*, ed. Joel B. Green and Max Turner (Grand Rapids: Eerdmans, and Carlisle: Paternoster, 1994), 164–80

Swinburne, Richard, *The Concept of Miracle* (London: Macmillan, 1970)

ed., *Miracles* (New York: Macmillan, and London: Collier Macmillan, 1989)

Welch, John W., 'Miracles, *Maleficium*, and *Majestas* in the Trial of Jesus', in *Jesus and Archaeology*, ed. James H. Charlesworth (Grand Rapids: Eerdmans, 2006), 349–83

16 Philosophers on miracles

MICHAEL P. LEVINE

THREE QUESTIONS

Philosophers have long been interested in miracles, but should they be? In what follows I argue that the question of miracles is philosophically uninteresting, and that recent work by philosophers on miracles often illustrates this. What is more, the central question of whether anyone is in fact justified in believing in miracles is often obfuscated or begged. Of course to say that miracles are largely philosophically uninteresting does not mean that they are uninteresting per se. I conclude with a brief account of the religious significance of alleged miracles.

Aquinas says 'those things are properly called miracles which are done by divine agency beyond the order commonly observed in nature [*praeter ordinem communiter observatum in rebus*]'.[1] This is the account or definition of miracles I shall adopt. There are basically three philosophical questions of interest about miracles. The first is whether miracles are possible.[2] The second is whether anyone can ever be justified, epistemologically speaking, in believing that a miracle has occurred. With regard to this question it is important to note that the fact one can imagine conditions in which belief in a miracle would be justified does absolutely nothing to show that anyone has been or now is so justified. The third question is whether anyone is or ever has been so justified.[3] These questions can be answered in short order. The first two questions have sheltered philosophers from dealing with the only philosophically significant question about miracles per se – the third question.

The first two questions lead to various questions concerning the nature of laws of nature, and naturalism versus supernaturalism. These issues may be worth pursuing in their own right, but they are of little consequence when it comes to the important third question about miracles. Is anyone epistemologically justified in believing in a miracle – for example, on the basis of Scripture and historical evidence?

The question is not the modal one of whether one *could be* justified, but of whether anyone is (or has been) so justified. It is this third question that Hume addresses in Part II of his essay, and it is this question that was of primary concern to him.

Hume's principal argument against the possibility of justified belief in miracles (Part I in 'Of Miracles') is the starting point for much subsequent philosophical discussion on miracles. Although the argument in Part I is unsuccessful, there has been no advance on his arguments in Part II. Instead, there has been backsliding and confusion by those who champion miracles. In Part II he argues straightforwardly and on the basis of ordinary everyday reasons – the kind used all of the time to dismiss such reports – that no one is justified in believing in miracles. On this view, Part I of Hume's essay is simply a misadventure.

In answer to the first question: if it is possible that God exists and that there is divine agency (not all theistic notions of deity imply divine agency), and if laws of nature (or the natural order of things) can be interfered with or overridden by divine agency – if laws of nature need not describe or account for everything that happens in the material world; that is, *if naturalism is possibly false* – then miracles are possible. This is an uninteresting tautology. Arguments against the possibility of miracles invariably focus on the plausibility of naturalism; on modal and metaphysical views about laws of nature, and sometimes about the nature of divine agency. Few philosophers argue that miracles are impossible, and those who do are in effect presupposing or else arguing for a thoroughgoing naturalism. Hence, Hume's empiricism commits him to naturalism, and if that goes unrecognized, his a priori argument in Part I of his essay against the possibility of justified belief in miracles is impossible to follow.

In answer to the second question: arguments to the effect that, contrary to Hume's view, one can conceivably be epistemologically justified in believing a miracle occurred generally do one of two things. Either they state the obvious in claiming that one can imagine conditions in which belief in a miracle would be justified. Or else they make Sunday school assumptions about the evidence for miracles, claiming for instance that Scripture provides such evidence in the form of his torically sound reasons for believing. These latter assumptions conflict with Hume's views in Part II of his essay.

Whether or not miracles are possible or even whether or not they occurred, and assuming we do not know whether or not they are possible, then it is clear – as illustrated below – that one can, in easily imaginable circumstances, be justified in believing that a miracle has occurred. Even if this comes as a surprise, this too is uninteresting given that no such circumstances can reasonably be shown to have occurred. The fact that one *could be* epistemologically justified in believing that a miracle has occurred does nothing to suggest that anyone is now or ever has been so justified on the basis of sound evidence rather than as a result of other unjustified or false beliefs they may have.

In answer to the third question: as Hume would have it, *even if miracles have occurred*, the wise theologian and believer realizes and accepts that no one is, or so far as we know, ever has been, justified on epistemological grounds, on sound evidential grounds, in believing that a miracle has occurred. The alleged historical evidence, including biblical and other so-called eyewitness accounts, does not justify such belief – not even if the alleged miracles occurred. Furthermore, no other kind of evidence justifies such belief in a miracle in any objective epistemic sense. The fact that a person might be subjectively justified in believing in a miracle given their other beliefs is inconsequential. Given certain mistaken background beliefs and lack of knowledge, people may justifiably believe (in a subjective sense) all sorts of things that are not the case and that are unwarranted given correct background knowledge and beliefs. I described this third question as the only one that is of philosophical interest, but this may be an overstatement. Once the issues are properly sorted, it is a question that appears to require historical expertise and judgment rather than philosophical analysis.

The question about miracles Hume addresses in Part II of his essay – and one that is arguably not particularly philosophical – is why so many people believe such things on the basis of such poor evidence. Here one can quibble about a few of the reasons he gives, like whether testimony to the miraculous (whether true or false) from different religions, mutually undermine the truth-claims of one another. However, the principal reasons he cites for people believing miracle stories cannot be beaten – though they can be added to (for example, narcissism and the need to feel special). Prominent among these are wishful thinking, gullibility, authority, superstition, and love of fantasy and notoriety. He cites just about all of the principal reasons, and of course these reasons for believing require further explanation.

John Haldane, Richard Swinburne, Nicholas Wolterstorff, and others have argued – contrary to Hume – that circumstances warranting justified belief in miracles not only have occurred, but that we can now justifiably, on objectively sound epistemic grounds – namely, the historical record – believe miracles have occurred.[4] The question then becomes whether the historical record supports such claims. Philosophical discussion about miracles frequently ignores the question (Hume's central concern) of whether there exists historical evidence, testimony – including testimony in the form of Scripture – or first-hand experience, that justifies belief in the miraculous. Those who wish to champion miracles either argue that such evidence exists or else they merely assume it. But the question of whether such evidence does exist, by itself, is the crucial question about justified belief in miracles.[5]

Is there a sound historical basis for supposing miracles did occur? No doubt one can find some historians (not many) who agree that miracles can be justifiably believed in on the basis of the evidence. But of course some historians deny the holocaust, or that anyone ever landed on the moon – much as some scientists reject evolution in favour of creation 'science'. The question that naturally arises is whether the belief that miracles can be and *have been* historically validated, much like the rejection of evolutionary theory in favour of creationism, is not the result of wish-fulfilment rejecting objective (in this case 'historical') scholarship. Claims that miracles can be historically validated or are historically probable, in accordance with contemporary canons of historical judgment, are false. Nor were they credible when Hume wrote 'Of Miracles'. The thesis of Part II of his essay is that historical enquiry does not support the case for miracles. Hume knew all about wish-fulfilment and the propensity to believe what we would like to, or need to, believe.

The question of the legitimacy of the historical claims is not merely academic but has implications for the principle of separation of church and state. If there is sound historical evidence for the literal truth of claims that miracles occurred, then not only should such truths be taught and accepted, but it would be no violation of the principle of separation to teach them as history. How could it be if it is what history confirms? It is a convenient route around the principle of separation of church and state. Elsewhere, Wolterstorff defends restrictive legislation based on religious belief.[6] There is something at stake and something to fear from such arguments, just as there is for accepting creation science as 'science'.

In stressing the historical case for miracles they also overlook what may be religiously important about miracle stories according to the academic study of religion. Ever since the nineteenth century, when modern biblical scholarship began, it is primarily theologians and biblical scholars rather than philosophers that have queried the significance of miracles to religion and faith. Like creation science which purports to advance the claims of religion and science while undermining both, those who claim that the Bible and other testimony provides us with sound historical evidence for believing miracles occurred, may undermine the character and significance of the claims. Arguments against justified belief in miracles are seen, perhaps rightly, as an attack on religious beliefs. However, at least since Darwin and nineteenth-century biblical scholarship, some have endeavoured to refashion their religious beliefs in view of their assumption that any epistemologically sound and reasonable faith must be consistent with science and consonant with historical evidence – not merely *claimed to be*. The enormous challenge to theology since Darwin, one bolstered by contemporary biblical scholarship and redactive criticism, has been to refashion an understanding of religious claims and the nature of faith, and even religion itself, to fit these facts. It is a very specific challenge and it is one that the parochialism of contemporary philosophy of religion generally forces it to shy away from in favour of literalism and that old-time religion.

Is there sound historical evidence to support the claim that miracles occurred? Perhaps it is worth looking at the issue more closely – just as it was once necessary, though now merely tiresome, to defend evolution against the claims of creation 'science'. I am, however, going to leave this question to one side. For one thing, it is less a philosophical question than an historical one.[7]

THREE-CARD MONTY; THE SHELL GAME; PHILOSOPHERS ON MIRACLES

Contemporary analytical philosophical literature on miracles, especially from the dominant Christian strain, spends an inordinate amount of time showing either that miracles are possible and/or that one could conceivably be justified in believing a miracle occurred. Barring conclusive arguments for naturalism, or against the existence of God, neither of these theses is particularly controversial. Arguments for the first in particular (that miracles are possible) invariably depend on higher-order theses like the view that 'violations' or exceptions to ordinary laws of nature are possible and that God exists (or could exist). They are problems in metaphysics or the philosophy of science, or *other* distinct problems in philosophy of religion.

The significant philosophical question about miracles is, however, as Hume recognized, epistemological. *Is anyone justified in believing in miracles – for example, on the basis of Scripture?* (Hume's argument in 'Of Miracles', Part I, that no one could be so justified, fails. However, his arguments in Part II, that no one is justified in believing that a miracle occurred, at least not on the basis of testimony, succeed.[8]) This is the question that many philosophers on miracles either (1) ignore or postpone[9] – while addressing questions about the laws of nature instead; (2) affirm[10] – despite what historical scholarship and sophisticated biblical (textual) criticism tells us; or (3) casually presuppose to be answered affirmatively.[11]

A close look at Beckwith's arguments will illustrate my contentions thus far. Beckwith attempts to refute two different kinds of argument against justified belief in miracles.[12] The two kinds are:

(a)   The argument from the impossibility of eliminating naturalism
(b)   The argument from a miracle's improbability

This approach, along with Beckwith's attempted refutations, highlights the strategies philosophers have adopted in either defending or refuting justified belief in miracles. They also further the claim that the so-called problem of miracles is not, by and large, a philosophical problem. Additionally, Beckwith's refutation of both these sorts of argument illustrates a distortion of the problem of miracles as Hume understood it.

Beckwith says, 'No particular theory, discovery, invention, etc., developed over the past 200 years casts doubt upon, or calls into question, the miraculous nature of any of the primary miracle-claims of the Christian tradition *if the accounts of them are accepted as historically accurate* [my emphasis]'.[13] Beckwith is here arguing against 'the argument [against justified belief in miracles] from the impossibility of eliminating naturalism'.[14] The assertion may be true, but it is beside the point. After all, even if one readily agrees, as we should, that there *could be* (easily) imaginable exceptions to Hume's contention that no reports of the miraculous should be accepted as historically accurate, the fact is that no such reports of miraculous events *should be* accepted as accurate. They should not be accepted for the reasons Hume gives in Part II of his essay; and (closely related) they should not be accepted on historical (or historiographical) grounds, including those ingredient in contemporary biblical scholarship and redaction criticism. Beckwith's inclusion of the condition '*if the accounts of them are accepted as historically accurate*' is meant to suggest, or may suggest, that they could or should be so accepted – that is, that there is no problem in doing so.[15] If so, it begs the only real question of philosophical interest with regard to justified belief in miracles.

Assuming one does not regard miracles as impossible, no argument is needed to reject the claim that a naturalistic explanation will always, necessarily, be the most plausible. One can make up a million cases in which it would be more plausible to accept an event as being a miracle. Some cases can of course plausibly be likened to Hume's case of the Indian where naturalistic explanations are more plausible. Hume relates the case of the Indian who refused to believe that water turned to ice.[16] According to Hume, the Indian 'reasoned justly' on the basis of his past experience. He refused, at first, to believe that water turned to ice, despite the fact that it was well attested to, because the event not only had the Indian's constant and uniform experience to count against it, but also because the event 'bore so little analogy' to that experience. The Indian 'reasoned justly' but he extended his judgments about the properties of water to cases where all the circumstances were not the same (i.e. the relevant circumstance here being temperature). In certain situations in which we hear testimony to extraordinary events we may be in a situation similar to that of the Indian, unaware of some relevant natural circumstance, and so suppose there is a naturalistic explanation for some extraordinary event.

It is *on the basis of experience* that when we are justified in believing in an extraordinary event we should liken ourselves to the Indian. That is why, in a case like the eight days of darkness, 'we ought to search for the [*natural*] causes whence it might be derived'. Experience demands it. When an extraordinary event is extraordinarily well attested to we have two options according to Hume. One is to accept the testimony and look for the event's natural causes. The other is to reject the testimony on the grounds that the event testified to bears no *significant* analogy to events as experienced. Hume thinks that testimony, no matter how reliable, *can never* establish the occurrence of a miraculous event, in accordance with the principles of a posteriori reasoning.[17]

That a miraculous occurrence could never be judged relevantly similar to anything in experience (i.e. that there must be 'a firm and unalterable experience' counting against belief in it) is something that on Hume's account we know, since we know that we cannot have an 'impression' of a supernatural cause. Impressions (sensations or their copies in ideas) are by their very nature empirical, and there is no ground for supposing them supernatural. The supernatural exceeds the limits of our experience.

Hume is thus constrained by his empiricism in such a way that had he been on the shore of the Red Sea with Moses, and had the Red Sea crashed to a close the moment the last Israelite was safe, Hume would still be constrained by his principles to deny that what he was witnessing was a miracle. If so, his argument against justified belief in miracles can be used as a *reductio ad absurdum*.

Apart from a commitment to Humean empiricism, the Indian-like cases leave untouched the question of whether there have ever been, or could be, cases that should not be likened to that of the Indian. If, for example, the Red Sea did part (as in the movie) that would be such a case – at least for those present.

Beckwith, however, implies that reports of such an occurrence not merely *could be*, but in fact *can be* justifiably accepted 'as historically accurate'. And this is false. The fact that it is possible that such a miracle occurred, and that it is also possible that there could be sound historical evidence for accepting the event as miraculous, does not support the view that such a thing has ever happened or that anyone is now justified, in the relevant epistemic sense, on the basis of historical evidence, for believing a miracle has occurred. In rejecting Michael Martin's bad argument[18] – bad because we can easily imagine cases in which one would be justified in believing a miracle occurred – Beckwith is suggesting that he has defeated an argument against accepting reports of the miraculous. But he has not. It is always possible to hold out for a naturalistic explanation, and, as we saw, Hume is compelled to do so. This does not mean that we cannot imagine far-fetched cases in which one would not – barring prior beliefs and assumptions such as the non-existence of God – be justified in doing so. I have given the example of standing at the shore of the Red Sea with Moses. Beckwith gives a different (and offensive) case illustrating the same point:

> Imagine if on the evening of September 11, 2001 – only hours after Muslim terrorists had crashed hijacked American airliners into the World Trade Centre buildings and the Pentagon – the stars were arrayed in such a way that there appeared to everyone who looked up in the night sky the following unmistakable sentence: 'Allah does not approve. All the hijackers are now burning in hell. Osama Bin Laden will be joining them soon enough.' It seems clear to me that a believer in miracles would be within her epistemic rights in maintaining that such an event was indeed miraculous.[19]

This constitutes an objection to Martin's argument, but it also shows the argument to be largely irrelevant.

The crucial question is not, and never has been, whether one could (assuming one knew miracles were possible) be justified in believing a miracle occurred, but whether one is. By highlighting the possibility of justifiably accepting a reported (or first-hand) experience of a miracle as *historically accurate,* that is, by correctly claiming one can *possibly* do so, Beckwith is intimating that Martin's argument can be defeated not merely in principle, by imagining some case as above, but also on historical grounds. If miracles are possible and we can know them to be possible (a big ask), then so too is it possible that we can justifiably believe that a miracle occurred and that the evidence can support such a belief. This is not an important philosophical finding. It is common sense.

Echoing Swinburne, Beckwith says that, 'I do not see why the believer is not within her epistemic rights in believing that a miracle has occurred (based on a convergence of independent probabilities)'.[20] But he deftly leaves the real issue untouched: whether anyone is or has ever has been, in the relevant epistemic sense, justified in believing in a miracle. Despite Beckwith's passing assumption that one can be – or that we are so justified, the answer is 'no'. No doubt, one can find biblical scholars and historians by the droves who claim the Bible to be historically accurate. Just seek out fundamentalist historians. This does not undermine the assertion that biblical scholarship and *acceptable* standards of historical evidence deny it. Arguing against the standards and against the views of such criticism is one thing, but what those views are is a matter of record. The idea that the Bible provides historically acceptable grounds for believing in miracles reflects a wish-fulfilling rendering of what constitutes evidence. For some, it also shows deep religious misunderstanding; failing to see for example how Scripture can be religiously authoritative or meaningful without being interpreted literally at every level.[21]

Søren Kierkegaard (1813–55) and Paul Tillich (1886–1965), for example, both regarded questions concerning the historicity of the Resurrection as impossible to prove and relatively inconsequential. On Kierkegaard's account, the Resurrection embodied a paradox (God becoming man or the infinite becoming finite) that was impossible to prove either speculatively (Hegel) or historically (the church). The 'truth' of Christianity is to be apprehended or 'appropriated' subjectively, by dwelling on the paradox, and in terms of the relationship between a person and their own thoughts.[22]

Nothing in this critique of Hume's argument suggests that miracles have ever occurred, or that we are justified in believing they have. But it would be surprising if some people at some time and in certain circumstances have not been, and will not again be, justified in believing in the occurrence of a miracle given other false beliefs (some objectively justifiable and some not) they have, along with what was or currently is commonly accepted and believed at the time. (This is to say nothing more than that it was at one time perfectly justifiable to believe, for example, in witches or that the sun revolved around the earth.) This does not mean that the evidence available for the occurrence of any alleged miracle warrants justified belief in miracles for most people now – including those who really do believe in them.

Haldane, for example, mistakenly believes that the Bible is generally an accurate source of information about the alleged events as they actually happened, and Wolterstorff's claims concerning Scripture and divine discourse are even more excessive. But their beliefs are not justified in any interesting or epistemologically robust sense. They are justified, if at all, only via other unjustified and some demonstrably false beliefs they hold. Objectively available evidence (historical enquiry and biblical scholarship) does not support them. Creationist views may have been justifiable for some before the facts of evolution were established, but they no longer are. Similarly, belief in biblical accounts of miracles may have been justified in the relevant epistemic sense before the advent of modern historiography, standards of historical evidence and biblical scholarship, but they no longer are.

The second kind of argument against justified belief in miracles that Beckwith is concerned to refute, the argument from a miracle's improbability, attempts to show that miracles cannot be known historically – that is judged probable on the basis of historical evidence. But again, given that in some circumstances one could justifiably believe a miracle has occurred, the only question that remains is whether anyone is now or ever has been justified in belief in a miracle on the basis of the evidence. All that Beckwith has shown is that Anthony Flew misstates his case by overstating it when (and if) he claims it is *impossible* to be justified on the basis of historical evidence.[23] Flew's conclusion is not philosophically interesting, it is just wrong. But again, the fact that it is possible to be justified in believing in miracles in some imaginable circumstances does nothing to show that there ever have been such circumstances.

Alternatively, Flew might be arguing against justified belief in a miracle by in effect insisting a priori that one is never justified, that is – cannot be justified, on pain of contradiction – in believing on historical grounds that an event 'contrary' to the law of nature occurred. If so, Flew can easily be refuted with a host of made-up examples that would send the a priori assumption scampering. These are fictional cases in which the likelihood that some event is a miracle (all things considered) vastly outweighs other hypotheses (like Hume's Indian case) suggesting that what we thought to be a true law of nature may not be one. Contrary to Hume's argument in Part I of his essay – and leaving his empiricism to one side – the case for a naturalistic explanation will not always be stronger than the case for a supernatural one, though again this does nothing to show that the supernatural explanation has ever been the more acceptable one. Beckwith says,

> Flew's argument may also be viewed as maintaining that the theist is inconsistent. Stephen T. Davis summarizes this interpretation in the following way: 'People who offer historical or probabilistic arguments in favour of the occurrence of a given purported miracle, Flew says, themselves presuppose the very regularity of nature and reliability of nature's laws that they argue against. Their position is accordingly inconsistent.'[24]

This interpretation has Flew arguing against justified belief wholly on conceptual grounds. In effect, Flew is presupposing the truth of naturalism and saying that if historical reasoning presupposes inviolable laws of nature, then we have to reject arguments that purport to show such laws to have been violated. He supposes that historical reasoning – inductive reasoning – requires this assumption of inviolability. But this just is not true unless one presupposes that nothing outside the provenance of such laws could occur. In different ways, Flew and Hume both presuppose naturalism. For both, the possibility of justified belief in miracles is ruled out because the possibility of the miraculous is ruled out.

Interestingly, discussion of Hume's view on miracles has focused less on whether he was correct than on exegetical issues. Thus, the question as to whether or not Hume concludes that one could never be justified in believing in a miracle on the basis of testimony is disputed. Hume concludes Part I by saying, 'If the falsehood of his testimony would be more miraculous than the event which he relates; then, and not till then, can he pretend to command my belief or opinion.'[25] But the idea that this sentence supports the view that Hume is claiming that one can be justified in believing in a miracle indicates not only a humourless reading of the text, but also a misinterpretation of the argument.[26]

Contrary to Anthony Flew, Richard Swinburne and Robert Fogelin, I have argued that Hume's argument in Part I is a priori, and, contrary to J. C. A. Gaskin, that Hume's argument applies to first-hand experience of a miracle as well as to testimony.[27] Fogelin insists that a close reading of the text does not support the view that Hume's argument is an a priori one. But the issue cannot be decided on how closely one reads the text or based on what Hume 'actually says'. The crucial issues are all interpretative. Fogelin's interpretative mistakes may result from a tactical error. Hume's essay and argument does not have to be placed in any historical context, but, as Hume did, in the context of his own (peculiar) empiricism. Given his view that divine activity is impossible to know, Hume's argument in Part I is in a sense superfluous. His a priori argument is logically pre-empted by his view on divine activity. If it were possible to know (have an impression of) divine activity as such, then it would be possible, on Hume's account, justifiably to believe a miracle.

The premise that 'a miracle is a violation of a law of nature' plays no significant role in Hume's argument. It is a gloss for the underlying supposition that one cannot have an 'impression' of a supernatural event.[28]

BAYESIAN ANALYSES OF HUME'S ARGUMENT CONCERNING MIRACLES

There are various versions of Bayes' theorem. For example, John Earman employs the following:

$$\Pr(H/E\&K) = \frac{\Pr(H/K) \times \Pr(E/H\&K)}{\Pr(E/K)}$$

Earman explains: 'The reader is invited to think of H as a hypothesis at issue; K as the background knowledge; and E as the additional evidence. $\Pr(H/E\&K)$ is called the posterior probability of H. $\Pr(H/K)$ and $\Pr(E/H\&K)$ are respectively called the prior probability of H and the (posterior) likelihood of E.'[29]

Bayesian analyses are prominent among recent interpretations of Hume's argument. Bayes' theorem is a formula that allows us to calculate the probability of one event given another if (1) we know the probability of the second given the first, and (2) the probabilities of each event alone. Since there is no consensus on just what Hume's argument (Part I) is, or exactly what he is trying to establish, it is impossible that any recasting of the argument in terms of Bayes' theorem will not beg issues of interpretation. In so doing, such analyses, in and of themselves, will also beg epistemological issues concerning, for example, evidence. Recasting Hume's argument in a Bayesian form cannot clarify the structure or substance of the argument without presupposing what the argument is. We do not know what we need to know to apply the theorem, and if we did we would not need the theorem.

On the interpretation of Hume's argument given above, a Bayesian analysis sheds no light whatsoever on the structure or substance of the argument, and can do nothing by way of either supporting or refuting the argument. Any Bayesian analysis of the question of justified belief in miracles must be otiose until the questions concerning 'evidence' in relation to an allegedly miraculous occurrence are resolved – at which point any Bayesian analysis will add little except the technical complexity of a formal apparatus that is unlikely to clarify Hume's argument.

One cannot balance probabilities until it is decided what goes into the balance – that is, what constitutes the evidence that is to be subject to the balancing of probabilities. Bayesian analyses beg the question by *ignoring* Hume's account of a posteriori reasoning in favour of accounts of their own. What is remarkable is not that Earman misconstrues the fundamentals of Hume's argument (most philosophers do) but that he and other Bayesians misconstrue the limits, and so in a sense the very nature, of Bayesian analyses. The point is this: apart from independent philosophical arguments – arguments that would undermine the relevance of a Bayesian analysis to the question of the credibility of reports of the miraculous, no such analysis can, in principle, prove that no testimony can (or cannot) establish the credibility of a miracle. So-called Bayesian analyses of Hume's argument are not analyses of Hume's argument; they are superfluous representations of it.

ARE MIRACLES RELIGIOUSLY SIGNIFICANT?

The question of how significant miracles are for religious belief and the religious life is perhaps the most important question of all. It is also a question largely ignored by contemporary philosophers in favour of the old war horses: whether miracles are consistent with science and how they relate to laws of nature.[30] These are far less questions about religion or miracles than they are about laws of nature, science and the supernatural. The question as to whether miracles are possible will be framed in terms of prior, and more problematic, conceptions of laws of nature and science, even though it is religious allegiances, or lack thereof, that arguably give rise to the conceptions.

Some biblical scholars and theologians claim that the issue of miracles has been largely misunderstood and co-opted by philosophers and critics of religion for their own purposes, specifically in order to deny – though sometimes to affirm – their occurrence as alleged in the Bible. Thus, David Strauss (1808–74) claimed that reports of miracles can be rejected, 'When the narration is irreconcilable with the known and universal laws which govern the course of events'.[31] Theologians have also pointed out, for example, that there is no word for 'miracle', in the Old or New Testament. What are described there as 'prodigies' or 'wonders' or 'effects of powers', are interpreted by philosophers, but not by the biblical writers, as 'miracles'. Flew says that according to Baruch Spinoza, as well as some contemporary theologians, 'conventional interpreters of the Bible read far more miracles into it than it contains, because they constantly read poetic Hebrew idioms literally'.[32]

Language, however, is hardly to the point. No matter how events such as a parting of the sea or a resurrection are described, whether as 'wonders' or as 'miracles', it is clear that they were understood in biblical times, as well as in contemporary times, to be in some remarkable sense contrary to the normal course of nature. People living at the time of Moses or Christ knew just as well as we do that seas do not normally part and that people are not, in the normal course of nature, resurrected. What is required for a notion of the miraculous is not a sophisticated notion of what a law of nature is, but a robust sense of what constitutes the natural, uninterrupted, course of events. This is something the ancients had just as much as those living in a scientific age.

Believers often regard the philosophical dimension, the epistemological one in particular, of the issue of miracles as insignificant. Indeed, philosophy of religion is for the most part regarded as inconsequential by believers as well as by those in the academic study of religion. Socio-scientific accounts of religion and belief (arguably) not only have implications for religious truth-claims; they also show both the believer's and the philosophy of religion's understanding of religion and religious truth-claims to be naive. Nevertheless, the philosopher's concerns may be more closely allied with those of religious people than, for example, are those of the social scientist. (At least they are more closely allied with what religious people think their concerns and interests are.) This does not make them more important, just more closely allied. The philosopher, in one guise, is allegedly interested in the truth about religious truth-claims and (though many would disagree on philosophical grounds) may pursue that interest more or less independently of dogma, tradition, and what socio-scientific study tells us about the various functions of religion.

Philosophical issues in religion are fundamental in a way that other modes of investigation are not. A system of beliefs may serve a variety of functions, personally and socially, but for the religious person these are, or are at least thought to be, consequences of the truth of what is believed. They believe their religion to be more or less coherent and true. It makes a difference, though not as much as one might expect, to most believers who are traditional theists whether or not miracles could occur, and whether one is justified in believing they did occur. One does not have to be a fundamentalist Christian, for example, to believe with Paul that the Christian faith is, in one important sense (though not in all important senses), a vain pursuit if the central miracles associated with, for example, Christianity did not occur. On this point David Hume, Bertrand Russell and Richard Swinburne would concur.

Apart from belief in miracles, one is left with a religious world view and ethos that remain significant. However, for those for whom these beliefs are important, religion could no longer function in quite the way it did if they became convinced of the falsity of such beliefs – not if those beliefs impacted on how they experienced and felt about life. There is a sense, albeit perhaps not a very important one, in which one is involved in pretence (not always a bad thing) if one practises a system of beliefs whose central tenets one denies. What one is practising may be similar to the religious tradition in question, but one will not be practising that religion, nor is one a believer.

Having said that, it is still the case that miracles are regarded as overly important by philosophers of religion. Some theologians, along with many in the academic study of religion, including philosophy, no longer regard truth-claims of any kind, let alone those about miracles, as central. They have relatively little role in the religious life, or to questions about God and meaning as taken up in philosophical theology. This perceived lack of importance is something that they seem incapable of conveying to others – most notably philosophers of religion.

Notes

1 Aquinas, *Summa Contra Gentiles*, III.
2 In 1748, David Hume, 'Of Miracles', in *Enquiries Concerning Human Understanding*, 3rd edn, ed. L. A. Selby-Bigge, rev. and notes

P. H. Nidditch (Oxford: Oxford University Press, 1975), 109–31, explicitly denies that he is arguing against the possibility of miracles. However, given his empiricism, there are reasons to doubt this. See Michael P. Levine, *Hume and the Problem of Miracles: A Solution*, Philosophical Studies Series 41 (Dordrecht: Kluwer, 1989), Part I.

3   A fourth question might be 'what is a miracle?' I do not, however, think that there is much of philosophical interest attached to this question. Aquinas' definition suffices. Following Hume, a miracle is frequently defined as a violation of a law of nature, but technically speaking this is a mistake. Laws of nature are meant to account for or describe natural events, not supernaturally caused events. Miracles, being outside the scope of laws of nature, cannot properly be seen as violations of them. See Levine, *Hume and the Problem of Miracles*, 65–74.

4   See J. J. C. Smart and J. J. Haldane, *Atheism and Theism* (Oxford: Blackwell, 1996); Nicholas Wolterstorff, *Divine Discourse: Philosophical Reflections on the Claim that God Speaks* (Cambridge: Cambridge University Press, 1995); Richard Swinburne, *The Concept of Miracle* (London: Macmillan, 1970); and Richard Swinburne, *The Resurrection of God Incarnate* (Oxford: Oxford University Press, 2003).

5   Swinburne, *Miracle*, ch. 4. Also see Swinburne, *Resurrection*; N. T. Wright, *The Resurrection of the Son of God* (Minneapolis: Augsburg Fortress and London: SPCK, 2003); Timothy McGrew and Lydia McGrew, 'The Argument from Miracles: A Cumulative Case for the Resurrection of Jesus of Nazareth', in *The Blackwell Companion to Natural Theology*, ed. William Lane Craig and James Porter Moreland (Chichester: Wiley-Blackwell, 2009), 593–662.

6   Robert Audi and Nicholas Wolterstorff, *Religion in the Public Square* (Lanham: Rowman and Littlefield, 1997), 67–120.

7   For a discussion of historical evidence and biblical interpretation, see Michael. P. Levine, 'Critical Notice' [of Smart and Haldane, *Atheism and Theism*], *Canadian Journal of Philosophy* 29 (1999), 157–70, and Michael P. Levine, 'God Speak', *Religious Studies* 34 (1998), 1–16; John Gager, *Kingdom and Community* (New Jersey: Prentice Hall, 1975); Richard Horsely, *Bandits, Prophets, and Messiahs: Popular Movements at the Time of Jesus* (New York: Seabury, 1985); Burton Mack, *Who Wrote the New Testament?* (San Francisco: Harper, 1999).

8   Hume's arguments are applicable to those who claim that the Bible can be read as an historical document; that it provides historical evidence for miracles or that it renders belief in miracles epistemically justified. Hume's claims in Part II have since been bolstered by historical studies, modern historiography, psychology, anthropology, sociology, aspects of religious studies and 'excavative' biblical scholarship.

9   Alvin Plantinga, 'Divine Action in the World (Synopsis)', *Ratio*, new series 19 (2006), 495–504.

10   Smart and Haldane, *Atheism and Theism*.

11   Francis Beckwith, 'Theism, Miracles and the Modern Mind', in *The Rationality of Theism*, ed. Paul Copan and Paul Moser (London: Routledge, 2003), 221–36.

12 *Ibid.*

13 *Ibid.*, 224.

14 *Ibid.*, 221.

15 *Ibid.*, 224, my emphasis.

16 Hume, *Enquiries*, 111–15.

17 *Ibid.*, 111–12.

18 Michael Martin, *Atheism: A Philosophical Justification* (Philadelphia: Temple University Press, 1990), 199.

19 Beckwith, 'Theism', 223. See Tamas Pataki, *Against Religion* (Melbourne: Scribe, 2007) for arguments suggesting an intrinsic connection between the character of what he calls the 'religiose' and violence. See also Damian Cox, Michael P. Levine and Saul Newman, *Politics Most Unusual: Violence, Religion and Sovereignty in the 'War on Terror'* (London: Palgrave Macmillan, 2009).

20 Beckwith, 'Theism', 227.

21 It reflects a *modus operandi* of philosophers of religion like Van Inwagen, Plantinga, Haldane, Wolterstorff, Swinburne and others. Let virtually nothing count against religious truth claims as more or less literally interpreted. In terms of this *modus operandi* treatments of the problem of evil are particularly noteworthy.

22 Søren Kierkegaard, *Concluding Unscientific Postscript*, trans. David F. Swenson, introduction and notes by Walter Lowrie (London: Oxford University Press, 1945); Søren Kierkegaard, *Philosophical Fragments: Johannes Climacus* (Princeton: Princeton University Press, 1985); Paul Tillich, *Systematic Theology*, 3 vols. (Chicago: University of Chicago Press, 1951–63).

23 Antony Flew, *God: A Critical Enquiry*, 2nd edn (LaSalle: Open Court, 1984), 14.

24 Beckwith, 'Theism', 234 n. 24; Stephen T. Davis, 'Is it Possible to Know that Jesus was Raised from the Dead?', *Faith and Philosophy* 2 (1984), 147–59 (149). Warwick Montgomery, *The Law Above the Law* (Minneapolis: Dimension, 1975), 52–8, interprets Flew's argument in a similar way.

25 Hume, *Enquiries*, 115.

26 Michael P. Levine, 'Hume on Miracles and Immortality', in *Blackwell Companion to Hume*, ed. Elizabeth Radcliffe (Oxford: Blackwell, 2008), 353–70.

27 Antony Flew, 'Miracles', *Encyclopedia of Philosophy* (New York: Macmillan and Free, 1967), vol. v, 346–53; Swinburne, *Miracle*; Robert J. Fogelin, *A Defense of Hume on Miracles* (Princeton: Princeton University Press, 2003); J. C. A. Gaskin, *Hume's Philosophy of Religion* (London: Macmillan, 1978); Levine, 'Hume on Miracles and Immortality', 353–70.

28 Levine, *Hume*, Part I.

29 John Earman, 'Bayes, Hume, and Miracles', *Faith and Philosophy* 10 (1993), 293–310 (307 n. 4); John Earman, *Hume's Abject Failure: The Argument Against Miracles* (New York: Oxford University Press, 2000), 27.

30 For example, Alvin Plantinga, 'Divine Action in the World (Synopsis)'.
31 David Friedrich Strauss, *The Life of Jesus Critically Examined*, Lives of Jesus series (Philadelphia: Fortress, 1973), 88.
32 Flew, 'Miracles', 347.
    My thanks to Brent Madison, Graham Twelftree and anonymous readers for their comments.

Further reading

Beckwith, Francis, 'Theism, Miracles and the Modern Mind', in *The Rationality of Theism*, ed. Paul Copan and Paul Moser (London: Routledge, 2003), 221–36

Burns, Robert M., *The Great Debate on Miracles* (Lewisburg: Bucknell University Press, 1981)

Earman, John, *Hume's Abject Failure: The Argument Against Miracles* (New York: Oxford University Press, 2000)

Flew, Antony, 'Miracles', *Encyclopedia of Philosophy* (New York: Macmillan and Free, 1967), vol. v, 346–53

*Fogelin, Robert J., *A Defense of Hume on Miracles* (Princeton: Princeton University Press, 2003)

Hume, David, 'Of Miracles', in *Enquiries Concerning Human Understanding*, 3rd edn, ed. L. A. Selby-Bigge, rev. and notes P. H. Nidditch (Oxford: Oxford University Press, 1975), 109–31

Levine, Michael P., *Hume and the Problem of Miracles: A Solution*, Philosophical Studies Series 41 (Dordrecht: Kluwer, 1989)

'God Speak', *Religious Studies* 34 (1998), 1–16

Locke, John, *A Discourse on Miracles*, published posthumously, 1706, ed. I. T. Ramsey (London: Black, 1958)

Martin, Raymond, 'Historians on Miracles', in *God Matters: Readings in the Philosophy of Religion*, ed. Raymond Martin (New York: Longman, 2003), 412–27

Plantinga, Alvin, 'Divine Action in the World (Synopsis)', *Ratio*, new series 19 (2006), 495–504

Smart, J. J. C. and J. J. Haldane, *Atheism and Theism* (Oxford: Blackwell, 1996)

17 Patient belief in miraculous healing: positive or negative coping resource?

NIELS CHRISTIAN HVIDT

Faith and hope in divine healing figure in most religious traditions. This chapter looks at faith in healing miracles and explores how following that faith may involve both risks and advantages. On the one hand, it may imply a risk by camouflaging a deferring attitude as when patients decline medical treatment on the basis of their belief in divine intervention, or demand utopian life-prolonging treatment so that God may be given time to perform a miracle. On the other hand, faith in miracles forms an important part of a well-integrated religiosity by inspiring hope and so helping patients to find meaning and initiative in situations in which they might otherwise be tempted to give up. Against the backdrop of such considerations, the chapter provides recommendations for health professionals and relatives on how to handle patient belief in miracles in practice.

FAITH IN DIVINE INTERVENTION AS A FUNDAMENTAL RELIGIOUS TENET

The majority of religious traditions profess faith in divine interventions such as miracles, signs, wonders or prophecies. All such traditions represent a fundamental belief that God can and does act in our world. Regardless of how different the suggestions may be as to *how* God has intervened and *what* he has achieved in doing so, religion is based on the idea that God can and has intervened in human affairs. If God had never intervened in this world in some way or another, people would not have had any knowledge of God, for people would have had no access to the realm of God. This is particularly true of the so-called Abrahamitic religions, that is, religions such as Judaism, Christianity or Islam, which believe in Abraham as their ancestor and that build on a foundational book.

The larger debate on divine intervention constitutes a broad and important arena of dialogue between theology, philosophy and science, and is usually summarized by the debate on divine action.[1] To present this debate is an enterprise that transcends the limitations of this chapter, whose aim is to focus on the impact of belief in miracles rather than on miracles per se. It should merely be noted here that the idea of divine intervention normally implies that God has done something in history that would not have happened without his special intervention. Whether this intervention should be said to break with the laws of nature or not is still a matter of debate, but much recent interpretation regards God as acting within and through the natural laws he has laid down, not violating but, on the contrary, confirming and working through the order he has created.

FAITH IN DIVINE INTERVENTION IN THE TWENTY-FIRST CENTURY

As the possibility of divine intervention is to a large extent considered a foundational feature of the origin and structure of much religious faith, we cannot be surprised that faith in such intervention thrives, even in the twenty-first century. Western societies have been profoundly affected by secularization, but sociologists of religion mostly agree that modernity has not displaced the human need for religion, including faith in divine intervention, especially when sickness and crisis call for extreme remedies.[2]

What has changed, however, is the way in which people live as religious beings. Organized religious institutions have lost some of their authority. At the same time, religious reflections and practices are becoming more individual, more private. When comparing the countries that are normally considered very religious (such as the USA and many developing countries) with those considered more secular (such as the northern European countries), the primary difference lies not in the number of people claiming to believe in God but rather in the way they practise their faith and the time they devote to it. In countries considered fairly religious, people are more used to practising their faith publicly with all the ramifications this has in public life. In the USA, for instance, the level of religious belief almost matches the level of religious practice. This is far from being the case in secular countries such as Denmark, where only around 2 per cent attend church on a weekly basis, although around 72 per cent consider themselves believers and more than 86 per cent are members of the Lutheran Church of Denmark.

This is very important for our topic, since in secular countries disease may become a relatively more powerful trigger for religious considerations and practices such as prayer for divine healing than in more religious countries. It has been said that the prayer houses in Denmark are no longer the churches but the hospitals.[3]

The sociology of religion has long tried to evaluate what catalyses religious change. The general conviction is that conversion to or intensification of religious faith is primarily the consequence of crisis such as that provoked by life-threatening disease or impending death. Not surprisingly, then, research confirms the fact that religiousness and religious need increase or at least change with age.[4] As M. E. Cavanagh writes, 'The cancer counterpart to the dictum "There are no atheists in foxholes" is "There are no atheists in oncology and bone-marrow transplant units".'[5] In one study, over 85 per cent of 337 patients admitted to the general medicine, cardiology and neurology services of Duke University Medical Center had strong, intrinsic religious attitudes. Over 40 per cent reported that their faith was the single most important factor that helped them cope with their disease.[6]

There are many reasons why patients tend to intensify their religiosity during times of disease. Research has identified many positive religious resources and confirmed that they may lead to increased quality of life for patients, may reduce the risk of depression following serious diagnoses and may bring patients better and faster through treatment.[7] Trusting prayer is generally viewed as an expression of a living, religiously based hope for positive prospects, and in many studies hope has proved to constitute a positive coping resource. It is not surprising, therefore, that patients express the wish to have their hope strengthened when they experience a major crisis.[8] Many patients express their hope through prayer that God will intervene and help them get well again.[9] We shall now look more closely at prayer for healing miracles as a particular form of divine intervention that is often invoked during illness.

Healing miracles appear to be the most common form of divine intervention in many religions.[10] This certainly is true for Christianity.[11] Healing miracles are normally considered divine interventions that lead to improvement or full recovery of a person suffering from disease. Experience of such miracles may range from the psychological to the physical sphere. It may only be experienced by the sufferer, but in many cases it comes to the attention of and invokes faith in larger groups of people.

HEALING MIRACLES INVESTIGATED
BY MEDICAL DOCTORS

Some healing miracles are of such a concrete and material kind that they can become the object of empirical investigation. A number of these have been recorded and investigated by the *Consulta Medica* in the Vatican Congregation for the Causes of Saints. In order for the Catholic Church authorities to beatify or canonize a believer, they require evidence of healing miracles occurring on the intercession of the candidate after his or her death.[12] Although the Catholic Church acknowledges the possibility of many forms of miracle, what these boards are investigating is a particular type of miracle whose effects are so tangible that they can become the object of medical investigation. The role of the doctors affiliated to the board is unique and somewhat curious. One of the fundamentals of the natural sciences, including the health sciences, is to employ empirical enquiry to propose explanations for phenomena that occur in the physical world. The role of these doctors, however, is the opposite, namely to employ traditional scientific methods to provide medical evidence that a given healing effect cannot be explained by natural causes alone.

In order for the theologians to proclaim a given healing experience as a miracle, the event must first match the following criteria that had already been laid down by Pope Benedict XIV in the sixteenth century:

1. The disease must be grave and, according to the judgment of doctors, extremely difficult or impossible to cure.
2. No medication may have been provided that could have healed the disease. Prescribed medication should have been proven to have no effect on the disease.
3. The healing should be instantaneous.
4. The healing should be complete. There could nevertheless remain consequences, such as scars.
5. The healing should be stabile and durative.[13]

It is important to note that the doctors in the *Consulta Medica* never venture to claim that a miracle has occurred. Their only purpose is to confirm that a given healing is in conformity with the criteria mentioned above. In the terminology of the Congregation for the Causes of Saints a healing miracle is, therefore, a medical event that is deemed inexplicable by the doctors but it only becomes a miracle in the religious and theological sense of the word by virtue of the religious culture, belief and practice in which it occurred. Once the doctors have reached their conclusions, therefore, it is still up to the theologians to determine whether the spiritual and religious requirements have been conformed with, such as sincere faith and prayer for healing prior to the experienced miracle. There is little doubt that these medical investigations, along with the biblical texts and anecdotes from church history, have encouraged prayer for miraculous healing and may explain why it is so widespread, at least in a Catholic setting.

PRAYER FOR THE ALLEVIATION OF ILL-HEALTH: A WIDESPREAD PHENOMENON

In the USA, a country that, as has been mentioned, is characterized by strong religious belief, surveys have repeatedly shown not only that faith in and prayer to God is widespread but also that a majority of Americans believe in miracles. According to a nationwide Gallup survey from 1995, 79 per cent of respondents believe in miracles, 8 per cent do not know what to answer, 12 per cent do not believe and 1 per cent have no opinion.[14] The figures are higher in the Afro-American south-eastern states of the USA. Here 87.5 per cent state that they believe in religious miracles and 63 per cent that they 'definitely believe' in them.[15] Belief in miracles is widespread not only among patients but even among healthcare professionals with 73 per cent of physicians in the USA believing that miracles are possible.[16] In a study made in Catholic Poland the figures are also relatively high. Here, 70 per cent of Polish students say that they believe in miracles defined as supernatural phenomena created by God.[17]

In the secular Scandinavian countries, the figures are significantly lower. The World Value Survey (WVS) and The International Social Survey Program (ISSP) both function as tools to evaluate and compare the variety of convictions across populations, including faith in miracles. Here it is clear yet again that the US population reports higher levels of faith in 'religious miracles' – 79 per cent versus 25 per cent in Denmark. In another survey 26 per cent of Danes testify to believing in the central biblical miracle, the resurrection of Christ, while only 16 per cent believe that Christ was conceived through the Holy Spirit. Data suggest, however, that the figures are higher for people who have undergone suffering or crisis. In a pilot study from the Danish Cancer Society on religious needs among women who survived breast cancer, 55 per cent responded that they believe in miracles.[18] Even secular Scandinavians seem to pray to God for a miracle, or at least pray that the doctor will perform one – with God's help.[19]

Along with praying for divine healing (see above), the ability to cope with disease seem to be the two oldest and most widespread complementary forms of expectation of intervention. As the Jewish rabbi J. D. Spivak pointed out 100 years ago, 'Wishing is praying, and who, if sick, does not wish with all the intensity of his soul for recovery?'[20] Since we tend to think of therapeutic traditions inspired by the East such as acupuncture, bio-kinesiology or Reiki healing when we talk of complementary or alternative medicine (CAM), we forget that in the parts of the world in which theistic religions such as Christianity, Judaism or Islam are most widespread, prayer has been the most commonly used form of CAM.

A number of surveys have established that around 75 per cent of the American population pray at least daily.[21] The National Center for Complementary and Alternative Medicine (NCCAM) sponsored by the National Institutes of Health (NIH) count intercessory prayer for divine healing as one of many complementary and alternative forms of health intervention.[22] An investigation of 2004 showed that 62 per cent of random (both healthy and ill) US Americans had used some kind of CAM over the previous twelve months. Two forms of prayer for health topped this list: prayers of individuals for themselves (43 per cent) and prayers for individuals by other individuals (24.4 per cent). Participation in a prayer group took fourth place (9.6 per cent).[23] Another study published in 2005 conducted among 493 patients in a hospital in Texas showed that 79.2 per cent of the patients reported that they prayed for their own health, whereas 71.9 per cent said that others prayed for them.[24] Similar results are found in European studies, although figures for so-called 'Mind–Body Interventions' such as spiritual healing, including intercessory prayer, are lower than in the USA. In one study, 31 per cent of the respondents had used prayer actively before they became ill, whereas 52 per cent of them used it after diagnosis.[25] Not surprisingly, then, medical interest in prayer is growing. A simple search in October 2009 on PubMed, the primary medical database, with the words 'prayer therapy' yielded 16,096 published articles.

POSITIVE AND NEGATIVE RELIGIOUS COPING

The question arises as to how this belief in miracles functions in the lives of the patients that pray and hope for them. The notion of religious coping is largely inspired by the psychology of coping as formulated by Richard S. Lazarus and others. Coping is the way people master, minimize, reduce or tolerate stress, such as stress inflicted by serious disease. Kenneth Pargament has carried out considerable research into the resources that religion may provide to help people cope, and substantial data suggest that religious coping may be positive or negative, depending on the way patients view God and their disease.[26]

Traditionally, many psychologists have looked down on patient belief in miracles. They have considered such faith to be an example of a deferring attitude or a denial of crisis that may be too frightening for the client and/or patient to handle. Psychologists generally agree that therapists are not obliged to regard such beliefs as obstructive to treatment, to encourage clients to 'face up to the truth' in order to evade the state of deferral, since such beliefs can constitute a healthy protective pattern when coming to terms with a major life event. However, it is necessary to help the patient when the denial assumes proportions that runs counter to patients' ability to cope in the long run. Such a pragmatic attitude is corroborated by research that suggests that negative religious resources, such as belief in God as an agent of retribution, may augment the risk of cancer-related depression.[27]

Faith in a God who is alive and active and interacts with people has been proven to be important to the way patients handle crises. Conceptions of God in which illness and crisis represent divine punishment have been shown to provoke stress and low self-esteem, whereas the opposite applies when patients believe that God enters into their suffering, bears it with them and supports them throughout their disease.[28]

The idea that God punishes through disease and traumas is, as Pragament's research shows particularly clearly, considered an example of 'negative religious coping'. Such negative coping has been associated with a decrease in psychological functioning, quality of life and longevity.[29] Some evidence suggests that the reason humans in crisis cling on to a vision of God as their judge just when they actually most needed support is because they are in need of an explanation. Sexton and Maddock see in this a form of self-judgment that they consider the worst and original sin from the Garden of Eden because it leads humans to deny God's deepest nature: his forgiveness and charity.[30] This destructive trend in human nature may lead to religious conflict, fear and depression, because the God who should give ultimate comfort has become the ultimate enemy. The result is anger against oneself or against God.[31]

The belief that God can perform miracles can clearly aggravate this negative coping pattern, leading sufferers to thoughts like: 'If God *can* perform miracles but chooses not to grant me one, it has to be because he does not *want* to, because he holds something against me'.

Negative religious coping tends to be aggravated by a patient's belief that God controls everything, even suffering. As belief in miracles is usually associated with belief in divine power, people who believe in miracles also tend to believe in divine control, albeit a control that can be influenced through intercession. The belief that God controls every event in world history is widespread in the Old Testament[32] and in the Qur'ān: 'Allah confounds whom He will, and guides to the Right Way whom He pleases' (Qur'ān 6.39). It continues in Jewish religious belief and thought (at least until the Nazi extermination camps), in Islam and in certain versions of Calvinism.[33] Belief that God controls all events, both good and evil, is today especially pervasive in developing countries. Over 80 per cent of Filipinos were convinced that God was the direct cause of the tsunami in 2004.[34]

A belief in God as the ultimate cause of all that happens becomes disruptive when combined with the idea that God uses suffering as a means of retribution, to punish sinners. Just as the Old Testament contains many reflections on the cause of suffering, so it presents many reasons for suffering. The primary answer to the reason for suffering is that God educates the believer through suffering. This reply is found primarily in the Old Testament[35] and in the Qur'ān. There are many examples of the belief that God sends accidents and suffering as punishments for misdeeds.[36] This faith continues today and is voiced by American TV Evangelists such as Pat Robertson, who repeatedly interpret events as expressions of divine retribution. Ariel Sharon's stroke and subsequent coma, for instance, were seen as God's punishment for vacating the Gaza Strip, something which contradicted Robertson's politico-theological convictions that Israel was to assume most of the Middle East based on Old Testament readings.[37]

Such convictions should come as no surprise, although we may not agree with them. They are widespread among believers in our time, whether Jews, Muslims or Christians. Psychological research has long been providing evidence that children can regard disease as 'immanent justice', that is they believe their disease is punishment for 'bad behaviour'. More recent data nevertheless suggest that a surprisingly number of adults share these notions. Three studies, summarized in an article in 2004, portray belief in 'immanent justice' as being more widespread among adults than among children.[38]

HEALING MIRACLES AS SUBSTITUTES FOR MEDICAL INTERVENTION?

Religious conviction may have an impact on more than mental well-being. It may lead patients to reject medical intervention. The best-known example is the rejection of blood transfusions by Jehovah's Witnesses and the dilemmas this often causes physicians. A simple search conducted July 2009 on PubMed with the words 'Jehovah's Witnesses blood' in the title yielded 742 published articles. Many of them discuss the medical techniques best employed to save Jehovah's Witnesses who need an operation while at the same time honouring their wish not to have a blood transfusion.

The belief in a God who can perform miracles can also lead patients to consider God's actions as an alternative form of therapy capable of replacing medical intervention. Such beliefs are familiar from the Christian Science movement, which distinguishes between faith healing and medical assistance. Here, the powers of faith are often preferred to those of the doctor.[39]

There are many other examples of how religious issues may affect patients' choice of medical interventions.[40] However, many believers share the common conviction that wanting to see a doctor is a manifestation of weak faith. Such a view is potentially disruptive, since behind it lies the idea that our faith in God's existence and action only shows itself to be truly serious when we abstain from actions we would have taken if we did not have this faith. The extreme version of this is found in The Church of God with Signs Following, also known as Snake Handlers.[41] This was a Christian sect, which originated in 1910, inspired by Mark 16.18: 'They will pick up snakes in their hands, and if they drink any deadly thing, it will not hurt them; they will lay their hands on the sick, and they will recover'. Believers brought poisonous snakes that they made writhe around their necks, or they drank poison. Here we have believers not only declining to act when met by a threat but actually adding a threat so that God's protective and active intervention may be manifest. The disastrous effects of such practices only go to show how unfortunate this interpretation of the New Testament belief in the God of miracles can be.

The danger of many attempts to prove faith in God's action is that faith becomes a matter of human effort in which the patient's action is required for God to work; belief in the God of miracles can become detrimental to health when it focuses on the patients' qualities and abilities instead of on God's love and support. The disappointment accompanying unfulfilled hopes of a miracle may become so overwhelming that it both can lead to severe crisis of faith and to demonstrable negative coping mechanisms.[42]

Just as patients' active faith in miracles can lead them to reject prescribed intervention, belief in miracles can in some instances lead patients or their relatives to demand senseless extension of regular treatment. In a well-known article in the *British Medical Journal*,[43] James Buryska provides an example of one such demand for extension of treatment because of a patient's hope of a miracle. It describes the case of a man aged seventy-five who has a stroke, is operated on but never regains consciousness. He has a wife and two sons. One is a hospital worker, the other is a pastor in the local Pentecostal church. The family keeps vigil around their comatose husband and father with song and constant prayer with the result that other patients gradually have to be transferred to other hospital locations to escape the disturbance. The family and especially the Pentecostal son pray and are convinced that the father will be miraculously healed by God and that they need to give God time, even though the doctors see no medical chance of the father surviving. Not only is his brain severely damaged but his liver and kidneys start to fail as well.

After three weeks without improvement, hospital management propose stopping life-support treatment and allowing the seventy-five-year-old to depart peacefully. The family has no health insurance so the very expensive treatment puts a strain on resources for other patients. The relatives nevertheless reject this proposal, forcefully demanding respect for their faith and threatening a court action if treatment is interrupted. Only after seven weeks does the patient die, and then in dramatic circumstances. In this case the relatives' hope of a miracle had induced stress and conflict for the health professionals, for other patients as well as for the family itself.

We have now seen some examples of how a faith in miracles can lead to unhelpful coping patterns. However, much evidence suggests that such faith in miracles is not always unhealthy but that, on the contrary, it normally acts as a positive coping resource that may help patients sustain their belief that they are not abandoned. Substantial psychological data suggest that belief in miracles proves surprisingly positive when coping with crisis.[44] Pargament proposed the theory that belief in miracles sustains believers by strengthening the relationship to the God to whom they pray for healing. Although the desired healing may not be achieved, a deeper relationship with God nevertheless results. In many studies such a relationship has in itself been shown to be the primary benefit of faith. Although patients praying for a miracle may not be granted the object of their prayer, they may obtain something they may not have sought that nevertheless proves very meaningful and powerful, namely that they encountered God and abandoned themselves to him on a deeper and more trusting level than they had done before.[45]

Although we have seen some examples of how belief in divine control and a God who can and does act can lead to unhealthy coping patterns, recent data suggest that such belief need not always lead to religious struggle. For instance, the Norwegian psychiatrist and trauma researcher Lars Weisæth ventured to perform the ultimate stress study. He came to the conclusion that the single most stressed group of people in the world at the time when he did his study had to be Iraqi police forces.[46] One of the surprising results of his study was that the primary factor helping the policemen cope with their daily encounter with death and destruction was the belief that God was behind all that happened regardless of how chaotic it seemed and that he knew best. Recent studies by Pargament and colleagues confirm this finding. In a recent survey study by Hisham Abu Raiya,[47] questions were included to evaluate belief in divine control, such as 'When I face a problem in life, I do what I can and put the rest in Allah's hands'. In Raiya's Psychological Measure of Islamic Religiousness these belief items were loaded onto one of the subscales called Islamic Positive Religious Coping and Identification that proved to be the most powerful predictor of positive outcomes. Hence, some knowledge of different types of faith in divine control is vital in order to know when religion will lead to struggle or comfort.

MIRACLE BELIEF IN PRACTICE

Let us now look at how the health services might tackle patient belief in miracles in practice. It must be emphasized that nothing indicates that a belief in miracles is in itself a sign of any religious pathology. As argued in the beginning, belief in miracles is an integral part of a belief in God as living, as creator and as maintainer of the universe, a belief that most religions and faiths have in common. Each individual has the right to decide whether they wish to follow such a belief but not the right to judge the faith of other people or to find fault with it just because it is different from their own. Whether religious or atheist, doctors are expected not to exploit the suffering of others to persuade or proselytize. First of all, this violates the patient's freedom of religion, which applies in hospitals at least as much as elsewhere in society. Second, research indicates that it may destabilize patients if their existential and religious universe, which constitutes the major ontological and psychological cohesive force to help them through their crisis, is shaken. Religious freedom and respect for the beliefs of the patient must remain a constant concern.

However, such concerns should not lead to neglect of religious needs in patient care. In fact, some researchers suggest that such neglect of religious issues is a larger problem than the imposition of doctors' values. Daniel Sulmasy, who is a professor of medicine and a Franciscan friar, argues that there is a resistance against moving into the religious sphere, which ironically is evinced by atheists and believers alike. Atheists avoid it because they regard the religious field as irrational, subject to matters of faith that are beyond them and in defiance of empirical and rational argument. Believers avoid it by referring to freedom of religious belief and respect for the religious world.[48]

In a renowned article Buryska suggests that three circumstances in particular have contributed to our reluctance to interact with the cultural, religious and spiritual spheres of patients:

1. The almost absolute value that we attribute to individual identity and personal autonomy.
2. The fundamental assumption that only conditions that can be measured empirically have clinical relevance.
3. The tendency to make personal matters private, thereby excluding them from public dialogue.[49]

The problem does not seem to be that religious freedom is violated. On the contrary, it seems that secularized fear of contact with the religious world sometimes leads to neglect of patients' religious needs. Religious patients often feel alone and left to their own devices when they find that no one is willing to touch on their faith. Real care and respect for people can never be expressed by keeping a distance. They are only realized when they include all spheres of the patient's world, including the religious sphere, even when the practitioners do not share the faith of the patients. As such, it is necessary to find ways to strengthen positive views of patients' attitudes, even when they include a belief in miracles that many health professionals trained in the natural sciences may not understand or may even find ludicrous.

Furthermore, most researchers interested in the religious coping resources of patients believe that the religious field must also be subject to a certain degree of pragmatic quality assessment, so that its positive resources can be respected and the negative resources countered, especially when they affect the well-being of patients. It is of vital importance to be able to have a dialogue with patients who make use of undesirable coping resources but without violating their freedom of religion and without unnecessarily destabilizing the meaning-making processes of patients.

Finally, we need to address the question of how to respond to patients who either reject treatment because they believe in miracles (such as Christian Scientists) or who demand extended treatment to give God the necessary time to perform the miracle that they are hoping for. In most countries legislation exists, usually modelled on the Amsterdam Declaration, which has a clear-cut approach to the issue. Rejecting treatment is what is called a negative right and is a right for all. Demanding treatment on the other hand is called a positive right and is not universal.

In the negative right of patients, patient autonomy takes precedence over the duty of care.[50] If the patient decides not to give his or her consent because he or she believes God will provide a miracle cure, there is no treatment. However, like other Health Acts, it requires truly informed consent.[51] In the case of senile patients, for example, it is not possible to speak of informed consent. In such cases the decision falls to the closest relatives or, if no relatives exist, to the practitioners who must carry out the best possible treatment. Neither is it a case of informed consent for children under the age of fifteen. As a consequence, parents who are Jehovah's Witnesses cannot employ the Health Act to demand that their children do not receive a blood transfusion. Patients aged fifteen to eighteen years may give their informed consent themselves, but their parents must be informed and can reject their consent if they judge that the patient does not understand the consequences of his or her choice.

It is a different matter with the positive right – the right to be treated – as it is not an absolute right. For instance, it is not possible to demand a treatment, which is disproportionately more expensive than another suitable treatment, as this would affect the finances of the hospital – and thereby other patients' access to health services.

It can be hard to know when a patient's rejection of treatment is a sign of religious neurosis or of healthy faith – when the judgment is truly 'informed' (by faith) or not. For example, not many practitioners would shake their heads if an old woman in her nineties after a long and fulfilled life declined potentially life-prolonging chemotherapy, for they would argue that the patient is ready to meet her Maker. Conversely, action must be taken if a young patient rejects vital treatment because of a religious faith that God will perform a miracle. This means that it will be necessary to evaluate individual cases and, as in medical ethics, to apply general guidelines to those very difficult individual cases that often lie in the grey area.

As to the wishes of some patients or relatives to extend treatment so that God can perform his wonders, things here are somewhat simpler. First, the patients or relatives have, as I have said, no positive right to choose the nature or length of the treatment, and the needs of other patients must be taken into consideration, so the arguments of health professionals will carry weight in the dialogue with patients.

When it comes to the concrete question how religious arguments should be dealt with in the context of hospitals, it is important to make clear that healthcare professionals sometimes have to engage in discussion with patients about religious matters. However, it would be better if they were able to call in people with religious qualifications, ideally a leader of the patient's religious community or, if the patient is not a member of such a community, the hospital chaplain.

It is important that hospital chaplains, psychologists, nurses and doctors do not brush aside or refute the beliefs of patients. Here, we are again touching upon the area of freedom of religion. Furthermore, studies show that it can be extremely destabilizing for patients if the foundation of their beliefs is questioned, even though followers of the majority faith view the minority faith as detrimental to health.

Daniel P. Sulmasy suggests that healthcare professionals should always call in a person with religious qualifications if they suspect that it is a case of injurious religiosity. Nevertheless, he offers a number of criteria to help healthcare professionals assess whether the faith in the intervention of God expressed by the patient is healthy or whether the patient is in a state of denial and is couching it in a belief in miracles:

1. If the patient praying for a miracle is able to pray that God's will be done and at the same time is aware that God might not want the healing to occur, then in all likelihood that faith is healthy. However, if the patient refuses to accept that possibility, then the danger of denial is significant.
2. If the patient believes that God is able to perform the miracle here and now, there is a chance that the faith is helpful. However, if the patient demands that the doctors continue with a treatment that they believe to be useless so that God may carry out his work, it is very likely that it is a case of denial and a deferring attitude.

3. What is the effect of the patient's faith in and hope for a miracle on the mood of the patient and on relations to relatives and practitioners at the hospital? If the patient is in harmony with him or herself and his or her God in the hope of divine intervention and if relations to others are healthy, then the faith is probably healthy too. If the patient's belief in and prayers for a miracle lead to tension for the patient, for relatives and for practitioners, then it is more likely that the faith is unhelpful.

4. Is the patient ready to accept input from other members of the patient's religious community, even when they interpret the faith differently from the patient? If so, it is probably a case of fruitful faith; otherwise it is considered unfruitful and may well be a case of an idiosyncratic faith, developed subjectively by the patient through a need to escape realities that, according to Sulmasy, may be too hard to face.[52]

Sulmasy argues, along with Buryska and others, against the faith of patients being beyond question when that faith runs counter to the well-being of patients. He believes that it is appropriate to examine whether the patients show signs of miraculous escapism according to the four criteria mentioned above. If this is the case, it might be a good idea to call in people with religious qualifications or psychologists with knowledge about religious matters to engage in dialogue with the patient and, based on the inner logic of the patient's religion, argue that the belief in question has to be adjusted.

CONCLUSION

In this chapter we have looked at patients' beliefs in miracles and discussed how practitioners should deal with such beliefs. We have seen that the belief in miracles in itself can in no way be viewed as pathological or as a sign of a deferring attitude, since it is an integral part of many important faith traditions that have a transcendent divine reality as their object of worship. According to the self-understanding of many religions, there could simply be no faith if God had not intervened in history to reveal himself and make people aware of his existence.

In the field of psychology, scholars have had justified concerns as to whether belief in miracles was beneficial to health or an expression of a deferring attitude, which in a worst-case scenario could result in the patient not taking his or her own crisis seriously and not acting to counter it. Like many other aspects of a religious credo, the belief in a living and acting God can have positive and negative effects – it can be a resource for both positive and negative religious coping.

All too often the religious sphere is seen as a private area of the patient's own world that no one else has access to. This attitude is encouraged by a naturalistic, scientific world view that regards the religious world as being irrational and closed to rational argument, as built on revelations, the validity of which cannot be tested or verified. Ironically, believers have also influenced this attitude by using freedom of religion and expression to maintain that everybody is allowed to entertain whatever beliefs they wish. However, most researchers in this field today believe that religious faith can and should be the subject of critical reflection, especially when people's well-being is at stake. Research suggests that the religious beliefs of patients may have a direct influence on their chances of recovering after an illness, on their risk of depression and on their perceived quality of life in general. Belief in miracles is included and it can and should be discussed – on a par with other beliefs – and be taken seriously, both to support the faith as an asset when it promotes health and to help patients think differently within their belief system if it proves to have negative consequences. To ensure the quality and integrity of such conversations, they should preferably be conducted between the patient and people with religious qualifications from the patient's religion.

From the perspective of their relevance for practice, religious issues cannot merely be characterized as private and irrelevant for health care. They are of direct importance to the effectiveness of health care and can be assessed against a series of classical health care outcomes tradition-ally used to measure the quality and the effect of treatment, such as quality of life, risk of depression, length of therapy and chances of recovery.[53]

Notes

1   Paul Gwynne, *Special Divine Action: Key Issues in the Contemporary Debate, 1965–1995*, Tesi Gregoriana. Serie Teologia 12 (Rome: Pontificia università gregoriana, 1996).
2   Pippa Norris and Ronald Inglehart, *Sacred and Secular* (New York: Cambridge University Press, 2004).
3   Jørgen Steens, 'Sygehuset er det mest religiøse hus i byen', Last Updated Date 2005 [cited October 2009]. Available from www.kriste-ligt-dagblad.dk/artikel/64672:Kirke–tro–Sygehuset-er-det-mest-religioese-hus-i-byen.

4 See the review in Christopher J. Mansfield, Jim Mitchell and Dana E. King, 'The Doctor as God's Mechanic? Beliefs in the Southeastern United States', *Social Science & Medicine* 54 (2002), 399–409.

5 Michael E. Cavanagh, 'Ministering to Cancer Patients', *Journal of Religion and Health* 33 (1994), 231–41.

6 Harold G. Koenig, 'Religious Attitudes and Practices of Hospitalized Medically Ill Older Adults', *International Journal of Geriatric Psychiatry* 13 (1998), 213–24.

7 Christopher J. Mansfield, Jim Mitchell and Dan E. King, '"Doctor as God's Mechanic?" Beliefs in the Southern United States', *Social Science & Medicine* 54 (2002), 399–409; Gene G. Ano and Erin B. Vasconcelles, 'Religious Coping and Psychological Adjustment to Stress: A Meta-Analysis', *Journal of Clinical Psychology* 61 (2005), 461–80; Kenneth I. Pargament *et al.*, 'Religious Coping Methods as Predictors of Psychological, Physical and Spiritual Outcomes among Medically Ill Elderly Patients: A Two-year Longitudinal Study', *Journal of Health Psychology* 9 (2004), 713–30.

8 Alyson Moadel *et al.*, 'Seeking Meaning and Hope: Self-Reported Spiritual and Existential Needs among an Ethnically-Diverse Cancer Patient Population', *Psycho-Oncology* 8 (1999), 378–85.

9 Laurence Binet Brown, *The Human Side of Prayer: The Psychology of Praying* (Birmingham, AL: Religious Education, 1994).

10 Kenneth L. Woodward, *The Book of Miracles: The Meaning of the Miracle Stories in Christianity, Judaism, Buddhism, Hinduism, Islam* (New York: Simon & Schuster, 2000).

11 Amanda Porterfield, *Healing in the History of Christianity* (New York: Oxford University Press, 2005); Jacalyn Duffin, *Medical Miracles: Doctors, Saints, and Healing in the Modern World* (Oxford and New York: Oxford University Press, 2009).

12 Similar investigations of possible healing miracles are also conducted at the Bureau Médical at Lourdes in France.

13 Benedict XIV, *Benedicti papae XIV doctrina de servorum Dei beatificatione et beatorum canonizatione in synopsim redacta ab emm. de Azevedo* (Brussels: typis Societatis belgicae de propagandis bonis libris, 1840); Andreas Resch, *Miracoli dei santi*, Sussidi per lo studio delle cause dei santi 5 (Vatican City: Libreria editrice vaticana, 2002), 9.

14 George D. Gallup, *The Gallup Poll: Public Opinion, 1995* (Wilmington: Scholarly Resources, 1996).

15 Mansfield *et al.*, 'The Doctor as God's Mechanic?'.

16 Jakub Pawlikowski, 'The History of Thinking About Miracles in the West', *Southern Medical Journal* 100 (2007), 1229–35.

17 *Ibid.*

18 Lone Zilstorff, *Kræft, tro og eksistens under lup*. Kræftens Bekæmpelse, Last Updated Date 2007 [cited 1 October 2009]. Available from www.cancer.dk/Cancer/Nyheder/2007kv1/tro±dallund.htm.

19 Fereshteh Ahmadi, *Culture, Religion and Spirituality in Coping: The Example of Cancer Patients in Sweden* (Uppsala: Acta Universitatis Uppsaliensis, 2006).

20 C. D. Spivak, 'Hebrew Prayers for the Sick', *Annals of Medical History*
    1 (1917), 83–5.
21 George D. Gallup and Timothy K. Jones, *The Next American Spiritu-
    ality: Finding God in the Twenty-First Century* (Colorado Springs:
    Cook, 2000), 178.
22 Marja J. Verhoef *et al.*, 'Reasons for and Characteristics Associated with
    Complementary and Alternative Medicine Use Among Adult Cancer
    Patients: A Systematic Review', *Integrative Cancer Therapies* 4 (2005),
    274–86 (275); National Center for Alternative and Complementary
    Medicine, *What Is Complementary and Alternative Medicine
    (CAM)?* National Institutes of Health (NIH), Last Updated Date 2008
    [cited October 2009]. Available from http://nccam.nih.gov/health/wha-
    tiscam/.
23 P. M. Barnes *et al.*, 'Complementary and Alternative Medicine Use
    Among Adults: United States, 2002', *Advance Data* 343 (2004), 1–19.
24 Mary Ann Richardson *et al.*, 'Complementary/Alternative Medicine
    Use in a Comprehensive Cancer Center and the Implications for
    Oncology', *Journal of Clinical Oncology* 18 (2000), 2505–14 (2506).
25 Alex P. Molassiotis *et al.*, 'Use of Complementary and Alternative
    Medicine in Cancer Patients: A European Survey', *Annals of Oncology*
    16 (2005), 655–63.
26 Kenneth I. Pargament, 'God Help Me (II): The Relationship of Religious
    Orientations to Religious Coping with Negative Life Events', *Journal for
    the Scientific Study of Religion* 31 (1992), 504–13; Kenneth I. Pargament
    et al., 'God Help Me-(I): Religious Coping Efforts as Predictors of the
    Outcomes to Significant Negative Life Events', *American Journal of
    Community Psychology* 18 (1990), 793–824.
27 George Fitchett, 'Religious Struggle: Prevalence, Correlates and Mental
    Health Risks in Diabetic, Congestive Heart Failure, and Oncology
    Patients', *The International Journal of Psychiatry in Medicine* 34
    (2004), 179–96; Kenneth I. Pargament *et al.*, 'Spiritual Struggle:
    A Phenomenon of Interest to Psychology and Religion', in *Judeo-Christian
    Perspectives on Psychology: Human Nature, Motivation, and Change*, ed.
    William R. Miller and Harold D. Delaney (Washington DC: American
    Psychological Association, 2005), ch. 13.
28 Kenneth I. Pargament *et al.*, 'Patterns of Positive and Negative Reli-
    gious Coping with Major Life Stressors', *Journal for the Scientific
    Study of Religion* 37 (1998), 710–24.
29 Gene G. Ano and Erin B. Vasconcelles, 'Religious Coping and Psycho-
    logical Adjustment to Stress: A Meta-Analysis', *Journal of Clinical
    Psychology* 61 (2005), 461–80; Kenneth I. Pargament *et al.*, 'Religious
    Coping Methods as Predictors of Psychological, Physical and Spiritual
    Outcomes among Medically Ill Elderly Patients: A Two-year Longitu-
    dinal Study', *Journal of Health Psychology* 9 (2004), 713–30.
30 Ray O. Sexton and Richard C. Maddock, 'The Adam and Eve Syn-
    drome', *Journal of Religion and Health* 17 (1978), 163–8 (163).
31 Pargament *et al.*, 'Religious Coping Methods'; Fitchett, 'Religious
    Struggle'.

32 Melanie Köhlmoos, 'Theodizee II – Altes Testament', *Theologische Realenzyklopädie* 33 (2002), 215–18.

33 Max Weber, *The Sociology of Religion* (Boston: Beacon, 1993), ch. 9.

34 Greg Bankoff, 'In the Eye of the Storm: The Social Construction of the Forces of Nature and the Climatic and Seismic Construction of God in the Philippines', *Journal of Southeast Asian Studies* 35 (2004), 91–111.

35 John M. McDermott, *The Bible on Human Suffering* (Slough: St Paul, 1990), 34–9.

36 John Aberth, *From the Brink of the Apocalypse: Confronting Famine, War, Plague and Death in the later Middle Ages* (London and New York: Routledge, 2001).

37 MSNBC, Reuters & Associated Press, *White House blasts Robertson's Sharon remark. Christian broadcaster said stroke is God's wrath for 'dividing God's land'*. Last Updated Date 6 January 2006 [cited October 2009]. Available from www.msnbc.msn.com/id/10728347/.

38 Lakshmi Raman and Gerald A. Winer, 'Evidence of More Immanent Justice Responding in Adults Than Children: A Challenge to Traditional Developmental Theories', *British Journal of Developmental Psychology* 22 (2004), 255–74 (255).

39 Larry May, 'Challenging Medical Authority: The Refusal of Treatment by Christian Scientists', *The Hastings Center Report* 25 (1995), 15–22.

40 Bernard Lo *et al.* and Working Group on Religious and Spiritual Issues at the End of Life, 'Discussing Religious and Spiritual Issues at the End of Life: A Practical Guide for Physicians', *The Journal of the American Medical Association* 287 (2002), 749–54.

41 Ralph W. Hood, 'When the Spirit Maims and Kills: Social Psychological Considerations of the History of Serpent Handling Sects and the Narrative of Handlers', *International Journal for the Psychology of Religion* 8 (1998), 71–96.

42 JoAnn O'Reilly, 'The Hospital Prayer Book: A Partner for Healing', *Literature and Medicine* 19 (2000), 61–83.

43 James F. Buryska, 'Assessing the Ethical Weight of Cultural, Religious and Spiritual Claims in the Clinical Context', *British Medical Journal* 27 (2001), 118–22.

44 Kenneth I. Pargament, *The Psychology of Religion and Coping: Theory, Research, Practice* (New York: Guilford, 1997).

45 Terry Lynn Gall and Mark W. Cornblat, 'Breast Cancer Survivors Give Voice: A Qualitative Analysis of Spiritual Factors in Long-Term Adjustment', *Psycho-Oncology* 11 (2002), 524–35; Lars Weisæth, 'Effekten av akutt invervensjon', in *Den 3. Skandinaviske Kriseterapeutiske Kongres* (Oslo, 2006).

46 Hisham Raiya Abu *et al.*, 'A Psychological Measure of Islamic Religiousness: Development and Evidence of Reliability and Validity', *The International Journal for the Psychology of Religion* 18 (2008), 291–315.

47 *Ibid.*

48 Daniel P. Sulmasy, 'Distinguishing Denial From Authentic Faith in Miracles: A Clinical-Pastoral Approach', *Southern Medical Journal* 100 (2007), 1268–72.

49 Buryska, 'Assessing the Ethical Weight', 118.
50 Helle Mathar, 'Når patienten afviser sygepleje', *Sygeplejersken* 4 (2008), 40–4.
51 Ministeriet for Sundhed og Forebyggelse. *LBK nr 95 af 07/02/2008, Kap. 5.* Last Updated Date 2009 [cited 1 October 2009]. Available from www.retsinformation.dk/forms/R0710.aspx?id=114054.
52 Daniel P. Sulmasy, 'Spiritual Issues in the Care of Dying Patients: "... It's Okay between Me and God"', *The Journal of the American Medical Association* 296 (2006), 1385–92.
53 Niels Christian Hvidt, 'Tro og praksis. Om troens betydning for patienter og læger i almen praksis', *Månedsskrift for Praktisk Lægegerning* 12 (2007), 1437–46.

Further reading

Ahmadi, Fereshteh, *Culture, Religion and Spirituality in Coping: The Example of Cancer Patients in Sweden* (Uppsala: Acta Universitatis Uppsaliensis, 2006)

Ano, Gene G. and Erin B. Vasconcelles, 'Religious Coping and Psychological Adjustment to Stress: A Meta-Analysis', *Journal of Clinical Psychology* 61 (2005), 461–80

Cavanagh, Michael E. 'Ministering to Cancer Patients', *Journal of Religion and Health* 33 (1994), 231–41

Duffin, Jacalyn, *Medical Miracles: Doctors, Saints, and Healing in the Modern World* (Oxford and New York: Oxford University Press, 2009)

Fitchett, George, 'Religious Struggle: Prevalence, Correlates and Mental Health Risks in Diabetic, Congestive Heart Failure, and Oncology Patients', *The International Journal of Psychiatry in Medicine* 34 (2004), 179

Gwynne, Paul, *Special Divine Action: Key Issues in the Contemporary Debate, 1965–1995*, Tesi Gregoriana. Serie Teologia 12 (Rome: Pontificia Università Gregoriana, 1996)

Hood, Ralph W., 'When the Spirit Maims and Kills: Social Psychological Considerations of the History of Serpent Handling Sects and the Narrative of Handlers', *International Journal for the Psychology of Religion* 8 (1998), 71–96

Mansfield, Christopher J., Jim Mitchell and Dana E. King, 'The Doctor as God's Mechanic? Beliefs in the Southeastern United States', *Social Science & Medicine* 54 (2002), 399–409

McDermott, John M., *The Bible on Human Suffering* (Slough: St Paul, 1990)

O'Reilly, JoAnn, 'The Hospital Prayer Book: A Partner for Healing', *Literature and Medicine* 19 (2000), 61–83

Pargament, Kenneth I., N. Murray-Swank, G. M. Magyar and G. G. Ano, 'Spiritual Struggle: A Phenomenon of Interest to Psychology and Religion', in *Judeo-Christian Perspectives on Psychology: Human Nature, Motivation, and Change*, ed. William R. Miller and Harold D. Delaney (Washington DC: American Psychological Association, 2005), ch. 13.

Pargament, Kenneth I., *The Psychology of Religion and Coping: Theory, Research, Practice* (New York: Guilford, 1997)

Porterfield, Amanda, *Healing in the History of Christianity* (New York: Oxford University Press, 2005)

Resch, Andreas, *Miracoli dei santi, Sussidi per lo studio delle cause dei santi* 5 (Vatican City: Libreria editrice vaticana, 2002)

*Sulmasy, Daniel P. *et al.* Special Section, 'Spirituality/Medicine Interface Project', *Southern Medical Journal* 100 (2007), 1223–54

Woodward, Kenneth L., *The Book of Miracles – The Meaning of the Miracle Stories in Christianity, Judaism, Buddhism, Hinduism, Islam* (New York: Simon & Schuster, 2000)

Index

THE CAMBRIDGE COMPANION TO REFORMATION THEOLOGY
edited by David Bagchi and David Steinmetz (2004)
ISBN 0 521 77224 9 hardback   ISBN 0 521 77662 7 paperback

THE CAMBRIDGE COMPANION TO AMERICAN JUDAISM
edited by Dana Evan Kaplan (2005)
ISBN 0 521 82204 1 hardback   ISBN 0 521 52951 4 paperback

THE CAMBRIDGE COMPANION TO KARL RAHNER
edited by Declan Marmion and Mary E. Hines (2005)
ISBN 0 521 83288 8 hardback   ISBN 0 521 54045 3 paperback

THE CAMBRIDGE COMPANION TO FRIEDRICH SCHLEIERMACHER
edited by Jacqueline Mariña (2005)
ISBN 0 521 81448 0 hardback   ISBN 0 521 89137 x paperback

THE CAMBRIDGE COMPANION TO THE GOSPELS
edited by Stephen C. Barton (2006)
ISBN 0 521 80766 2 hardback   ISBN 0 521 00261 3 paperback

THE CAMBRIDGE COMPANION TO THE QUR'AN
edited by Jane Dammen McAuliffe (2006)
ISBN 0 521 83160 1 hardback   ISBN 0 521 53934 x paperback

THE CAMBRIDGE COMPANION TO JONATHAN EDWARDS
edited by Stephen J. Stein (2007)
ISBN 0 521 85290 0 hardback   ISBN 0 521 61805 3 paperback

THE CAMBRIDGE COMPANION TO EVANGELICAL THEOLOGY
edited by Timothy Larsen and Daniel J. Trier (2007)
ISBN 0 521 84698 6 hardback   ISBN 0 521 60974 7 paperback

THE CAMBRIDGE COMPANION TO MODERN JEWISH PHILOSOPHY
edited by Michael L. Morgan and Peter Eli Gordon (2007)
ISBN 0 521 81312 3 hardback   ISBN 0 521 01255 4 paperback

THE CAMBRIDGE COMPANION TO THE TALMUD AND RABBINIC LITERATURE
edited by Charlotte E. Fonrobert and Martin S. Jaffee (2007)
ISBN 0 521 84390 1 hardback   ISBN 0 521 60508 3 paperback

THE CAMBRIDGE COMPANION TO LIBERATION THEOLOGY, SECOND EDITION
edited by Christopher Rowland (2007)
ISBN 9780521868839 hardback   ISBN 9780521688932 paperback

THE CAMBRIDGE COMPANION TO THE JESUITS
edited by Thomas Worcester (2008)
ISBN 9780521857314 hardback   ISBN 9780521673969 paperback

THE CAMBRIDGE COMPANION TO CLASSICAL ISLAMIC THEOLOGY
edited by Tim Winter (2008)
ISBN 9780521780582 hardback   ISBN 9780521785495 paperback

THE CAMBRIDGE COMPANION TO PURITANISM
edited by John Coffey and Paul Lim (2008)
ISBN 9780521860888 hardback   ISBN 9780521678001 paperback

THE CAMBRIDGE COMPANION TO ORTHODOX CHRISTIAN THEOLOGY
edited by Mary Cunningham and Elizabeth Theokritoff (2008)
ISBN 9780521864848 hardback   ISBN 9780521683388 paperback

THE CAMBRIDGE COMPANION TO PAUL TILLICH
edited by Russell Re Manning (2009)
ISBN 9780521859899 hardback   ISBN 9780521677356 paperback

THE CAMBRIDGE COMPANION TO JOHN HENRY NEWMAN
edited by Ian Ker and Terrence Merrigan (2009)
ISBN 9780521871860 hardback   ISBN 9780521692724 paperback

THE CAMBRIDGE COMPANION TO JOHN WESLEY
edited by Randy L. Maddox, Jason E. Vickers (2010)
ISBN 9780521886536 hardback   ISBN 9780521714037 paperback

THE CAMBRIDGE COMPANION TO CHRISTIAN PHILOSOPHICAL THEOLOGY
edited by Charles Taliaferro, Chad Meister (2010)
ISBN 9780521514330 hardback   ISBN 9780521730372 paperback

THE CAMBRIDGE COMPANION TO MUHAMMAD
edited by Jonathan E. Brockopp (2010)
ISBN 9780521886079 hardback   ISBN 9780521713726 paperback

THE CAMBRIDGE COMPANION TO SCIENCE AND RELIGION
edited by Peter Harrison (2010)
ISBN 9780521885386 hardback   ISBN 9780521712514 paperback

THE CAMBRIDGE COMPANION TO GANDHI
edited by Judith Brown and Anthony Parel (2011)
ISBN 9780521116701 hardback   ISBN 9780521133456 paperback

THE CAMBRIDGE COMPANION TO THOMAS MORE
edited by George Logan (2011)
ISBN 9780521888622 hardback   ISBN 9780521716871 paperback

Forthcoming

THE CAMBRIDGE COMPANION TO THE TRINITY
edited by Peter C. Phan

THE CAMBRIDGE COMPANION TO THE VIRGIN MARY
edited by Sarah Boss

THE CAMBRIDGE COMPANION TO BLACK THEOLOGY
edited by Dwight Hopkins and Edward Antonio

Made in the USA
Middletown, DE
17 January 2020